Migration and Development

World Anthropology

General Editor

SOL TAX

Patrons

CLAUDE LÉVI-STRAUSS
MARGARET MEAD
LAILA SHUKRY EL HAMAMSY
M. N. SRINIVAS

MOUTON PUBLISHERS · THE HAGUE · PARIS
DISTRIBUTED IN THE USA AND CANADA BY ALDINE, CHICAGO

Migration and Development

Implications for Ethnic Identity
and Political Conflict

Editors

HELEN I. SAFA
BRIAN M. DU TOIT

MOUTON PUBLISHERS · THE HAGUE · PARIS
DISTRIBUTED IN THE USA AND CANADA BY ALDINE, CHICAGO

ISBN 90–279–7549–3 (Mouton)
0–202–01153–4 (Aldine)
Jacket photo by Douglas K. Midgett
Cover and jacket design by Jurriaan Schrofer
Printed in the Netherlands

211158

To the migrants of the world
whose struggle for a better life
is an inspiration to us all

General Editor's Preface

In all of anthropological history no set of phenomena have interested us more than the migration of peoples, the interplay among their cultures, and the transformation of smaller societies into larger urban and national agglomerations. Yet it was appropriate to await a major International Congress for a full review of our knowledge from a post-colonial point of view. This is one of two complementary volumes which look at modern migrations as they relate to ethnicity. The other — *Migration and urbanization*, edited primarily by Brian M. du Toit — deals particularly with problems of migration theory and adaptive patterns. The two together bring to the social sciences a new and very rich corpus of case material from every continent, synthesized in a series of essays by editors and commentators.

Like most contemporary sciences, anthropology is a product of the European tradition. Some argue that it is a product of colonialism, with one small and self-interested part of the species dominating the study of the whole. If we are to understand the species, our science needs substantial input from scholars who represent a variety of the world's cultures. It was a deliberate purpose of the IXth International Congress of Anthropological and Ethnological Sciences to provide impetus in this direction. The *World Anthropology* volumes, therefore, offer a first glimpse of a human science in which members from all societies have played an active role. Each of the books is designed to be self-contained; each is an attempt to update its particular sector of scientific knowledge and is written by specialists from all parts of the world. Each volume should be read and reviewed individually as a separate volume on its own given subject. The set as a whole will indicate what changes are in store for anthropology as scholars from the developing countries join in studying the species of which we are all a part.

The IXth Congress was planned from the beginning not only to include as many of the scholars from every part of the world as possible, but also with a view toward the eventual publication of the papers in high-quality volumes. At previous Congresses scholars were invited to bring papers which were then read out loud. They were necessarily limited in length; many were only summarized; there was little time for discussion; and the sparse discussion could only be in one language. The IXth Congress was an experiment aimed at changing this. Papers were written with the intention of exchanging them before the Congress, particulary in extensive pre-Congress sessions; they were not intended to be read aloud at the Congress, that time being devoted to discussions — discussions which were simultaneously and professionally translated into five languages. The method for eliciting the papers was structured to make as representative a sample as was allowable when scholarly creativity — hence self-selection — was critically important. Scholars were asked both to propose papers of their own and to suggest topics for sessions of the Congress which they might edit into volumes. All were then informed of the suggestions and encouraged to re-think their own papers and the topics. The process, therefore, was a continuous one of feedback and exchange and it has continued to be so even after the Congress. The some two thousand papers comprising *World Anthropology* certainly then offer a substantial sample of world anthropology. It has been said that anthropology is at a turning point; if this is so, these volumes will be the historical direction-markers.

As might have been foreseen in the first post-colonial generation, the large majority of the Congress papers (82 percent) are the work of scholars identified with the industrialized world which fathered our traditional discipline and the institution of the Congress itself: Eastern Europe (15 percent); Western Europe (16 percent); North America (47 percent); Japan, South Africa, Australia, and New Zealand (4 percent). Only 18 percent of the papers are from developing areas: Africa (4 percent); Asia-Oceania (9 percent); Latin America (5 percent). Aside from the substantial representation from the U.S.S.R. and the nations of Eastern Europe, a significant difference between this corpus of written material and that of other Congresses is the addition of the large proportion of contributions from Africa, Asia, and Latin America. "Only 18 percent" is two to four times as great a proportion as that of other Congresses; moreover, 18 percent of 2,000 papers is 360 papers, 10 times the number of "Third World" papers presented at previous Congresses. In fact, these

360 papers are more than the total of ALL papers published after the last International Congress of Anthropological and Ethnological Sciences which was held in the United States (Philadelphia, 1956). Even in the beautifully organized Tokyo Congress in 1968 less than a third as many members from developing nations, including those of Asia, participated.

The significance of the increase is not simply quantitative. The input of scholars from areas which have until recently been no more than subject matter for anthropological respresents both feedback and also long-awaited theoretical contributions from the perspectives of very different cultural, social, and historical traditions. Many who attended the IXth Congress were convinced that anthropology would not be the same in the future. The fact that the next Congress (India, 1978) will be our first in the "Third World" may be symbolic of the change. Meanwhile, sober consideration of the present set of books will show how much, and just where and how, our discipline is being revolutionized.

This book (and its companion volume) profited from conferences held in Oshkosh, Wisconsin, immediately before the Congress. Many of the authors could attend, and the presentations to the Congress itself could be prepared. The participants could also take advantage there of similar conferences leading to other books on related subjects in this series on *World Anthropology*. Readers of this book will also be interested in the equally rich material the other volumes provide on such subjects as ethnicity, urbanization, population, class competition, and historic developments in all parts of the world.

Chicago, Illinois   SOL TAX
July 11, 1975

Preface

Migration today is part of a world-wide process of urbanization and industrialization which has brought about severe dislocation in the national economy of advanced industrial as well as developing Third World nations. Migration is no longer limited to shifts of families from country to city, but now involves wholesale population movements across national boundaries and into different cultures and economies. The ethnic minorities created as a result of this new form of migration are increasingly rejecting assimilation as a mode of adaptation and seeking instead to maintain their identity within a new pluralistic framework.

This volume seeks to explore the implications for ethnic consciousness and political conflict of this new form of massive migration. The authors, drawn largely from anthropology and sociology, met at a conference on Migration and Ethnicity held in conjunction with the International Congress of Anthropological and Ethnological Sciences in Chicago, Illinois in August 1973 and organized by Helen I. Safa from Rutgers University and Brian M. du Toit of the University of Florida. The papers presented at this conference have resulted in two volumes, one entitled *Migration and urbanization: models and adaptive strategies*, edited by Brian M. du Toit and Helen I. Safa, and the present volume, dealing primarily with migration and development, and its implications for ethnic identity and political conflict.

In the area of ethnic identity, the participants in the conference addressed such questions as: Does migration foster maintenance or abolition of ethnic identity? Under what circumstances? What are the functions of ethnicity in the new setting to which the migrant has moved? What are the interrelationships between race, class, and ethnic identity among migrants? What are the structure and rationale behind pan-ethnic movements such as Black Power in the United States and Great Britain or cooperation among various American Indian groups. Clearly the motive for this drive for unity is not only to reaffirm the sense of ethnic identity, weakened by parochialism, but to use this unified strength to gain more political leverage on the local and national level.

Discussion of ethnic identity and class structure cannot therefore be divorced from the political implications of massive intra- and international migration. Political conflict arises out of the growth of regional imbalances and income inequality as well as the sociocultural conflicts between migrant ethnic groups and their host societies. Thus the division of this book into two sections is, as in most cases, somewhat arbitrary; if we wish to move towards an integrated social science, we can no longer treat topics such as politics, ethnicity, and class structure as if they were separate issues, particularly when they stem from a similar root cause like migration.

Nor can we continue to analyze migration at a strictly micro-level. The increasing movement of migrants across national boundaries, as in the papers given here analyzing the consequences of West Indian blacks migrating to London and New York or Spaniards migrating to Switzerland foree us to view migration within an international as well as a national context. What we are witnessing is the "internationalization of the proletariat," as the labor pool upon which modern industry draws extends from the "native reserves" of South Africa to the slums of London and New York. As Bryce-Laporte points out in his commentary, this labor pool is largely and increasingly non-white, and reinforces the sense of exploitation felt by Third World peoples whose land and now labor are being exploited for the benefit of advanced industrial societies.

Migration, therefore, becomes another link in the chain binding the fate of Third World and non-white people to the vicissitudes of industrial capitalism. This volume is a preliminary attempt to understand the implications of this movement on a global scale. Much of the data represents fresh field material gathered within the last few years and hopefully will offer new insights into the field. The conference and this volume clearly indicate the need for more comparative research in this area, particularly studies that will link migration to the larger issues of social change and economic development.

In closing, I would like to extend my appreciation to Dr. Sol Tax of the University of Chicago, whose commitment to the "internationalization of anthropology" made the Congress possible, against almost impossible odds. I would also like to thank all the participants in the conference, who attended at their own expense and demonstrated such interest and enthusiasm, not only at the conference but throughout the preparation of this volume. Last, I would like to thank the staff of the International Center at Rutgers University and, particularly Ms. Tiffany Nourse, for her invaluable help and cooperation at every stage of this endeavor.

Rutgers University   HELEN I. SAFA
New Brunswick, New Jersey

Table of Contents

Introduction

HELEN I. SAFA

Migration is normally viewed as an economic phenomenon. Though non-economic factors obviously have some bearing, most studies concur that migrants leave their area of origin primarily because of a lack of employment opportunities and in hopes of finding better opportunities elsewhere.

However, the wider economic ramifications of migration are often overlooked. Migration can no longer be viewed as simply a question of individual choice, though this may still have some bearing on selection in a migrant population (see du Toit 1975). The massive movements taking place today within as well as across national boundaries are due to major structural transformations in the economies of developed and Third World countries. Migration is a manifestation of a world-wide shift from a rural agrarian base to an urban-industrial base in the economies of most Third World countries.

Industrialization is viewed as the key to economic growth and modernization in Third World countries, as it was in the West. Much of this industrialization is rationalized as "import-substitution." That is, Third World countries argue that they are freeing themselves from dependence on industrialized Western nations by producing themselves what they formerly had to import from abroad. On the contrary, however, industrialization in Third World countries has fostered a new form of dependence on the industrialized West, since most industrialization in these countries is financed by foreign capital and is heavily dependent on foreign technology. This dependency has been accentuated by the growth of multinational corporations with their highly sophisticated and capital-intensive technology (cf. Sunkel 1974).

The counterpart to the emphasis on industrialization in Third World countries is the virtual total neglect of rural economy. Scarce government resources are poured into industrialization and the urban infrastructure needed to support it — roads, ports, plants, hydro-electric power, as well as other amenities such as housing, schools, hospitals, etc., all concentrated in the urban area. Other incentives are offered to industry in the form of low-interest loans, tax exemptions, reduction of tariff barriers, etc. The result in most Third World countries has been increased public and private investment in industrialization and a reduction in capital available for agriculture. It has been estimated, for example, that in Africa, where over 70 percent of the labor force is still agricultural, more than half the countries allocate less than 20 percent of total investment to agriculture (Hunter 1972:47). The poverty engendered by the stagnation of the rural sector is described by Richardson in his article on Guyana and Trinidad, where peasants are forced to supplement their meager income from the land by wage labor on nearby plantations, a common phenomenon in Latin America.

THE RURAL EXODUS

This policy of government-supported urban concentration has led to a massive exodus from rural to urban areas in most Third World countries. In Latin America as a whole, for example, the percentage of persons employed in agriculture decreased from 53.4 percent in 1950 to 42.2 percent in 1969, with a growth rate between 1960–1969 of only 1.5 percent (Pompermayer 1973:65). Some reduction in the agricultural labor force can be accounted for by mechanization, but the slow rate of growth in agriculture during the same period suggests rather the displacement of investment and the labor force into non-agricultural sectors. The rural-urban exodus has been further accentuated by the concentration of land ownership accompanying agricultural mechanization and modernization.

The discovery of important mining or other natural resources may also lead to the expulsion of the indigenous rural population. Whitten's article illustrates how Indians in lowland Ecuador are being squeezed out of their land as a result of highland colonization following the discovery of oil. This process is now being repeated in many areas of Latin America, particularly Brazil, which now has the highest growth rate in the southern hemisphere. Not content with expulsion or "pacification," Brazil is reported to have slaughtered whole communities of Indians in the Amazon area standing in the path of a new trans-Amazon highway, and has even crossed over into Paraguay for the construction of a huge hydro-electric plant and into Bolivia for the exploitation of new iron ore deposits. Thus, whole countries, like Bolivia and Paraguay, with very weak national economies, are being absorbed into the Brazilian industrial orbit.

It was expected that industrial employment would absorb the surplus labor from the rural area in Third World countries, as it had earlier in Western industrialized economies. However, this has not happened, and unemployment continues to grow in these countries at an alarming rate, along with rural-urban migration. Thus, according to a United Nations study, the gap between the rate of growth of industrial output and employment was about 3 to 4 percent for all Third World countries for which data were available over the period from the mid-1950's to the mid-1960's (United Nations 1968). In Latin America, the number of unemployed rose from 2.9 million in 1950 to 8.8 million in 1965 and the unemployment rate from 5.6 percent to 11.1 percent of the labor force over the same period (Pompermayer 1973:63). Again, part of this increase in unemployment can be attributed to a tremendous population increase, especially in Latin America, which increases the pressure on the cities and on the urban labor force.

One reason industrialization has been unable to absorb this surplus agricultural labor is because it has been geared largely to the consumer needs of the middle and upper classes, which still constitute a limited market in most Third World countries. The purchasing power of the rural and urban poor is far too low in most countries to enable them to buy expensive manufactured goods, except for the ubiquitous transistor radios, plastics, and other mass-produced items now displacing local handicrafts in many areas. At the same time these newly industrializing nations are unable to compete in a highly competitive export market with the advanced industrial nations. The problem of labor surplus is intensified where countries have elected to adopt new capital-intensive technologies, yielding high productivity but requiring little manpower. Thus, in Latin America, while the industrial sector has been the leading contributor to growth of the gross national product (together with construction and basic infrastructure), its share in total employment DECLINED between 1950 and 1969 (Pompermayer 1973:63).

Where, then, has this surplus labor been absorbed? Primarily in an ill-defined tertiary or services sector, which in Latin America is usually referred to as a marginal labor force. It is difficult to define the marginal labor force on the basis of occupation, because most work at a variety of odd jobs, including domestic service (especially for women) and petty trade, characterized as in the traditional bazaar economy by extensive fractionalization of risk and profit. Although this marginal labor market is able to absorb large numbers of people, they are poorly paid, under-employed, and often unemployed for long periods of time. Thus, the "shared poverty" once so characteristic of the rural areas of Third World countries, has now shifted to the cities, where people try to scavenge off each other as they survive on a bare hand-to-mouth existence.

Many economists, including Hirschman (1958) and Hoselitz (1955) feel that the growth of this large underemployed and essentially unproductive labor force is temporary and will balance itself out as economic growth proceeds and industry is able to absorb a larger labor supply. However, economic growth, dependent as it is on the export economy, seems only to foster the expansion of parasitic primate cities which continue to demonstrate record-breaking population increases. In most Third World countries, urbanization has far outpaced industrialization. In Latin America, even where the rate of industrial output has remained relatively stable or slightly declined between 1960 and 1970, urbanization rose by between 15 percent and 72 percent during the same period (Pompermayer 1973:64).

As noted earlier, the ability of industry to absorb labor is theatened by the accelerating trend toward highly technological capital-intensive industry introduced largely by multinational corporations "the basic economic institution of the postwar capitalist world." (Sunkel 1974). Thus the highly productive, high income petroleum sector in Venezuela accounts for over 20 percent of the gross domestic product (GDP), but barely 2 percent of employment; bauxite in Jamaica accounts for 16 percent of the GDP but only 4 percent of employment. Workers in these capital-intensive industries typically earn between four and ten times the normal wage in similar employment in another sector (Girling 1973:89). They have become a new "labor aristocracy."

Income differentials between the marginal and stable labor force in Latin America have accentuated the growing income inequality in these countries. Not only is the income gap growing between the Third World and developed countries, but the INTERNAL inequalities within these Third World countries are also increasing. Thus, in Latin America in 1965, the top percent received 33.4 percent of total income, while 80 percent of the population received only 37.5 percent of total income (Girling 1973:83). Most of the poor still reside in the rural area, where incomes are at least two to three times less than in the urban areas (1973:90). Industrial development policies have thus failed to alleviate persistent poverty in the rural areas while they have contributed greatly to the rise in rural-urban migration, leading to further unemployment and underemployment in the cities. Industrialization and the need for a cheap labor force also help account for migration across national boundaries, such as the migration of laborers from Spain to Switzerland, described by the Buechelers in their article, or of West Indians to London, described by Midgett.

The end results of a policy of rapid industrialization in Third World countries has thus been an increase in rural-urban migration, the stagnation of agriculture and the rural economy in general, growing regional imbalances, increasing inequality of income and living standards between the rural and urban poor and the urban elite, now expanded to include a growing middle class and a new labor aristocracy. While industrialization has undoubtedly contributed to the growth of the gross national product in these countries, the primary beneficiaries of this higher productivity have been the urban elite, not only in terms of more jobs and higher incomes, but in terms of greater production of consumer goods such as automobiles, telephones, washing machines, television sets, etc. In fact, the high propensity of these elite sectors to consume has been criticized even by conservative economists who, following the Keynesian model, argue this money should be reinvested to generate further economic growth. It has also contributed to spiraling inflation, which bears particularly hard on the urban and rural poor with low and unstable incomes. Price and subsidy policies tend to favor the urban consumer, while the profits from this consumption flow largely to foreign-owned corporations, which supply these products. As Lloyd's article documents for Nigeria, the post-independence elite is consolidating itself into a self-perpetuating group, reserving for itself the top jobs (many in government bureaucracy), the best university educations, and other avenues of social mobility.

ASSIMILATION OF URBAN MIGRANTS

Seen in this light, the assimilation of an impoverished rural population into urban life takes on a different dimension from that normally posed by anthropologists. The barriers to assimilation are not only cultural, though this continues to pose problems, particularly when the migrant group is of different nationality, race, religion, or linguistic stock from the host culture, as several of the articles in this volume demonstrate. Cultural barriers may make it more difficult for them to find new jobs in the host society, and certainly increase the problems of housing, schools and general acceptance by the host society. Heller's article points out how even in Israel, set up as an immigrant society, Oriental Jews have been discriminated against because of their low educational and skill level.

However, even when migrants are from the same culture, the problems posed by the absorption of this large mass of unskilled labor into the urban economy is formidable, and tends to increase as the rural exodus accelerates and the skill level of the migrant is lowered (cf. Cardona 1975). Migrants pose a problem to planners and other government officials in at least three areas:

1. Finding jobs for this mass of largely unskilled workers and the consequences of unemployment and underemployment.
2. The provision of housing and other public services.
3. The political significance of this large "lumpen proletariat" for the urban and national power structure.

We have already discussed the problem of employment in the first section. We have seen that the mass of rural migrants is not absorbed into urban-industrial employment, but ekes out a living in a variety of service occupations which form the core of the marginal labor force. At the same time, the presence of this huge labor reserve tends to depress wages in all but the most skilled sectors of the working class because it is very easy to replace one employee with another. This is also a great hindrance to the formation of unions among workers in Third World countries because competition for jobs is very high and employment is very unstable. Most workers tend to take whatever job they can find, and only the most skilled find steady, remunerative employment.

Migrants are the main source of the squatter settlements or shanty towns which have sprung up at an alarming rate around the periphery of Latin American cities and other parts of the Third World in the last two decades. In Santiago, Chile, for example, it is estimated that about 70 percent of the squatters and slum dwellers are migrants (Lozano 1973:2). The process of urban land invasion, by which squatters seize land illegally, accelerated in Santiago from an aggregation of individual families before the 1950's to massive, planned seizures backed by political organizations and technical assistance in the 1960's. Even in Puerto Rico, where shantytowns had normally grown by gradual accretion, there have been organized land invasions involving whole communities since 1968.

Initially at least, most of these squatter settlements lack any form of public services. They have no water, electricity, sewers, or paved roads, not to speak of schools, hospitals, or recreational facilities. In Latin America, as squatter settlements develop, they often acquire some of these services through political pressure put upon the government and through self-help methods. In San Juan, Puerto Rico, for example, the *barrio* committees were responsible for bringing in running water and electricity to each house, while street lights were put up with local voluntary labor (Safa 1974). Because many shantytowns in the San Juan Metropolitan Area lie along the canal, the land has to be filled in periodically to prevent flooding, and this too was performed with local labor. Though originally deemed unfit for residential use, this land eventually began to acquire greater value because of its central city location. As a result, the shantytown was cleared for commercial use, and the residents forced to seek shelter in public housing or private, modest income subdivisions, now increasingly located on the periphery of the metropolitan area, making the journey to work even more costly and time consuming.

The bulk of public expenditure in most developing countries does not go toward the provision of public services for the poor, but toward the improvement of an urban infrastructure which will encourage private investment and make the cities, particularly the capital, a showcase of modernization with superhighways, subways (now under construction in several Latin American cities), modern office buildings, etc. The eradication of squatter settlements from the central city in countries such as Puerto Rico, Brazil, and Peru is also in line with this new "modern" image that the cities wish to project to the outside world. Thus, in Chile under the Christian Democrats, only 26 percent of the average public investment from 1965–1968 went to productive sectors, with the bulk, 74 percent, going to infrastructure. This was "coherent with the notion that the public should support and encourage the private sector, but should never attempt to replace it" (Lozano 1973:8). The concentration of investment in the Santiago Metropolitan Area is shown by the fact that it received 53.6 percent of the national investment in housing, 46 percent of the investment in electricity, gas and water, 36.6 percent of the investment in education, 27.9 percent of the investment in health, and 22.7 percent of the investment in transportation (Lozano 1973:8).

Most Third World countries spend a considerable portion of their budgets on education, which is universally viewed as the prime vehicle for social mobility and modernization of the illiterate rural population. Yet the growth of educational facilities in developing countries has been unable to bridge the gap between the privileged and poor segments of the population. Education has served principally to create a new and growing middle class of white-collar workers to staff the burgeoning urban economy and, especially, the government bureaucracy which often is one of the principal sources of employment in the cities. Many of the new middle class in developing countries have risen from the ranks of the unskilled working class and take such pride in their new positions that they become strong supporters of the status quo (Safa 1974).

Thus, education in Third World countries has been geared largely to preparation for jobs in the relatively small modern sector of the economy and has contributed considerably to the exodus from the rural area. As Curtain points out in his article, even in Papua New Guinea, school leavers tend to migrate to the city because there are no jobs for their skills in the rural area. Attempts to stem this tide by a "rurally biased" curricula are absurd if there is no corresponding investment in the rural economy. As Hunter noted for Africa:

...no amount of "rurally biased" curricula could persuade young people to remain in an unimproved agricultural sector or in a rural economy deprived of even minor investment — feeder roads, telephones, electricity, storage space for agricultural produce, water supply, health services, and transport and petrol for the extension and other staff trying to improve the situation (1972:40).

THE REVOLUTIONARY POTENTIAL OF MIGRANTS

Unemployment, poor housing, inadequate public services, and other ills might be thought to foster an explosive political situation among urban migrants. This ties in with the thesis of Fanon (1962) that it is the "wretched of the earth" that will form the vanguard of revolutionary movements in the Third World, rather than the industrial working class as in more orthodox Marxist ideology. Certainly the marginal labor force is more numerous in the Third World and has more reason to complain: compared even to the industrial work force, they are underemployed, poorly paid, and lack even minimal security of employment. Even social security and other fringe benefits which are now being extended to workers in Third World countries accrue largely to the stably employed white- and blue-collar class (cf. Mesa-Lago 1973).

However, the very insecurity of marginal workers in Third World countries may prevent them from becoming a potent political force for radical change. They are too concerned with the struggle to survive to organize politically, and the lack of a stable place of employment makes organization along trade union lines virtually impossible (cf. Goldrich 1965). It may be possible to organize marginal workers in their place of residence, chiefly the shantytowns, which also include a large number of the stable working class. The success of the MIR and other revolutionary leftist parties in organizing the *campamentos* of Concepción, Santiago and other cities in Chile for the support of the socialist government of Salvador Allende seems to support the feasibility of this form of political mobilization (cf. Vanderschuren 1973:281–282; Center for Urban and Regional Development 1971).

However, the possibilities for political mobilization among the urban poor in Third World countries must again be analyzed within the context of the vast structural transformations now engulfing these societies. It would seem that, despite the serious dislocations it has engendered, economic growth in the form of industrialization and urbanization can retard the formation of political movements among the urban poor, at least temporarily. My work among the urban poor of Puerto Rico has shown that expanded employment and educational opportunities create the myth of an "open society," in which it is assumed there are limitless possibilities for social mobility for all those who are willing to work hard and save, get an education, etc. (Safa 1974). This is especially true of first-generation migrants, who tend to view mobility in terms of their own life history rather than in terms of their socio-economic position in the larger society. In his article, Lloyd has referred to this personalistic view of social mobility or stratification as the ego-centered model, one formed by the individual through his network of personal relationships. Lloyd, working among the Yoruba, also finds this model to be predominant over the externalized analytical model used primarily by western observers, which attempts to view the social structure objectively as a whole.

Despite growing evidence of social inequality, then, most studies fail to substantiate the fears of Pye (1969) and others that migrants are a potentially disruptive force. Cornelius (1971), in an extensive study of cityward migration in Latin America, concludes that the poor are content with relatively minor improvements, and that despite the hardships faced in the new urban setting, cities represent for them an advancement over the stagnant rural environment. Nelson (1969) found much the same results in her extensive survey of the "disruptive potential" of migrants in Latin America, but felt there was greater potential discontent and political tension among second-generation migrants, who have not experienced the dire poverty of the rural area. My data from Puerto Rico suggest this may be true because the expectations of the second generation are considerably higher than those of their parents, while opportunities are stabilizing, or in some cases, even shrinking. (Safa 1974:56). Thus, children with a high school diploma may find it more difficult to find a job commensurate with their educational level than their parents did with much less education. This is because in Puerto Rico, as in most Third World countries, educational opportunities have expanded at a much faster rate than employment, making it possible for firms to upgrade continually the requirements for even relatively unskilled employment.

Contrary to those who cast dire predictions about the politically disruptive potential of migrants, Horowitz (1969) and others maintain that internal migration has served to reduce revolutionary discontent in several

Latin American countries by offering an alternative to rural poverty. However, Horowitz adds:

Only when cities do in fact relieve social and economic sources of discontent by enlarging upon industrial opportunities do the mass agencies of revolution become shriveled. And this withering away of the revolutionary impulse is not so much a function of ecological mobility as it is of industrial mobility (1969:144).

In short, revolutionary discontent may be averted as long as economic growth continues to offer expanding employment opportunities, even if only to the minority.

However, this is why the trend toward capital-intensive industry is politically as well as economically significant. As we noted previously, capital-intensive industry tends to absorb far less labor, while those employed are paid considerably higher wages because of their higher productivity. This division in the working class between the privileged workers of capital-intensive industries and the marginal workers largely employed in service and petty commerce could reduce even further the possibility of a unified political movement emerging from the working class (cf. Safa f.c.). The division could follow a pattern similar to the United States, where the "hard hats" have turned against the welfare poor, whom they feel represent a tax burden and a threat to their jobs and neighborhoods. This division in the United States is exacerbated by the racial antagonisms between the largely white "hard hats" and the popular misconception that the welfare poor is made up primarily of blacks, Puerto Ricans, or other racial minorities.

Ethnic or racial antagonisms naturally serve to augment divisions in the working class. In fact, where ethnic or racial groups have been systematically excluded from participation in the fruits of economic growth or from possibilities of upward mobility, we may expect revolutionary discontent which generally takes the form of ethnic nationalism. Several articles in this volume document various forms of racial and ethnic discrimination, among blacks in the U.S. (Green; Sutton and Makiesky), in Great Britain (Midgett; Sutton and Makiesky), and in South Africa (Magubane), among Oriental Jews in Israel (Heller), among Spanish migrants in Switzerland (Buechler) and among Indians in the United States (Hodge). As Gugler notes in his article on Africa, strong differences in access to resources reinforce ethnic and/or racial differences, often leading to political or economic opposition. Racial or ethnic differences are often exploited by the ruling elite as a "divide and rule" strategy to maintain the powerlessness of the poor and heighten intra-class hostilities. Magubane's article clearly describes the strategy of the white South African government in physically separating the black population into *bantustans* from which the adult population is forced to leave periodically in order to eke out even a marginal existence in towns or mining camps.

However, migration has not only served to heighten ethnic and racial antagonisms, it has also led to the development of new "pan-ethnic" movements encompassing larger ethnic groupings such as the black movement in the United States and the Caribbean, described by Sutton and Makiesky and the growing black identification among West Indians in Great Britain, described by Midgett. As Bryce-Laporte comments, "The world is witnessing the emergence of new levels of blackness, the universalization of black ethnicity, a new meaning to the Black Diaspora." These new linkages will hopefully provide a wider basis for political as well as cultural solidarity, so that ethnic groups such as blacks and Indians may work more effectively toward the elimination of exploitation and inequality. Certainly the limited success of the black movement in the United States is due largely to the unity and self-confidence which enabled blacks to press their demands upon a racist white power structure.

Ethnic nationalism is a far more prevalent form of protest in most Third World countries today than the class struggle forecast by orthodox Marxists. Ethnic and racial groups have a cultural basis for solidarity which class groups lack, and as we have seen, ethnic differences may even serve to obscure class antagonisms, and to prevent crucial class alliances.

As the articles in this volume demonstrate, most migrants are a long way from achieving the kind of class consciousness which can make them a meaningful political force in developing countries. Most recent rural migrants, uprooted from their families and villages, are struggling for an existence in the city. Most suffer ethnic and racial discrimination as well as class oppression. Traditional vehicles for creating class solidarity such as unions and political parties are generally weak and fragmented, and serve largely to perpetuate the dependency upon a paternalistic government or charismatic leader.

CONCLUSIONS

Until the urban and rural poor in Third World countries do achieve greater political power, however, it is unlikely that present development policies resulting in urban concentration, rapid industrialization, continuing rural-urban migration, and rural poverty will change. The only countries in Latin America where significant reversals in this trend have been seriously undertaken are Cuba and Chile under Allende, both socialist governments with a political power base in the urban and rural proletariat. Analysis of their policies goes beyond my intention here, but can be obtained elsewhere (Acosta and Hardoy 1973; Lozano 1973). Suffice it to say that they go far beyond the growth pole strategies advocated by planners such as Friedmann (1970), which stress the development of alternate urban centers to absorb rural population and stimulate regional development. However, it is unlikely these policies could ever be implemented in capitalist countries, developed or underdeveloped, because they run counter to the interests of the power elite who continue to benefit from a continuation of present policies. Urban concentration and rapid industrialization mean greater profits, especially for multinational corporations, more consumer goods and urban amenities for the middle classes, and continuing massive migration for the poor.

REFERENCES

ACOSTA, MARUJA, JORGE E. HARDOY
  1973   *Urban reform in revolutionary Cuba.* New Haven, Connecticut: Antilles Research Program, Yale University. (Translated by Mal Bochner.)
CARDONA, RAMIRO, ALAN SIMMONS
  1975   "Toward a model of migration in Latin America," in *Migration and urbanization: models and adaptive strategies.* Edited by Brian M. du Toit and Helen I. Safa. World Anthropolopy. The Hague: Mouton.
CENTER FOR URBAN AND REGIONAL DEVELOPMENT (CIDU)
  1971   "Reivindicacion Urbana y lucha politica: los campamentos de pobladores en Santiago de Chile." Catholic University of Chile.
CORNELIUS, WAYNE A., JR.
  1971   The political sociology of cityward migration in Latin America: toward empirical theory. *Latin American Urban Research*, volume one. Edited by Francine Rabinovitz and Felicity Trueblood. Beverly Hills: Sage Publications.
DU TOIT, BRIAN M.
  1975   "A decision-making model for the study of migration," in *Migration and urbanization: models and adaptive strategies.* Edited by Brian M. du Toit and Helen I. Safa. World Anthropology. The Hague: Mouton.
FANON, FRANTZ
  1962   *The wretched of the earth.* New York: Grove Press.
FRIEDMANN, JOHN
  1970   *The future of urbanization in Latin America.* Studies in Comparative International Development 5. Beverly Hills: Sage Publications.
GIRLING, ROBERT
  1973   "Dependency and persistent income inequality," in *Structures of dependency.* Edited by Frank Bonilla and Robert Girling. Nairobi, California: Nairobi Bookstore.

GOLDRICH, DANIEL
1965 "Toward the comparative study of politicalization in Latin America," in *Comparative cultures and societies of Latin America*. Edited by Dwight Heath and Richard Adams. New York: Random House.

HIRSCHMAN, ALBERT
1958 *The strategy of economic development*. New Haven: Yale University Press.

HOROWITZ, IRVING LOUIS
1969 "Electoral politics, urbanization and social development in Latin America," in *Latin American radicalism*. Edited by Irving L. Horowitz, Josue de Castro, and John Gerassi. New York: Random House, Vintage Books.

HOSELITZ, BERT F.
1955 Generative and Parasitic Cities. *Economic Development and Cultural Change* 3(3).

HUNTER, GUY
1972 Employment policy in tropical Africa: the need for radical revision. *International Labour Review* 105 (1).

LOZANO, EDUARDO E.
1973 "The regional strategy of Unidad Popular in Chile." Princeton University, Dept. of Architecture and Urban Planning. Mimeographed manuscript.

MESA-LAGO, CARMELO
1973 "Social security stratification and inequality in Latin America: the case of Peru." Paper presented at the Fourth National Meeting of Latin American Studies Association, University of Wisconsin, Madison.

NELSON, JOAN M.
1969 *Migrants, urban poverty and instability in developing countries*. Harvard Occasional Papers in International Affairs 22.

POMPERMAYER, MALORI J.
1973 "Dependency and unemployment: some issues," in *Structures of dependency*. Edited by Frank Bonilla and Robert Girling. Nairobi, California: Nairobi Bookstore.

PYE, LUCIAN W.
1969 "Political implications of urbanization and the development process," in *The city in newly developing countries: readings on urbanism and urbanization*. Edited by Gerald Breese. Englewood Cliffs, New Jersey: Prentice Hall.

SAFA, HELEN I.
f.c. "Divisions in the working class: the political implications of industrialization in Puerto Rico," in *The American working class*. Edited by Irving Horowitz, John Leggett, and Martin Oppenheimer. Transaction Books.
1974 *The urban poor of Puerto Rico: a study in development and inequality*. New York: Holt, Rinehart and Winston.

SUNKEL, OSVALDO
1974 Transnational capitalism and national disintegration in Latin America. *Comparative Studies in International Development* 9 (1).

UNITED NATIONS
    1968   *Industrial development survey*, volume one. New York. Table 1 and
           Table 78.
VANDERSCHUREN, FRANZ
    1973   "Political significance of neighborhood committees in the settlements
           of Santiago," in *The Chilean road to socialism*. Edited by Dale L.
           Johnson. New York: Doubleday, Anchor.

PART ONE

Immigrants and Forms of Group Identity

Los Suizos: Galician Migration to Switzerland

HANS C. BUECHLER and JUDITH-MARIA BUECHLER

Traditionally, ethnic identity has been seen as an explanatory principle associated with the adherence of individuals to a defined social group that could be delimited in space and time by specific cultural features. Upon migration such identification was maintained in cultural enclaves within host societies until such time, a few generations later, when permanent assimilation took place by the gradual dilution of the original cultural peculiarities and the acceptance of the main tenets of the dominant culture. Accordingly, the resurgence of ethnic identity in such minority groups signified the last, desperate reactions of the subculture to an extremely stressful situation in which assimilation was blocked.

More recently, studies have tended to separate the cultural and social aspects of ethnic identity. Thus, as Cohen's study of Hausa migrants (1969) and Mitchell's seminal work on the Bisa (1956) have shown, ethnic identity cannot be explained as sheer cultural continuity, for identification may continue even when a migrant group has lost most of its cultural traditions. In such cases, the continuity of interpersonal linkages that migrants maintain among themselves and with individuals in their place of origin may be more important in explaining ethnic identification than are continuities in cultural tradition (i.e. language, clothing, customs) *per se*. Furthermore, the manifestation of ethnic identity or solidarity (as in the *kalela* dance) depends on the economic, political, and social situation. If ethnic identity is viewed as a concomitant of social ties rather than of cultural continuity, it is not surprising that ethnic identity

Research (1972–1974) on which this article is based is supported by the Swiss National Science Foundation. H. C. Buechler was on sabbatical leave from Syracuse University during the academic year 1972/1973.

among Hausa urban migrants should have been strengthened rather than weakened by their new adaptations, which were quite different from those of their fellow tribesmen at home.

The persistence of Spanish Galician ethnic identification in the face of large-scale emigration to the Americas, other European countries, and Australia poses a similar problem. Like the Hausa and the Bisa, Galicians who inhabit the northwest corner of Spain ascribe to themselves a number of characteristic and identifiable traits including the Gallegan language, stewed foods, and oxcarts. Intellectuals and other middle class Galicians, and to some extent the peasants themselves, add to the list of typical Galician traits the *moriña gallega* or homesickness and love for the homeland, the avoidance of generalizations, a slipperiness in dealing with civil authorities, and an astuteness in getting ahead in the world. As in the case of the two African tribes the FACT of ethnic identification is more important than the professed basis for identification. We shall hypothesize that this fact is related to regularities of interpersonal behavior. We should not assume, however, that these regularities must necessarily be associated with the characteristics of a territorially bounded group but may be the result of non-localized social forces. More specifically, we shall contend that Galician ethnic identity is a function of regularities of social interaction developed as a consequence of an age-old migratory pattern which is in turn related to Galicia's geopolitical position within Spain and Europe.

Major migratory movements from Galicia are centuries old. As early as the sixteenth century, a large number of Galicians migrated to the newly reconquered Granada. In the eighteenth century they harvested grain in Castille and worked as longshoremen in the ports of Portugal, France, Italy, and England. (Meijide Pardo 1960:465, 467). Then as today, migration grew out of land scarcity, which at that time was compounded by heavy taxes, tithes, and other contributions and levies that the peasants were forced to pay to the landlords, the church, the crown, and the army. The early part of the nineteenth century witnessed many Galicians working in the mines of Seville (Meijide Pardo, 1960:570). But seasonal labor migration to other Spanish provinces declined toward the middle of the nineteenth century, being replaced mainly by migration to Latin American, specifically to Cuba, Uruguay, Brazil, and later Venezuela, which began in the eighteenth century but reached major proportions only during the latter half of the nineteenth century (García Fernández 1965). Declining in the early part of the twentieth century, it reached another high after World War II.

According to Sánchez López (1967:55) La Coruña, the province in which we conducted our intensive research, had the highest rate of migration in Galicia and perhaps in all of Spain. The 354,525 persons from La Coruña who migrated overseas from 1910–1960 represented more than one third of the population in 1960 (i.e. 991,729 persons). However, THIS form of migration decreased abruptly in the early 1960's. Although initially migration to other parts of Europe was popular mainly among laborers from Southern Spain, Galician labor migration has grown at an accelerated rate since 1961. By 1963 it had by far surpassed migration to South America in importance. In terms of continental emigration from Galicia, La Coruña ranked second (following Orense) from 1963–1970 but by the beginning of 1971, this province experienced the heaviest migration in all of Galicia and Spain. (Congreso regional de la emigración gallega, 1971:56–57). Migration thus has been and continues to be an integral part of Galician life.

The following figures may give some idea of the magnitude of present-day Galician migration: in 1970 Galicia, a region half the size of Switzerland, had 2,583,674 inhabitants. Since 1960 the census points to a net loss of 233,856 or 8 percent due to emigration. Because contemporary migrants to other European countries (in contrast to earlier migrants) often return home for Christmas and a census reflects the population on December 31 of the census year, real emigration and temporary population loss is, in fact, much higher. Currently, (i.e. in 1972, 1973) according to Instituto Nacional de Emigación (La Coruña) records, the highest percentage of migrants from the province go to Switzerland, the country of destination that we selected for intensive study.

Our sample of 154 households in Santa Maria, a parish in the province of La Coruña, reflects the history of Galician migration sketched above. Ninety-six or 62 percent of the households included members or children of members who were or had been out of the country, and an additional five had members who had emigrated to other parts of Spain. If one adds migrant siblings and parents of household heads, this figure would be much higher still.

Our preliminary findings corroborate Beiras (1970) and Sánchez López (1967) in that we too found that more men than women migrate. This difference was particularly pronounced in the migration to the Americas in the early part of this century. Similarly the age of migration has changed. The latter increased until 1950, whereupon it decreased again slightly. In Santa María the reason for these changes is quite clear. Between 1920 and 1930, when most of our older informants migrated to the Americas (especially to Cuba and Uruguay), they were as young as fifteen when they left, returning some five to ten years later when they had saved enough to establish an independent household. After marriage, some emigrated again, usually alone, while most settled down permanently in Galicia. Today the pattern is different. Young men and, in lesser proportions, young women migrate to other European countries, predominantly Switzerland, Germany, and France, before they marry. The men usually return for military service, then migrate again until they marry, whereupon the couple often migrates together. Many migrants avoid having children in the beginning of the marriage. Others return just before or after the birth of the second child, who has usually been left behind with the maternal grandparents. Women rarely remain away after the birth of the third child, while men may continue to migrate for a few more years. Small children are rarely taken abroad, but when they are, they are generally sent back to Spain to be educated.

The demographic composition of the migrant colonies is predominantly male with an extremely narrow age distribution. In 1972, in Thun, Switzerland with a Galician migrant population numbering 262 only 74 (or 28 percent) were female. Their average age was 29.4 (Eighty-four percent of them were between the ages of eighteen and thirty-five). Similarly, the average age of the 188 male Galician migrants in the same city is 31.2 years with 68 percent in the same age grade. Many of the migrants were married (159 or 59 percent) but only 28 percent were accompanied by their spouses. The official records show that all of their 173 children were absent: 167 in Spain and six in Italy; but our observations and school records indicate that there are at least ten Galician children in Thun.

In contrast the parishes of origin are inhabited mainly by persons aged under eighteen and over forty, plus some younger women with two or more children and a few young men who commute to work in towns and cities or who have established small construction enterprises and other small businesses in the parish. The contrast is all the more marked because people in Galicia are very long-lived.[1]

The migratory process is made possible through a wide range of interpersonal ties. The scope of these ties is important in understanding Galician ethnic identification. First demographic complementarity of the home and migrant populations make for close socioeconomic linkages between migrants and their relatives at home. Grandparents rear the migrants' firstborn children, and although the Galician households, at

---

[1]   Of thirty-eight persons whose deaths were reported in the parish records of Sta. María in the three years between 1970 and 1972 (including a member of the parish who died in Germany) four were ninety or more years old, fourteen between eighty and ninety, eight between seventy and eighty and three between sixty and seventy (Of the remaining nine, two were infants and two had died in accidents.)

least in the area of Santa María, are still largely self-sufficient in their basic food requirements, the money sent by the migrants and the presents they give when they come home during vacations provide the household with clothing, home furnishings, appliances, a few luxury foods such as fruit, and improved housing.

The amount of money which migrants send home varies according to the financial circumstances of the family involved. Thus migrants may send home from $25 to $100 for the care of a child. One grandmother who takes care of two children aged three and ten, with migrant parents working near Zurich, received 3000 pesetas ($50) a month in addition to presents. She said that this is what her other working daughter-in-law pays for child care in La Coruña.

The economic ties with the home community are further enhanced by the fact that migrants whose parents own sufficient land often provide their children, especially the daughters, with a plot of land to build a house, perhaps the principal goal of emigration. Because a lot situated on a road may cost $2500 or more, this form of assistance is a powerful incentive to maintain ties with one's place of birth. For example, an older informant, a return migrant from Cuba, with two sons (one in Venezuela and another in Switzerland), gave his two daughters who had worked in England, house plots on the main thoroughfare, in addition to raising one of their sons. One of his daughters employed her savings from emigration to build a house and bar, and the other established herself as a seamstress in her new home. One may also use such ties to establish other small service enterprises (such as restaurants, grocery stores, gas stations, garages and construction firms). The money so invested of course provides work for those who choose to remain at home.

Finally, ties between migrants and relatives at home are a safeguard for those left behind. One of the great fears of Galician women is abandonment. Indeed our sample shows a considerable number of women whose husbands left for the Americas and were never heard from again. These cases are much rarer today. Relatives and friends are quick to advise wives of men who establish liaisons in their host country, and easy communications in Europe make rapid action possible. For instance, in one case a husband was urgently called back to Spain, and his family refused to let him emigrate again; in others, reluctant migrant bridegrooms are pressured into marriage.

Secondly the migration process is associated with a complex network of ties among migrants themselves. Since these ties are in turn based upon ties among those who have remained at home or who have returned either to their communities of origin or to nearby cities, we must first describe the nature of the ties among Galicians within their home region.

The ties linking migrants with related households in Galicia cut across geographic, hamlet, parish, district, as well as class boundaries. Although the hamlets have some social cohesion (e.g. mutual aid in agriculture is usually restricted to hamlet members, and joint decisions regarding road building and other facilities must occasionally be made at the hamlet level), this is not the case on the parish level, at least not in Santa María. There is a great deal of social interaction between individuals belonging to neighboring hamlets whether or not they belong to the same parish. Conversely, persons living in distant hamlets within Santa María may enjoy little social intercourse apart from that engendered by sharing a common cemetery. It is not unusual for an individual to sponsor a mass in the neighboring parish, and young parishioners attend dances and regularly marry into parishes located ten to fifteen miles away. Of 178 marriages recorded in the parish records between 1963 and 1972, 112 (or 62 percent) were parish exogamous. Social ties also extend to relatives and members of the same group of hamlets who have moved to nearby towns and to La Coruña and Santiago. So, parishioners regularly become clients of townsmen and urbanites who have established small businesses and services at the same time that they partake in family celebrations and mobilize legal aid in both places. A small number of them may even sell or abandon land at home and settle wherever conditions are more favorable, whether relatives live in the area or not, while others live and work in other areas of Spain for shorter spans of time.

Numerous family histories and our annotated census also revealed the broad range of occupations, educational background, and lifestyle for both women and men which cut across traditional classifications of class. In most larger families one finds agricultural laborers, industrial skilled and clerical workers, traders, businessmen and women, as well as a few professionals especially in the service professions: the clergy, teaching, nursing, agricultural extension, and other kinds of technical assistance. The range was associated more with "middle peasants" but was not limited to them alone.

Galician society, then, provides a geographically widespread and socially diverse range of ties. This range is essential for all Galicians who must leave the parental home and are not able to reside in the spouse's home, as well as for those whose parents have little land. Multiple ties allow them more choice to cope with a life full of uncertainties. In Galicia, stable employment is difficult to find. Even those who never leave their area of origin have often lived in different parishes and worked in three or more professions during their lifetimes.

It is this same broad network of ties that is available to the migrant in the migration process. Except in the first years of migration to other European countries, formal channels of gaining employment, e.g. the workers' union, were largely shunned by the migrants studied. Relatives and friends ask migrants to find jobs for them, and foreign employers avail themselves of the same channels to recruit workers. In some instances migrants with numerous connections at home may even act as semi-official paid job agents. As a result, individuals from the same area of Galicia may be concentrated in the same locality abroad and even in the same enterprise.

Over the last ten years both the official registration of foreign inhabitants and the employee records of major enterprises in Switzerland indicate such clustering. Thus the records from 1961–1972 of one large hotel on the Lake of Thun reflected not only the phenomenal increase in Spanish employees and the concentration of Galicians, but also the growth and attribution of persons from a limited cluster of parishes. In that ten year period the increase had been from two to thirty-six (twenty-nine of whom were Galicians) from five parish clusters. Frequently individuals from the same or adjacent parishes who did not know one another in Galicia work or live together abroad because some mutual friend or relative aided in placing them or their "go-betweens." Later, because Gallegos are hard bargainers and use their connections effectively to improve their salaries, they may use other ties to move to better situations and/or to put pressure on their employers. Unlike Europe, in countries like Venezuela, migrants are allowed to ensure a constant labor pool for their own purposes. Thus Eleuterio, presently on a vacation in Santa María to find a wife, frequently visited the Club de Amigos de Santiago in Caracas, which was attended mostly by migrants from his province, in order to recruit workers for his own construction venture.

The need for contacts for job recruitment is especially true for seasonal laborers who are often unable to return to their previous work the following season, and who often must wait for months for new contracts. Those with the largest number of well placed contacts obtain the jobs.

Not only jobs but rooms or apartments are next to impossible to find in overcrowded Swiss cities without personal contacts. According to the police files in Geneva, where the address changes of all inhabitants are recorded, migrants often change their residence two or three times a year.

Since, contrary to a popular Swiss stereotype, Galician migrants do not live to work and save money alone, the foregoing ties are the basis for their social life both in Switzerland and upon their return. In Switzerland the little free time available is spent in each other's company. As more Galician migrants are found in any one place, social life has changed from the interaction with Spaniards in general, common ten years ago, to activities with kin and individuals from the same region of origin. Such affiliations are reinforced upon return. For example men from one parish in the province of La Coruña who worked in a large tobacco factory in Switzerland regularly played cards together on market days in town, on vacation, and upon their permanent return home.

One might argue that for a migrant a viable alternative to relying on other Galicians would be to multiply his ties with them. But many factors militate against this. The legal restrictions on bringing nonworking relatives, including infants, into such countries as Switzerland and the uncertainties about future limitations of foreign laborers inhibit making a break with the home country and settling permanently in the host country. In European nations where the labor supply can be increased and reduced almost at will, it is difficult to entice a selected group of migrants to burn their bridges and to assimilate completely. Because of the rapid labor turnover (for instance only 130 of the 225 Galicians living in Thun in 1973 had been present a year earlier), assimilation can only be a rather solitary venture. Thus most of the persons who came with one of our informants who has lived in Thun for ten years have either returned to Galicia or moved to other Swiss localities. Nor do they have any intimate contacts with either Swiss or Italian workers beyond those they obtain in the work situation. The only migrants who do enjoy close ties with their hosts are the few longer term migrants who work in small Swiss family enterprises and in small geographically isolated locations.

Ethnic identification may be considered as the symbolic expression of the two aspects of adaptation to a migration situation: the fact that in order to migrate in the first place one must maintain a network of ties with other migrants and with individuals in the place of origin on the one hand, and, on the other, the difficulty of establishing multi-purpose ties, i.e. ties which affect more than a small aspect of life in the host country with members of the host population. These two factors reinforce one another because isolation by the hosts makes it essential to fall back on those ties which made migration possible, and these latter ties in turn reduce the need to assimilate into the host population by learning the language, or investing one's resources. This interplay explains why the identification of the migrant is segmentary in nature. While one could assume that social and economic isolation from the host population taken alone would further the development of class consciousness among all migrants regardless of origin, the ties activated and created in the process of migration separate migrants of different origins.

Let us now examine the reasons for the extent of this segmentation in terms of ethnic identification. Why do migrants stress their Galician identity rather than a provincial or national one?

The province turns out to be a somewhat artificial administrative unit. Although persons from our parish, which is located in the center of the province, did have most of their ties within the province, this would not be true for individuals living closer to the borders of other provinces. Although Spanish identity is stressed in certain contexts, Galicians regard themselves as having been neglected by the political and economic centers of power, indeed deliberately isolated by them. The mistrust of authority which in the last analysis is tacitly recognized as synonymous with the center and therefore with Spain as a nation, makes it difficult for Galicians to identify with their country in a direct and immediate manner. The Gallegan language, their common background as small landholders, and the shared lot as a region of migrants provide a more significant emblem by which to justify their actions. For both the migrant and for his dependents who have stayed behind, Galician identity is, first and foremost, coterminous with being a member of a migrant population that has adapted to its age-old plight by relying on its members to face life in strange lands without expelling them inevitably from their homeland. It is a justification of ties which has proven to be a viable means of adapting to life in Galacia, to migration, and to the return home, for most Galicians expect to return to their native region.

The meaningfulness of Galician identity is, however, highly situational. Thus, Galicians in Switzerland stress their particular food habits. They look down upon the Italians for eating spaghetti and take every opportunity to cook for themselves. Swiss chain food stores even provide such Galician delicacies as octopus because of migrant demand. And yet when they come home, they are often quick to criticize Galician cooking. Such innovations as dried soups are certainly related to European migration. The migrants also delight in veal, which is bred but rarely eaten by Galician peasants. Indeed, homecoming migrants vaunt the conditions of life in Switzerland as much as abroad they criticize the inadequate and expensive lodgings, the food, and the inhospitality of the Swiss. Their identification with migrant life in Switzerland earns them the epithet of *los suizos* among those who have stayed at home.[2] Their identification is symbolized by considerable linguistic play, for migrants delight in puns in

[2] We have never heard equivalent terms for migrants to other countries. The term seems to designate migrants to Germany as well. (Similarly the term *hacer las Americas* [do the Americas] applies to migration to Central Europe too).

both languages and jokes about the pitfalls and misuse of foreign terms.

At home Galician identity is a relative concept too. It is stressed when deploring discriminating government policies regarding milk and meat prices and the importation of agricultural products from other European countries. It is stressed when one speaks of the lack of industrialization in northwestern Spain and of the slowness with which an adequate infrastructure is being created. The limits of meaningfulness are difficult to ascertain, because emigration to other European countries is too recent a phenomenon. It is quite obvious that second-generation Galician migrants frequently intermarry. Identifying as a Galician in social intercourse in certain contexts in the host country is most certainly continued in that generation and perhaps beyond. In other instances it may have a rather hollow ring. For example, the wife of a first-generation migrant who had just come back from Australia was introduced to us as being from Lugo, although she was born in Montevideo. The visit sparked a heated conversation in which the husband criticized Australia while the wife defended the country. It soon became apparent that the two had entirely different goals in mind with respect to migration. While his idea of a good migration situation was being able to save money quickly and then return to Galicia, she would have preferred to settle wherever she felt the conditions were best. She had willingly left Montevideo for a higher standard of living in Australia. Then having persuaded her parents to come from Montevideo to Australia, she had been perfectly happy there. She could not imagine why her husband wanted to return to Galicia and then look for another job in Switzerland where they would be faced with yet another language. In contrast, HE saw in migration to Switzerland a logical step toward saving more rapidly in order to build a house on a lot they had already bought in a nearby town. Her label as a Gallega in this context was tenuous indeed. Questioning the basic tenet, i.e. that no matter how long you stay in another country, your basic mission is to save in case you want to (or have to) return home, was tantamount to denying Galician identity.

In contrast, the behavior of a spinster from the Galician province of Lugo who owns a small hotel in Montreal was more in accord with that concept. She had come to Montreal in 1949 and had first worked in other hotels until she was able to establish her own business. Her employees were Spaniards, albeit not Galicians. Nevertheless, she persuaded one of them to visit her family in Galicia when he went to Spain on vacation. She obviously wanted to retain her ties to Galicia for she planned to retire there eventually. Similarly the young man who came to Switzerland as a child with his parents, who speaks the local dialect, and is seriously thinking of taking the unheard of step of marrying a Swiss girl, is following the precept of Galician identity. He plans to return to La Coruña with her.

Given the nature of Galician identity, it is not surprising that there is a fear of losing one's cultural characteristics by becoming too accustomed to the way of life in the host country. Our informants were fond of telling of pathetic cases such as that of a relative who, upon her return to La Coruña vainly searched for a hairdresser at 8 A.M., a time when all Swiss businesses are open but two hours before Spanish ones are. With equal alacrity one informant recounted a story about a friend who used English words in a letter she wrote home. The migrant had written that her boss had been so kind as to make a gift of clothing left by the "boys" in the boarding school where she worked. This filled her mother with awe and amazement, for *bois* signifies bulls in Gallego. "Do bulls in England really wear clothing?" she asked. For the same reason Gallegos avoid sending their children to Swiss schools, even when they have resided in Switzerland long enough to acquire the right to take their children along. The fear that the children could not adapt to Spanish schools again should they return to Galicia is an often repeated theme.

The Galician fear of the loss of ethnic identity has its counterpart in the greater Swiss fear of *Überfremdung* (overforeignization.) Max Frisch (quoted in Braun, 1970) has remarked: "We called for a labor force, and human beings came." The quote reflects the tension surrounding the sensitive issue created by the fact that there are some 900,000 foreign workers to 5,200,000 Swiss citizens. Although most Swiss recognize the necessity of the contribution of the immigrants to economic prosperity, they are equally afraid of overpopulation and unwilling to bear the cost of expanding social services. Characteristic of this fear is the denial that the migrants could contribute anything apart from labor. The only possibility of closer contact is seen as total assimilation on the part of the migrants. (Thus we were unable to obtain any literature on migrants and the cultures to which they belonged in Swiss book stores although this literature is quite extensive; in contrast books on *Überfremdung* abounded.) During our school visits children of foreigners were never asked to contribute information about their own cultural background. It was also automatically assumed that the children of foreign workers lived in a socially and culturally impoverished environment, which was defined by some of our teacher informants as an environment lacking nature walks or trips to the zoo. The Galicians are well aware of these Swiss attitudes which if anything serve to reinforce their ethnic identification.

In conclusion, the Galician case may shed some light on the meaning of identification along linguistic and cultural lines. First, ethnic identification is contextual. In Galicia, ethnic identification is a statement about isolation from the political and economic centers of power and, with reference to migration, it describes the multiple dependencies among migrants and between the latter and their relatives at home as well as the separation from the host population and from other migrant groups. This does not mean that ethnic identification can be likened to a theatrical act in Goffman's sense of "face-work" (1967:4–46) or "performance" (1959:15), i.e. that individuals put up the front of ethnic identity whenever it best suits them. Goffman's view implies a consciousness about one's actions that we do not think applies in most situations. Barth's interpretation (1969) of ethnic identity as a set of cultural norms that are accepted or rejected by individuals belonging to groups that are in contact according to the advantages they perceive seems equally unsuitable, for it clouds the social processes, the creation, maintenance, and abrogation of social ties, which precede or accompany changes in ethnic identity. Rather, it seems to us that ethnic identity is an expressive mechanism that employs certain cultural continuities as symbols to communicate certain broadly based social ties. One may expect a configuration of social ties (or transformations of this configuration) in any given social context to be expressed in one manner or another. Ethnicity is simply one form of expression particularly appropriate to network regularities that have persisted over long periods of time.

REFERENCES

BARTH, F., *editor*
1969   *Ethnic groups and boundaries.* Boston: Little, Brown.
BEIRAS, J. M.
1970   *Estructura y problemas de la población gallega.* La Coruña: Graffinsa.
BRAUN, R.
1970   *Sozio-kulturelle Probleme der Eingliederung italienischer Arbeitskräfte in der Schweiz.* Zurich: Eugen Rentsch Verlag.
COHEN, A.
1969   *Custom and politics in urban Africa: a study of Hausa migrants in Yoruba towns.* Berkeley: University of California Press.
CONGRESO REGIONAL DE LA EMIGRACIÓN GALLEGA
1971   *Problematica de la emigración gallega.* La Coruña: Oficina de relaciones con los galletos en el Exterior.
GARCÍA FERNÁNDEZ, J.
1965   *La emigracion exterior de España Barcelona.* Ariel.

GOFFMAN, E.
1959   *The presentation of self in everyday life*. New York: Doubledav.
1967   *Interaction ritual: essays on face-to-face behavior*. New York: Double-
        day.
MEIJIDE PARDO, A.
1960   *Emigración, sociedad y economía en la Galicia del siglo XVIII*. Estudios
        de historia social de España, Consejo Superior de Investigaciones
        Científicas Instituto Balmes de Sociología, Madrid. Volume 4.
MITCHELL, J. CLYDE
1956   *The Kalela dance: Aspects of social relationships among urban
        Africans in Northern Rhodesia*. Rhodes Livingstone Paper 27.
SÁNCHEZ LÓPEZ, F.
1967   *Movimientos migratorios de Galicia*. Vigo: Editorial Compostela.

Ethnicity as a Factor in Modern American Indian Migration: A Winnebago Case Study with References to Other Indian Situations

WILLIAM H. HODGE

The question of ethnicity as a factor in modern American Indian migration is an important but difficult relationship to study. The implications of both variables are so extensive that they must be arbitrarily reduced to manageable proportions. The situation is further complicated by the fact that the full significance of Indian activities cannot be understood without viewing them in the context of the larger non-Indian society. Neither comprehensive data nor appropriate methodology are available for such a task.

Accordingly, this analysis is arranged along the following lines. For present purposes, the highly generalized, interrelated, eclectic terms, "identity," "ethnicity," and "self-conception" are regarded as being similar if not identical. Migration is viewed as movement both in space and time and as having a wide variety of subtle implications discussed in an earlier publication (Hodge 1971:346–391).

Central emphasis is given to a single case study of a Winnebago man whose life history exemplifies the thesis of this study: migration when carried out by an individual from a society having a loose social structure heightens and extends his sense of ethnic identity as an Indian. This increased sense of identity or ethnicity can have primarily tribal implications, assume a pan-Indian frame of reference, or incorporate both dimensions should a particular situation require it. Conversely, if migration occurs where the society of a migrant has a tight social structure, the opposite end result is likely to be produced: Indian ethnicity or identity becomes muted and distorted, often with unsatisfactory immediate or long-term effects for the particular individual.[1] Such a

---

[1] The possibility of comparing tight and loose types of social strcture vis-à-vis migra- and ethnicity was suggested to me by Gerald L. Gold.

result is exemplified by a brief consideration of the migration differentials within a single family living at Bear Pueblo. A family is considered here because given the pueblo context, it is a far more viable social unit than a single individual. Some of the personal and place names I have used are fictitious. In an attempt to indicate partially the range of variation, a number of other Indian migration situations are considered in more succinct fashion.

P. J. Pelto (1968:37–40) has argued that the dimension of tightness and looseness can characterize entire societies and that these features are related to other important aspects within a society such as personality or types of deviant behavior. During the past thirty-five years, a number of other anthropologists in one way or another have also pointed out the possibility of various kinds of correlations. While tightness or looseness is a matter of degree and both variables constitute opposite poles of a continuum, a wide variety of societies, or "social structures," throughout the world can be usefully characterized in terms of this continuum.

According to Pelto (1968:38) a tight social structure or society has twelve distinguishing elements: (1) permanent recognized political control; (2) legitimate use of force; (3) political authority differentiated within the community; (4) some conscription of economic goods, including taxation; (5) priests and/or religious societies; (6) some conscription of labor; (7) hereditary recruitment to a priesthood or religious society when they exist within the local community; (8) curing of illness in the hands of community or sub-community leaders, priests, or a religious society or of other persons identified with leadership; (9) mainly corporate ownership and use of production property; (10) some corporate ownership of stored food in the community; (11) some corporate control of incorporeal property; and (12) theocracy.

On the contrary, a loose social structure or society would exhibit considerable tolerance for deviant behavior with little emphasis placed upon the values of group organization, formality, permanence, durability and solidarity. In addition such structures would require little cultural commitment on the part of individuals and would have a relatively high degree of cultural adaptability. Among representative societies having a tight social structure are the Hutterites of North America, the Hano of Arizona, and the Lugbara of Uganda. Examples of societies having a loose social structure are the Skolt Lapps of Northeastern Finland, the Cubeo of Brazil, and the !Kung of South Africa.[2]

---

[2]   Tom McFeat has independently carried out an unpublished analysis similar to mine using the Zuñi as an example of a tight social structure and the Micmac representing the loose variety.

This study has two central aims: first, to suggest that the concepts of tight and loose social structure can be related in a significant way to migration and ethnicity; and second, to illustrate this fact by showing how many of the variables within the tight-loose construct operate with respect to specific individuals.

The materials presented here are by far more descriptive than theoretical, but such a presentation is necessitated by the sparse and often distorted conceptions of contemporary American Indians. To date there are too few adequate descriptions of contemporary Indian behavior. Finally, it is my intent to raise questions that would suggest various directions for future reserach.

AMERICAN INDIANS TODAY AND MIGRATION

I would estimate that at least 60 percent of American Indians are full or part-time residents of cities. Obviously, then, in studying these people the urban environment is of great importance. However, attention must also be given to Indians who live on reservations or in other kinds of rural communities because for most Indians urban and rural living are part of one pattern of life or one system. Both kinds of residence must be considered if either is to be understood. Much stress should also be devoted to the examination of modern Indian life as movement *per se*.

One of the central integrating aspects of all Indian life is travel. Travel is conceived as a necessity to gain that which makes life possible and also as a great good in itself. To be Indian is to seek new vistas and challenges but then to return home. Indians would agree with Robert Frost who defined home as "a place where, if you go there, they got to take you in."

I believe that this perpetual wandering and camping is a very old endeavor for Indians. It is as old as North American cities themselves. From Jamestown, Virginia, to the concrete wilderness of Los Angeles, Indians have come, looked, briefly lived in cities, and then moved on to be replaced by others of their kind. Throughout this process, most have remained Indians, first, last, and always.

This desire for travel, used as a frame of reference and placed in sharper focus, centers around the interrelationship of three variables: migration, residence, and behavior as they relate to fluctuations in resources. Fluctuations in resources, in turn, are correlated with a variety of social and cultural changes, the instability of resources, and an expanding population. These changes cannot always be readily predicted by those most closely influenced by such developments. Hence, Indian life is based upon a variety of subsistence patterns as they vary through time, and it consequently assumes a plastic, effervescent kind of texture characterized above as movement, travel, or migration.

The Indian population has been increasing at a significant rate for at least the past fifty years. The resouces that Indians have had to rely upon within the confines of their reservations and/or rural communities during this period have either remained constant or decreased in magnitude. The various modes of subsistence such as pastoralism or limited dry and wet farming supplemented by a modicum of hunting and gathering have proven to be woefully inadequate to support the increasing population numbers. Accordingly, wage labor and some form of welfare support have been relied upon with greater frequency, both generally being sought outside the home. The utilization of wage labor and welfare imply some form of migration, often to an urban area, on the part of individuals or individuals as members of families.

A further observation should be made before presenting the specific data provided below. To understand migration, defined generally as movement through time and space, its reciprocal, non-migration, should be analyzed. Both are regarded as intrinsic aspects of the same process. If some understanding is to be gained as to why a given Indian moves from one place to another at a particular time, one should know why he remains elsewhere at another time. The two kinds of behavior, movement and non-movement, often result from the same influences, but in each case their arrangement or combination varies. Migration by a member of a loose society heightens the sense of ethnicity while migration by a member of a tight society significantly decreases it. Continuous residence or non-migration influences the degree and direction of ethnicity according to the nature of the migration which antedated and followed it.

THE WINNEBAGOS

More than 3,000 Winnebago Indians live in the states of Wisconsin, Minnesota, and Nebraska. At least half of this number are Wisconsin residents. Sieber and Lurie (1965:1–10) provide a useful summary of Winnebago contact with whites beginning in the first quarter of the nineteenth century. Under heavy dures by the federal government, the Winnebagos ceded their land in southern Wisconsin and northwestern Illinois to whites. About forty bands were gradually pushed to the north and to the west until 1837, when a large number of these Indains, then in cental Wisconsin, refused to move again and thus acquired the status of squatters. The remainder agreed to abide by their treaties and eventually were located on a reservation in eastern Nebraska in 1865 after having previously lived in Minnesota and South Dakota.

The "disaffected bands" who would not leave Wisconsin were finally granted forty-acre homesteads by the federal government in 1874 if they would relinquish claims to the Nebraska reservation. The Winnebagos readily agreed to do this. Unfortunately, most of the land which they acquired in this manner had limited utility for agriculture or hunting and gathering. Fall and winter trapping could provide only a supplementary form of income. Therefore, an itinerant crop-harvesting economy was developed which was buttressed by limited sales of timber and occasional wage work in mills or factories or on roads. Small seasonal amounts of cash were produced by selling baskets and other handicrafts to tourists.

Many of these homesteads were lost through tax default after the twenty-year tax-free provisions expired. The remaining homesteads in the majority of cases now have been divided beyond any practical utility by the complications of heirship extending over four or more generations. Miller and Lurie (1963) characterize the current residence pattern and some of its implications as follows:

Beginning in the 1870's little communities of Winnebago began to spring up around missions, on remaining homestead plots and on land rented or bought from Whites. During the depression of the 1930's, as an emergency measure, the federal government acquired some land — less than 100 acres — where homes were built for a few homeless Winnebago families to live. The Winnebago communities are now scattered over an area of several hundred miles from Wittenberg in eastern Wisconsin to LaCrosse in western Wisconsin, with the largest community near the town of Black River Falls, and other towns and cities in the region. In effect, the Winnebago have developed a modern counterpart of the old band organization with scattered communities forming headquarters for groups of families who spend varying periods of time elsewhere in order to find sources of income. These modern bands, like the old ones, are tied together socially by bonds of kinship, friendship, common culture and language....

Mizen (1965–196:361) states that Winnebagos "are located within or adjacent to" Tomah, La Crosse, Black River Falls, Wittenberg, and Wisconsin Dells. Winnebagos are also found living "near" Friendship, New Lisbon, DeSoto, Willard, Mauston, Onalaska, Merrillan, Neillsville, Vesper, and Holmen. All of these cities are in Wisconsin.

From 1874 to the present, the Winnebagos' economic base seems to have remained the same with a gradually increasing emphasis upon wage labor. This, in turn, has entailed a steady increase in urban residence on both a full- and part-time basis.

However, urban residence does not constitute a highly desired form of living. Miller and Lurie (1963:28–29), after talking with 1,384 people representing 313 households scattered throughout the state, conclude that while most Winnebagos who live in a variety of large and small cities located in the Midwest achieve financial independence, the dependable cash income associated with urban living cannot compensate for its attendent disadvantages such as the frenetic pace of living occasioned by the demands of urban employment and the necessity of maintaining satisfactory relationships with friends and relatives away from the city.

Dan Jackson, a tall, well-built Winnebago with a relatively dark complexion, is thirty-eight years old. He is fluent in both the Winnebago and English languages. He often wears black-rimmed glasses. His quiet, well-modulated voice sounds remarkably like that of the actor Henry Fonda. The majority of his friends and associates like and respect him for what he is, an intelligent, self-reliant, traditionally-oriented Indian who has come to terms with a turbulent, challenging environment. That environment reaches from his mother's home to the north of Red Pond, south to the Racine-Kenosha area, where several of his blood and affinal kinsmen work. The places where Dan has lived and worked are indicated on Map 1. The order of residence is indicated by Roman numerals.

The texture of his life is a startling blend of Winnebago and white elements. One hot, sultry night in August of 1968, we sat in his comfortably air-conditioned living room watching, on his new color television set, the riots that were associated with the Democratic convention then being held in Chicago. After several minutes of viewing, he shook his head, turned to me, and said: "You know I'm Bear clan. One of our jobs is to keep order in the community. Something like this could never happen back up home." He then gestured to the north with his lips. As I looked at a well-made peyote rattle on a shelf over the television set, I could only nod my head in agreement.

How did such a man come to be as he is? Much of his past life seems to amount to a series of invitations to personal disaster rather than reward on any basis. The themes of conflict and reward are inextricably intertwined throughout his life. The elements of danger and tragedy form a strong countermotif to the progression of places, people, and events as they are linked together by time.

I was born in LaCrosse, Wisconsin, August 2, 1932, and we lived in the LaCrosse Indian settlement called Hunter's Bridge. There was my older brother and sister and my mother and dad. We lived there until I was about school age.

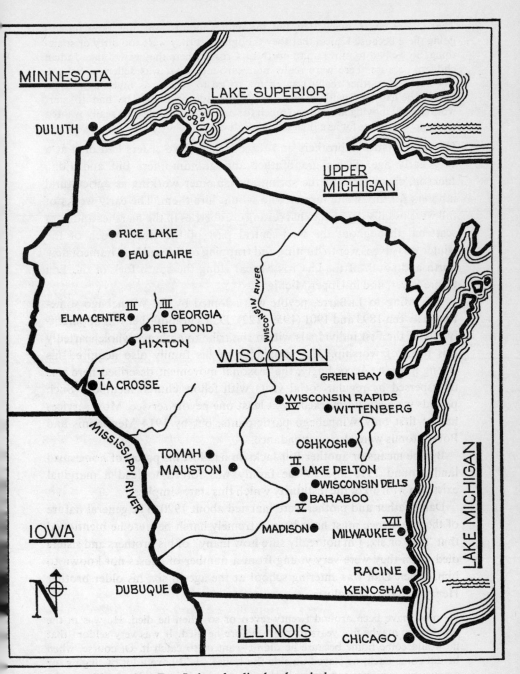

Map 1. Places where Dan Jackson has lived and worked
(order indicated by Roman numerals)

That school was Council Bay, but the whites didn't want any more Indians going there because I guess that they thought that they were too dirty or something. So we had to move up to north La Crosse where they would take Indian childern because there were really none around. That was Jefferson School. My dad and mother really wanted me to go to school as much as I could because he had only made it past the third grade and then he had to start working and moving around too much for any more school so he really wanted me to get at least as far as a high school diploma.[3]

His father had five brothers and three sisters. Two sisters had died at a very early age. Dan's grandfather and grandmother, Bill and Edna Jackson, spent most of the spring and summer working as agricultural laborers for any white farmer who would hire them. The early weeks of fall were usually devoted to harvesting cranberries in the marshes and bogs scattered throughout the west-central part of the state. Much of the winter was given over to hunting and trapping on federal land immediately north and south of the La Crosse area, along the south fork of the Eau Claire River, and in Upper Michigan.

According to LaBarre, peyote was adopted by the Winnebago sometime between 1893 and 1901 (1959: 122). Dan's grandfather was apparently one of the first individuals within the tribe to embrace wholeheartedly this form of worship. The remainder of his family also acquired his strong interest. Accordingly, the seasonal movement described here was interspersed by regular social visits with fellow church members. Such periods were always marked by at least one peyote service. Most services had at first only Winnebago participants, but by 1914 Menominis and Potawatomis were also in attendance.

By one means or another Bill Jackson had lost his parcel of homestead land around 1915 and so the family was forced to lead a marginal existence with all of the insecurity which this status implies.

Dan's father and mother were married about 1920. The general nature of their existence must have been extremely harsh because he mentioned that "five or six, I'm not really sure how many" of his brothers and sisters died when they were very young from a number of causes not known to him. When Dan was entering school at the age of six, his older brother Henry died of tuberculosis.

He must have been around twenty-seven or so when he died. He was in the sanatorium maybe five years or more before he died. It was very seldom that he would come home because he didn't want us to catch it. Of course, when he did come back, he stayed outside the house. He'd have a lot of singing, or a powwow or maybe something to do with the Medicine Lodge. I guess maybe he thought that things like that might cure him where the white doctors at the

---

[3] Hereafter, an asterisk * indicates a tape-recorded conversation.

sanatorium couldn't. My mother said he always told her she must boil all his eating utensils and his towels and everything else that he used. Then one time after he hadn't been home for real long, someone came and told us that he was dead.*

Despite the pall which Henry's death cast over the family, Dan did well in school and enjoyed his associations with his white school mates. He was the only Indian student enrolled and, as such, must have been something of a welcome diversion to the other students and teachers. His parents urged him to have nothing to do with other Indians outside the family who lived in the La Crosse area because such associations would only make trouble for him, and he carefully followed this advice. His mother worked intermittently as a seamstress in a La Crosse clothing factory. The six years at the La Crosse school passed quickly, but despite this strict, voluntary isolation from other Indians who were not close relatives, he was never allowed to forget his heritage as a Winnebago.

My folks always made sure that I had plenty of chances to see how the Winne-bagos all lived years ago because we used to visit with my parents' older rela-tives a lot. All the old people, they talked about war and fighting. All the Indians in them days knew how to live and they fought each other all the time. There was this one old man Jake Redbird who was my father's mother's brother, and he'd tell me about the times when some of the Chippewas would come down to the Black River area to steal horses and anything else that they could from Winnebagos. You really had to watch out all the time back then or you could get killed real easy. Old man Redbird said that you could just go out in the woods to pick some berries and there might be enemies waiting there to kill you. I think that I would have really liked to have lived during the days before the white men came around.

Besides Redbird, my folks left me for several weeks at a time with my grand-father Bill Jackson. He used to live for a while around the Mississippi between some tributaries where the Black River came in. There were little creeks all around and lots of marshes. Plenty of game. Nobody else around. That really made me feel like an Indian even though I was just nine or ten years old maybe. He lived in this wigwam with a hole in the middle of the roof for the smoke from the fire to go through. At night he built up a fire and he would tell me stories for as long as I could stay awake. The next morning there was a pile of snow that had drifted in through the hole in the roof during the night. That wigwam was just a frame of poles with a lot of canvas over it, but it was warm enough. Then, after a few days there, we'd get in his Model A Ford and drive to wherever my folks happened to be.

We also visited a lot of other old people who must have been some kind of relatives but I can't remember them well at all. They lived in some places that aren't there anymore like Sicklerville and Shrunkville (?). There used to be plenty of other old people around places like Merrill, Hixton, and Blair, but the ones that we visited have been dead for years now.*

In 1945 his family moved to Lake Delavan north of Wisconsin Dells. Dan was about thirteen at this time. The family moved to this community so that his father and sister could work in a defense plant there. He attended high school for the first two years at Wisconsin Dells. These two summers were spent eleven miles north of Red Pond near the small community of Georgia, where his father sold baskets woven from splints of black ash wood. The family liked the area so much that their savings from their wages at the defense plant were used to buy twenty acres of land that were well-wooded and close to good locations for the tourist souvenir business.

My father always was a great hustler. He really wanted to be because he thought that it was an awful disgrace to go on welfare like so many of the other Indians did as often as they could. My dad was proud of the fact he almost never had to ask for help. Only a few times that I can really remember. Nobody ever gave my family nothing, and he didn't want to ask anybody for anything else either. But sometimes in the middle of winter, things were really rough. One winter especially about 1948. There were only a couple of pieces of bread in the house and just enough gas in the car to get to town. My mother and dad went to town to the welfare to ask for help. They gave them a whole car load of groceries and money for gasoline and they even told them to go up to a certain farm and get a couple of cords of wood for the stove that we used for cooking and heating. But it made my dad mad and me too that the Winnebago tribe and the mission never would help us like they did Winnebagos who were still living on homestead land and close to the mission. They would tell him that since he bought his own land, he really didn't need any help. But except for owning those twenty acres, we were as bad off as a lot of people who had help all the time were. I grew up in the wigwam, the one that is out front of that two-room wooden frame house that my folks live in now. That isn't more than thirty-five feet long and fifteen feet wide. We'd have to have a wood fire burning on the dirt floor all the time during the winter. I never lived around where there was electricity and running water until I was about eighteen years old. When I was in high school, I almost never had any spending money like the white kids.*

Probably the most influential person in Dan's life has been his father, and it was from him that he acquired his ambivalent attitude toward whites, one which seems to consist of equal parts of respect, envy, and distrust.

My mother's brother Willie Lynx was our babysitter. They said that I needed somebody to wake me up in the morning and see that I was all right. Sometimes my folks would leave oh, maybe two or three weeks at a time and go all over trapping. Lots of times they'd go over to up north of LaCrosse along the Mississippi River trapping for muskrats and beaver. Often they'd be back on weekends, or sometimes in the middle of the week to check up on us and see that we had enough food in the house. Then they'd go right out again. My dad was in his fifties then and so was my mother and sometimes they didn't feel too good, but they'd always go out if they could possibly make it.
Once during the winter my mother and dad were out visiting some bunch of relatives and trapping and left me at home with my sister. This big snow

storm came up and they were really stuck. So they got up to this farm house where some whites lived and they let them stay there for about six days until the storm was over. Dad helped the farmer chop wood and do chores. Every night that farmer would read the Bible aloud and then he talked about who was going to Heaven and who would have to go to Hell. Finally the weather was good enough for them to get home and that white man even gave them some food and about $5.00 in cash to get back on. My folks have always been grateful for that help. A few years later my dad saw this farmer on the street in LaCrosse and offered to give him his $5.00 back but the man didn't want it. Then my dad told him, "Well, that's the way that you should feel because you whites took everything away from us Winnebagos and we didn't get nothin' for it." Then the farmer said, "Well, if that's the way you feel, you are really goin' to Hell." Then my dad told him, "Hell is for whites only. You whites have turned this earth into a hell for us Winnebagos." Then that white farmer just walked off real mad. My dad has always said that there was getting to be less and less room for Indians and since that is the way it is, we really have to work everything as hard as we can. You got to have money or you won't survive. He is right about that. As I see it, the more money you make and the more things that you have that you want, the better Indian you are. There is just no excuse for any Indian to be poor. There are too many opportunities to get money.*

Dan completed his last two years of high school at Elma Center, the school nearest his father's land. During the summer he helped his father with the souvenir business, worked for brief periods of time in nearby vegetable canneries, and worked for the state highway department. He worked as much as possible because he had to buy his own clothes, and he felt that he had to have a car. All of his school friends were white, and most of them had cars. He soon bought a two-door sedan and began driving over most of central and northern Wisconsin, "just to look around, but sometimes I could find ways to make money." He made his own engine repairs and soon developed a strong interest in auto mechanics. In his last year of high school he was offered a football scholarship to Eau Claire State College, but he rejected this since he would have to provide money for room and board.

So then I spent the next year just running around with my dad. We'd make souvenirs, mostly small drums out of old tire inner tubes and coffee cans, then find some other Indian where you could get bead work and baskets cheap from and boost up the prices for the white tourists. That was mostly summer, and then that fall we went over to Wisconsin Rapids to harvest cranberries. We waded around in hip-deep water with one of these big rakes from dawn to sundown sometimes. You get out of there so damn cold and tired you can hardly breathe. And then that winter, this was about 1950–1951, we went out on his trap lines, caught some mink, muskrat, and other things, but you really couldn't get much for the pelts.*

Then that spring he went over to La Crosse and tried to get a job with

Allis-Chalmers, but the plant had no vacancies for unskilled laborers. He then went to Baraboo and got a job as a general helper in the garage of the powder plant.

Through the Winnebago grape vine I heard that they were hiring over there and that was really my first big break. I was too young to work on the assembly line where they made the gun powder. I was nineteen and you had to be twenty-one, so they put me in the garage, especially when I told them that I like to fix cars. So I worked there for four years and for one semester I even commuted down to Madison for this night vocational school in auto mechanics, but the winter driving was too tough, so I didn't go any more after that. I was able to learn a lot and keep up with everything that I was supposed to do by watching other people work on jobs in the garage. But then the Korean War slowed down enough and they started laying people off and the job came to an end after four years there. This was 1954.*

While he was at Baraboo, he married Rose, a Winnebago. This marriage proved to be an unfortunate one that was to end three years later when his wife walked out of their apartment leaving him with a three-year-old son, Jeff. Probably because of the unpleasant memories associated with this time, Dan refused to talk about life with Rose beyond saying that his brothers-in-law helped him to find a job in Milwaukee. After looking around Chicago for one month and failing to find a job as a truck mechanic, he went to Wisconsin Dells and hunted unsuccessfully for work there for another month and then returned to his wife's brother's home in Chicago. This man knew of an opening in Milwaukee for a truck mechanic, and Dan and Rose moved there. It was shortly after this that she disappeared and Dan began divorce proceedings. His first job lasted one month, but his supervisor was sufficiently impressed with him to recommend him for a similar position as a truck mechanic at Mack Trucks. In the fall of 1956, he began work there as a "garage helper" and now (1972) is an assistant foreman in a shop devoted to repairing truck cabs and engines. He married another Winnebago woman, Judy, soon after he was divorced from his first wife. His marriage and present job have lasted fifteen years.

Now at Mack, I'll stay there until they either fire or retire me. If I stay until I retire, we'll go up north around Georgia and maybe I'll open a small garage and filling station. I never did look hard for another job up north after I left the powder plant at Baraboo. I wouldn't want to be up there now because it's just like my dad says. If you're an Indian and live around where there are a lot of other Indians, everything that you do good and especially bad is magnified one hundred times by the whites. You get blamed for something a drunken Indian slob does. With farming, hunting, and trapping and anything else that Winnebagos used to do no good now for earning a living, you got to work with whites. I feel that if I'm going to do this, it might as well be someplace where I can have a good job and not get blamed for the bad things that some other Indian does. I'm the only Indian where I work, and I like it that way. Some of these guys under me get a little jealous sometimes since I was made assistant foreman, but I got ways of handling that. Like I manage and play on one of the softball teams that they have and I'm always telling jokes around the shop. I like the job I guess because it really keeps me jumping. Just not anyone can do this. Every repair job that comes into our place is assigned to one mechanic and like if I have to replace a clutch I know that I have only so many hours and minutes to do that job. Then I have to be finished and ready to work on something else. And after the job is done, it had better be right because they keep a record of who has repaired what and if that truck has clutch trouble too soon again, I get called to the office to explain what went wrong. If that happens too many times, I'd get fired.*

With his second marriage, Dan's life seems to have assumed a regular but demanding pace. Two incidents have marred this portion of his life. Since Judy cannot have children, they adopted in 1965 a Winnebago infant who died a few months later. No additional adoptions have been made. In April, 1970, his father died at the age of seventy-eight after a long illness. Dan's devotion to the sacrament of peyote has provided a large measure of solace during these crises. In fact, the use of peyote seems to be an increasingly dominant part of his life as time goes on. This seems to be one of the few aspects of his existence that he was reluctant to discuss during our interviews. He would seldom talk about peyote while the tape recorder was in operation and would not discuss with me to any extent his ideas about its significance for him during the interviews. Most of the following is a synthesis of a variety of offhand remarks that he made to me over a period of eighteen months. My recall here is reasonably accurate but far from total.

The worship of God through the use of peyote in company with other Indians has been a prominent and significant influence on Dan's life since he began participating in peyote services at the age of thirteen. His father had convinced him that all men need a guide to follow through life. This guide should generally provide aid and comfort in time of distress and should also supply specific rules to follow in given difficult situations. Such a guide should also provide a plan for people to live out in times of order and prosperity. Peyote was not the only such plan and others available to other men were equally good, but peyote was something that he used because his father had told him that it had helped him.

Dan's grandfather had initially been introduced to peyote by a delegation of Indians from Oklahoma and had relied upon it for the rest of his adult life. Most of Dan's Winnebago friends used peyote, as did his wife and sixteen-year-old son. He was firmly convinced that peyote had given him his house in Milwaukee, his good job, his car, his marriage, and the tranquillity to view life as a series of positive and negative episodes experienced in the fellowship of other Indians along the peyote road. Peyote had given him these things by teaching him that he must work hard, provide for his family, and attempt to live in harmony with all other men and the inanimate universe. Peyote would not have given him these things if he had not supplied a great deal of concerted effort over a long period of time. Life for him at times is difficult and terribly unfair. Virtue and hard work are not always rewarded as they should be since both can make him vulnerable to the machinations of other men. However, such behavior on their part does not discredit the essential validity of the peyote road for him or other Indians.

His consumption of peyote during a service can be as great as thirty-five or forty buttons. He goes to the Red Pond area at least twice a month for services. Chewing the dry, hard pieces of cactus has worn down enough teeth so that he now has a complete upper plate and his remaining natural teeth are in poor condition. Yet his interest in peyote continues to be great. He uses a good quality, portable tape recorder to record unfamiliar songs used during a service, and then plays the recorded tapes when he is at home in Milwaukee so that he can learn this new music. He is a "captain" for many of the Milwaukee Winnebagos who use peyote. As a captain he is responsible for helping to maintain communication between Milwaukee Winnebagos and their fellow church members up north during times of crisis. During one relaxed conversation, he made the following statement:

We believe that church members should help each other all they can, especially when somebody dies or is very sick. This can be quite a problem if you live in the city and other friends are 250 miles away. You have to organize something special. Suppose a peyote man dies up north and he and his family have a lot of friends living down here in Milwaukee. Those people need help fast and you can't depend entirely on the white ways to give the help that's needed. What happens is that somebody close to the family up there calls on the telephone down here and they reach two or three captains. Now each one of these has the responsibility to contact ten or twelve families, all Winnebago and all peyote, down here. He tells them that this man has died and his family needs help and asks them how much money can they give to send up there. A captain can do this in twenty-four hours. So he gets this money and then calls this man up north and that guy gets a total of the cash collected here in town. Then he takes that sum out of his own bank account and gives it to the family. He can do this because the captains have told him that their personal checks are in the mail to him, and he will have his money back, less whatever contribution that he wants to make, in a day or two. The dead man's family gets some help fast and they also know that we are all pulling for them down here. Then in two or three weeks, when everyone can get off, they go up north for a memorial service on Saturday night. Everybody does their part because we all know that we'll get help like that when we need it.*

Looked at in broad perspective, Dan's life now moves at an incredibly rapid pace as he attempts to meet the demands of his Winnebago friends and relatives up north, his Indian colleagues in the city, and his employer. The fact that his efforts are usually successful is a great tribute to his energy and resourcefulness. Taxing eighteen-hour days seven days a week are the rule, not the exception, in his household. Because his wife, Judy, works at a full-time job as a secretary, many of the routine duties of housekeeping fall on his son. Times for total relaxation and quiet are rare. Both Dan and his wife frequently mentioned that if they sat down to watch television in the evenings, they would usually fall asleep. I attribute this reaction to physical exhaustion rather than to the usual poor-quality entertainment that television provides.

I asked Dan to describe the family's activities during a typical week:

Monday's about the worst day of the week to get up and go to work, but on Monday evening I don't do anything because I am recuperating from the weekend up north. Tuesday's not much different. We get up at 6:00 a.m. I leave the house for work at 7:00. In about fifteen minutes, I'm at work. I have time to change clothes and have some coffee before we start at 8:00 a.m. At 9:30 we have a ten-minute coffee break and at noon we have half an hour for lunch. In the afternoon we have no breaks at all. During lunch we talk about football if it's that season, then after that in the winter it's basketball and then baseball in the spring. Or sometimes we talk about how to fix things about the house that break. During the working time the guys will help each other out if necessary on fixing a part of an engine that they haven't seen before. Sometimes we borrow each other's tools, but we always give them back at the end of the day. Then at 4:30 we quit, stack up our tool boxes, and wash up. I go pick up the wife at her job and we get home about 5:30 and she fixes supper or if we're a little money ahead we might go get some hamburgers. On Tuesdays or Wednesday nights we often drive to Racine to visit my sister down there. Thursday is pay day night so we have to go out and shop for groceries and anything else that we need. Friday is a busy night and we go shopping again for what we didn't have time to get the night before. Then we used to leave Friday night late for up north, but since we bought this house we can't get started up there until sometimes on Saturday and sometimes not at all because I have the yard to clean up and there's always something around the house to fix. To take up the time we watch television if we're home weekends. Sports mostly. Once in a great while some Indian friends will drop in, but not very often.

The neighbors around here don't bother us, but only the lady across the street is at all friendly. The people across the alley are real old and the husband is blind so they almost never get out. But if people don't want to be friendly with me, it doesn't bother me because I don't need them. I got other interests.

My boy Jeff minds his own business and doesn't fight with other kids. He'll be big enough for football next year.

Sometimes we drive up to see my wife's folks around Wisconsin Dells or Wausau. Her folks have always been great to me and Jeff too. Sometimes we go to their Lutheran Church with them. But usually if we go out of town, it's up around my place for our church (peyote). When my dad was alive, I took him to powwows all over the Midwest so that he could sell his souvenirs. Sometimes I set up a refreshment stand at one of those places and made some extra money. Then Dad always liked to look for bargains to buy. We'd go down to Maxwell Street in Chicago where on Sunday people would sell just about anything at a low price. They have something like this south of Milwaukee at this Seven Mile Fair. After he got too old to work his trap lines, he and Mother would come down and spend a few weeks with us in the winter. Then he'd go all around and collect junk and keep it in the wigwam in front of the house and try to sell some of it. He had forty old tires there, lots of old furniture that he picked up at city dumps, and piles of rags. Sometimes I took him around to places in my car so he could look. Sometimes he'd make genuine Indian souvenirs out of that stuff. Maybe I got some of my restlessness from him. We sure never keep still around here.*

I found Dan to be not only an intelligent, conscientious informant, but a very likable individual as well. Many other whites also have the same attitude toward him. However, we all noticed the muted but firm distance which he maintained toward non-Indians and even non-Winnebagos. Other Winnebagos knew what he was thinking and how he felt. Around them he was forced to "explain" little or nothing as to his general attitudes toward almost all aspects of his existence. "Winnebagos are Winnebagos and other kinds of people have their own ways too. This will never change."

In spite of the intense, earnest nature of his life style, his delightful, infectious sense of humor is usually evident. One evening we were discussing the high cost of Milwaukee living. Dan concluded that portion of conversation by saying in a very solemn but bogus fashion:

Yes, it's certainly true that everything around here costs a lot of money, and it usually turns out not to be worth it. Now I remember last year this summer festival that they had down by the lakefront. Those dancers from Mexico. There was this woman in the group and at the end of the program, she is standing on top of this high pole and she takes all her clothes off. And there I was standing and I couldn't see nothin'. I paid $2.50 to see this weird female standing way up there. That made me so mad that I decided to be Indian about this. I went right home and laid down on the couch in the living room, started smoking a big cigar, and told my wife, old Judy, to go in the bedroom, take off all her clothes and then come and stand in the living room. Then I looked her over real good and it didn't cost me nothin'. Now that just goes to show that the Indian way of doing things is the best.*

I was impressed by the essential validity of his statement.

The events of Dan Jackson's life history do suggest that voluntary migration can support and increase a sense of ethnicity. Essentially, it can be argued that migration is a means used by him ultimately to maintain and extend an Indian identity. He has moved from one place to another to take advantage of varying resources as these have fluctuated through time. What resources have been used at a particular place and time depend in turn upon the position which he occupies in his life cycle and the perceived demands of the situation. He can be regarded as an active, healthy, middle-aged individual who requires a relatively dependable wage income in order to satisfy a variety of needs of a personal and familial nature. For a number of reasons, this wage income can be most readily obtained in Milwaukee. He will probably leave Milwaukee and return to an Indian rural community situation when he becomes too old to maintain his place in the urban labor force. Dan by that time will have done all that he can for his son, Jeff, who in turn will be an adult potentially able to help his aging parents if so required. Armed with savings, Social Security, and his job pension, he will probably retire to the twenty-acre "farm" he will inherit from his mother.

Dan Jackson appears to have developed an economically secure niche for himself in Milwaukee. He has had a reasonable amount of success in developing varying degrees of social and personal security as well. With the aid of resources available only in the city, he seems to have obtained, if only in a temporary sense, the best of all possible worlds. In his earlier years there were many aspects of his home community which he disliked. Many of these conditions still persist, often in an aggravated form. There are also many aspects of the urban situation which he does not like, but which he must accept or at least tolerate. His history of urban residence amounts to a slow, halting selection of preferred behavior patterns which can be maintained. This selection is based generally on how similar a particular form of behavior in the city is to that which he enjoyed doing back home. In short, Dan Jackson to date has met with a reasonable degree of success in being an Indian in an urban situation. It also seems evident that for now he can be an Indian in a much easier and more extensive manner than if he were to return home immediately or if he had never left his birthplace. Hence, within the narrow limits described above, he remains an urban resident.

Dan still traps, hunts, and exploits the tourists, as he did as a boy and as his father did before him. But now he successfully hunts and traps money over an area much larger than his father was ever able to do. His and his wife's combined incomes exceed $15,000 per year. He has acquired many of the rewards which urban living potentially offers, e.g. a physically comfortable home, equal or superior to that used by many urban whites, and a balanced, realistic conception of the positive and negative features of city life. If anything, he is a much more active member of his peyote church because he now must work harder to prove his allegiance to his faith than if he had remained in a place where he could conveniently manifest the outward signs of superficial religious commitment, this place being, of course, the Red Pond area.

Because he has to drive at least 450 miles and commit 90 percent of his weekend leisure time to insure merely the attendance at a single service, his devotion to peyote has become greatly heightened in his own eyes as well as those of his rural peers. His activities as a peyote captain in Milwaukee further structure and direct his faith. His immediate and indirect urban contact with a wide variety of other institutionalized religions has led to a number of insightful comparisons whose conclusions hinge around the fact that as an urban resident, Winnebago, and an Indian, he should and can continue to follow the peyote road.

He has concluded that while many whites are admirable human beings in a wide variety of ways, they are not Winnebago, and thus their primary interests lie in directions different from his own. He can avoid those non-Winnebagos he does not like, and he allows such people to avoid him. The superficial nature of general urban social interaction permits him to use advantageously and occasionally even to enjoy urban contacts with most whites whom he meets and those few whom he regards as friends. Yet he need make little or no commitment to those in either category. His strong allegiance to tribal affiliation and the sacrament of peyote helps deter unwanted contacts with other Indians. He can keep in mind that he has a place up north to which he can retire when he thinks it best.

MIGRATION AT BEAR PUEBLO

Bear Pueblo is a settlement of Indians located about forty-five miles north of Mesa, New Mexico. The direct, lineal ancestors of these people have been living in the area for at least 350 years. The lives of the village inhabitants are lived out against the background of an extremely uncomfortable paradox. While the pueblo maintains a social and political independence from the larger non-Indian society, it is closely integrated with it in an economic sense. The social and cultural integrity of the community are perpetually threatened by this fact.

About 1,800 individuals consisting of 310 households live on a reservation of approximately 140 square miles of land. The village is governed by a religious hierarchy of officials who maintain a pervasive control over most of the social and political lives of the people. These officials are responsible for the maintenance of an elaborate series of ceremonies associated with a kind of agriculture which used to provide the basis for the community's existence. Because of a critical shortage of suitable farming land, a rapid increase in population and a number of other crucial factors, cash from wage labor done away from the pueblo is now the basis of the pueblo's economy. However, those who work for wages outside the pueblo must also continue to fulfill a demanding number of ceremonial obligations. Such obligations can be met, for the most part, only by assuming pueblo residence and living by a behavioral code deeply rooted in tradition and perpetuated relentlessly by the religious oligarchy.

To be a Bear Indian means to reside within the geographical bounds of the village and reservation for the better part of one's life. Demands fall hardest upon men, but women also play important supplementary roles in the dancing, prayers, and feasts which occur throughout the year and are believed to be vital to a satisfactory continuation of pueblo life. All healthy men are expected to fill ceremonial positions which require full time residence at the pueblo at least every three or four years. This imperative alone makes it impossible for Bear men to obtain well-paid permanent employment outside the village.

It is estimated that well over half of the men and women between the ages of eighteen and fifty-five have full- or part-time jobs away from the pueblo. Most of these people maintain pueblo residence but commute to jobs in the cities of Mesa or El Palacio. A few are able to obtain rural-based employment away from the pueblo, usually on a seasonal basis. A number of informants stated that about 200 people lived and worked outside the Southwest. The religious hierarchy realistically expects most of these individuals to return eventually to the village to assume full-time residence, since such migrants for a variety of reasons find that they lack the emotional and vocational preparation necessary for a satisfying life in an urban non-pueblo setting. While these migrants are away, they are expected to support the pueblo by spending their vacations there and by the regular contribution of money to friends and relatives living in the village. Ideally the recipients of this cash will meet the urban pueblo residents' ceremonial obligations by using these funds in various ways to support the religious and secular activities of Bear. If migrants or other pueblo residents fail to meet their dictated responsibilities, they run the risk of suffering a social death in the eyes of the community. On very rare occasions, if their irresponsibility is sufficiently flagrant, they face the possibility of biological extinction as well.

Given this situation, the migrants and wage-work commuters find themselves forced to experience in many respects the abrasive aspects of both white urban and rural pueblo life. For the most part, the economic resources found at Bear are allocated to older individuals who have demonstrated their fidelity to the pueblo over a period of years. The rewards of community membership on the part of the younger adults are limited to less tangible returns of a social and spiritual nature. Many of those in this category regard such compensation as inadequate and unsatisfactory. Their dissatisfaction is often mirrored by a marked decrease in pueblo and/or Indian ethnicity, which often takes the form of permanent out migration from Bear to a city.

The Wilson family provides a number of vivid examples of diminished ethnicity or identity which is largely the product of migration within the setting of tight social structure. The family consists of Mike and Eloise Wilson and their children, three sons and five daughters. These people are regarded by the community with mixed feelings since the parents measured against the most rigid conservative standards of the pueblo are "good Bear people." However, the majority of their children are not, since, for a variety of reasons, they have avoided adequate participation in the secular and religious spheres of community life.

The oldest son, John, was active in a number of medicine societies, but had trouble finding enough temporary, full-time wage work to support his large family on even a marginal basis. As a result, he was given to fits of moody, erratic behavior and heavy drinking which eventually led to a fatal traffic accident while he was traveling in the Midwest. Before his death, John often mentioned to me how dull Bear life was, but "living in town somewhere would only make things worse."

One of his brothers, Peter, is epileptic. He too objected to the implacable demands of the community leadership but was unable to establish satisfactory urban residence partially because of his physical disability but mainly because of his unwillingness to "sweat it out at a job in a town somewhere and satisfy the old people out here." His difficulties have been supplemented by alcoholism, which in turn resulted in a near fatal car accident which left him a paraplegic. When not drinking, he can be found sitting in his wheel chair immersed in the problems of his difficult future.

The remaining son, Alfred, after a distinguished term of military service and a very successful training period in Cleveland sponsored by the federal relocation program, returned to Bear to marry a conservative pueblo woman with a large number of equally conservative brothers. He works at a well-paid job in Mesa, commuting from Bear, and appears to be well-satisfied with his life. He confided to me that it was no accident that he returned to the pueblo from Cleveland immediately after his wife's parents announced that she was ready for marriage. He knew that she would make an ideal wife since she had a congenial disposition and a large number of close relatives who would help him meet his community obligations. Apparently, such families with daughters eligible for marriage are uncommon at this pueblo. His general behavior, whether at Bear or while working in town, strongly suggests that he finds his life as a young pueblo man a rewarding one.

For the most part, the daughters of this family have used the mechanism of marriage to avoid burdensome community obligations. Two married Montana Indians whom they first met while attending a nearby federal boarding school. They have accompanied their spouses to Montana and have well-established households there. They help support their aging parents with small, irregular amounts of money, but have not visited the pueblo since their marriages.

Another daughter attempted to marry a white man from Indiana, but was deterred by his unexpected marriage to a white woman in the Midwest. This daughter now lives in Mesa and seems grimly determined to achieve the status of permanent spinsterhood. She visits her parents at Bear a few weekends out of the year, but attempts to avoid other contacts with her home. As a long-time employee of the Bureau of Indian Affairs, she has modest but secure financial support. Her acceptability in the eyes of the pueblo community is tenuous, and may well soon result in a permanent exile, unless she would return to Bear now to live and marry a Bear man. As she is almost fifty years old and has a well-established albeit barren existence in Mesa, her voluntary exile will probably become permanent and irrevocable.

The youngest daughter's relations with men have produced children but not marriage. Two non-Indians have fathered three of her children and a Navajo, the fourth. She encountered these three men during an erratic series of adventures which kept her away from the pueblo for several years. She lives in an anomalous household with her elderly parents and is regarded by the community as a good housekeeper and a useful member of the pueblo. But since she has no husband and only one brother active in the village, she cannot take part fully in the events of the pueblo. The few bachelors at Bear seeking wives do not regard her as a potentially desirable spouse. This collective judgment is not likely to change in the future.

It can be safely argued that while the Wilson family may not necessarily be typical of all other Bear families, they are far from unique.

ETHNICITY AND MIGRATION IN OTHER AMERICAN INDIAN SITUATIONS

Ethnicity as a factor in migration can assume different guises or nuances among other Indian groups, and the influence of tight social structure with regard to migration and ethnicity can vary from the relationship described for Bear Pueblo. A significant number of men and women from the Eastern Keresan Pueblo of Santo Domingo, a clear example of tight social structure, are renowned traders; they often travel long distances to trade and sell a remarkable volume of goods. The pueblo has long had the reputation among the general Indian population for producing efficient, but often unscrupulous traders. Such trading has been going on at least since the second decade of the nineteenth century. Their presence can be noted at most Indian and non-Indian public events throughout the Southwest. Their business activities generally consist of the trading and sometimes selling of Indian crafts such as Navajo rugs, silver and turquoise jewelry, shell necklaces, etc., to Indians and non-Indians. At present their trading activities seem to be expanding.

As mentioned before, Dan Jackson frequently sells Indian crafts to whites and occasionally to other Indians. Most of these sales take place at powwows held on weekends. He recently described an encounter with a Santo Domingo woman:

I was down at the Rock Island, Illinois, powwow selling stuff and I met this Santo Domingo woman who was doing the same thing. When I told her that I was headed down to the Southwest to buy and trade, she got real interested and wrote me out a letter of introduction to take to her father who is married in at the pueblo of Cochiti which is just a few miles north of Santo Domingo. So when I got down there — but I stopped off at Anadarko, Oklahoma, first and got a lot of peyote things from the Kiowa — I went to Cochiti and found this man. He read the letter and that really turned him on. We drove down to Santo Domingo and those people started running out of their houses like crazy with stuff to trade. I could have traded ten times over what I had brought with me. They sure trade hard, but I guess since I was with this woman's father, they were fair about it. I can't wait to get back down there again.

The anthropologist Howard (personal communication, 1971) told me of one Santo Domingo man who obtains Hopi *katchina* dolls from these Indians in Arizona and eventually exchanges or sells them to both Indians and whites for tropical bird feathers and varying amounts of cash. He conducts many transactions with whites and Indians in a number of locations between Arizona and Florida and spends a great deal of time trading in Oklahoma.

A number of informants are convinced that these traders are among the most zealous members of the pueblo in meeting their ritual and social obligations. The timing and duration of their trading activities are determined by the part they must play in the ceremonial functions of the season. Much of the profit from trading eventually are used to support the community as a whole.

Freilich (1958, 1963) and Mitchell (1965) have described the activities of some Mohawk and other Iroquois men who travel throughout the United States and Canada as construction iron workers in high steel. The Iroquois seem to occupy an intermediate position on the tight-loose continuum. Freilich and Mitchell argue cogently that such well-paid, dangerous work involving travel over great distances enables these modern Iroquois to demonstrate their identity as worthy Indian males. Apparently such individuals, at the end of their working lives, retire to Iroquois communities in upper New York state or on the Six Nations Reserve near Brantford in Ontario, Canada, During their working years, however, they maintain financial and social commitments to their kinsmen friends, and communities.

DISCUSSION AND CONCLUSIONS

The central argument presented here can be said to have been given considerable support by the illustrative data. While the limits of its extrapolation are obviously narrow, the analysis has now been moved beyond the bounds of informed speculation. One obvious next step in the consideration of ethnicity and migration vis-à-vis tight and loose social structure would be to develop a series of verifiable hypotheses based upon the present study and subject them to large amounts of data taken from various tribal contexts. Statistical inference would play a vital role in such a procedure. Unfortunately, such materials are not now available and will not be developed for a number of years. The burgeoning difficulties involved in doing significant research with contemporary American Indians, plus the reluctance on the part of many anthropologists to recognize and accommodate their research methods to these hazards, preclude an immediate significant advance in our understanding of the comprehensive implications of ethnicity and migration within the dimensions of contemporary Indian life.

However, with regard to the data here, it is evident that Dan Jackson, operating from a loose structural base, has been able to control the nature of his migration. He has also developed a correspondingly greater sense of tribal and general Indian ethnic identity. His experiences away from his birthplace have given him penetrating insights into the non-Indian white world, but at the same time, sharpened the desire to use only those aspects of it that will reinforce and extend the likelihood of his remaining a Winnebago.

The nature of his migration alone, however, is not responsible for his present situation. More important perhaps have been the teachings of his father and other close Winnebago kinsmen. Under their tutelage, most of his early years must be regarded as a thorough preparation for living as a Winnebago in an often indifferent and frequently hostile world. Meeting and overcoming these challenges has increased his sense of being Winnebago. Many of his tribesmen, including a number of collateral relatives who did not have such careful preparation, lack this strong feeling of identification with the tribe and the general Indian population. An interesting additional facet of their current situations is that while they have moved around the western Great Lakes area as much or more than has Dan, they are far less successful in terms of economic achievement than he is. Does this result imply that a vital part of modern tribal identity hinges around economic achievement in the white sectors of society? Indeed, this may well be the case. In short, it would appear that Dan Jackson is a conservative Winnebago living in a largely white world because he has been able to create a distinctive Winnebago orbit using selected white elements, particularly money from wage labor, to make a Winnebago life. Other Winnebagos have been far less successful in their attempts to do this because they lacked his preparation and, perhaps equally important, his luck.

For Dan, "home" is a place that he is still making and that will not be complete until he retires from his Milwaukee job and moves to his inherited farm up north armed with his urban-acquired economic supports, e.g. his pension, savings, and federal Social Security payments. Since this "home" is not now a fixed geographical place, Dan is immune from various disruptive influences that could make his current life an unpleasant one.

Since the pueblo of Bear has rigid spatial dimensions, and Bear life must be structured within its confines, the members of the Wilson family are vulnerable to all negative as well as positive stimuli which affect that community. It may well be that certain demographic features of their family, such as the unequal proportion of adult daughters to functioning adult sons, the unusually wide gap in years between parents and offspring, and a number of other variables, place the behavior of most of the family out of focus with the general community structure much of the time. With the possible exception of Alfred Wilson, the degree of tribal ethnic identity in this family is far less than it is in the case of Dan Jackson.

One of the more intriguing questions posed but not answered by this study is the relationship between tribal and pan-Indian identity at both the individual and community levels. They appear, at least in the situations discussed here, not to be mutually exclusive. Unfortunately, data are not available now as to the specific dynamics of this relationship.

The considerations of Hertzberg (1971), Howard (1955), Corrigan (1970), and Schusky (1957) on pan-Indianism could be carefully studied and extended with great profit.

REFERENCES

ABERLE, DAVID F.
  1963 Some sources of flexibility in Navaho social organization. *South-western Journal of Anthropology* 19(1):1–8.
CORRIGAN, SAMUEL W.
  1970 The Plains Indian powwow: cultural integration in Manitoba and Saskatchewan. *Anthropologica*, n.s. 12(2):253–277.
FREILICH, MORRIS
  1958 Cultural persistence among the modern Iroquois. *Anthropos* 53: 473–483.
  1963 Scientific possibilities in Iroquoian studies. *Anthropologica*, n.s. 5(2):171–186.
HERTZBERG, HAZEL W.
  1971 *The search for an American Indian identity: modern pan-Indian movements*. Syracuse: Syracuse University Press.
HODGE, WILLIAM H.
  1971 "Navajo urban migration: an analysis from the perspective of the family," in *The American Indian in urban society*. Edited by Jack O. Waddell and O. Michael Watson, 346–391. Boston: Little, Brown.
HOWARD, JAMES H.
  1955 Pan-Indian culture of Oklahoma. *The Scientific Monthly* 81(5): 215–220.
LABARRE, WESTON
  1959 *The peyote cult*. Hamden, Connecticut: The Shoe String Press.
MILLER, HELEN MINER, NANCY O. LURIE
  1963 *Report on the Wisconsin Winnebago project: the contribution of community development to the prevention of dependency*. Privately printed and distributed by the Wisconsin Winnebago Business Committee.

MITCHELL, JOSEPH
  1965   "The Mohawks in High Steel," in *Apologies to the Iroquois*. New York: Vintage Books.
MIZEN, MAMIE L.
  1965-1966   *Federal facilities for Indians*. United States Senate Committee on Appropriations. Washington, D.C.: U.S. Government Printing Office.
PELTO, PERTTI J.
  1968   The differences between "tight" and "loose" societies. *Transaction* 5(5):37–40.
SCHUSKY, ERNEST
  1957   Pan-Indianism in the eastern United States. *Anthropology Tomorrow* 6(1):116–123.
SIEBER, NADINE DAY, NANCY O. LURIE
  1965   *Report on the Wisconsin Winnebago project: the contribution of community development to the prevention of dependency*, volume two. Privately printed and distributed by Wisconsin Winnebago Business Committee.

West Indian Ethnicity in Great Britain

DOUGLAS K. MIDGETT

> It have people living in London who don't
> know what happening in the room next to
> them, far more the street, or how other
> people living. London is a place like that. It
> divide up in little worlds, and you stay in
> the world you belong to and you don't
> know anyting about what happening in the
> other ones except what you read in the
> paper
>
> SAMUEL SELVON, *The Lonely Londoners*

> London, all that was mix up; Cyprus,
> Hungarians, Indians, Morocco, Africans,
> Jamaicans, Trinidadians, Dominicans, Bar-
> badians, all that was mix up
>
> P.G., a repatriated St. Lucian

I have examined the criteria relating to ethnic identification of West
Indian migrants resident in London and the factors contributing to
changing definitions in this realm. Although the data are with respect to
one specific aggregate, the migrants from a single locality, generalization
to a wider West Indian context is consistent both with the published

This article is based on fieldwork in St. Lucia and London initiated in 1965. The
research in Great Britain during 1970–1971 was supported by a grant from the National
Institute of Mental Health. I would like to thank Richard Frucht, Dennis Forsythe,
Enid Schildkrout, and Connie Sutton for comments on earlier versions. I would also
like to thank a number of St. Lucians who have allowed me to share a little of their
identity in those situations when it made sense to them.

accounts of this migration and with descriptions of migration and migrant community formation in general. It ought also to be pointed out that most remarks and generalizations are with respect to a certain sector of the West Indian migrant population, namely, those who come from lower class rural and urban backgrounds in the islands. Thus, what I have to say may not necessarily apply to students or middle-class professionals, whose orientations and expectations in British society may be considerably different. However, the population in question does comprise the great bulk of West Indian immigrants, and any valid generalizations I may make concerning them ought to be considered in view of that fact.[1]

BACKGROUND, THE HISTORY OF A MIGRATION

West Indian labor migration has been a prominent feature of the demographic history of the area since the abolition of slavery. Successive migrations have seen movements of people from the British islands to Panama, Cuba, Venezuela, the Guianas, the United States, Aruba, and Curaçao, and, since World War II, to the United Kingdom and the American Virgin Islands. The case of the United Kingdom migration, under consideration here, is the most extensive in that greater numbers are involved and the migration has consisted, eventually, of whole families.

The movements of ex-slaves commenced soon after emancipation in 1838 in the British islands. Caused in part by the end of the slave trade and in part by the refusal of ex-slaves to engage in plantation work, labor shortages became acute, particularly where plantation agriculture developed late, in such areas as Trinidad and the Guianas. Smith tells us of the incentives which were quickly offered to attract workers to Trinidad (1962:26–30). In an historical study of Barbadian migration Roberts relates how continuing motivation for migration kept the island, already densely settled by 1850, at a fairly constant population level for over half a century (1955:245–246). Again the primary thrust of migration was aimed at Trinidad and British Guiana, where planters held out inducements for agricultural laborers. The attraction was so strong that restrictive measures were enacted to attempt to curb the labor drain from the smaller islands (Roberts 1955:247).

[1] For greater elaboration on the role class has played in West Indian migrations, see Frucht (1968). Despite the fact of a continuing orientation to migration, selection factors have the effect of stamping certain individual characteristics on each successive migrant population.

Through the latter quarter of the nineteenth century and the first half of the twentieth century, West Indians continued to be a mobile population. It was particularly the male sector of the population that was recruited in large numbers to work on the Central American canal projects and other Latin American schemes. This migration took significant numbers away from some islands, for many of the migrants remained as permanent settlers in these Spanish-speaking countries. Roberts notes that about 20,000 workers from the island of Barbados were under contract during construction of the Panama Canal (1955:271).

Another target for large numbers of migrants from the British islands was Cuba, where a seasonal work force was needed for annual sugar harvesting. Again, even though the work was seasonal, the number of permanent migrants was high, particularly from Jamaica (Maunder 1955:40). Other important routes of migration during the early 1900's took many West Indians to other islands, to the South American mainland, and to the United States. The tempo decreased after 1920, and repatriation of migrants from Cuba, following restrictive legislation in that country, reversed the tide of movement in many islands.

More recently, i.e. after 1945, there has been heavy migration to the United States. This has been of a temporary nature, the recruiting of agricultural laborers under contract for specified lengths of time. Permanent migration to the States, an important movement during the early part of the current century, was effectively choked off by restrictive legislation. Would-be migrants then turned to Great Britain, where a number had spent time during the war while serving with the West India Regiment; the number of immigrants to British soil from the Commonwealth has now passed the half-million mark.[2]

This migration has not been a steady flow, but until 1962 seemed to conform rather closely to fluctuations in the British economic picture (Peach 1968). Following 1962, when the Commonwealth Immigrants Act was passed, the magnitude of the movement was considerably reduced, with the majority of subsequent migrants consisting of dependents traveling to join portions of families which were already situated in Great Britain.[3]

[2] Enumeration of immigrants seems fraught with problems as Peach (1966) demonstrates. Thus, while the figure I use may be higher than some other estimates, I suspect it is quite close to the real number.
[3] Prior to the Commonwealth Immigrants Act, members of the Commonwealth were free to move in and out of Great Britain. Increasing racial tension and a number of incidents coupled with a dramatic rise in the numbers of colored immigrants during 1960 and 1961 prompted passage of the act. Peach (1968) suggests that the threat of a ban, in the air in the late 1950's, precipitated the rush in 1960–1961, in turn hastening

West Indian Settlement in Great Britain

The pattern of migration and settlement of West Indians in Great Britain followed that of many other cases which come under the heading of "chain" migrations (MacDonald and MacDonald 1964; Price 1969). Moreover, the vast majority settled in large urban areas, moving into occupational categories being vacated by British working-class labor (Peach 1968). A third factor influencing the settlement of West Indians is the discrimination they encountered in seeking housing (Daniel 1968). Each of these will be discussed in turn, but first it is instructive to examine the literature which concerns this migration in its earlier days.

Migration and the situation of migrant groups in Great Britain has been the subject of a number of studies written in recent years. These studies may be considered in two groups according to their points of departure. The first group consists of a number of primarily demographic studies conducted by sociologists from the University of the West Indies. Because they deal with the causes and consequences of the movement from the island and have little to say about the situation in Great Britain, they are of secondary concern here.

The second group of studies has focused on the condition of the immigrant, Asian as well as West Indian, and on his reception by the British host community. Although some earlier work had been done on the position of racial minorities in British society, little more was accomplished with reference to the most recent newcomers until 1958, when the shock of the Notting Hill and Nottingham race riots woke the hosts to the fact that race might just be a divisive issue in British society. From that point the studies multiplied, the recently formed Institute of Race Relations embarked on a far-reaching survey of the subject, and the race relations industry in Britain boomed. Early works examined the position of the migrants with reference to existing theory on race relations and the stated policies of governmental bodies (Griffith et al. 1960) and also sought to provide information for service agencies that might aid in the adjustment of the immigrants to British life (Ruck 1960).

These studies concentrated on the urban situation and on the progress being made in assimilating these new minorities into the majority society. The concentration upon assimilation led to two assumptions that occur in much of the literature that followed and that often lead to erroneous and occasionally ridiculous conclusions. The first of these is the assump-

---

the restrictions. For a complete picture of associated legislation up to 1969, see Mac-Donald (1969).

tion that the immigrants cluster in response to threats from the host society. Although this is not entirely false, the corollary, that ethnic clustering is therefore a threat to good race relations, suggests that it is the immigrants themselves who are responsible for poor relations because of their clannishness. Stated in this way this appears absurd, and yet both Glass (1960) and Patterson (1963), in two of the better early studies, express apprehension at the growth of ethnic communities and the failure of West Indians to articulate with various areas of British society outside the work situation.

This xenophobic trend in sociological writing has continued such that one writer sees in "ethnic exclusiveness and group consciousness... the seed of considerable future tension and hostility between the ethnic groups and the host society" (Hylson-Smith 1968:476). He goes on to suggest that this situation is likely to be particularly intensified in the case of West Indians because of "perceived" racial prejudice (1968:476).

The second assumption follows from the first in that it is assumed that assimilation will take place with the inclusion of the immigrants in the working and lower classes. It was also frequently suggested during the early 1960's, when Britain was agonizing over the fact that a race problem might exist, that, in fact, the problem was only the old one of class, albeit with a slight new twist. Thus, one writer could seriously state of unemployed black school leavers that, "some were unemployed because they were of LOWER CLASS ORIGIN, dirty and OF UNPREPOSESSING APPEARANCE BY WHITE STANDARDS" (Maddox 1960:14, my emphasis). This continuing emphasis on the assimilative process and consequent dread of expressions of ethnic solidarity has characterized much of the work that has focused on the British situation and has in turn led to remedial approaches which are highly paternalistic in their conception (Rose et al. 1969).

When West Indians arrived in Great Britain, they began to cluster in certain areas and to initiate a process which would lead to precisely the kinds of expressions of ethnic solidarity noted above. This is not an unusual phenomenon in those cases of human population movement generally referred to as chain migrations. These are defined as movements "in which prospective migrants learn of opportunities, are provided with transportation, and have initial accommodation and employment arranged by means of primary social relationships with previous migrants" (MacDonald and MacDonald 1964:82). Moreover, this type of migration is described by Price (1969:210–212) as being characterized by a series of stages which involve the establishment of ethnic communities replete with "folk" institutions that come to define the community. Although West Indian immigrants have not been resident in England long enough to determine whether they will pass through these stages, Patterson has already noted some progression in terms of residential selection correlating to economic upward mobility (quoted in Deakin 1964).

West Indian settlement is highly urbanized, a characteristic that is directly related to the kinds of employment sought by and offered to migrants on their arrival in Great Britain. Indeed, Peach (1968) relates the characteristics of migration flows and ebbs and patterns of settlement to labor demands in Great Britain. Not only did the migrants move into the more menial, undesirable, unskilled positions that British workers were vacating in a booming post-war economy, but they also settled in areas which the British were abandoning in order to move to those parts of the country where new industry was being established (Peach 1968: 62–82).

Migrants also encountered racial discrimination in housing, a factor which severely limited their choices of residence, particularly during the early years of the migration (Burney 1967; Daniel 1968). This served to limit the areas in which West Indians could find accommodation and, because only certain houses in "twilight zones" were available to non-white renters, made heavy overcrowding the general case for immigrant tenants (Rex and Moore 1967). The result of the interplay of all of these factors was a situation in which West Indians came to be settled in areas of old, frequently dilapidated housing, often in overcrowded conditions, located primarily in the largest urban areas in Great Britain, and clustered in groups comprised of people who had multiple ties to one another both before and throughout the migration.

ETHNICITY AND COMMUNITY

In discussing the topic of ethnicity among West Indians a prefacing statement relating to the general issue of ethnicity is in order. Barth has suggested that the critical feature relating to ethnic identification is "the characteristic of self-ascription and ascription by others" (1969:13). It seems to me that this is a statement that can be extended somewhat. Initially, the inclusion of people within an ethnic category is an issue of self-definition, the ways in which the individual categorizes himself. However, this self-definition is either validated or denied by members of the category in question, that is, the individual's decision is dependent upon decisions by members of the category to acknowledge or deny his membership. Moreover, I think we must ask what it means if, in the case in which individual and other members agree upon his inclusion, outsiders who recognize the category refuse to deal with the individual in terms of the stereotypic behavior which they extend to other members.

Another point emerging from studies of ethnicity in urban, complex situations is that ethnic relations are conceived of as basically segmentary in nature, although this characteristic may be confined to just these kinds of situations. Ethnic affiliation is seen as an ordered phenomenon with categories of the same order in opposition. This opposition need not necessarily be symmetrical from the standpoint of the outside observer but is most likely so in the view of actors who are involved. Finally, there are no set criteria for differentiating categories at various levels of opposition. These categories may themselves be based on various characteristics, at one time a notion of descent, common language, or origin, or combinations of these and other markers. But again, these criteria need be valid only from the point of view of the actors.

Another closely related concept employed in this discussion is that of community. When community is used as in "West Indian community" or "Two Friends community" the term refers to what Pahl has termed "a locality-based social network" (1970:105–110). That is, inclusion within the community may not be confined to residents of a locality, nor are all residents of the locality included within the community. It may also be the case, as with the notion of "West Indian community," that there are numerous localities which serve to define the community.

West Indian Ethnicity – General Observations

For West Indians living in urban Great Britain there are a number of possible self-identifications, the choices of which are dependent upon context and strategic value. For most, the choices include at least affiliations based on island identity or on community of origin within that island, as well as some generalized West Indian identity.[4] For some, the choices may be influenced by real or putative affinities between certain islands; Grenadians may invoke the relationship with Trinidad which results from their long-standing social ties through migration to the larger island (although Trinidadians may not reciprocate), or Dominicans and St. Lucians may give expression to the close cultural and

[4] It is most likely that the situation in individual islands affects the kinds of affiliations found in Great Britain. For example, Lowenthal notes the presence or relative absence of well-defined local communities in various islands (1972:8–9).

linguistic affinities between the two islands. In addition, all West Indians have to deal with yet another category, that which is imposed upon them by the host society. This is a racial category, that is, like all ethnic classification it involves stereotyping but in this case stereotyping based on phenotypic criteria, on deviance from a white British norm.

All of this is portrayed in schematic fashion in Figure 1, in which two characteristics of ethnic relationships are indicated. First, all identifications based on community of origin are subsumed under the island affiliation and these are in turn contained within the West Indian category. Thus, at least for West Indians in Great Britain, ethnicity displays a certain basic order that relates to geographical origins. Other criteria for ethnic inclusion, such as those mentioned in the above paragraphs, may then be considered. The second characteristic concerns the amount of information and fineness of distinctions relevant for any particular actor. Notice that for members of the categories designated by "X" there are whole areas (shading) about which little may be known in terms of internal differentiation and about which little need be known.

The ethnic categorization and distinctions outlined above are expressed and reinforced through various patterns of interaction. It is this ongoing interaction which provides the vehicle for the relational component of ethnicity; in this area solidarity within the categories is expressed and the definition of boundaries is manifested by the kinds of interaction which take place within and across these boundaries. For West Indians in Great Britain, this kind of activity can be observed in a number of contexts exemplifying various spheres of identification.

One type of activity not frequently occurring among the West Indian sector is that which is associated with the formation of well-defined, corporate groups. Most writers have noticed the relative absence of organized bodies, such as voluntary associations, operating along ethnic lines and mobilizing group support in some political arena. Institutions which have served this kind of organizational function for other migrant populations are rarely present in the West Indian community in England.

As an example, the church often serves as a significant community-defining institution in localities in the islands, but these religious bodies in most instances have their counterparts in England. The result is that the West Indian Catholic who was used to a church that in many ways united and defined his community through attendance and rites of passage finds himself in a London church, run by Irish priests, and meaningless in terms of its significance for the community with which he has come to identify in the new setting. Calley (1965) has commented on this situation and the importance it has for the growth of predominantly West Indian

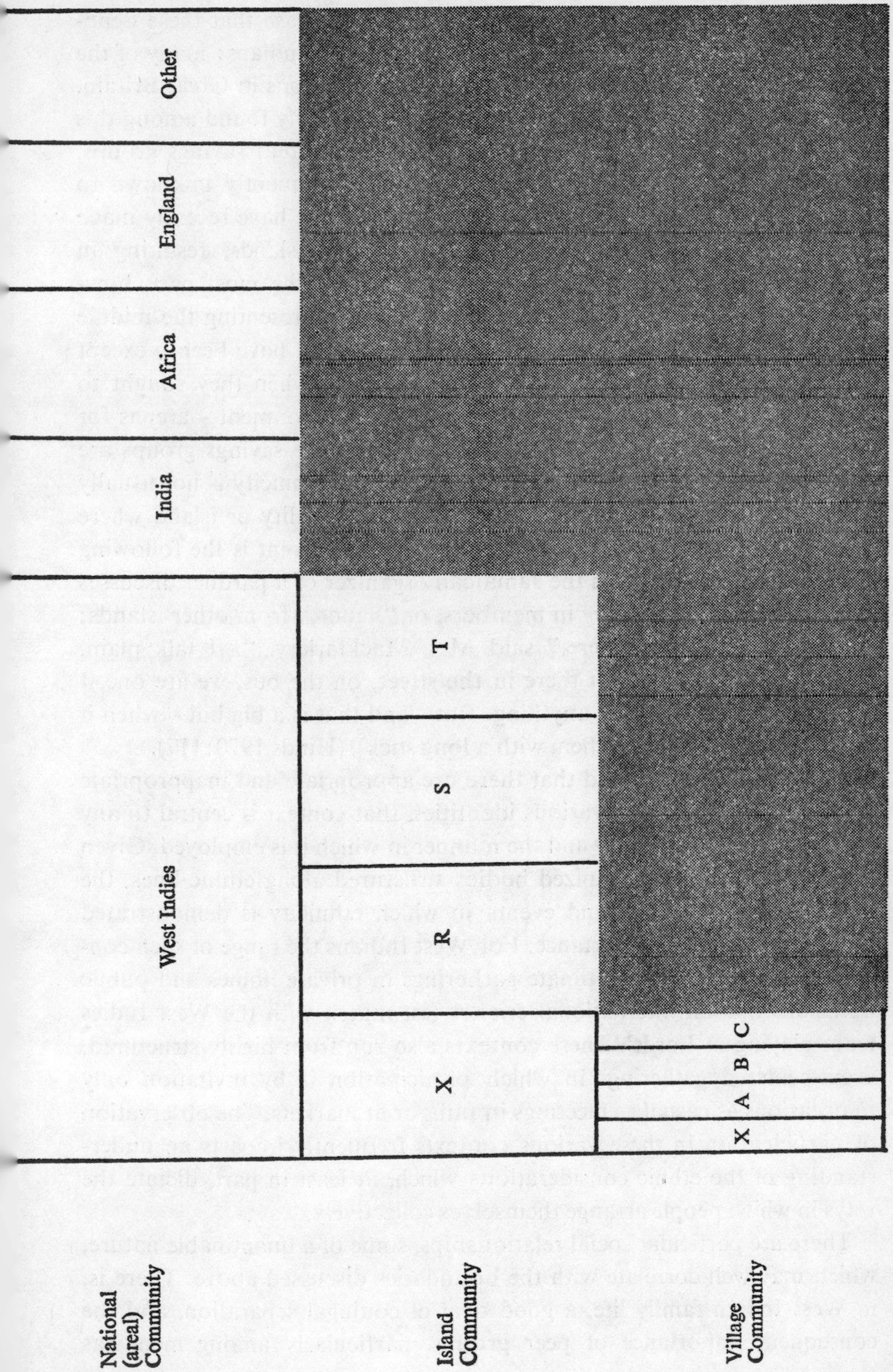

Figure 1.   Generalized West Indian ethnic identity

pentecostal groups in London, but it remains the case that these deno-
minations account for but a small minority of West Indians; many of the
rest have come to have very tenuous church affiliations in Great Britain.

Other kinds of corporate organizations occasionally found among this
migrant population are island associations and mutual savings groups,
called "pardners." The island associations are frequently unknown to
the majority of West Indians except insofar as some have recently made
available charter flight accommodations to the islands, resulting in
considerable savings for prospective visitors. For the most part, however, associations have been run by individuals representing the middle
class or elite sectors of the islands' populations and have been – except
for a period of time following the riots in 1958 when they sought to
represent the interests of islanders in a hostile environment – arenas for
political struggles among their active members. The savings groups are
organized either at the work place, in which case ethnicity is not usually
a factor, or among migrants from a particular locality or island where
ethnicity is a paramount consideration. A case in point is the following
fictional example in which the Jamaican organizer of a pardner discusses
the advisability of bringing in members, or "hands," from other islands:
"We are all Jamaicans here," said Mrs. Mackfarlery. "...I talk plain.
I not fighting Bajans. Out there in the street, on the bus, we are one. I
ready to stand by them in anything. But – and that is a big but – when it
come amongst us I touch them with a long stick" (Hinds 1970:117).

I have already suggested that there are appropriate and inappropriate
situations for expressing various identities, that context is central to any
understanding of ethnicity and the manner in which it is employed. Given
a relative paucity of organized bodies structured along ethnic lines, the
examination of context and events in which ethnicity is demonstrated
becomes of singular importance. For West Indians the range of such contexts includes the most intimate gatherings in private homes and public
occasions like an international cricket test match with the West Indies
team playing at Lords'. These contexts also run from highly structured,
event-centered gatherings in which participation is by invitation only
to occasions as casual as meetings in pubs or at markets. The observation
of participation in these various contexts frequently imparts an understanding of the ethnic considerations which, at least in part, dictate the
ways in which people arrange themselves collectively.

There are particular social relationships, some of a quantifiable nature,
which may well correlate with the boundaries discussed above. There is,
in West Indian family life, a good deal of conjugal separation, and the
consequent importance of peer groups, particularly among men, has

been noted (Wilson 1971). In Great Britain these groups or cliques are often indicators of feelings of ethnic inclusion or exclusion, for apart from kinsmen, it is from within these circles of very close friends that aid and support are sought and given in times of crisis.

The other social relationship that provides an index of the strength and perseverance of boundaries is marriage. Again the occurrence of marriage within the categories of local community, island, and the West Indies can be an indicator both of the degree to which these categories have reality for their putative members and of the perseverance of these patterns or, conversely, of changing attitudes. Statistical profiles of marriage are not in themselves expressions of ethnicity, however, but suggest the kinds of question that such an inquiry ought to address.

Finally, West Indians in Great Britain generally maintain close links with their home communities through remittances, letter writing, and exchanges of goods and services, primarily with relatives. Philpott (1968) has shown how these networks serve not only to keep the identification with the home community strong but also to reinforce the bonds which exist among the migrants from that community. The maintenance of these bonds with home are very closely tied with expectations of eventual return and, although predictions are unsure of just how many may actually return (see Davison 1966:104–121), it is certainly a fact that either large-scale repatriation or abandonment of this goal will have considerable effect on home community solidarity in Britain.

Two Friends Villagers in London

Among West Indians, St. Lucians are reputed to be some of the greatest travelers, a reputation which is well deserved as a result of thier participation in all of the earlier migrations, in addition to their frequent sojourns to neighboring French islands. The greatest flow of St. Lucian migrants lagged somewhat behind that of the Jamaicans and Barbadians, who were the first to leave in large numbers. Within St. Lucia some communities took advantage of the putative benefits offered in England as early as 1954. In the village in question, which I shall call Two Friends, the first emigrant bound for London did not leave until 1955, but others followed so quickly and in such numbers that there was soon a greater proportion of migrants from the village in London than from any other community in St. Lucia. Their numbers have continued to grow such that presently the total of island-born and their offspring resident in London exceeds the population of the village.

Two points concerning the migration are noteworthy. First, there was only one primary settlement area for migrants from Two Friends, a locale popularly known as Paddington, to which nearly all villagers first gravitated. The immediate requisites of the migrant population, housing and employment, abetted this pattern because these were met through the assistance of relatives and friends. In addition, there are certain physical characteristics of this area which served to inhibit outward movement of expanding families seeking better accommodations. The second point is that in this case, as with most West Indian migration to England, wives and sisters followed closely on the heels of men, so that approximate sexual parity obtained fairly soon after the movement was initiated.

Paddington – The Place and the People

The area I refer to as Paddington has long been a reception area for immigrants and, consequently, one which has had a transient population. The area, which corresponds roughly to the Harrow Road ward, is built in three- to four-story terraced houses, mostly dating from the 1880's. Many of these are poorly kept up and overcrowded but some sections have been improved as a result of Greater London Council and local borough projects.[5] Other similar areas are found to the north in Kilburn and to the south in North Kensington and Kensal New Town but these are separated from Paddington by railways and a canal, which serve to create social as well as physical boundaries.

The population of Paddington is decidedly mixed. In addition to the native English, the area contains many Irish from Eire, who came to London after World War II. Among immigrants from the colored Commonwealth, only West Indians are represented in large numbers, there being few Indians, Pakistanis, and Africans. Within the West Indian population it is notable that Jamaicans, who comprise a majority in many areas of West Indian concentration, account for less than one-quarter of the black population of Paddington. On the other hand, St. Lucians and Dominicans probably outnumber all other West Indians in the area. They, in turn, are not nearly as numerous in Brixton, which has a large black population.[6] The point to be made here is that in the

[5]   Leech (1967) notes that from the 1961 census the heaviest overcrowding in London occurred in the Paddington area. He also observes that the overcrowding in colored immigrant households was much greater than for the area as a whole.

[6]   Although Davison puzzles "why Jamaicans tend to concentrate in Lambeth where-

formation of migrant communities, the ethnic composition of different areas of settlement is likely to reflect nothing more than the idiosyncratic choices of the groups involved. Clearly, this uneven distribution of migrant populations has implications for a study of ethnicity.

In the Paddington area the West Indian population is characterized by a virtual absence of corporate organization beyond the family level. There are mutual saving groups, which may or may not be comprised entirely of West Indians, and island associations, which are not local, i.e. Paddington, organizations, and about which most Paddington residents know little. Consequently, the most significant ethnic affiliations are those based upon island and home community origins.

A resident of Paddington who comes from Two Friends defines his ethnic identity in terms of a number of categories or spheres, each of which is included in successive ones (see Table 1). He identifies with any one of these depending upon the situation – the person to whom he is speaking or the context. That is, in conversation with an Englishman he may identify himself as a West Indian, realizing quite correctly that to refer to himself as a St. Lucian would likely be puzzling. The category "West Indian" in its London context is one which is generally held to include all people who have come to England from the Commonwealth Caribbean, including East Indians from the islands but exclusive of whites. Moreover, there are certain cultural attributes held to be characteristic of members of this category in contradistinction to members of other categories of the same order, such as British, Africans, Indians, or Irish.

On a different scale, the same man identifying himself for another West Indian would refer to himself as a St. Lucian. To call himself a West Indian would be merely stating the obvious, while to identify with his home community would be meaningless for the listener. Again there are a number of attributes believed to be associated with residents from each of the islands and from Guyana, and stereotyping along with stereotypic behavior are frequently employed.

At the intra-island level, identification is on the basis of community of origin, and distinctions similar to those noted above are made between members of different communities; at the same time there is the recognition of the common social and cultural ties which bind them in the category "St. Lucian." Important as the island category may be, it is

---

as people from other parts of the Caribbean are more strongly concentrated in Paddington" (1963:67), given the nature of the migrations, it should come as no great surprise that the distribution reflects some selection on the part of the migrants.

Table 1. Spheres of identification

Spheres	Named community?	Expressions	Relevant others	Recognized commonalities
Two Friends	Yes	"all the same people" "We are we" other expressions of common descent	Other St. Lucian villages and communities	Almost total mutual social knowledge High degree of interrelatedness Group cohesiveness and mutual aid throughout migration Paddington as center for sense of community Reputed character traits in contra-distinction to other St. Lucians
St. Lucia	Yes	expressions of common origin and generalized descent	Other West Indian islands	Island of origin Language and dialect Generalized knowledge of island geography and limited acquaintances in other communities Reputed character traits in contra-distinction to other islanders
St. Lucia and Dominica	No	"Same as we" "We are all French"	Non-patois speakers (West Indian)	Language Other cultural affinities Fiction of frequent prior interaction
Small Islands	Yes[1]	None	Jamaica	Reputed character traits in contra-distinction to Jamaicans
West Indies	Yes	"Black people"	Other nation-alities or gross collectivities	Same general area of origin Mutual recognition of dialects Race Former state of political integration (rarely) Cultural affinities – expressive culture, food, certain putative social attributes
Colored immigrants	Yes[2]	None	Whites	Political category Sociological category

1 "Small island" is not a term of self-reference but rather a somewhat pejorative term employed by Jamaicans.

only within the group of migrants from Two Friends that one will find people who have detailed knowledge of each other's social backgrounds. The importance of this category is maintained through the maintenance of ties with the village and through participation in events and activities mostly carried out in Paddington (See Table 1).

Within the Two Friends community in London the contexts and modes of expressing community identifications may be more frequently expressed in contexts which lie outside the area (see Table 2). Every weekend villagers from other parts of London come to Paddington to spend time with families, attend social affairs, or just meet friends in the pub. Contexts for this interaction are parties, often connected with rites of passage such as first communions and marriages, most frequently held in private homes or church halls, and dances, which range from intimate gatherings in homes to large, publicly advertised events.

Such affairs are instructive for an examination of ethnic relationships in that they demonstrate a progression of the various criteria for inclusion and, conversely, exclusion. To elaborate, at any given event one might identify a category of people whose attendance is welcomed, even expected; another category who, while not expressly welcome, may come; and others who would be decidedly out of place. The notable feature here concerning this rather general rule of social gatherings is that the bases for categorizing are frequently the kinds of ethnic criteria described above.

In addition to these organized events, both public and private, there are a number of public contexts which are not event-centered. Examples include pubs, betting shops, laundromats, and markets. In contrast to the contexts mentioned above, these are places where St. Lucians are frequently brought into contact with English and Irish as well as other West Indians. Pubs provide an especially instructive example, in part owing to their segmented physical structure. It is often in Paddington pubs that drinkers of different ethnic origins have appropriated different sections of the pub. In one pub, every weekday during midday opening hours domino games are played in the private bar area. All conversation is carried on in patois, the French Creole of St. Lucia and Dominica, a situation which serves to exclude all others.

Ethnic self-identification is also expressed in a number of ways, the degree of interaction and affect serving to underline the differential nature of inclusion. Among both men and women, peer groups are important and are, in the case of Two Friends villagers, drawn mostly from fellow villagers. A relationship which gives a more graphic picture of the processes of inclusion is that of marriage (see Tables 3 and 4).

Table 2.   Spheres of interaction

Spheres	Contexts	Type of interaction
Two Friends	Parties (private, in homes) Private house dances Wakes Home visitations	Peer group formation Intermarriage (60 percent) Selection of godparents Information exchange (home) mutual support - money, accommodation, child care
St. Lucia	Parties (outside homes, semi-private, as in rented halls) Public house dances Pubs (often special "reserved" section) Betting shops Laundromats Markets (local)	Limited peer group formation Intermarriage (20 percent) Exchange of island news Limited mutual support (within neighborhood)
St. Lucia and Dominica	Parties (outside homes) Public house dances Betting shops	Limited peer group formation
Small Islands	None	Nothing exclusive
West Indies	Public dances (halls) Pubs (general) Betting shops Markets (central, i.e. Church Street, Portobello Road) "On the street"	Casual acquaintanceship Formation of mutual savings groups, "pardners" (at work place)
Colored immigrants	None	Nothing exclusive

Among villagers who have established conjugal relationships in London, a majority have selected spouses from the village. Although the tendency to select partners from home is evident, younger people display an increasing tendency to select from outside the village. Two factors seem relevant here. First, this trend is an expression of a wider range of interaction among younger people, and second, there is a greater probability that younger people have never been resident in Paddington, having joined their parents after the latter had moved out to other areas. As a result, some of these late arrivals to London never become part of that close community of villagers which focuses in Paddington.

In the area of extramarital, extraresidential relationships, there is a definite preference for partners outside the village circle. The anonymity

Table 3. Two Friends' marriages – by age, location, and spouse's origin

	Men							
	In St. Lucia		In England					
	Two		Two	Other		West		
Age	Friends	Other	Friends	St. Lucia	Dominica	Indian	Other	Total
60+	1	0	0	0	0	0	0	1
50–59	8	0	1	2	0	0	0	11
40–49	19	2	7	4	0	1	1	34
30–39	4	3	17	6	3	2	2	37
20–29	0	0	5	0	2	3	3	13
Total	32	5	30	12	5	6	6	96

	Women							
	In St. Lucia		In England					
	Two		Two	Other		West		
Age	Friends	Other	Friends	St. Lucia	Dominica	Indian	Other	Total
60+	1	0	0	0	0	0	0	1
50–59	2	0	1	0	0	0	0	3
40–49	18	2	4	1	0	1	0	26
30–39	11	4	13	0	2	0	0	30
–29	0	0	12	7	1	1	1	22
Total	32	6	30	8	3	2	1	82

Table 4. Two Friends' marriages – by location and spouse's origin

	In St. Lucia		In England					
	Two		Two	Other		West		
Sex	Friends	Other	Friends	St. Lucia	Dominica	Indian	Other	Total
Male	69	9	66	24	7	13	15	203
Female	69	10	66	18	5	5	2	175
Total	138	19	132	42	12	18	17	378

one can assume in a city the size of London ensures the maintenance of the secrecy of such a relationship, particularly important in cases in which one or both of the parties is married or living with someone else. These arrangements take place in the nearly complete absence of those situations, occasional in the West Indies, in which a man has polygynous relationships, maintaining more than one household in a community.

When marriages are made with people outside the category "villager," there may result a problem of inclusion of the outsider. If the spouse is a St. Lucian, this is of minimal concern, but if he or she is from another island or is white, the resulting arrangement may mean that one partner is separated, often physically, from family and community. This separation, especially during times of stress, can be very difficult for people who customarily depend heavily on kinsmen and friends; it is more so for women, who are generally much less mobile than men. In the case of a community such as the Two Friends community, which displays considerable vitality and solidarity, the outsider is most likely to be brought in rather than vice versa.

For villagers from Two Friends the ties with the village are maintained through a number of mechanisms: remittances, correspondence, and visits in both directions, an increasing trend with the availability of cheaper charter flights. Many migrants remit large sums of money regularly and are virtually the sole support of a number of households in the village. There are equal numbers, however, whose help, in some cases much needed by their kinsmen in Two Friends, is intermittent and sparing. These people, who are failing in an obligation which most acknowledge, are usually reminded not only in the letters from their families but also by friends and kin in London who are made aware of this state of affairs. The only way out of this obligation or the sanctions of harrassment is literally to drop out of the community, to move without telling one's own brother or sister, and simply to avoid the Paddington area and any other locations where one might encounter villagers. This kind of drastic behavior occurs very seldom in this community and most often the harrassment has at least temporary results.

I have drawn a portrait of the Two Friends migrants which emphasizes the solidarity and multiple ties existing within and giving definition to this community. As I noted at the outset, this may not be a typical case; in fact, from other observations I am sure that it is not. I would suggest that migrants from most West Indian communities are not involved in a community so closely defined by their previous residence; for many, the village community identification may have no meaning whatsoever. But the example is instructive in that I suggest that these migrants demonstrate their ethnic affiliations in most ways that other West Indians do and in many ways that others do not.

GENERATIONAL DIFFERENCES

I have indicated above that there is a tendency on the part of younger immigrants to take less note of the narrower frameworks for ethnic inclusion than do their parents and older brothers and sisters. One cannot speak strictly of generational differences here because most second generation West Indians born in London are still in school and under fifteen years of age. Moreover, generational differences are too gross to characterize accurately the changes taking place in this area. One must instead speak of age, age at the time of migration, domestic situation at the time of migration, and amount of schooling in London.

A particularly important context for influencing interactional patterns is the London school. In peer groups formed at school, separation according to island or village origin occurs very infrequently and cultural differences such as language are leveled out. This, of course, is perfectly in keeping with the assimilative orientation of the British schools, but this process is abetted by many West Indian parents who have been slow to demand that the schools take account of the cultural background of their children. As to language, there has developed a youth dialect, a kind of generalized West Indian English, which is not directly attributable to any single island but which has numerous Jamaican and Cockney elements.

In the areas of work and housing, young people's approaches differ considerably from those of their elders. Rather than seek jobs and accommodation through relatives and friends, they are more likely to use the labor exchange or the youth employment services at school and to seek rental housing through the local authority or a housing trust. This use of bureaucratic channels suggests that for these people at least some of the potential support from kinsmen and friends is no longer employed. Other contexts for interaction differ from those previously mentioned, predictably being less centered in the home. The youth club becomes the most important context for social interaction among those in their late teens and presents a distinctly heterogeneous picture in terms of its habitués. Close friends of both sexes are more frequently drawn from such social contexts and from the work situation.

Even in situations in which all age groups are present, there is a fairly rigid separation along age lines. Talk among older people revolves around subjects having to do with family, old friends, and the village or island, whereas younger people have only slight interest and sometimes vague recollections about these topics. This reflects another division, for young people differ from their elders in their attitudes toward the village and island and the possibility of an eventual return. Whereas most older villagers see themselves returning home within the next ten years, often to reoccupy homes left behind or to move into residences built with remittances, the young have no intention to return except perhaps to visit. This tendency will be reinforced if older villagers return home after their children finish school and take jobs in England, a course of action that many seem committed to follow. Such eventual action would result in a situation which poses questions for the study of adult socialization.

For those children who have either been born in England or who came there when very young, the categories of Two Friends villager or St. Lucian are simply meaningless. Culturally, they have very little to distinguish them from any other black children in London. They cannot speak patois, the language of their parents; they have no recollection of an island or village home; and they even reject the cuisine of their parents in favor of fish and chips.

Implications for Race Relations

It should be quite obvious at this point that ethnic categories based on village or island origin are likely to have little meaning for young people of West Indian background now resident in London. This raises the question of what criteria for identification are likely to emerge among this population.

As the importance of village or island background for ethnic identification fades, one might suppose that the category "West Indian" would emerge as a primary identification. In fact, this is a category now employed in census tabulations and has been used by other writers as if it were a socially significant criterion for the people subsumed under it. I would argue, on the contrary, that this has proved to be a category far more relevant for the census abstractor and the sociologist than for the people themselves. It has also been a category which has relevance for the bulk of the white population, often as a euphemism for more derogatory terms. Because the majority white population does not choose to make distinctions of any finer degree, for these distinctions would not be sociologically meaningful for them, and because the category "West Indian" represents a racial stereotype, and stereotypic behavior is accorded to persons of West Indian origin, this results in a situation having sociological significance for West Indian people. But it is not significant because of self-identification as "West Indian" and self-attributes defining that category; rather it is significant because of attributions made by others about people variously identified as "West Indian," "colored," "black," "nigger," or "wog."

As a self-identification, "West Indian" has seldom been of considerable importance. Although there are some organizations which employ the term in their names or seek to be a voice for migrants of West Indian origin, they seldom operate as representative bodies and are scarcely known to their presumed constituents. Individual exceptions to this general rule are few. Writers, artists, and students have evinced a greater identification with an entity larger than an island unit, and during the brief existence of the West Indies Federation perhaps more people identified as West Indians, thus validating Lamming's claim in 1960 for an emerging pan-West Indies consciousness (1960:214–215).[7]

West Indian identity has also occasionally been asserted in something less than positive terms, that is, in situations in which black people were reacting to overt expressions of racism in British society. The most notable example of this occurred in the late 1950's when those expressions took the form of violent physical attacks directed primarily against West Indians. As a result, organizations mushroomed, seeking to safeguard the interests of all West Indian migrants in Great Britain. Other indications of West Indian unity appeared; the *West Indian Gazette* had a considerable readership as it sought to build a group consciousness. But now the *Gazette* is defunct and the remaining organizations with a West Indian orientation are no longer much involved with consciousness raising.

Some scholarly work still suggests that these migrants and their children will be eventually assimilated into British society in a process that involves their becoming incorporated in the class system. Such explanations, inevitably discounting the paramount importance of racial domination, have been supported by more recent research. For example, Singham's conclusion is that West Indians' "political integration in the society will probably be achieved without undue stress..." and that they will be "organized ... as members of the working class" (1967:196). This is directly countered by Katznelson's (1972; 1973) demonstration of West Indian political impotence brought about through the formation of buffer organizations established by the British government as a result of a bipartisan effort by both major parties. As another example, the obscurantism of a notion like "housing class" (Rex 1971; Rex and Moore 1967) to account for the tenor of race relations is demonstrated by studies which indicate the racist attitudes and color prejudice prevalent in the society (Daniel 1968; Richmond 1970).

In dealing with the question of changing identity, it may be well to examine how black people, and young ones in particular, perceive this

---

[7] The factor of numbers is surely important here; as immigration increased, internal differentiation in the West Indian population became more characteristic. The significance of a chance encounter between two anonymous West Indians, depicted in Stuart Hall's story (1960), would be understandable in the early 1950's, unlikely now.

society and their position in it. One fact that becomes clear is that West Indians of all ages are becoming increasingly aware that the threat to their well-being today comes not so much from random violence by white hoodlums but more from government policies buttressed by police enforcement. There is a recognition that British racism has become less personal and more institutional in nature, that the problem is not in terms of the recurrence of Notting Hill but in the proliferation of political trials, police harrassment, and increasingly restrictive immigration laws. The argument is made that the Commonwealth Immigrants Act and subsequent legislation carry a racial bias, both in conception and practice, and that, consequently, people from the colored Commonwealth have been defined as constituting a particular category, singled out for differential incorporation within British society.[8] The response of young black people has been in accord with this definition.

Much evidence points to very conscious attempts to focus on blackness as the basis for identification. In addition to the drawing of attention to the position of black people in British society, there is an emphasis on the positive aspects of this identity, much in the same way as this has occurred in the United States. Many of the models for depicting British society and for orienting political and social action on the part of black people have their analogs on the American scene.

In some quarters there is a developing Third World consciousness as well, and in the columns of the liberation newspapers that have sprung up are found stories on the FRELIMO movement in Mozambique and the Viet Cong. In terms of cultural symbols, much that is emphasized lies in the expressive realm and, as such, has had an appeal to a wider audience, many of whom have yet to develop a radical political awareness. Reggae, the latest Jamaican popular music, has become THE urban black sound in England, spreading even beyond the limits of the black population (see Lewis 1971).

All of this, then, suggests that an identity based on blackness is emerging, that this is taking the form of a movement very much along the lines of those which preceded it in the United States, and that this movement is not merely some form of reaction in response to overt expressions of racism in British society, but that it carries positive aspects and seeks to establish this identification as based on criteria which blacks themselves define.

[8]   MacDonald (1969) discusses the biases in legislation affecting the migration. For an example of the discrimination in the application of immigration legislation, see Gish (1968).

REFERENCES

BARTH, FREDRIK
  1969 "Introduction," in *Ethnic groups and boundaries*. Edited by F. Barth, 9–38.Boston: Little, Brown.
BURNEY, ELIZABETH
  1967 *Housing on trial: a study of immigrants and local government*. London: Oxford University Press.
CALLEY, M. J. C.
  1965 *God's people: West Indian Pentecostal sects in England*. London: Oxford University Press.
DANIEL, W. W.
  1968 *Racial discrimination in England*. Harmondsworth: Penguin.
DAVISON, R. B.
  1963 The distribution of immigrant groups in London. *Race* 5:56–69.
  1966 *Black British: immigrants to England*. London: Oxford University Press.
DEAKIN, NICHOLAS
  1964 Residential segregation in Britain: a comparative note. *Race* 6:18–26.
FRUCHT, RICHARD
  1968 Emigration, remittances and social change: aspects of the social field of Nevis, West Indies. *Anthropologica* 10:193–208.
GISH, OSCAR
  1968 Color and skill: British immigration, 1955–1968. *International Migration Review* 3:19–37.
GLASS, RUTH
  1960 *Newcomers: the West Indian in London*. London: Allen and Unwin.
GRIFFITH, J. A. G. *et al.*
  1960 *Coloured immigrants in Britain*. London: Oxford University Press.
HALL, STUART
  1960 "Crossroads nowhere," in *West Indian Stories*. Edited by Andrew Salkey, 186–188. London: Faber & Faber.
HINDS, DONALD
  1970 "Small islan' complex," in *Island Voices*. Edited by Andrew Salkey, 117–122. New York: Liveright.
HYLSON-SMITH, K.
  1968 A study of immigrant group relations in North London. *Race* 9: 467–476.
KATZNELSON, IRA
  1972 "The politics of racial buffering in England, 1948–1968: colonial relationships in the Mother Country," in *Racial tensions and national identity*. Edited by E. Q. Campbell, 63–87. Nashville: Vanderbilt University Press.
  1973 *Black men, white cities*. London: Oxford University Press.
LAMMING, GEORGE
  1960 *The pleasures of exile*. London: Michael Joseph.
LEECH, KENNETH
  1967 Housing and immigration, crisis in London. *Race* 8:329–343.

LEWIS, GORDON K.
1971   An introductory note to the study of race relations in Great Britain. *Caribbean Studies* 11:5–29.

LOWENTHAL, DAVID
1972   *West Indian societies.* London: Oxford University Press.

MAC DONALD, IAN
1969   *Race relations and immigration law.* London: Butterworth.

MAC DONALD, J. S., L. D. MAC DONALD
1964   Chain migration, ethnic neighborhood formation and social networks. *Milbank Memorial Fund Quarterly* 42:82–97.

MADDOX, H.
1960   The assimilation of Negroes in a dockland area of Britain. *Sociological Review* 8:5–15.

MAUNDER, W. F.
1955   The new Jamaican emigration. *Social and Economic Studies* 4:38–63.

PAHL, R. E.
1970   *Patterns of urban life.* London: Longmans.

PATTERSON, SHEILA
1963   *Dark strangers.* London: Tavistock.

PEACH, G. C. K.
1966   Underenumeration of West Indians in the 1961 census. *Sociological Review* 14:73–80.
1968   *West Indian migration to Britain: a social geography.* London: Oxford University Press.

PHILPOTT, S. B.
1968   Remittance obligation, social networks and choice among Montserratian migrants in Britain. *Man* 3:465–476.

PRICE, CHARLES
1969   "The study of assimilation," in *Migration.* Edited by J. A. Jackson, 181–237. Cambridge: Cambridge University Press.

REX, JOHN
1971   The concept of housing class. *Race* 12:293–301.

REX, JOHN, R. MOORE
1967   *Race, community and conflict: a study of Sparkbrook.* London: Oxford University Press.

RICHMOND, A. H.
1970   Housing and racial attitudes in Bristol. *Race* 12:49–58.

ROBERTS, GEORGE
1955   Emigration from Barbados. *Social and Economic Studies* 4:245–288.

ROSE, E. J. B., *et al.*
1969   *Colour and citizenship: a report on British race relations.* London: Oxford University Press.

RUCK, S. K., *editor*
1960   *The West Indian comes to England.* London: Routledge and Kegan Paul.

SINGHAM, A. W.
1967   The political socialization of marginal groups. *International Journal of Comparative Sociology* 8:182–198.

SMITH, M. G.

1962   *Kinship and community in Carriacou.* New Haven: Yale University Press.

WILSON, PETER

1971   Caribbean crews: peer groups and male society. *Caribbean Studies* 10:18–34.

Racial versus Ethnic Factors in Afro-American and Afro-Caribbean Migration

VERA GREEN

Fredrik Barth maintains that ethnic status is "superordinate to most other statuses" and that "...it is imperative, in that it cannot be disregarded and temporarily set aside by other definitions of the situation" (1969:17). He considers the critical or determining factor in defining ethnicity to be "the characteristic of self-ascription and ascription by others" (1969:13). Ethnic identity is expressed by certain "overt signals or signs and basic value orientations" (1969:14) with the relative weighing of these factors varying considerably between differing types of sociocultural systems. Unfortunately Barth has not shown what he considers to be the relationship between "race" and "ethnicity." "Race," in the sense of "inbreeding populations" (Berreman 1971:31: Garn 1971:5), and "ethnicity" at times coincide, which explains in part why the terms are often used interchangeably. Consequently, we frequently find such statements as the following: "Thus, in the U.S., the Negroes are more properly called an ethnic rather than a racial group, as M. F. Ashley Montagu urges persuasively in his *Man's most dangerous myth*" (Gould and Kolb 1964: 243–244).

Other scholars opt for a distinction between race and ethnicity. For example, van den Berghe defines race as "...not a subspecies of homo sapiens but a group of people who in a given society are socially defined as different from other groups by virtue of certain real or putative physical differences" (1970:10), and he maintains that distinct types of stratification can result from physical versus cultural differences. Van den Berghe indicates that although systems of race and systems of ethnic relations are similar in many ways, the distinction between the two is important. Dobzhansky has stated:

...one may hate an ethnic group as virulently as a race. But the propriety of using such subterfuges in science is questionable. Speak of ethnic groups if you like, but a statement such as "man has no races, he has only ethnic groups" is misleading. Ethnic groups are biologically the same phenomenon as races, subspecies and breeds (1964:268).

If, however, race and ethnicity are considered basically different, even though related phenomena, how relevant is Barth's statement for the New World where racial factors *per se* are often of primary importance? The following is a brief analysis of data from the United States, Aruba and Curaçao in terms of racial versus ethnic primacy, with a discussion of the implications of these findings for various types of change studies.

UNITED STATES

It has been stated that discrimination in the United States is on the basis of origin or genetic ancestry, whereas the discrimination found in the Caribbean and Latin America is primarily that of rank or sociocultural position (Harris 1964, 1970; Wagley 1965; Nogueira 1955). It is clearly observable that in the United States the factor of race operates so that locality, class, or ethnic differences are minor in comparison. However, there are certain instances where it is possible for ethnicity to take precedence over race. This may occur when individuals present the phenotypical appearance of a derided group, but clearly indicate by outward signs such as language and mannerism evidence of "foreign" birth. There have been numerous cases in which Africans and West Indians have received differential treatment from that of the United States-born Negroid population UPON presentation of the "proper credentials" or behavioral signs, both in the northern and southern sectors of the United States (Reid 1969; Coombs 1970). Note that the concept of passing, with the connotation of hiding identity or masquerading as a member of another group was not applicable in these circumstances. The term passing was only utilized by members of the Negroid community when describing behavior of the members of the United States black population who adopted different behavioral credentials to change their identity in order to gain access to better socioeconomic conditions and services.

It is therefore evident that social race or discrimination by mark did at times operate openly in the United States for individuals of obvious foreign status. In effect, then, it is possible for ethnicity to supersede race in the case of non-United States nationals.

The only problem is that many darker foreigners resent and often refuse to wear a sign (i.e. extra emphasis of behavioral and linguistic differences) to indicate foreign status in order to be accorded what they consider to be normal treatment.

Interestingly, those in the dominant culture ignore similar types of "ethnic" differences when they occur WITHIN the primary United States black population. Narroll's definition of an ethnic group specifies persons who share basic cultural values and interactional spheres and are biologically self-perpetuating; further, they recognize themselves and are recognized by others as constituting a different group (Barth 1969:11). Barth considers the recognition by themselves and others as distinct to be the critical organizing feature of ethnicity (1969:13). Shibutani and Kwan define an ethnic group as "those who conceive of themselves as being alike by virtue of their common ancestry, real or fictitious, and who are so regarded by others "(1969:47). Utilizing the definitions of both Narroll and Shibutani and Kwan, the native-born French-speaking blacks of Louisiana can definitely be considered an ethnic group. Indeed, when outside their home areas they appear to have problems of adjustment and acceptance that are similar to those of European immigrants in the United States.

Louisiana was of course French until 1803, when the area was sold to the United States. Consequently, French culture has remained strong in parts of the state, especially the more isolated former French strongholds. As Louisiana was a slave-holding state, the population descended from French freemen and freedmen would have been predominantly "French" in culture and speech. To date, Creole-speaking blacks can be found throughout Louisiana. As a result of the romanticizing of affairs such as the quadroon balls, and the practice of Plaçage, there is a tendency to think that only mulattoes, quadroons, octoroons, et cetera are "French" in culture. This is of course not correct any more than it would be correct for areas such as Martinique or Guadeloupe. There is the same phenotypical and genotypical variation among French blacks that exists within the United States black population as a whole. The gamut from "jet black" to "stark white" is available with accompanying socioeconomic variations. Although to my knowledge few scientific studies exist regarding this group, and my data do not focus on this problem, I would venture to predict that class lines would be more sharply drawn among French-speaking as compared to English-speaking blacks as a partial reflection of French structure in Louisiana prior to the United States purchase. Charles B. Rousseve, author of *The Negro in Louisiana*, states that in recent years the French and the English elements of the black community in New Orleans have been drawing closer together paralleling the pattern of *rapprochement* between the whites in the area (personal communication).

While I was conducting research in Houston, Texas, the presence of the French-speaking as a definable element within the black community became very clear. Houston has received migrant workers from a number of southern states and there is a rather clear rivalry between those from Louisiana and Texas. Many Texans hold a generalized stereotypic view of those coming from Louisiana. For example, they are said to be hard workers and to work for less money than Texans. The Louisiana stereotype of the Texan is that they are not good workers, are too interested in having a good time, and have an easy-come-easy-go attitude.

There are apparently two basic stereotypes of the black people of French-speaking background from Louisiana. One appears to be applied primarily to the poorer families, while another operates for those who are better off financially. At times the term "French Creole" appeared to be used by some of the local English speakers to refer to the phenotypically lighter, mixed types. These were reported to consider themselves better than anyone else, and they attempted to isolate themselves from others, particularly the darker, non-French speakers. However, even lighter English individuals maintain that the "Creoles" or lighter French-speakers prefer the company of others from Louisiana. In short, they were considered both snobbish and "color struck." The poorer Frenchmen with less education were often said to be stupid, mulish, or stubborn but hard workers. Both the lighter and the darker French-speakers were considered clannish and family-oriented. Some of those coming from heavily French-speaking areas were often ridiculed because of their lack of fluency in English. Apparently the ordering of English words and the strong accents caused some English speakers to conclude that French speakers were "dumb" because they could not understand or "talk" English. Those with the strongest French accents were primarily from rural areas or were older persons. Those from educated families and those from urban areas were able to speak standard English. A number of younger informants from French families often prided themselves on the fact that they could not speak Creole, but would admit that when their relatives of their parents' and grandparents' generation got together Creole was generally the language used. The same young informants would often indicate that there was an old grandmother or elderly aunt in their home who could "hardly talk English."

Although at times there appeared to be some confusion in the minds of English blacks about the very dark French-speaking individuals, the French were considered to be different from the English-speaking Louisiana migrants. Both French and English Louisiana families tended to settle close to relatives or friends from their former localities so that a number of Protestant churches, as well as Catholic churches, were composed primarily of Louisiana-born persons.

It became clear that the French were careful about discussing the matter of differences between themselves and the English-speaking. However, after they recognized that my motive was simply to understand the situation, it was evident that they adhere to the division that was important immediately after the sale of Louisiana to the United States. Even young non-Creole-speaking informants spoke of "we Frenchmen" versus the Americin (the English-speaking) negroid population. One young Texas-reared informant confided that one could tell immediately after entering a house if it belonged to a "Frenchman." Further discussion revealed that objects in a French home were usually arranged differently and that Catholic pictures were frequently visible.

Both English and French informants indicated that the Frenchmen stressed family life more than the Americans. One well-known philanderer even stated, "We take better care of the family," when questioned as to whether there were differences between the English and Creole-speaking United States blacks. Of course, since little information is available on the French-speaking, to say nothing of a comparison between the French and the English, it is difficult to judge whether this is actually the case or not. It does appear that many of the French social activities are family-involved to a greater extent than in comparable English-speaking families, but this, too, must be confirmed by intensive study.

The Frenchmen and other Houston residents state that the first French arrivals settled in a sector which is now known as French Town. The Catholic church within the area still has primarily French parishioners, although Louisiana Catholics are also represented in other parts of Houston. One educated French-speaking Catholic, preferred to speak of himself as a Cajun (i.e. speaking mainly Cajun French vs. the African-based Creole), thereby revealing a distinction within the French-speaking Negroid sector. He stated that many of the Frenchmen had been lost to the Catholic church since there had been no local French-speaking priests in the past. A number of the priests brought in from other areas such as French Canada "did not understand our people"; consequently French Catholics either shifted to Protestant churches or simply did not take part in the local religious life. In the former case, Frenchmen would become even more involved with the dominant English element in Houston. In fact, there are a number of instances where individuals have anglicized their names, become Baptists or Methodists and subsequently important pillars within the English community.

Both the French- and the English-speaking Louisiana migrant would undergo varying degrees of adjustment to the Texas situation; but the Frenchmen often were faced with an additional hurdle involving some degree of language and cultural adjustment.

Unlike the foreign-born phenotypically dark individuals, the presence of obvious Creole and even the standard French language or different mannerisms and expressions do not serve as sufficient credentials to obtain full rights in the society as a whole. Whether or not these individuals, especially the lighter, are able to leave the area and go elsewhere and "pass" is not the issue here. The fact is that Frenchmen, even the mulattoes, quadroons, et cetera, many of whom attempted to isolate themselves from others, were all assigned or restricted to the same status as the black "Américain" by the whites at large. This was especially true after the Civil War. Consequently, in this case, racial status assumes primacy over undeniable ethnic status.

Both Leach (1961:306) and Barth (1967) have discussed the importance of considering cultural behavior in reference to the total context and strategic self-interest:

People's allocations are adjusted and adapted in terms of what they experience as the observed outcome of their behavior. The strategic constraints of social life also enter and affect behavior: people's activities are canalized by the fact of competition and cooperation for valued goods with other persons and thus by the problems of adapting one's behavior to that of others (Barth 1967:665).

Barth also states that we should not necessarily assume that categories and values have changed when we observe changing patterns of activity: "...we can also look at the changed circumstances that may well make allocations optimal when evaluated by the SAME standards" (Barth 1967:667).

The French-speaking in Houston are under constraints to adjust to both white and black English-speaking expectations to some degree, and at least two strategies are apparent. A number have reacted by doing all within their power to curtail the use of Creole by their children, and they strive to replace aspects of their French culture with English elements. Other Frenchmen

Keep the traditions for the intimacy of the home, the company of other Frenchmen and for visits to Louisiana, but assume the standard [English] forms for operation within the greater Houston Black society (Green 1971:11).

Although there are the subtle pressures by whites to view all Negroid persons in the United States as one undifferentiated mass and to coerce all others to do likewise, it is ironic that in many instances the French-speaking were subjected to much the same types of ridicule by black English speakers as European immigrants were within the total white society.

ARUBA, NETHERLANDS ANTILLES

Race and not ethnicity has generally been considered the vital factor in Caribbean relations. In Aruba, as in Latin America generally, color assumes more importance than race *per se* and ethnicity, in the sense of local island identification, at times is the most salient feature on both an emic and etic basis of study. How does a situation arise which brings ethnicity into relief?

Aruba is a former Dutch island located off the coast of Venezuela. As a result of the establishment of oil refineries on the island in the late 1920's, the population increased from approximately 5,000 to 60,000 in 1960. In 1951, 28,500 of a population of 56,000 were born off the island. Prior to the location of the refineries, economic life had been very precarious. Consequently, large numbers of native Arubans were forced to seek employment elsewhere. The opening of the refineries resulted in the return of many native Arubans to the island as well as the influx of masses of migrant laborers from other countries. By far the largest numbers came from neighboring islands and countries such as Colombia, Venezuela, the British and French West Indies, Surinam, Bonaire, Curaçao, and the Windward Islands.

The local language, Papiamentu, was the effective business and social language, and due to historical factors Spanish was utilized in place of Dutch as the "intellectual" language. As a result of the fact that few among the masses spoke Dutch and Papiamentu was not a standard language, Standard Oil of New Jersey, in consultation with the Aruban elite, selected English as the language of the refinery. This circumstance worked to the advantage of British West Indians, educated Dutch subjects from Curaçao and Surinam who had learned English, and the Dutch Windward Islanders whose local language was English. The language factor, the low economic base and the previous relative lack of educational facilities on the island placed the masses of mestizoid native Arubans at a comparative disadvantage in terms of skills required during the formative period of the refineries. The elite native Arubans were able to maintain and reinforce their positions as the merchant class in the island capital of Oranjestad.

On Aruba, all the groups occupy visible occupation niches, and with the exception of the Americans, the Chinese, Netherlands Dutch, and Portuguese groups, include various phenotypes within their ethnic confines. The native Arubans themselves consisted of a number of Caucasian, mestizo, Amerindian and mulatto types with fewer, but some Negroid phenotypes depending on the area of the island. Individuals coming from Colombia, Venezuela, and Bonaire might exhibit Caucasoid, Negroid, mulatto, even Amerindian types, while Caucasoid, mulatto, Negroid, East Indian, and Chinese phenotypes were possible from Surinam, Guyana, and Trinidad. There were a few mestizo types from Curaçao; and they, like the Windward Islanders, included not only mulatto and Negroid phenotypes but also the Caucasian. The relative percentages of each type varied between the groups, and some denied the existence of particular phenotypes. For example, the native Arubans, due to the smaller number of African slaves when compared with Curaçao and Bonaire, insist they lacked the African element. Given these conditions, and the fact that over the years many residents became fluent in two or more of the languages utilized on the island – Papiamentu (the local Creole language), Spanish, Dutch, and English – the simple reliance on phenotypical distinctions could not serve as an accurate indication of ethnicity. The surname became the important ethnic indicator as certain surnames abound on given islands.

Also due to the economic system there were individuals of all colors and races at each sociocultural level. Although a majority of Caucasoid types were at the peak, there were also Caucasoids at the bottom of the socioeconomic ladder. Some individual poor white Windward Islanders (i.e. Sint Maarten, Saba) and the Portuguese as a group were consigned to the lower levels with the result that terms "to work like a Portugee" and "Portugee work" originated, although some Portuguese individuals were ranked higher. Conversely, there were a number of phenotypically darker Negroid and mulatto types in the middle economic realm and a few in the upper, especially in St. Nicolaas, a village near the seat of the refinery which, after the influx of migrants, grew to rival the capital city of Oranjestad where the majority of the "strangers" were located. After the peak of refinery production, there followed a decline, later retrenchment and eventual automation of the Lago facilities. It was during the decline that relations between Arubans and strangers were intensified. The masses of native Arubans, formerly considered shy and isolative if not actually backward by a number of the outsiders, were preparing to take over positions in government and business formerly occupied by non-natives. As a result of the retrenchment and Arubanization of the economy, numbers of strangers repatriated or moved to St. Croix for employment.

In 1967, during the writer's period of residence on the island, it was noted that on the emic level, first color and secondly ethnicity were important in ordering the relationships between native Arubans and nonnatives. Many foreigners, white and black, maintained that Arubans "don't like black people." However, an equal number of white strangers complained that native Arubans did not like them, either. It was explained that "they don't like outsiders," "they stick to themselves." One black Windward Islander voiced the opinion of many when she commented, "They're shy people. Friendly... but up to a point..." At the etic level it appeared that primarily propinquity and personal relationships and secondarily ethnicity were important in ordering relationships. In effect there was a noted difference in the verbalized norm and actual observable behavior. Also there was a difference between the official governmental immigration policy toward strangers (for example problems encountered by foreigners continuing residence on the island during periods of unmployment) and individual personal relationships between native Arubans and the strangers.

The research data revealed numerous examples on the behavioral level, indicating that propinquity and personal relations were vital. Older native Aruban informants reported that, at one time in certain localities, even native Arubans were suspect when they entered other communities. Native Aruban parents have been known to interfere with the marriages of their children to dark non-Arubans, as well as to other native Arubans. In some cases the interference has been against a native Aruban prospective spouse in favor of a non-native with whom there has been a close family relationship. One particular organization on the island was, according to verbal reports, the stronghold of the native or "real Arubans." "They don't tolerate non-Arubans around there." Personal interviews with the board of the organization indicated that at least two of the principal members were relatively darker, phenotypically Negroid and mulatto type non-native Arubans who lived nearby. Some of the local children taking part in activities were definitely phenotypically Negroid.

One might state that ethnicity served to structure relationships at the categorical level (Mitchell 1966), for although everyone was necessarily placed in an ethnic group, the specific classifications were sometimes wrong. For example, a Venezuelan friend was classified as a Surinamer even though the latter were generally disliked as a group. The native Arubans generally were closer to Venezuelans and there were a large number of intermarriages in this group. In general, they also liked Bonairians, who were considered gentle and polite. Windward Islanders and Britishers were lumped together in a category, "the English," and were considered loud and rude. Interestingly, this group was most often the one considered and referred to as black. Verbalized resentment against Surinamers and natives of Curaçao was quite strong. The statements against the former were because they were "little Dutchmen," occupying posts directly under the Dutch, and more importantly they were reputed to go against a friend for a job. The latter were supposedly loud and pushy, tried to dictate to Arubans, and were "cheap" (frugal) like the Dutch. Although a number of younger native Arubans married Dutch wives, the masses tended to avoid the Dutch also.

When faced with a situation of this complexity it might be understood why race as a category appears to be of less importance than ethnicity and color. In such a context, sociological color in the sense discussed by M. G. Smith (1965) becomes important. It is not so much the phenotype, but the structural, behavioral, and associational color which are crucial. Hence individuals, Arubans as well as non-native Arubans and strangers, might complain loudly that they did not know or associate with black people when it could be observed that one or more of their close friends and possibly even a parent was phenotypically Negroid. Under these circumstances, ethnicity may be said to take precedence over color. For example, there are cases where darker Venezuelans, Bonairians, and Colombians have been selected for close personal relationships, while Curaçalenans and Surinamers of the same phenotypes were not.

Actually propinquity and the development of personal rather than categorical relationships appear to be as important as ethnicity in certain realms of activity. If individual Curaçalenans, Surinamers, and Windward Islanders, et cetera were in close proximity and exhibited the personal qualities prized by native Arubans, such as a quiet manner, not "pushy" or authoritarian, and generous, close relationships frequently resulted. In the past there was a differential location of ethnic groups on the island due to the fact that foreigners were located primarily around St. Nicolaas near the refineries. Consequently, the native Arubans living in other parts of the island had less contact with foreigners. Also, foreigners in St. Nicolaas had comparatively limited contacts with native Arubans as the former operated in what was actually an international setting during the years when employment was at its peak. Native Arubans in St. Nicolaas were consequently more knowledgeable about strangers than were their countrymen in other areas. Likewise, the strangers living in other areas were drawn more into the local island atmosphere.

As a result of the rather complex cultural and linguistic atmosphere on Aruba, and the rather close ties with Venezuela and Colombia, one finds the great majority of residents, especially the educated and the younger age groups, able to operate effectively within a number of different cultural settings as a matter of expediency without any concomitant loss of ability to operate efficiently within their original group.

CURAÇAO, NETHERLANDS ANTILLES

Is it possible to assume that the same relationship between race and ethnicity operates in all the Dutch-influenced Caribbean?

Curaçao was the larger of the two islands and actually the administrative center for the Dutch West Indies. The faltering economy received an impetus with the establishment of the Dutch Shell Refinery on the island in the mid-twenties. The socioeconomic life on both Curaçao and Aruba was dominated by the refineries and members of virtually the same ethnic groups sought employment on both islands. As Shell was a Dutch concern, there was no question of instituting other than Dutch as the official language, in spite of the fact that Papiamentu was the local language. This meant that primarily the Surinamers, the Netherlanders, and only the educated Antillians were eligible for higher posts as Papiamentu had been the language of the masses. The English-speaking were less favored and as a whole, like the Bonairians, occupied positions farther down the status ladder, in comparison to the position of many members of these same ethnic groups on Aruba.

The traditional Caribbean population pyramid was much more evident on Curaçao than Aruba during the pre-refinery days. As the Curaçalenan population base was African, there were the darker masses and the coloreds in addition to essentially three groups of whites. The white Protestants were divided into an elite and a lower or poorer Protestant group, and there was the elite Sephardic Jewish element. As a result of the plantation system, color categories and class lines in pre-refinery days appeared to have been more rigidly drawn on Curaçao than on Aruba, although there is evidence that sociological color was also operative then as now (Hoetink n.d.:167). What was the implication for the migrants of the different color pyramid on Curaçao as opposed to that of Aruba?

The masses of strangers, no matter how dark, were able to blend in phenotypically with the Curaçalenans to a much greater degree than in Aruba, although ethnicity was still determined primarily by surnames.

Due to the larger native population on Curaçao, the local Curaçalenan never suffered the psychological threat of inundation by the entry of large numbers of strangers that was possible on the part of native Arubans. However, after retrenchment and automation by Shell, interethnic friction was accentuated in a fashion similar to that which developed on Aruba.

A shorter period of fieldwork with approximately the same types of associations and ethnic groups and essentially the same questionnaire revealed basically the same attitudes; indeed similar statements from the strangers about the Curaçalenans were given by their countrymen in regard to the native Arubans. The essential difference was that darker strangers in Aruba practically always brought in the color factor as an explanatory mechanism, whereas it was generally lacking when strangers spoke about Curaçalenan exclusiveness. This was presumably due to the variation in the pre-migration color pyramids of the two islands. Curaçalenans were considered to be isolative, preferring their own company, hesitant about taking advantage of opportunities, and inclined to avoid positions of authority. As in Aruba, the strongest interethnic connections were with Venezuelans and, as a result of intermarriages, there were a number of connecting family and business relationships between the two areas.

The data collected on Curaçao indicated that at the emic level first propinquity and personal relations and second ethnicity were important in ordering interethnic relations. At the etic level class, propinquity and personal relations, and ethnicity were important in that order.

Color, of course, was an omnipresent factor on Curaçao as in Aruba or Houston or indeed in any New World former plantation-slave area! The fact is that color problems were of even more psychological import on Curaçao among the indigenous populations than among the native Arubans. On Aruba color was used primarily to distinguish between natives and non-natives after the influx of migrants. On Curaçao color had been utilized historically to distinguish between the natives themselves. Note Paula's work on the color factor and the presence of the local concept of "Drecha Raza" (improve color by marrying lighter) which is deeply imbedded in island lore (1967). In spite of these factors, color did not always take precedence over ethnicity, nor was ethnicity in Barth's terms ALWAYS the imperative force. In Curaçao class or socio-economic status was a powerful force.

As on Aruba, members of the various ethnic groups are able to utilize the languages and behavior of other groups to operate effectively within different cultural contexts. That is, Britishers or Surinamers may speak fluent Papiamentu and Dutch and operate within the Curaçalenan, Bonairian, or Dutch context, while maintaining their own languages and behavioral characteristics to be exhibited within their own British or Surinam context. There are others who became "assimilated" to varying degrees in the sense of releasing the old in order to obtain the new. But this is not always the case and there are apparently as many instances in both Curaçao and Aruba where the effective language and behavioral usage is evidence of situational change and not "assimilation" as such.

SUMMARY AND CONCLUSION

This has been an attempt to discuss relationships between migrants in three areas of the New World within the framework of race and ethnicity. While it is recognized that the factors of race and its offspring color are omnipresent in areas where large numbers of persons of African descent were confined, it is not always the crucial factor. Authors such as Noguiera (1955), Harris (1964), M. G. Smith (1965), and Wagley (1965) have shown that socioeconomic factors can operate as mitigating forces. The data in the three cases presented above suggest that ethnicity be added to such sociocultural factors as class and behavior, et cetera, as a possible mitigating force.

The fact that ethnicity can supersede race in such a racialistic society as the United States – IF foreign-born blacks are willing constantly to stress, if not parade, their "foreignness" – indicates the basic power of Barth's assertion. Nevertheless, the same white society considers the ethnicity of French-speaking blacks in the United States as secondary to their racial status. Consequently the assertion that ethnic status is "superordinate to most other statuses" is not universally true and must be qualified. Further, the data from the Netherlands Antilles and the United States indicate that ethnicity is not universally imperative – it can be "disregarded and temporarily set aside by other definitions of the situation" (Barth 1969:17).

REFERENCES

BARTH, FREDRIK
    1967   On the study of social change. *American Anthropologist* 69:661–669.
BARTH, FREDRIK, *editor*
    1969   *Ethnic groups and boundaries.* Boston: Little, Brown.
BERREMAN, G, *et al.*
    1971   *Anthropology today.* Del Mar, California: Communications Research Machines.

COOMBS, O.
1970   *Do you see my love for you growing?* New York: Dodd Mead.
DOBZHANSKY, T.
1964   *Mankind evolving: the evolution of the human species.* New Haven: Yale University Press.
GARN, S. M.
1971   *Human races.* Springfield, Illinois: Charles C. Thomas.
GREEN, V.
1971   "Situation of change and selection versus assimilation in understanding multi-ethnic societies." Paper presented at the seventieth annual meeting of the American Anthropological Association.
GOULD, J., W. KOLB, *editors*
1964   *A dictionary of the social sciences.* New York: Free Press.
HARRIS, M.
1964   *Patterns of race in the Americas.* New York: Walker.
1970   "Referential ambiguity in the calculus of Brazilian racial identity," in *Afro-American anthropology.* Edited by N. Whitten and J. Szwed. New York: Free Press.
HOETINK, H.
n.d.   *Het patroon van de oude Curaçaose samenleving.* Aruba: De Wit N.V.
LEACH, E.
1961   "Pul Eliya, a village in Ceylon." Cambridge University Press.
MITCHELL, J. CLYDE
1966   "Theoretical orientations in African urban studies," in *The social anthropology of complex societies,* volume four. Edited by M. P. Banton. New York: Praeger.
NOGUEIRA, O.
1955   "Preconceito racial de marca¡ e preconceita racial de origem," in *Anais do XXXVI Congresse Internacional de Americanistas, São Paulo* 1:409–434.
PAULA, A. F.
1967   *From objective to subjective social barriers.* Curaçao: Boekhandel Salas.
REID, I.
1969   *The Negro immigrant, his background, characteristics and social adjustment, 1899–1937.* New York: Arno Press and the New York Times.
ROUSSEVE, C.
1937   *The Negro in Louisiana.* New Orleans: Xavier University Press.
SMITH, M. G.
1965   "A framework for Caribbean studies," in *The plural society in the British West Indies.* By M. G. Smith. Berkeley: University of California Press.
VAN DEN BERGHE, P.
1970   *Race and ethnicity: essays in comparative sociology.* New York: Basic Books.
WAGLEY, C.
1965   "On the concept of social race in the Americas," in *Contemporary cultures and societies of Latin America.* Edited by D. Heath and R. Adams. New York: Random House.

Ethnic Differentiation among the Jews of Israel

CELIA S. HELLER

Six months before the Yom Kippur War of 1973 Israel came very close to having a Sephardic Jew assume the elevated post of president. The hope of many non-Ashkenazim was that at last the fourth president of the country would be a Sephardi. But as various candidates emerged, influential Israelis put forth the concept that the question of Sephardic background was irrelevant to the issue of who should be president. For example, a group that organized to push the candidacy of Professor Yigael Yadin (an Ashkenazi) stressed that ethnic considerations should not be involved in making the choice. The reasons given by the leaders of this group are noteworthy. These organizers, including three Technion professors, expressed their objection to seeking a candidate of Sephardic background "simply for the sake of his origin" (*Jerusalem Post Weekly* February 13, 1973:4).

The implications of such statements, which reflect the concept that ethnic background is irrelevant, bring us to the heart of the problem: the discrepancy between the objective reality and the subjective interpretation of ethnic differences among the Jews of Israel. On the one hand, there is the objective reality of economic, political, and social inequality between the Jews of European and non-European background. But on the other hand, there is the subjective dimension of persistent refusal on the part of the Israeli establishment and influential Israeli to recognize explicitly that ethnicity counts among the Jews in Israel. As a young Israeli sociologist of "Oriental" background, Smooha (1972:31-36) observed, Ashkenazim are willing to listen only when the problem "is defined in traditional social class terms," not in ethnic terms. Both dimensions of this problem — the objective and subjective — are reflected in the fact that the first four presidents were Ashkenazim, while more than half of the Jews in Israel are non-Ashkenazim. In view of the fact that the role of the president is mainly ceremonial and symbolic, it is especially significant that no Sephardic or Oriental Jew has occupied this post. This state of affairs is indicative of a larger problem: ethnic inequality among the Jews of Israel.

How did this problem come into being and what are its important dimensions? It should be recalled that Sephardim formed the bulk of the Jewish community living in Palestine before the start of immigration from eastern Europe in the 1880's. Still, most of the Sephardim came after World War I. (Eisenstadt 1967:50). Also coinciding with the main waves of central and east European immigration was the arrival of Jews from Oriental countries. It might be fitting to note here that, contrary to common usage, the terms Sephardic and Oriental are not synonymous. The term Sephardic originally applied to all the Jews originating in Spain and Portugal who after the Inquisition lived both in Europe and in "Oriental" countries, Egypt and North Africa. They were bound, in addition to country of origin, by common religious rituals and a common Judeo-Spanish language, *Ladino* (mainly derived from old Spanish dialects and written in Hebrew letters; it is comparable to the Yiddish of the Ashkenazim). If the Sephardim differed in cultural characteristics from the bulk of European Jews who were Ashkenazim, they also differed thus from the bulk of Oriental Jews. (And yet today the term Sephardic is often applied to the masses of Jews from the Arab countries, most of whom are not Sephardic.)

But most of the Jews who came to Palestine during the English Mandate were Ashkenazim, Jews from eastern and central Europe. As a matter of fact when Israeli scholars speak of the major waves of immigration prior to independence, the *aliyot*, they usually refer solely to these immigrants who were inspired by Zionism to return to Zion. In contrast to these pre-independence *aliyot*, the post-independence immigration from Europe, as well as from the Oriental countries, was not primarily Zionist: it consisted largely of refugees seeking a haven. (Some point to the Russian Jews' coming to Israel now as the first post-independence Zionist immigration.) Prior to independence, Zionists argued the issue of selective versus indiscriminate immigration. Those who were bent on creating a utopian society favored ideological commitment as a necessary prerequisite for entry. However, their argument proved irrelevant in face of the tragedy of the Holocaust. Thus, the right to return became the prevailing philosophy of post-independence immigration. First to be brought were the survivors from the displaced persons camps from eastern

Europe. The doors were also opened to the Jews from the Islamic countries who feared Arab violence in retaliation for their defeat in Palestine. In terms of numbers, the immigration was almost equally split: half of the immigrants (54.6 percent) during the years 1948–1962 came from the Middle East and Africa, north of the Sahara. Conformity to the way of life established by the Zionist pioneers during the English Mandate was expected of both categories, but neither worked out in accordance with this expectation. "Neither of the two types of new immigrants," to quote Professor Talmon of the Hebrew University, "had much training, aptitude, or taste for the utopian collectivist endeavor" (1970:161). And yet in the first case, the Israeli scholars speak of successful absorption and in the latter of failures in absorption. The fact is that the European immigrants succeeded in transforming the society and steering it away from the collectivist endeavor along the path of modern development. As Talmon expressed it: "An extremely egalitarian society, based on voluntary teamwork, changed almost overnight" (1970). The rhetoric of the governing elite remained egalitarian; the social structure of the country was no longer so.

It was to a rapidly industrializing society that the immigrants from the underdeveloped Arab lands had to adjust. They were preached to in terms of egalitarian and collectivist ideals; they were often treated in terms of divisive, rugged, and impersonal individualism. The implementation of the goals of the "ingathering of exiles" was assigned to bureaucracies, in contrast to the direct contact between oldtimers and newcomers which was characteristic of the pre-state period. And how did the bureaucracies implement the "ingathering of exiles"? Upon arrival the immigrants were given housing, some financial aid, and assistance in finding work. But shortly after, they were left more or less to their own devices with little continuous guidance or help. Left to themselves, the immigrants from Europe were able to cope comparatively well in the Israeli society that they were shaping along the lines of industrialization, with emphasis on consumption as a prime measure of social accomplishment. They possessed the necessary technical skills to a much greater extent than the immigrants from the Islamic countries. Their central values tended to be secular, universalistic, and achievement-oriented. Conversely, the deeply-rooted value orientations of the Oriental immigrants were not conducive to effective functioning and advancement in a rapidly changing industrial society, however praiseworthy on other grounds. The extended family, with strong ties spread through a number of generations in a large web of kinship, prevailed among them. These ties imposed obligations of mutual responsibility and aid. Loyalty was primarily to a person's own kinsfolk, not to impersonal organizations. Such loyalty, such values, which served them well during centuries in exile, proved to be obstacles to advancement in Israel (Weintraub 1971:257–258).

Another factor that must not be overlooked is that most of the groups arriving from the Islamic countries had become separated from their modern and intellectual elites. For example, the Jews who came to Israel after Moroccan independence was achieved were the poor Jews; the richer chose to remain or to take up residence in France and other parts of Europe (or even in Montreal). The same was true of Algerian Jews. Albert Memmi in his *Portrait of a Jew* alludes to this phenomenon; André Chouraqui discusses it in his *Les Juifs d'Afrique du Nord entre l'Orient et l'Occident*. Separated from their intellectual elites, the Oriental Jews lacked the leaders to pave the way and guide them on the road to modernization. A notable exception to this pattern were the Yemenites and their "absorption" was rather "successful," to use the standard Israeli terms (Deutsch 1958:328–339). Nevertheless, they tended to be subsumed under the label Oriental and subjected to the differential treatment accorded to Orientals.

A large proportion of the immigrants from Europe received money from the German government as compensation for their suffering under Nazism. The total of these personal restitutions amounted to twice what the Israeli government received from Germany as part of the Reparations Treaty. Needless to say, no comparable compensation was forthcoming from the Arab states. And so the economic gap between the European and Oriental immigrants became wider through the "blood money" received from Germany.

The gap in terms of objective criteria is now substantial: there is considerable occupational, income, and wealth inequality between Jews of Oriental and European background. Orientals are markedly underrepresented in professional and scientific occupations and overrepresented in unskilled and semiskilled occupations. The per capita income of Oriental Jews is only half that of the Ashkenazim. (It was 45 percent in 1965, 47 percent in 1970, and 48 percent in 1971). Even if a statistical refinement is introduced, weighting by "family size," which raises the per capita figure of Oriental Jews, the ratio does not increase much above half. A refinement was done by Dr. Oded Remba on the assumption that "a four member family does not need twice as much income to maintain a certain level of consumption as a two-member family" (1973:210). (According to his calculations, the thus adjusted gross income per person of Oriental Jews was 50.8 percent of the income of European Jews in 1963–1964 and 54.8 percent by 1970.) This marked income difference is due both to the occupational differences noted above and to the fact that their families are much larger. We could fill this article with statistics to demonstrate the range of economic inequality, for extensive materials exist on this subject (Ben-Porath 1971; Lissak 1969:16–31; Hannoch 1961). Suffice it to say here that all these statistics point to high correlation between one's being Oriental and belonging to the lower class. One of the most recent studies shows that even if the level of education is statistically held constant, high occupational positions correlate significantly with European background (Hartman 1973) The Oriental Jews are heavily concentrated in the lower social strata, irrespective of length of stay in Israel. However, the actual gap in the standard of living of the two groups would have been still wider were it not for the welfare policies pursued by the government and the Histadrut. The importance of such programs as free medical care and government subsidies of essential foods — bread, milk, etc. — must not be overlooked.

Apart from the economic inequality, which finds expression in the standard of living, there is the marked political inequality between the two groups of Jews. Only 'twenty of the one hundred and twenty members of the present Knesset (Parliament) are non-Ashkenazim. In the nineteen-member National Cabinet, there are only two persons of Oriental background: Shlomo Hillel, Minister of Police and Interior, and Aharon Uzan of Agriculture. Similarly, the Oriental Jews continue as a small minority in intermediate political posts, although they are making headway on the local leven as exemplified by the Mayor of Beersheba, Eliahu Navi (Weiss 1970). The inequality in power between the two Jewish ethnic groups is of growing significance because political posts are increasingly becoming sources of prestige and avenues of access to higher economic positions (Eisenstadt 1969:443, 447–494). Notice, for example, the phenomenon of *protectzia* (well-placed connections), its importance and its acceptance in Israel as a natural arrangement. The general conviction is that only by the use of *protectzia* can one break through the bureaucratic maze. Israelis consider it indispensable in every aspect of civilian life. To obtain a good job, to have a certain rule overlooked when applying to a university, to have a telephone installed when there is a shortage of lines, the common answer is *protectzia*.

Another important factor in the formation of ethnic divisions among the Jews of Israel is the over-all goal that the *vatikim*, the Ashkenzaic old-timers who pioneered the country, and especially the leaders of the new state, set for the large number of immigrants who came after Israel was established. This goal is to some extent implied in the much-used Israeli term "absorption" of immigrants: They expected the immigrants to shed the values and behavior in which they were socialized and to conform to the values and behavior of the existing secularized pioneering community. (This was very similar to what has been characterized as the philosophy of "Anglo-conformity," applied to immigrants in the United States.) The elite failed to take cognizance of the fact that many of the immigrants from the Islamic countries came to Israel with a different over-all goal, a pluralistic one. Their way of life was strongly traditional and they expected that, having held on to their traditional ways while living among Gentiles, they would find it much easier to practice them in a Jewish land. Before coming to Israel, they identified with the European Jews as Jews. Their traditional Jewish faith and Messianic hopes embraced all Jews irrespective of the country in which their *galut* ('exile') was spent. They assumed that in the resurrected Israel they would pursue their way of life without incurring social degradation, segregation, and political subordination. But their assumptions proved wrong. They were expected to shed their ways which were perceived as inferior. The same is occurring today with the Jews from Soviet Georgia who are arriving in Israel.) Yehuda Ninni, an Israeli writer and poet of Yemenite background, conveyed to us the arrogance in this pattern by recounting an experience he had at the time of the large immigration from the Islamic lands. In an article in a Kibbutz periodical, he told of his encounter with a highly placed Ashkenazi woman who had heard of the dangerous missions he had gone on to help bring Jews to Israel from the Arab countries. "*Kol hakavod*, all honor to you," she said, "You have brought them here and now we shall make civilized human beings out of them." When he asked her whether she ever studied Maimonides, her answer was: "What has he got to do with our current problems? He died hundreds of years ago." Ninni said that he turned from her with the words: "They read Maimonides with reverence and think that he is relevant. Please don't make your kind of 'human beings' out of them" (Hadary 1972:13).

This exemplifies the other aspect of the ethnic problem of the Jews in Israel today, beside the economic and political inequality. The elite and not so elite Ashkenazim pride themselves on their "Western" culture and look down on the others, when in fact the culture of some of the Sephardim and Orientals "was in many ways more refined than that of many European-born Israelis" (Segre 1971:193). The dignity and honor of their traditional ways are outside the field of perception of most Ashkenazim, who often refer to the Jews from the Islamic countries as "backward" or Levantine. In Israel one frequently hears remarks about the danger of "Levantinization" of Israel, especially because of the high birthrate of Oriental Jews. "Many lived among the Arabs and they became like them. We had to teach their children European culture. This is a modern country and we don't want it to become just another Levantine country," a young teacher explained when discussing the difficulties of her work. The result of such attitudes has been the failure to incorporate into the national culture of Israel important esthetic values as well as traditions of the Sephardic and Oriental Jews. Israeli culture could have been that much richer had there been from the very beginning respect for what Orientals and Sephardim could give to it. The treatment given Oriental Jews is sometimes labeled by radicals outside of Israel as "racial" prejudice. I would prefer to call it "culturalism," not racism, because it does not entail the notion of biologically inherited superiority or inferiority. In Israel, the Ashkenazim are increasingly rationalizing and justifying their behavior towards Oriental Jews by invoking the idea of culturally inherited superiority or inferiority. It is intriguing, and would merit investigation by social scientists, that the very Jews who suffered so much in Europe and now live in Israel take such pride in European ways and values and look down on the non-European Jews, even when the latter display traditional Jewish ways and values. Not infrequently such superiority is claimed by individuals whose manners or speech would hardly win them in Europe the designation of "cultured."

The disregard of the cultural heritage of the non-Ashkenazim is clearly reflected in the elementary and secondary-school curricula and textbooks. Little can be found in them to give the children and youth of non-European origin a sense of pride in their past. The students learn about such things as the *shtetl* (village) life of eastern Europe, about the major social movements among the Ashkenazim, etc. They learn little about Jewish communal life in the Islamic countries. No appreciation of the aristocratic elements of Sephardic culture nor of the esthetic elements so predominant in the culture of the Sephardic and Oriental Jews is developed in school.

It will now be easier to comprehend the widespread use of negative stereotypes of Oriental Jews in Israel. How they came into being has hardly been studied by the social scientists in Israel. Of special interest would be an exploration of how the negative stereotypes originally attached to specific geocultural groups with the greatest problems of adjustment — Moroccans and Kurds — have become extended to the broad ethnic category of Orientals. These stereotypes, sometimes completely erroneous, more often consist of inflexible exaggerations of actual tendencies or attributes. They constitute the predisposition to respond to individuals considered to be Orientals in a different way. In the everyday unguarded conversation of Ashkenazim one hears frequent allusions to the supposedly undesirable traits of the Orientals. For example, at a friendly gathering I heard a woman lament that her niece was bent on marrying an "Arab." Upon probing, I discovered that she referred thus to a Jewish youth who was brought as a child from Egypt. And a respected builder who tried to sell an apartment to my parents said to them in my presence: "We would like you to live in this house. You know, let them be well, but we don't like *Frankim* in our houses." By the way, *Frankim* and *Shehorim* (blacks), are the derogatory labels used by Ashkenazim to designate the other Jews, who in turn call them *voos-voos*. Both the derogatory labels and prejudicial remarks can easily be noticed by any perceptive visitor to Israel. Thus the denials of the existence of prejudice in Israel sound rather hollow. For those who want more precise documentation, the quantitative study of the Israeli sociologist Yochanan Peres, based on questionaire data, demonstrates that a considerable amount of prejudice exists against Oriental Jews. It shows that this prejudice contrasts sharply with the usually favorable attitudes of the Oriental Jews toward the Ashkenazim (Peres 1971:1021–1048).

Hand in hand with prejudice is the manifestation of discrimination: the differential treatment of individuals who are considered to be Orientals. As far back as 1962, the Israeli sociologist Judith Shuval spoke of "growing evidence of certain forms of scapegoating," but hastened to add that "only rarely have these assumed extreme forms of expression." She specified that prejudice and discrimination generally manifest themselves "on the level of exclusiveness, unwillingness to maintain social relationships with certain groups, stereotyped perception..., verbal hostility" (Shuval 1962:323–329). Professor Shuval and other Israeli sociologists have pointed to the absence of quotas or formal discrimination on jobs to emphasize how mild the pattern is. But what I want to stress is that although the manifestations in Israel may not be as extreme as the discriminatory practices in many other societies, the people subjected to them experience them acutely precisely because the perpetrators are Jews and Israelis. In the countries where they formerly lived they were victims of prejudice and discrimination because they were Jews; now in Israel it is because they are Orientals. The latter, although milder in form, may often be just as hard or harder to endure. The cry of wounded pride has been translated into words by Yehuda Ninni in his controversial article entitled "Reflections on the third destruction," which appeared in a 1972 issue of *Shdemot*, a Kibbutz periodical. It would appear from this challenging indictment of the ethnic *status quo* in Israel, that what pains the author even more than the economic disadvantages is the injured pride of his own community (Ninni 1972).

The injured pride, as well as the economic and political inequality, is not confined to those born abroad: It is shared by *sabras* (native-born Israelis) whose parents were born in Afro-Asian countries. For in Israel there are also two distinct categories of *sabras*, whose life chances are different. The extent of differences among them is minimized by official statistics which treat Israeli-born as one category that is compared with two others: those born in Europe or America, and those born in Asia or Africa. But the few sociological studies that break down the Israeli-born category by parents' country of birth, show that the inequality is in the process of being perpetuated from generation to generation. There is some evidence that the occupational and income differences might be as large, or even a bit larger, among the two groups of *sabras* than among their parents (Ben-Porath 1971). The reason for this is that there is considerably less upward mobility among *sabras* of Oriental descent. Crucial here is the tremendous inequality in educational attainment between the two groups, a subject that has been fully explored. Perhaps it can be summarized in the following figures: Orientals constitute 60 percent of the children entering primary grades, 25 percent of those in secondary schools and 10 percent of the university students. It is true that the absolute level of educational attainment of those born in Israel is substantially above that of the parental generation. The gap, however, between the *sabras* of Oriental-born parents and those of European-born parents is greater than between young immigrants from these two geographic areas (Kleinberger 1969:284). Symptomatic of the actual differences in achievement is how each group view their opportunities in the country in which they were born. For example, a study conducted among urban youth in the sixties by the Israeli sociologist Moshe Lissak found that only 2 percent of those of European origin but 29 percent of those of Oriental origin thought that there were NO possibilities for their advancement in Israel (Lissak 1969:66).

Now, these last figures can also be treated as indicators of the feelings of relative deprivation that characterize people of Oriental background. Ashkenazim often resort to any criticism of the material conditions of the Oriental Jews by the following two responses. They accuse them for their inferior conditions. After all, so goes the rationalization, both groups started in Israel from the same point. The other frequent response of the Ashkenazim is to retort how much better off the Oriental Jews are today as compared with the past. It is true that their standard of living is often far superior to what it was in the Arab countries or to what it was at the beginning of their stay in Israel. But the main point missed in such arguments is: they are now in Israel and they compare themselves with other Israelis. And when they do so, the Oriental Jews feel relatively deprived *vis-à-vis* the Ashkenazic Jews. It must be recognized that their perception of their relative lack in things that count in Israel is especially heightened by the changing life-style of the country. The simplicity in style of life, so characteristic of the pioneering days, is being rapidly replaced by a preoccupation and fascination with consumer goods. Such goods are being imbued with great symbolic value and are displayed conspicuously by the *nouveau riche* and others who emulate them. As Ben Aharon, former Histadrut Secretary General, expressed it, "the *nouveau riche* wax fatter like a cancer in our national bloodstream." While some might object to his language as too dramatic, he did convey the effect that the rise of the newly rich has had on the social climate of Israel. In such a climate, the feelings of relative deprivation of the Orientals are heightened. This manifests itself, among other things, in resentment of what they perceive as preferential treatment of recent immigrants from Russia. They point to these immigrants as living in "luxury apartments" and sporting cars and other goods which they cannot afford (Gitelman 1973:67–95).

The feelings of relative deprivation of the Orientals probably exceed their actual lack of things. As Emile Durkheim (1951:246–247) noted long ago, what is needed for people to be content with their lot is not that they have more or less, but that they be convinced that they have no right to more. But the Orientals are convinced that as Jews in a Jewish land they have the right to expect all the things that the Ashkenazim have. In light of these feelings, as well as the existence of objective inequality, the manifestations of growing ethnic consciousness among the Jews of Oriental background are not surprising. While formerly they were linked to each other, to some extent, by common values and religious traditions, they now also share a common situation of economic, political, and social disadvantage *vis-à-vis* the Ashkenazim. And this growing "we" feeling among them is expressed not only by the rise of *Pantherim Shehorim* but also in the way these Black Panthers of Israel were viewed by the bulk of Oriental Jews who never became actively involved with them. Having resided in Israel during the time of the rise of Black Panthers, I must say that I have never encountered an Oriental Jew who thought that their grievances were wrong or who did not justify their actions. The only objection of some with whom I spoke was to the choice of the name, Black Panthers, since they, like Israelis in general, tended to associate the name with anti-semitism in America. Diametrically opposite was the reaction of the Ashkenazim to this phenomenon, which received wide coverage in the mass media. Their overall response was that of surprise and even shock. (Cohen 1972:93–103). And yet, why the surprise? Is this really the first time that Jews have been involved in class conflict against Jews? Jewish radicals in Russia did not hesitate to use militant tactics against Jewish capitalists. And the present governing elite of Israel are the radicals of that time or individuals who had sufficient contact with them to know. To understand this reaction, it is helpful to bring to mind the sociological theorem that dominant groups in general tend to identify their interests and values with those of society as a whole. An organization — like the *Pantherim* — which disturbs the stability of the dominant group is then perceived by members of that groups as endangering the stability or existence of the nation. Add to this the specific Israeli factor: the egalitarian ideology which for at least a decade after independence prevented even the acknowledgement of the existence of the ethnic problem. The presence and the activities of the *Pantherim Shehorim* brought the problem to the forefront. They also helped to bring about a recognition that, in contrast to what was believed before, the problem is not withering away. That most of the Panthers were *sabras* was living proof that integration was not achieved *ipso facto* in the second generation. The conscience of some Ashkenazim was stirred to the extent that they became aware of and a bit troubled by the conditions of the Orientals. Prior to the rise of the *Pantherim*, the governing elite and the respectable intellectuals mostly denied the existence of this problem. Professor Eisenstadt, the leading Israeli sociologist and the 1973 winner of the Israel Prize, on that occasion fittingly characterized the 1960's as showing

the growing tendency to sweep problems under the rug, in the obvious hope that they would simply disappear in time from benign neglect. Meeting social problems head-on, it was felt, could only undermine national solidarity. In fact, the result was to deepen existing division (Eisenstadt 1973).

But there is a long road between recognizing the problem and concerted action to solve it. One of the main reasons for the failure to mobilize prior to the Yom Kippur War the resources to solve the ethnic problem (even within the possibilities left after the national defense expenditures were met) was the fact that the ethnic consciousness of the Oriental Jews had not yet become translated into effective political organization. True, by 1971 the Sephardic and Oriental politicians who worked within the framework of the Israeli power structure displayed a degree of political boldness unthinkable before. At the Labor Party convention they held a caucus and demanded a 35 percent representation of Sephardim and Orientals in all positions of power. Their demand was rejected (Smooha 1972:31–34). Such rejection is understandable in view of the nonexistence of a mass political movement among them. It also explains why no imaginative breakthrough had been made to provide adequate housing for the slum dwellers in the major cities of Israel. And this was the case, notwithstanding the periodic hunger strikes and protests of slum dwellers.

The factors that worked against the Sephardic and Oriental Jews' becoming highly politicized were the same factors that accounted for the fact that the *Pantherim* did not develop into a mass movement, despite the sympathy with which they were regarded by those Jews. The decisive factor was the threat of the Arab countries and the constant danger of war. This constituted a strong cementing force for the whole nation which overcame ethnic divisions. Another important cohesive factor was the Israeli army, a people's army, the source of pride for all Israelis. Certainly up to the Yom Kippur War no other institution commanded equal respect or affection from the whole nation. The charge of ethnic discrimination in promotions had never been leveled against the army, and this despite the fact that there was not one general of Oriental background. There was full confidence among Israelis, irrespective of ethnic background, that the army promoted its personnel according to impartial criteria. To illustrate, the only grievance that the *Pantherim* leveled against the army was that the delinquent records of a substantial number of Oriental youths made them ineligible for army service! (As a result of their protest, the army revised its policy and decided to draft those with criminal or police records.)

It is too early to judge whether the experiences of the October 1973 Yom Kippur War have resulted in substantial changes in these attitudes toward the army as well as toward the ethnic problem in Israel. According to Abba Ebban, "the war has shaken Israelis out of the images and ways of thought in which they lived for six years... We are summoned almost overnight to a far-reaching reconstruction of our conceptual world" (1973:10). If such a reconstruction will take place will it in turn lead to fundamental changes in the ethnic stratification structure that was jelling in Israel? Such changes would be more likely to occur if the Sephardic and Oriental Jews were better organized to press their demands. However, this level of political organization has little chance of developing as long as the country is threatened by war. Therefore, I maintain that breakthrough in the solution of the ethnic problem is more likely to come with peace. But this did not seem to be the prevailing view in Israel prior to the attack by the Arab countries which caught the Israelis by surprise. There was then a growing apprehension that the time of relative peace, with its Black Panthers' manifestations and slum dwellers' strikes, were previews of the civil disorders to come with real peace. Israelis seemed very fearful of internal conflict. For example, Eli Eliachar, the head of the Council of the Sephardic Community in Israel, is reported to have commented on these events by predicting: "If we ever get peace in the

Middle East we will have civil war at home" (Grose 1971). But I saw in these manifestations reasons for hope (Heller 1973:330). I am still convinced that if peace is achieved in the Middle East and if the Oriental Jews succeed in organizing themselves in Israel, they will succeed not only in improving their situation but in realizing to a large degree the ideal of a unified people. It is true that they are today relatively powerless *vis-à-vis* the dominant Ashkenazim. However, much potential power is vested in them. First of all, they are numerically a majority (60 percent of the Jewish population) and their proportion in the Jewish population is growing due to their much higher birth rate. Secondly, in fighting for equality they could hold up the principles of the egalitarian ideology to which the dominant group subscribes, even if it violates them in practice. The cogent argument of the Israeli government today is less likely to be accepted in time of peace: the argument that with the defense expenditures being what they are, the abolition of economic inequality is beyond the financial capability of the state of Israel. And finally, the failure of the dominant group to respond positively to the demands of strongly organized Sephardic and Oriental Jews would threaten the existence of the nation.

To conclude, the dominant group in Israel, like dominant groups everywhere, does not comprehend the urgency of the problems of the subordinates. Only the demands of the subordinate group, the Sephardic and Oriental Jews, backed by strong political organization, could bring about a radical transformation in the existing institutions that would reduce ethnic inequality and hasten integration. This is more likely to occur in time of peace because peace would allow for a certain amount of conflict, a prerequisite for change, which the nation threatened by war cannot afford. And the society that the Jews have built in Israel, is flexible enough to accommodate substantial change. I therefore believe that in time of peace the challenge presented by conflict will prove to be superable for the Israeli nation that has again and again demonstrated its extraordinary quality of rising to challenge and emerging victorious despite tremendous odds.

REFERENCES

BEN-PORATH, YORAM
 1971   On East-West differences in the occupational structure of Israel. *Report of the Committee on Income Distribution and Social Inequality*, 215-237. Tel Aviv.

COHEN, ERIC
1972   The Black Panthers and Israeli society. *Jewish Journal of Sociology* 14:93-103.
DEUTSCH, AKWA
1958   The character of the elite in a Yemenite suburb. *Megamoth* 9:328-339 (In Hebrew.)
DURKHEIM, ÉMILE
1951   *Suicide.* New York: Free Press.
EBBAN, ABBA
1973   "The windows should be opened." *Jerusalem Post Weekly*, December 4.
EISENSTADT, S. N.
1967   *Israeli society.* New York: Basic Books.
1969   "The emerging pattern of Israeli stratification," in *Structured social inequality.* Edited by Celia S. Heller. New York: Macmillan.
1973   "Change and continuity." *Jerusalem Post Weekly*, June 5.
GITELMAN, ZWI
1973   "Absorption of Soviet immigrants," in *Israel: social structure and change.* Edited by Michael Curtis and Mordecai S. Chertoff. New Brunswick: Transaction Books.
GROSE, PETER
1971   "Internal issues cloud Israeli New Year mood." *New York Times*, September 22.
HADARY, AMMON
1972   "Shedmot: new voice from the kibbutzim." *Jerusalem Post Weekly*, May 2. Quotations taken from an article by Yehuda Ninni in *Shedmot* (1972). Tel Aviv: Davar.
HANNOCH, GIORAH
1961   Income differentials in Israel. *Fifth Report: 1959 and 1960.* Jerusalem: The Falk Project for Economic Research in Israel. (In Hebrew.)
HARTMAN, M.
1973   "Occupational differences between ethnic groups in Israel." Unpublished paper presented at Annual Meeting of the Israeli Sociological Association, Bar-Ilan University.
HELLER, CELIA
1973   "The emerging consciousness of the ethnic problem among the Jews of Israel," in *Israel: social structure and change.* Edited by Michael Curtis and Mordecai S. Chertoff. New Brunswick: Transaction Books.
HELLER, CELIA, *editor*
1969   *Structured social inequality.* New York: Macmillan.
Jerusalem Post Weekly
1973   February 13.
KLEINBERGER, AHRON
1969   *Society, schools, and progress in Israel.* Oxford: Pergamon Press.
LISSAK, MOSHE
1969   *Social mobility in Israel society.* Jerusalem: Israel Universities Press.
PERES, YOCHANAN
1971   Ethnic relations in Israel. *American Journal of Sociology* 76:1021-1048.

REMBA, ODED
 1973 "Income inequality in Israel: ethnic aspects," in *Israel: social structure and change*. Edited by Michael Curtis and Mordecai S. Chertoff. New Brunswick: Transaction Books.

SEGRE, V. D.
 1971 *Israel — a society in transition*. London: Oxford University Press.

SHUVAL, JUDITH
 1962 Emerging patterns of ethnic strain. *Social Forces* 40:323–329.

SMOOHA, SAMMY
 1972 Black Panthers: the ethnic dilemma. *Society* (Transaction) May:31–36.

TALMON, J. L.
 1970 *Israel among the nations*. London: Weidenfeld and Nicolson.

WEINTRAUB, D.
 1971 *Immigration and social change in Israel*. Jerusalem: Israel University Press.

WEISS, SHEVACH
 1970 *The typology of local representatives and the problem of the stability of local government*. Jerusalem.

Migration and West Indian Racial and Ethnic Consciousness

CONSTANCE R. SUTTON and SUSAN R. MAKIESKY

Though West Indian emigration during the 1950's and 1960's constitutes but the latest phase in the diaspora of English-speaking West Indians, this recent exodus differs from previous migrations in a number of ways. In scale, it has surpassed previous migratory movements. Its direction has shifted from other Caribbean countries to the urban industrial centers of the imperial powers which colonized the Caribbean in the past and continue to dominate it today. And it is an exodus that has taken place during a period of considerable racial and political conflict in both the host societies and the West Indies. Its impact on the racial consciousness and political awareness of both the migrants and those who remain behind is the major concern of this paper.

We shall explore the character of West Indian migration to England and the United States since World War II* and consider its contribution to the development of a positive black identity and a political solidarity directed at achieving autonomy and equality at home and abroad. Our comparisons of the West Indian presence in England and the United States draw mainly on the existing literature and, in the case of New York City, on our informal observations. In considering the impact of this emigration on the sending societies, we shall confine ourselves to Barbados, where we both carried out extensive fieldwork during two different

The authors wish to thank Dr. Samuel Sutton for his helpful suggestions and critical reading of this paper. We also wish to thank Dr. St. Clair Drake and Dr. Muriel Hammer for calling our attention to points that needed clarification.

* Though this migration has brought large numbers of West Indians to Montreal and Toronto we do not have sufficient information to include Canada in our discussion.

time periods — the late 1950's and the early 1970's.[1] Our fieldwork was conducted in the same village, and though directed to other problems, it nevertheless provided us with some data for comparing the effects of emigration at the village level at two periods in the development of Barbadian society.

We shall focus on an aspect of the migration process that has been relatively neglected — namely, its impact on the knowledge, concerns, and perceptions of Barbadians, both on the island and overseas. It is generally recognized that migration exposes migrants to new ideas and creates the need for them to define themselves and the terms of their relationship to the host society. Under certain circumstances, this process tends to transform vague feelings of common ethnicity into a more articulated racial and political consciousness. There has been little attention given, however, to the ways such developments actually occur or to how they are affected by the expectations of the migrants and in turn feed back into the ideological conceptions of those who remain at home. Our emphasis is on migration as a bidirectional rather than a unidirectional phenomenon, sustained by social networks and exchanges between migrants and those they leave behind.

Most studies to date have focused on one or the other end of the migration continuum. Early work on the migration experience in the host societies was concerned with the immigrants themselves and the institutions they brought or created for coping with their new environment. More recently, studies have been cast in a macrosociological framework which calls attention to the ways societal economic and political structures define and incorporate immigrant groups (Schermerhorn 1970; Zubaida 1970; Katznelson 1973; Blauner 1972). Looking at the other end of the continuum, we find that studies of the effects of emigration on the sending society have either dealt with the institutional adjustments made to accomodate population loss or have emphasized the overall conservative impact of emigration which siphons off skilled and potentially dynamic leadership, exports internal pressures, and channels discontent into hopes for salvation elsewhere.

The need to consider both ends of the migration continuum for the same group has become increasingly apparent as modern means of

[1]   Support for field research came from the Research Institute for the Study of Man (C.S.), Population Council (C.S.), the Wenner-Gren Foundation for Anthropological Research (C.S.), New York University Arts and Science Research Fund (C.S.), and the Foreign Area Fellowship Program (S.M.). Support for other aspects of research whose findings are incorporated in the paper was obtained in part from the National Institutes of Health Biomedical Sciences Support Grant to New York University (C.S. and S.M.) and New York University Arts and Science Research Fund (C.S. and S.M.).

transportation and communication have drastically altered the nature of migration, especially between Caribbean countries and the United States. Some studies of Caribbean migration processes have sought to relate what happens at home and abroad by focusing on how social networks operate to maintain ties, interests, and social control across international boundaries. Returned migrants, who have by these means stayed hooked into their home societies while away, are said to invest their acquired assets in the already defined economic and status systems, rather than challenging them or serving as carriers of social and cultural innovations (Philpott 1970: 18).

Our evidence from Barbados suggests that return migration has a rather more dynamic impact on the home society. This is most evident in the realm of ideology — the ideas, perceptions, and evaluations that people have of themselves and their society. This view of emigration as change-producing is one that Barbadians themselves hold. Even in 1956, when the outflow of people to the metropoles of England, Canada, and the United States had not reached the volume it did during the following decade, Barbadians from all walks of life asserted the importance of leaving the island in order to acquire a new view of life and a different and better understanding of Barbados. Exposure to ideas and ways of doing things abroad was said to be the main way to increase one's understanding of the oppressive nature of Barbadian society and the "narrow-mindedness" of its customs and beliefs. These observations, concretized in specific examples and illustrations, formed a major conversational theme during lengthy "rap" sessions, and became a central topic of interest among villagers whose fund of knowledge and political awareness were shaped by this talk. Racial identity was not an issue of major concern. But the Barbadian novelist George Lamming, with the liberties that a novelist can take in projecting images and articulating possibilities that may be only faint stirrings, forecast what the migration experience to the United States could mean. In his early novel on Barbadian village life, entitled *In the castle of my skin*, published in 1953, Lamming has the young Trumper, returning from a stay in the U.S., tell his village friend:

"'Twas what I mean when I say you don't understan' life," Trumper said. "An' I didn't understan' it myself till I reach the States. If there be one thing I thank America for, she teach me who my race wus. Now I'm never goin' to lose it. Never never."

"There are black people here too," I said. I hadn't quite understood him.

"I know," said Trumper, "but it ain't the same. It ain't the same at all. 'Tis a different thing altogether. 'Course the blacks here are my people too, but they don't know it yet. You don't know it yourself. None o' you here on the islan' know what it mean to fin' a race. An' the white people you have to deal with won't ever let you know. 'Tis a great thing 'bout the English, the know-how. If ever there wus a nation in creation that know how to do an' get a thing do, 'tis the English. My friend in the States use to call them the great administrators. In America I have see as much as a man get kick down for askin' a question, a simple question. Not here. That couldn't ever happen here. We can walk here where we like if 'tis a public place, an' you've white teachers, an' we speak with white people at all times in all places. My people here go to their homes an' all that. An' take the clubs, for example. There be clubs which you an' me can't go to, an' none o' my people here, no matter who they be, but they don' tell us we can't. They put up a sign, "Members Only," knowin' full well you ain't got no chance o' becomin' a member. An' although we know from the start we can't go, we got the consolation we can't 'cause we ain't members. In America they don't worry with that kind o' beatin' 'bout the bush" (Lamming 1953: 296).

In this passage, Lamming captures the comparisons that engage black West Indians as a result of their migration experiences. The passage indicates, too, the ambivalence with which Barbadians regard the English – "clever" and "deceitful" on racial issues – and how the United States racial situation unmasks for them the true nature of their own situation. Lamming then goes on to show that discovery of "one's race" via identification with the black American leads the West Indian to feel for the first time a transcending racial pride:

He had found something to cradle his deepest instincts and emotions. He was a Negro and he was proud. Now he could walk in the sun or stand on the highest hill and proclaim himself the blackest evidence of the white man's denial of conscience (Lamming 1953:299).

At the time Lamming wrote, Barbadians were renowned for being a "proud" people. But this was based on a national identification that emphasized their English-like traits and virtues and discouraged the assertion of racial pride. Not until the mid-sixties did public expression of a pride in blackness begin to emerge. The form this took, the meaning it had to villagers, and conditions that gave rise to this situation must all be seen in the context of the broader social field within which islanders increasingly operate, and that social field extends beyond Barbados.[2]

The more general theoretical issue at stake in this analysis is the relationship between objective structural reality and conceptions of that reality. We are concerned with the nature of the social experiences, either direct or mediated, which act as an intervening variable between objective reality and its conceptualization and result in the formation of new conceptions. This theoretical formulation falls in the same category

[2]   Robert Manners (1960, 1965) has called attention to the need to view Caribbean societies in the context of a wider social field and has illustrated this point in his discussion of the West Indian emigration-remittance pattern (1965).

as the problematic relationship between structure and belief, class position and class consciousness, forms of inequality and forms of group identity or consciousness. Our efforts to explore this in terms of the West Indian migration experience are, at this stage, at the level of analytic observations intended to stimulate future field research.

The role of emigration in West Indian societies and the experiences of West Indians abroad have been shaped by a number of factors. Important among these are the structure of the West Indian society, the expectations and perceptions of the emigrants, and the social and political structure of the host society. We briefly review the nature and consequences of Barbadian emigration prior to World War II and contrast the dimensions of that movement with the post-World War II migration. We then take a comparative look at the structure of Barbadian society and the differing perceptions and expectations of England and the United States that prevailed in Barbados during the late 1950's and the early 1970's. Next, we move to the two metropoles themselves. We discuss (a) structural differences which affect how West Indians are incorporated; (b) the ways these structures are experienced by West Indian immigrants; and (c) the nature of the consciousness which emerges from these experiences. Finally, we return again to our island point of departure and consider the impact of the immigrants' experiences on the societies left behind.

BARBADIAN EMIGRATION PRIOR TO WORLD WAR II

Emigration has always been an integral feature of Barbadian society, intimately tied to its history as an exporter of sugar. In 1660, a generation after Barbados converted to cane cultivation and became known as the richest colony in English America, there was a flight of small proprietors and ex-indentured servants, as a small class of large planters gained control of the majority of the island's property (Dunn 1969). At the same time, large numbers of enslaved Africans were being imported to meet the labor needs of a thriving sugar economy, so that only thirty years after Barbados was first settled, its population density exceeded that of England by four times (Lowenthal 1957:451).

By the mid-nineteenth century, the island's superabundant population caused the government to pass legislation promoting emigration in order to relieve overcrowding, unemployment, and poverty. This was the same period during which other British Caribbean colonies were busily recruiting foreign labor. Beginning in 1861, the island witnessed the first large-scale outward movement of black Barbadians who went mainly to British Guiana (now Guyana) and Trinidad. A second migratory movement of significant magnitude began in 1904 when work on the Panama Canal was resumed, and lasted until 1914 when this work ceased. Migration was then redirected to the United States until 1924 when restrictions on entry there were imposed. Between 1921 and 1946 there was a steep decline and a reversal in direction as more migrants returned than left the island. The total number of emigrants between 1861 and 1921 equalled the size of the island's population in 1921 — 150,000 (Roberts 1955 :276). Even more significant than relief from demographic pressures was the contribution of emigration to the island's economy in the form of remittances which equalled the value of between one tenth and one fifth of annual imports between 1904 and 1920 alone (Roberts 1955 :282).

The impact of these early phases of Barbadian emigration on the island's black majority was to increase their options and change their attitudes. Remittances and the savings of returned migrants were applied to the purchase of land and houses and resulted in a rapid growth of freehold villages throughout the countryside. Emigration also worked to decrease the near-total dependence of the population on the plantation for loans and employment. This in turn gave plantation workers enough of a margin to engage in a series of spontaneous sugar strikes that first began in the 1920's. Moreover, the returned working class migrants brought with them radical ideas that helped fuel the riots which broke out throughout the West Indies in the late 1930's and which came to be the watershed between the old social order and the new one that was emerging (Reid 1939). Repatriation of ideas also occurred as West Indian professionals educated abroad returned to assume leadership of the struggles for social and political reforms on the islands.

The emigration orientation of Barbadian society led islanders to accord prestige and power to those with knowledge of the world outside, and out of the comparisons – specific and general, between Bajan* and foreign ways – there developed a framework for viewing Barbados in a more critical light. But while this comparative, relativistic view of the island society gave rise to new kinds of political consciousness and to demands for improvements, emigration also reinforced the notion that solutions to problems were to be sought outside the society. For the black majority, it meant that though things were hard at home, elsewhere there were opportunities they might seize. This in part explains why one of the most dispossessed of agro-proletariats maintains an optimistic attitude about the possibilities for individual socio-economic mobility.

* "Bajan" is the colloquial term for Barbadian. It is also used to refer to the folk language and culture of the black majority.

During this early period, the success of Barbadian immigrants contributed to the growth of an ethnic consciousness based on proverbial island pride and gave support to their deeply held conviction that if you give a Bajan half a chance – just a start – he or she will make good![3] Reputed to be hard-working, law-abiding, and well-educated, Barbadians were favored by recruiting agents, and in the societies to which they went they gained ascendancy in the two occupations that carried authority and were open to black and colored people at that time: they became known as the teachers and policemen of the West Indies.

As immigrants to other Caribbean territories, Barbadians maintained an ethnic identity at the same time that they became part of the West Indian community of the host society.[4] This was not possible for the Barbadian immigrant community which formed in New York City, as is indicated in Paule Marshall's novel, *Brown girl, brownstones* (1959). Here it is revealed how their relations to black Americans and the racial identity assigned to them by the wider society constantly intruded on their efforts to view themselves simply as another immigrant-ethnic group. But to consider this difference more fully, we turn to the context and nature of emigration after World War II.

POST-WORLD WAR II MIGRATION

World War II and the years immediately following brought changes within West Indian societies, in their relations to North Atlantic metropolitan centers, and in the patterns of migration between them. The war itself had produced an accelerated flow of Barbadians to both metropoles where agriculture, industry, and the armed forces utilized their services to meet the emergency of war. The novelty of this migration to the United States lay in the large numbers involved, but in Britain not only the size, but the character of the movement was new. West Indians who migrated to England previously were almost entirely of middle and upper class

[3] Barbadian confidence on this score is quite remarkable, and those who come to know it first-hand are amused, awed, and envious. It is exemplified in the person of Shirley Chisholm, daughter of Barbadian immigrants to New York City, who received her schooling on the island. In 1972, she offered herself as a candidate for the Presidency.
[4] There are untapped opportunities for comparative research on migration and ethnicity provided by the West Indian communities created through voluntary migration to other colonial areas. R. S. Bryce-Laporte has made an important beginning with his studies of West Indians in the Panama Canal Zone (1970) and in Costa Rica (i.p.). The work of Nancie González on the Black Caribs in Guatamela, though focused on problems of migration and household structure, contains more general observations of interest with respect to these communities (González 1969).

status, but war service for the first time brought working class and lower middle class West Indians to Britain.

The economic situation and immigration policies of the North Atlantic industrial countries were the primary determinants of the direction that the post-war outflow from the West Indies took. In the United States, a sharp drop in agricultural recruitment programs and the passage of restrictive legislation in 1952 curtailed West Indian immigration. At the same time, labor shortages in Britain and an open immigration policy attracted increased numbers of West Indians to that country, particularly from 1952 to 1962. With the exception of the large number of Barbadians who, after 1956, came under contract arrangements their government had established with London Transport and the British Hotels and Restaurant Association, most West Indian arrivals came without prior certainty of employment. But the levelling off during the 1956–1959 recession in the British economy indicates that information about the state of the labor market affected migration patterns (Rose 1969). The West Indian immigrant population in England grew from an estimated 15,300 in 1951 to 171,800 a decade later, and was expected to reach 572,000 in 1971 (Deakin 1970 :136). Barbados, from its population of less than a quarter of a million, contributed 23,000 between 1955 and 1965 (*Barbados development plan* 1965–1968).

Beginning in 1962, Britain began to impose restrictions on the immigration of Commonwealth citizens from the colonies. These restrictions, which were followed by more stringent ones in 1965 and 1971, made clear Britain's political stance on race relations and served to deflect the direction of outflow from the West Indies toward the United States, which liberalized its immigration policies in 1965. Because of the large number of illegal entries, it has been difficult to get reliable figures on the volume of West Indian migration to the United States. Official figures record that during the past 150 years, over a million West Indians have come to settle here. During the last two decades alone, it is thought that some 600,000 West Indians have taken up residence in the United States, mainly in New York City (*Antillean Caribbean Echo* 1971 :3). Figures for Barbados alone are even more difficult to obtain, but one estimate placed their number at 32,000 in 1970. However, if one includes second and third generation Barbadians, it is rumored that there are as many Barbadians living in New York as there are on the island itself – almost a quarter of a million. Though this may seem unreasonably high, it is supported by our calculation that the village of 2,500, in which we both did our fieldwork, has contributed about 2,000 – original villagers and their descendants – to the Barbadian population of New York.

Barbadian Society

In Barbados during the late 1950's the contours of a sugar-producing colonial plantation society were still deeply etched in landscape and social structure. The island's 166 square miles held a population of just under a quarter of a million, making it one of the most densely populated areas in the world. Some 150 white creole families owned 85 percent of the canefields stretching across most of the island, and the remaining small plots owned by colored and black families were also planted in cane. Interspersed along the edges of estates and crowded together at highway intersections were dwellings of a large wage-earning rural population.

Most of the black majority lived in these rural settlements with easy access to the main town by bus, bicycle, or car. The community we studied, was adjacent to the island's largest plantation. We have pseudonymously named it Endeavor because of its reputation as a district of aggressive, enterprising individuals. The plantation owned a quarter of the land occupied by villagers and employed, either seasonally or year-round, some 45 percent of Endeavor's working population. Another 15 percent worked at other plantations, and the remainder worked "all about" as artisans, tradespeople, shopkeepers, or domestics. Of Endeavor's working population, 40 percent were women.[5]

Our household census taken in 1958 indicates that the more than six hundred dwellings in the village housed a population totalling more than 2,500 persons, who were bound together by ties of kinship, common residence, similar experiences, and shared sentiments. There was an outward-looking quality to life reflected in the daily dispersal of the working population during the week, and in the fact that 173 villagers, or 11 percent of those over the age of fifteen, had lived and worked abroad some time in the past. Sixty percent of this returned emigrant group had lived in Panama or other West Indian islands, 30 percent in the United States (the majority as contract laborers), 5 percent in England (emigration to England had just begun a few years earlier) and the remainder in a variety of far-off places.

Though information on remittances is less reliable, the census showed that one quarter of the adult population was receiving money from relatives abroad. Amounts varied from total support for an individual to cash supplements for purchasing specific items, covering school fees, or contributing to celebrations of births, marriages, and other rites of passage. Interestingly enough, 60 percent of the remitting relatives were at

[5] For a fuller account of Endeavor in 1956-1958, see Sutton (1969).

that time living in England or Canada; the balance were evenly divided between the United States and other West Indian countries.

By the late 1950's, the paternalistic control of plantation days was being seriously eroded as trade unionism and mass politics brought the black majority into the political process. The new island leadership had committed itself to raising living standards, creating new opportunities and resources, and breaking the dependency ties that were part of the plantation past. Progress was occurring in this direction. Nevertheless, for the black majority, education and emigration were still the two main avenues for "rising a notch above," and the target societies for the hopeful emigrants were England, Canada, and the United States.

When we returned to the island a decade later, the most striking change that had occurred was the shift of the Barbadian economy away from its three-hundred-year-old near-total dependence on cane cultivation. Though sugar remained the primary earner of foreign exchange, by the late 1960's it was rivaled by tourism and light manufacturing, which had experienced spectacular growth in the last half of the decade. These developments, important in weakening the economic control of the Barbadian planter-merchant class, were marked by significant intrusions of North American capital into this formerly British preserve. Encouraged by incentives offered by the new black government, North American investors and tourists alike were attracted by the island's reputation for political stability – an image Barbadian leaders were successful in cultivating and vigilant in maintaining. Ironically, the island's release from exclusive economic dependency on sugar – and thus on the creole whites and the protected market England offered to sugar exports – coincided with the growth of new economic dependencies which brought the island more fully into the American sphere of influence.

There were parallels in the political domain. In 1966 the processes set in motion three decades earlier culminated in Britain's granting to Barbados the status of independent nation within the Commonwealth. But though the political leaders of independent Barbados significantly increased their role in the administration of the island's education, health, and welfare services, the ultimate economic control of the island receded overseas where it has continued to elude their grasp.

While foreign capital and tourists were entering the island in increasing quantities, the large-scale emigration begun in the post-war years continued to take unprecedented numbers of Barbadians to England, Canada, and the United States. Thus the elaboration of the island's links to metropolitan centers at the national political and economic level had parallels in the increased involvement of working class Barbadians in the countries which dominated them. By the early 1970's Barbados was more firmly than ever ensconced in an international network of trade, politics, and migration, its destiny and maneuverability more than ever dependent on these external linkages.

The villagers of Endeavor, though happy to participate in the annual ritual of independence celebrations, saw the island's new independent status as having little impact on their own life chances. One plantation worker summed up community attitudes when he said, "Independence? As for me, it ain't come yet." More significant to them was the proliferation of "wall"houses, refrigerators and other consumer goods now available to villagers as a result of an increased volume of remittances from abroad and the expansion of consumer credit through hire-purchase programs at home.

One of the most important changes was the marked decrease in villagers' involvement in the surrounding plantations. By 1970, few young people were willing to work in the sugar industry. The average age of the agricultural labor force was over fifty, and it became necessary for the plantation adjacent to Endeavor to import two hundred workers from St. Vincent and St. Lucia to assist with reaping the cane crop. The building boom occasioned by tourist developments and the growth of light manufacturing and assembly plants absorbed some of the unskilled and semi-skilled labor that in earlier years would have had no alternatives to the plantation. Expanded educational facilities had prepared a number of young women and men to fill new clerical posts in banks, business, and the civil service. However, unemployment was high, and emigration provided, even more dramatically than before, the most realistic avenue for meeting the social and economic aspirations of an increasingly consumption-oriented population. We turn now to Barbadian preconceptions of the societies they hoped to immigrate to, for these influenced the ways villagers interpreted their social encounters as immigrants in the host countries.

Perceptions of England and the United States

Most of the literature on West Indian preconceptions of England emphasizes the cultural affinities West Indians feel for the "mother country," and the sense of disillusion and rejection the immigrants experience when they find that the English do not share this view of West Indians (Brown 1970; Deakin 1970; Lewis 1969, 1971; Midgett 1971; Rose 1969; Tajfel and Dawson 1965) .Our fieldwork bore out these notions. But to leave the matter there would seem to imply that West Indians come to Britain with no knowledge of or concern about racism and discrimination. This grossly distorts the realities of social life in the West Indies, and perpetuates the myth of the islands as a paradise of racial harmony. It has become increasingly evident that West Indians at home experience considerable conflict and discomfort about racial identity, in part due to the historic white bias of their societies. It does not seem, however, that these conflicts entail the internalized self-hate and inferiority complex that has been attributed to West Indians in many recent writings (Lowenthal 1972; Fanon 1967). Especially at the village level, we found little evidence that people saw their disadvantaged position as due to inherent inferiority. Instead, they would assert that their difficulties lay in being denied the opportunity to achieve socially valued goods and positions of esteem.

Though villagers felt equal, if not superior, to whites in inherent abilities, they granted social superiority to the local white elites and race and color were far from irrelevant in their social evaluations. In fact they were at the heart of Barbadian social stratification, which is built on an invidious grading of status distinctions, described interchangeably in terms of either chromatic shade or power and prestige. It is a system in which consciousness of race has been a divisive rather than unifying force. This is quite different from what immigrant experience in Britain (or USA), where the racial identities assigned to them ignore differences in shade and status.

Another factor affecting Barbadians' preconceptions of England is their tendency to assume that the racial prejudice of Barbadian whites represents a perversion of the "true" metropolitan culture. The history of the West Indies has given support to the notion of England as protector against their own white elites. In Barbados, this belief triggered off the "Federation Riots" of 1878 (Hamilton 1956), and continuous conflict between the colonial office and the Barbadian plantocracy was viewed by the masses as further proof of its validity: the enemies of my enemies are my friends. Barbadians, then, did not generalize their experiences of invidious racism at home to England or to all white people, and maintained an open, if somewhat skeptical, mind about what they might encounter in England.

Their lingering faith in British fair-mindedness left many Barbadians unprepared for the differences between their nineteenth century textbook versions and the twentieth century realities of English culture. Nor, more importantly, were they prepared for the indifference or contempt which many British people feel for their colonial citizens. By 1971, these earlier conceptions had been replaced by newer perceptions based on the incidents of racial conflict in England, the rise of Enoch Powell, and the passage of restrictive immigration laws. But by this time, the influx to

England had been sharply reduced as a consequence of British policies.

Images and expectations that potential immigrants have of the United States are somewhat more complex and have been generated by more diverse sources than the monolithic colonial apparatus of cultural indoctrination. The primary element in the Barbadian view of "America" is a vision of riches and high standards of living which is variously perpetrated by American television shows, Hollywood movies, and upper middle class tourists, as well as by earlier emigrants who have returned home to build large houses and develop new lifestyles.

Economic expectations are complemented by the recognition of less attractive features of United States society. Violence and danger, muggings and murder, are graphically portrayed in the media and elaborated by returned migrants. More important, though, is the knowledge of American racism which has an important place in Barbadians' perceptions of United States society. They are conscious that the white majority has brutally treated its own black minority. There is a tendency, however, to rest part of the blame on black Americans themselves for not behaving in ways that are more "self-respecting" and for not showing more "initiative" in the face of opportunities. Evidence of the successes of earlier migrants lends credence to their view that West Indians can "get through" despite American racism.

The images of economic opportunity, violence, and a troublesome black minority are to a large extent images which white America projects of itself. These have been modified and counteracted in recent years by cultural imports from black America: music, dress, hair styles, verbal expressions, and the ideology of Black Power. The result in Barbados has been both an increased consciousness of American racism, and a new admiration for black American militancy, especially among younger Barbadians who have developed a heightened interest in coming to the scene of the action.

These preconceptions affect how Barbadians interpret and react to their encounters with English and American society, but it is the structuring of race relations in the two societies that determines the nature of these encounters. We shall look briefly now at some of the structural differences between England and the United States and then consider their impact on West Indian experiences.

English and American Structures of Incorporation

Despite the similarities of England and the United States as industrial, capitalist, urban societies, in their social composition and in the political structuring of social differences, the two metropoles exhibit contrasting patterns. England has been largely an ethnically and culturally homogeneous society. Its salient divisions have been those of class. These have been given political recognition, but within an institutionalized framework of basic consensus. Political participation is on an individual basis and the political legitimacy of ethnic group interest is denied (Deakin 1970; Katznelson 1973).

By 1958, racial disturbances had caused the issue of race to emerge with all of its potentiality as a key political issue. The immigration restrictions of the 1960's further crystallized the different status of the immigrants from the colonies. Summarizing the responses of English society to colonial immigration, Gordon Lewis writes:

There has taken place a massive escalation of white racist attitudes in the society. The decade of the 1950's, which can be seen as a period of immigrant arrival, was characterized by the myth that the English and the immigrants could peacefully co-exist with each other in a sort of host-guest relationship. That myth was effectively destroyed with the 1958 race riots in Nottingham and Notting Hill. Those riots …were followed by the decade of the 1960's, which can be seen as a period of immigrant settlement and was in turn characterised by the myth that racialism was a product only of the right-wing lunatic fringe of British politics. That myth was effectively destroyed by the process by which, after 1962, both major political parties took over, in one way or another, racialist policies, ending with the emergence in the figure of Enoch Powell, of a white populist demagogue located at the heart and not simply on the margins of the Conservative party.

The history of how the party machines surrendered to the crypto-racialist majority of their electorates is the history of the legislation dealing with immigration and race-relations put through, first, by the Conservatives and, secondly, after 1964, by the Labour Party cabinets (1971:12–13).

However, the British political elites (and the new West Indian leadership) had a stake in depoliticizing the race issue. As Katznelson (1973) documents in a recent book, what developed in England were buffering institutions between the immigrants from the colonies and the larger society. West Indian cultural brokers sprung up to reassure the British that the "dark strangers" from the West Indies, who were working at jobs the British working class no longer cared to fill (Peach 1968), were an intelligent, responsible, and stable people – qualities that by implication could be equated with docility and political quiescence. Paternalism was to be perpetuated as the major form for dealing with West Indians, thus domestically reproducing a quasi-colonial relationship.

Unlike England, the United States has, throughout its history, experienced large-scale immigration and has been aptly described as a nation of immigrants. Despite the predominance of WASP ingredients in images of "the American way of life," ethnic diversity is a recognized fact of existence – particularly in the large urban centers. More significant for West Indians, however, is the overriding institutionalized racial division between black and white, and the presence of a large native black population in the cities to which they migrate.

Ethnic differences in the United States have been given informal political recognition in practices such as "balancing tickets" but have never received explicit formal legitimation in law. Racial differences, on the other hand, HAVE been formally recognized, and non-white groups throughout American history have been "differentially incorporated" into the polity. Slavery and Jim Crow set black Americans apart as a group with a special political status, as did reservation policies for native-Americans and the World War II internment of Japanese-Americans. No parallels of formal differential incorporation can be found in the history of white ethnic groups, and the unique treatment the United States has reserved for non-white citizens justifies designating their relationship to the larger society as "colonial" (Blauner 1972; Katznelson 1973). While Britain until recently kept its colonies overseas and the issue of race at arms length, the United States internalized its colonies from the beginning and created a society pervaded by racial division.

Experiences in England and the United States

ENGLAND   Barbadians moving into the homogeneous white society of Britain have rather different experiences than their compatriots going to the racially divided United States, though in both cases they meet poor housing, job discrimination, and inferior schooling for their children, as well as personal hostility from sections of the white population. Written accounts and statements of numerous West Indians in Britain document their quick realization that however acculturated they may be, their color and colonial status set them apart from the English and evoke different treatment from landlords and employers (see for example, Tajfel and Dawson 1965). It is not necessary to idealize the racial patterns of West Indian societies to appreciate the impact of this on the newcomers. As Gordon Lewis writes:

As recently as the 1950's it was a cardinal article of faith among the newcomers that they were coming "home" to the "mother country," and particularly so for the West Indian, so much more culturally English than his Asian counterparts. The literature of disillusionment...is of recent growth, and to read it is to be made poignantly aware of the general figure of the West Indian, immeasurably saddened by the unexpected humiliations of his daily experience.... There can be little doubt that, as that reservoir of goodwill slowly evaporates, he becomes increasingly radicalised in his attitude to the total problem.... More and more, to put it succinctly, the immigrant sees himself less as a West Indian or a Sikh in English society, and more as a black man in a white society (1969:428).

At the same time that Britain provides a setting for the growth of West Indian racial consciousness, it also promotes knowledge of an interaction between West Indians from different islands in a context of shared position and experiences. Though these interactions are often far from harmonious, recent reports indicate that improved relations develop over time. A Nevisian is recounted as saying in the late 1960's:

"When I first came here in 1958, the feeling was terrible. At parties, in particular, there was always fear of trouble. You never knew when arguments and fights would spark off.... It's quietened down now, and there's far more mixing. Even mixed marriages between Jamaicans and Barbadians, those most at loggerheads. Ten years ago, that would have been impossible. Everyone kept to his own kind" (Brown 1970:105).

Midgett (1971) notes that new understandings arising out of this interaction, particularly among the English-born children of immigrants, are defined in terms of blackness, not West Indianness. In either case, they serve to break down some of the insular prejudices that have marked failures to achieve unity at home.

Just as the white racism that has emerged within British society has taken over some forms of expression from the American experience, so too do West Indians find in the struggles of black Americans the forms in which to express their response to the racism they encounter in Britain. Thus the new racial consciousness that arises out of daily realities in Britain owes much of its rhetoric and symbols to the Black Power movement in the United States. Black Power in England has been a preeminently West Indian phenomenon in which black American forms have been transplanted and reworked in a new environment. Aside from providing a ready-made vehicle for expressions of black consciousness, such American borrowings have served to emphasize common features of the African diaspora on both sides of the Atlantic.

Although West Indians move into Britain as black foreigners in a white society, they are not the only exogenous elements disrupting traditional homogeneity. The same post-war period has involved substantial migrations from other former British colonies as well. The largest numbers have come from India and Pakistan, but West Africans are also well-represented. Studies of British racial attitudes indicate an awareness of differences between the several immigrant groups (Deakin 1971), though for many purposes they are lumped together by the British public and race relations scholars alike under the umbrella term "colored people."

While recent studies have compared the community and organizational life of Indians, Pakistanis, and West Indians, we know of no work addressed to the question of contact or relations among them, or the extent to which recognition of their common problems has led to organization for united action. In the mid-sixties, an Afro-Asian-West Indian Union existed and took an active stand opposing immigration restrictions and British paternalistic handling of racial problems, but we know little of the extent of its support among the immigrants. It is clear, however, that England provides a unique setting for contacts between diverse sections of the Afro-Asian Commonwealth and that this tends to introduce a Third World orientation into the political ideologies West Indians develop in England, an emphasis somewhat different from that developed either in the islands or in the United States.

UNITED STATES   West Indians immigrating to New York travel a rather different route to racial consciousness than that taken in England. They bring with them not a notion of their likeness to Americans, black or white, but rather an awareness of their distinctness – as Barbadians, Jamaicans, Grenadians, etc. Theirs is a kind of ethnic consciousness that parallels that of earlier European immigrants, though they are initially less concerned about adjusting to the larger society, since unlike the white immigrants, most West Indians intend ultimately to return home. West Indians arrive with some foreknowledge of white attitudes of racial superiority and with experiences with problems of racial inequality. However, life in New York soon teaches them that the same characteristics of race which make them such a visible immigrant minority in England, make them invisible as immigrants in the already racially divided system of the United States (Bryce-Laporte 1972).

In their dealings with each other and with black Americans, distinctions of shade and features and differences of nationality and island background retain some of the significance they had back home. But these have little relevance to the larger white society which, if it acknowledges them at all, sees them as internal divisions in a group whose primary categorical identity is as black people – with all that implies in the history of United States black-white relations. As a result, both the problems and the achievements of West Indians are viewed by the dominant white majority, and come to be viewed by West Indians themselves, in the context of black America.

The West Indian response to this situation is ambivalent. It involves consciously emphasizing their distinctness from black Americans in some contexts and moving to establish closer ties and an identification with them in others. In neither case, however, do they escape a heightened consciousness of themselves as a black minority enclosed within a sometimes menacing, sometimes friendly, world of more powerful whites. In recent years this new consciousness has been articulated in ideologies which stress the world-wide common fate of black people – often generalized to Third World colonized people. The concept of "common fate" is not unknown in the West Indies, but it takes on a new salience in the United States, for here West Indians learn its implications in their daily lives as they compare and contrast their own experience with those of other black people and with whites. Their own relationschip with white America also leads them to reinterpret United States actions elsewhere. Thus Barbadians at home had opposed United States involvement in Indochina as a case of a big country bullying a small one, while Barbadians in New York saw it as an example of a white country suppressing a "black" one.

A further element in the development of West Indian racial consciousness in America is the new experience of interactions with West Indians from other islands and with people from Haiti and the Hispanic Caribbean. Employment, housing, and school all provide settings for this contact, and though island rivalries and jealousies may be aired, there is also a recognition of similarities of background and shared experiences as non-white immigrants in United States society.

In bringing together workingclass Barbadians, Trinidadians, Jamaicans, Guyanese, etc., in situations of extended exposure the process in New York parellels that which occurs in England. Though a recent study of Barbadian marriage patterns in New York indicates that this group remains highly endogamous and carries on its social life primarily within group bounds (Maynard 1972), our informal observations suggest that encounters with other West Indians in the neighborhood, classroom, and workplace provide a context for building relations between them. On one construction site in the Bronx, Barbadian and Jamaican workers observe, provoke, and antagonize each other, but *vis-à-vis* white workers on the job and in the bar on the corner after work, they form a united West Indian front. It seems that New York offers more opportunities to build common understandings among West Indians than all the pro-Federation pronouncements of West Indian leaders at home.

A similar process operates, though one step removed, in bringing together West Indians with other Caribbean peoples. Puerto Ricans, Dominicans, and Haitians are visible parts of New York's social landscape, and though they are "foreigners" *vis-á-vis* West Indians, similarities of life style and in position with respect to the dominant society create shared understandings which are beginning to be articulated in the growing interest in the Caribbean as a region and in community forms of political action and socializing. Just as England provides a unique context for merging West Indian concerns with broader notions of black Commonwealth and Third World issues, New York constitutes a parallel environment for nourishing among working people a latent Caribbean consciousness which has not been actively promoted by Caribbean leaders among their own populations at home. What we are describing here is the well known fact that social identities vary with circumstances and are situationally defined. However, as others have noted, they are not without patterning and can be described, following Despres (1973), as segmentary in character, and they are activated by the unifying and dividing forces of inequality.

While West Indians are coming in contact with others from the Caribbean, they are also encountering white Americans in unprecedented settings, though with rather different results. West Indians in England discuss their initial feelings of strangeness at seeing white people perform manual work. Barbadians in New York have expressed similar reactions, for even though a racial division of labor exists in the United States, it is nowhere as complete as it is in the West Indies. One might expect that comparable occupational status among some white and black workers would lead to a coalition of interests emphasizing class, not race. In fact, quite the reverse occurs. For in their contacts with white workers, West Indians often encounter direct expressions of racist attitudes and learn that their white co-workers enjoy in the wider society privileges and opportunities denied to them. Thus while their view of white men and women working serves to demystify the racial division of labor and class privilege back home, the experience also makes clear the independent racial basis of the oppression of blacks in America.

Both our own observations and data from the literature thus indicate that West Indian experiences in England and the United States result in converging developments of racial consciousness. West Indians go to England with no developed sense of ethnic distinctness and only a submerged racial consciousness and acquire in England a consciousness of being different – of being "black people in a white world." In the United States, to which they go with a distinct ethnic feeling and apprehension over their racial identity, they lose much of their sense of ethnic difference as the full meaning of being black in a white society is driven home to them. Their arrival at similar forms of racial consciousness via different routes is significant. It suggests that England and the United States share a common way of structuring their relationships to black and colonized peoples despite their different historical ties to the colonized world.

Feedback Effects

One of the most interesting elements of the West Indian experience in the metropoles is its feedback effect on the island societies. The new forms of racial and political consciousness that have arisen among West Indians in England and the United States are relayed back to the islands through direct and indirect channels. For Barbados, we are able to report on some of these feedback effects that we noted among the villagers of Endeavor in the 1950's and again in the early 1970's. Our information on Endeavor can be taken as more or less typical of the hundreds of rural villages throughout Barbados which are similar in structure and in culture. We explore how the experiences and ideas of West Indians abroad were perceived by villagers and operated, along with other factors, to bring about changes in their own racial consciousness.

Politics is a prominent theme in village rumshop debates, casual roadside discussions, and in general conversations at work, at home, and at social affairs. During the 1956–1958 period, though village political talk was primarily concerned with local issues, the interest shown in events outside the island was remarkable in its range. The case of Julius and Ethel Rosenberg, accused and executed as Soviet spies by the United States four years earlier, was still being debated, as was the British treatment of Cheddi Jagan of British Guiana. Knowledge of methods of cutting cane in Cuba was put forth, and views on the "soviet syst'em" acquired by a cane worker who had been in Cuba during the period of radical activity on the sugar estates there in the 1930's, were discussed and compared to ideas in the Bible or with practices alleged to be followed in England.

During this period, villagers followed with interest local newspaper and rediffusion (wired radio) reports on the progress of school integration in the United States and the white reaction it provoked in Little Rock, Arkansas. It was the latter incident that gave the Barbados government the impetus to seek the resignation of a British aide-de-camp, who was accused of racial prejudice when he placed his daughter in an island secondary school known to cater to the children of the white plantocracy. His resignation over the issue was referred to as the local "Little Rock" incident, but with the moral that Barbados did not tolerate anything resembling the United States pattern of race relations. The population was very pointedly reminded how different their position was from that of black Americans.

However, the issue of color and race on the island was not so easily buried. The following year, 1958, was marked by racial disturbances in the town of Nottingham and in Notting Hill, London, areas where the West Indian immigrant presence was being felt. The English put the riots down to the doings of irresponsible fringe elements in the society – the Teddy Boys or small native fascist groups – and denied that there was any racial feeling in England or that the two incidents had a racial basis. There were also reassurances from members of the British government that the incidents would not influence Britain's open immigration policy – reassurances which hindsight has shown to be as untrue as the proclaimed absence of racial feeling in England.

These British interpretations of events were conveyed to Barbados where they did not go down so easily. Instead, the riots galvanized a sentiment of West Indian racial unity as ministers from all the unit territories flew to England to look over the situation. Local newspapers featured lengthy accounts of what life was like for West Indian immigrants in England and insular differences were momentarily forgotten as indignation ran high over the treatment they were being accorded. Latent hostility toward British colonial rule surfaced as islanders compared the hospitality shown British officials and expatriates to the rejection West Indians were experiencing in England. One of the local commentators wrote that Britain could never repay her debt to the West Indies which had provided her with the wealth to dominate the rest of Europe.

The riots had evoked sentiments of both anger and relish – anger that black people were attacked, but relish at the opportunity this afforded to embarrass white people on the island and to expose British hypocrisy. A few villagers voiced the feeling that "we live with race hatred all our lives, but now our boys in England are holding out and giving them limeys a tough time." This combative view of the situation was not widely shared, however, and one woman told a group standing about chatting:

I feel real bad and hurted over this in truth! These things, can they be fair? What are we black people to do? We only ask for a chance to make a living and help ourselves and our families when they want to push us under the ground. It look like they want to kill all the nigger people out of the world. But that can't happen because the white people can't do without we... even when they try to keep we down.

In Barbados the resentment provoked by the riots was channeled by the black governing elite into programs aimed at preparing emigrants for what to expect in England. There was also a concerted effort to emphasize the alleged differences between the English incidents and the acts of race hatred that typified the situation in the United States. In addition, Barbadians were informed that of all the West Indian groups in

England, they were the best liked, were doing well economically, and were most successful at accommodating to the new scene.

Thus while race was an issue that lurked around the corners of all other issues in the West Indies – the question of the color-class hierarchy, of economic hegemony and international alignment, of emigration, and of a distinct national identity reflective of the history of their own societies – the elites followed the past policies of caution and avoidance of conflict, continuing to hold up the British and their ways as models to emulate.

By the late 1960's, Endeavor had experienced more than a decade of large-scale emigration to England and the United States. This, combined with the entry of the recently independent nation into the international political arena, intensified the already-existing outward-looking orientation of islanders. Two consequences of the past decade's emigration were particularly significant in directing the attention of villagers to events in the metropolitan urban centers. First, the dramatic increase in the numbers of friends and relatives abroad gave information from these areas immediacy and personal relevance. Events such as the British postal strike of 1971 had an obvious impact on villagers because it severed the channel through which remittances flowed. But some villagers thought it had wider implications: they linked it to the concurrent debates in England about immigration policy and interpreted the strike as a ruse to force West Indians, cut off from news of their kin and friends at home, to return to their islands and thus satisfy those segments of the English population who clearly wished them gone. Second, in addition to their concern for friends and relatives, villagers viewed what happened in the metropoles with an eye to its implications for their own potential future abroad. News of criminal violence in the United States evoked hypothetical accounts of their own strategies for dealing with such things, while pregnant women debated whether the benefits of United States citizenship conferred by birth there outweighed the possibility that their as yet unborn sons might someday be drafted to fight in Vietnam.

The mass media and the returned migrants served different roles with respect to information about the metropoles. While media coverage kept the community up to date with the daily happenings in those countries, interpretations of these events were provided by villagers who had themselves been there. The traditional respect Barbadians express for knowledge gained "outside" was augmented in this case by the recognition that at least some of what was occurring in America and England had parallels in Barbados. This was particularly true for issues of race and

Black Power. The awakening racial consciousness of black Americans drew early responses in the West Indies.

Though the university campuses of the West Indies have been the source of some of the more articulate expressions of the new racial and political consciousness, its impact on life at the village level deserves more attention than it has received. What occurred during the late 1960's in rural Barbados was a fairly autonomous reaction to the joint impact of local conditions and international racial disturbances, and owed more to the return of villagers from urban centers in the United States than to the tenuous links of villagers to middle class and student radicals.

Our first inkling of this change came in 1968 when, returning to Endeavor after a ten-year absence, we found a new mood of racial concern which entered into the always lively political conversations. "Tell me, is God a black man or a white man?" a thirty-five-year-old mechanic challenged his rum-shop audience. Parents expressed concern with the younger generation which flaunted openly their rejection of established norms of respect and deference behavior. And among the young people themselves, information about black America and Africa was actively solicited. Afro hair styles and dashikis, though not yet commonplace, were beginning to make an appearance, and black American soul music took precedence over calypso at country brams and house parties. Small beginnings, perhaps, but striking departures from the 1958 village scene.

The most dramatic indication of the new mood was the formation by a group of young men in the community of an organization dedicated to achieving economic autonomy for black villagers. Though the members of this group were not unanimous in their conceptualizations of Black Power, the concept included for them a commitment to placing economic control of the island in the hands of the black majority and opposition to the island's present black leadership for their self-interested approach to politics and collaboration with the white oppressors. They expressed solidarity with the struggles of black people elsewhere – particularly in the United States – and sought to bring the concept of black unity closer to home by asserting solidarity with West Indians in other islands as well. "We got to adjust ourselves to all of us are brothers," one young man said, "and not treat the St. Lucians like the white man treat the black man." Finally, there was unanimous concern with the right of black people to personal dignity and respect. While condemning their elders for their desire to "please the white man," they personally defied village norms of social deference which recognized minute status differences. Instead they asserted their right to evaluate and validate themselves on their own terms.

What is of interest in this development is that it occurred among semi-skilled artisans who did not trust or accept the leadership or motives of middle class Black Power advocates on the island. They sought their models for leadership further afield in black America, and the impetus for their formulations came from there.[6] They quoted Malcom X, not West Indian Walter Rodney, and in 1971, the trial of Angela Davis, "a beautiful black woman made into a political prisoner," generated active discussion. The local leaders were, predictably, villagers returning from the United States, but the issues to which they applied their new insights were predominantly those of their own community: the local plantations and sugar factory and their personnel, the village "greats," and even their own parents were the focus of attack – though national leaders came in for their share of abuse. Moreover, they sought contact with groups similar to theirs which had formed in other villages on the island.

By 1971, then, the new knowledge had affected both behavioral styles and assessments of their own local situation. The demand in the village for books by Eldridge Cleaver, Malcolm X, and George Jackson, as well as writings on Africa, Cuba, and China was symptomatic of the attempt to place their local experience in a broader context. The result was a broadened consciousness of colonialism and the standards it imposes. "Ten years ago," one young militant said, "ninety percent of the Bajans thought that the white man was superior. Today, I would say that seventy percent think he just another man – or another crook – or 'tief,' we call it. And with some help by the outsiders, I think we'll make it." The outsiders referred to here are black Americans, who were cited as models not only of ideology but personal life-style as well.[7]

---

[6]   We do not deal with the feedback of the Black Power movement that developed in England because its impact was not as apparent. This is in part because there were fewer migrants who had returned from England but also because the movement in the United States was setting the pace and was the focus of attention on the island. In England, the race riots, immigration restrictions, and reported incidents of racial discrimination fed back into racial and political consciousness at home by changing the public image of England in the eyes of black Barbadians and considerably reducing their identification with English culture.

[7]   We do not mean to imply that the influence was one-way. West Indian symbols and forms of expression such as *reggae* music, bangles, and "*Rasta*" hairdos have diffused to the United States and have been incorporated by a black America involved in asserting symbolically its own heritage. But though the diffusion was two-way, the political symbols and analysis during this period were largely the articulations of black Americans. It requires a longer, historical perspective to appreciate fully the reciprocity that exists between West Indians and black Americans in the leadership and cultural framework for carrying out their long-term struggle for equality.

The community's reaction to the rhetoric of Black Power was not uniform. Cautious acknowledgements of the fact of racial oppression were followed quickly by disparagement of the disrespect and violence thought to characterize Black Power. A forty-two-year-old plantation worker found Lord Kitchner's rather moderate calypso "Black Power" too "wicked" for his children to hear, but privately confessed that it was enjoyable "for people with understanding." Though activists were admonished to concern themselves less with Black Power and more with hard work to increase their buying power, there was at the same time a grudging approval of the audacity of the youth, tempered by fear of its consequences.

The ambiguous response to Black Power at the village level was paralleled at the island level by the reactions of political leaders. To some extent the receptiveness to American-style Black Power that their own populations exhibited could be seen as a continuation of the earlier struggles of the island which began in the 1930's. But the enthusiasm of the leaders was tempered by the fact that for the first time, racial pride and demands for independence were being turned against the black leaders themselves, who were viewed – at least by the more system-oriented of the Black Power advocates – as reneging on their promises of independence by equating their own political ascendancy with the autonomy and control over West Indian destinies that true independence should signify.

The black leaders who brought the island to independence did so with minimal disruption of the old social structure. They discouraged any stress on racial pride as a basis for national identity. Not surprisingly, then, they have reacted to the Black Power movement by proclaiming its irrelevance to West Indian realities and asserting that "Black Power" already exists in the guise of their own leadership. They have sought to allay the influence of foreign appeals to racial consciousness by forbidding or controlling their entry into island society. Book bans in Jamaica, Barbados' alarm at Stokely Carmichael's visit and the subsequent passage of a Public Order Act forbidding public meetings without police permission, are examples of the governments' responses, as is the denial of entrance visas to West Indian radicals from other islands. All were ploys to contain the migration of ideas by restraining their carriers.

But reactions at home required justification for such actions, and the rationale was phrased in nationalist terms: Black Power was portrayed as an example of United States cultural imperialism and placed on a par with CIA intervention and multi-national corporations. This attempt by the political elite to obscure the very different relationship of Barbadians to black and white America was a response to the real threat that a sense of unity between Caribbean and United States blacks posed to their leadership and policies. Rather than supporting American dominance in the Caribbean, the alliance of Barbadian and American blacks was predicated on opposition both to that domenance and to their political leaders' acquiescence to it. But in addition to its ideological counter-assertions, the black American influence provided a model of behavior and leadership that was explicitly proletarian. This contrasted with the anglified styles of local leaders who tended to perpetuate the traditional social distance between leaders and followers.

The introduction of Black Power ideology and writings into the village community directly involved only a few of the returned migrants. However, even those villagers least involved in political action or ideology abroad returned from the United States as conveyors of political messages, however inadvertently. This was so despite their avowed reluctance to emphasize the hard times and difficulties they faced abroad. What they did impart of their experiences, however, reinforced in unintended ways the use of black people as a reference group. When they talked about AMERICA, they referred to subways and tall buildings, to expressways and snow – features of the landscape. But when they talked about AMERICANS, the reference was primarily to black Americans. However, Jamaicans and Puerto Ricans, Italians and Jews – these groups also figured prominently in their conversation, and the traits and characteristics of these new "significant others" were dissected, analyzed, and merged into the available stock of information about the world outside. Just as older villagers, including many who have never left the island, speak authoritatively about Panama and Panamanians, Cuba and Cubans, so increasingly is the awareness of relevant features of thought, habit, and life style of the groups with whom they are in contact in New York permeating consciousness at home.

In Barbados, the village-level expressions of racial consciousness were at their zenith in 1969. The later subsiding of interest in and organization around Black Power concepts can be attributed partly to governmental intimidation and cooptation,[8] and partly to the fragmentation of the movement in the United States. Barbados did not experience the more dramatic expressions of Black consciousness that have occurred in

[8] The unrest of this period gave the Barbados government the leverage to compel local and foreign companies to take on non-white Barbadians at levels of management and decision-making formerly closed to them. Though entry into these positions benefited only a few, their assuming such positions gave many black Barbadians the feeling, at least for the moment, that there was some room for them at the top.

Trinidad, Jamaica, and some of the smaller islands. However, the brief period of activity was not without its impact. Fragments of the new consciousness persist and have modified local behaviors, and much that is now submerged lies latent, but available for elaboration and development. What events are necessary to activate these directly and vicariously experienced levels of identity and consciousness remains to be seen, but surely they cannot be ignored by those who are fashioning new concepts of West Indian, Afro-American, and Third World identity.

SUMMARY AND IMPLICATIONS

Historically, West Indian societies have been migration-oriented, and this pattern has been especially pronounced in the case of Barbados. Since the 1860's migration has been an important avenue of socioeconomic mobility for increasing numbers of colored and black Barbadians. Though the effects of this migration-mobility pattern on the island's economy and demography have been given considerable attention in studies and policy-making, its impact on Barbadian racial and political consciousness has been treated only incidentally. In this paper we have explored how migration, in interaction with other factors, has produced a heightened sense of racial identity and political awareness among Barbadians and other West Indians.

Though there are few studies of West Indian immigrants comparable to those of European and Asian immigrant communities, the available data have led us to suggest that during the nineteenth and early twentieth centuries, when Barbadian emigrants went primarily to other West Indian colonies with similar racial and social structures, they retained a pride in their national origin but tended to merge with the host population. It is possible to characterize this period as one in which Barbadian immigrants used an ethnic identity to distinguish themselves as individuals but tended to merge with other West Indians rather than form distinctive ethnic enclaves in their host societies. Immigration to Panama and the United States, where West Indians had a racial minority status imposed upon them, constituted exceptions to this situation.

After World War II the main flow of migration was directed to the industrial centers of England, the United States, and Canada. West Indian experiences in these countries led to an emphasis on racial rather than ethnic identity, and this growth of racial consciousness had parallels on the islands. It is our contention that these parallel developments were not independent but were linked by the migration process. We claim that migration provided an important channel for the bidirectional flow of peoples and ideas in such a way that political events at home, such as independence, had an impact on the migrant communities abroad, while the experiences of the emigrants were relayed in the opposite direction. The combined movements in both directions have generated a framework of knowledge and understanding that has led Barbadians to react in similar ways to related but different situations at home and abroad.[9] The result has been a broadening in the scale of group identity for most Barbadians, and presumably other West Indians as well.

In the case of Barbados, we were able to observe the shift in the nature and content of the racial and political consciousness of villagers from the late 1950's to the early 1970's. This shift was toward a greater emphasis on and concern with blackness and race as a dominant idiom by which Barbadians were coming to see themselves in opposition to those with power, whether in their own society or outside. In the late 1950's, race was a latent factor in political consciousness which focused more prominently on the need for class unity to extract concessions from the planter-merchant class that still dominated the economy. The challenge to the negatively ascribed characteristics associated with the status of being black only began to make itself felt after the mid-1960's.

The new racial awareness stirring Barbadians abroad and at home differed from other earlier expressions of either national or ethnic identity in significant ways. Most important, it was not simply an expression of national or ethnic pride but rather of cultural opposition – an explicitly countercultural assertion against the dominant values both at home and in the metropoles. As such, it has merged with other Third World movements in which assertions of group identity have been directed at the common goal of overthrowing Western cultural as well as economic and political hegemony.

A complex number of elements have operated along with migration to create this shift in group identity and political consciousness. We have outlined the situation of Barbadians at home and how it predisposed

---

9   A most dramatic example of this was the relation between the West Indian students' protests in 1969 at Sir George Williams University in Montreal where they took over a computer center and caused damage to the computers before leaving, and the Black Power revolt that took place in Trinidad a year later when some of the Montreal students returned to the island. West Indian sociologist Dennis Forsythe makes the connection between the two events explicit in his analysis of the Sir George Williams episode. He views both conflicts as part of a single liberation struggle (Forsythe 1971). Accounts of the Trinidad Black Power revolt can be found in Best (1970) and Oxaal (1971).

them to have certain expectations concerning their place in the societies of England and the United States. We turned then to examining the structures of incorporation in these two countries and how these led Barbadians and other West Indians to find that their status as colonized races overrode other aspects of their background and became the salient dimension of their social encounters. We pointed out the political events of the 1960's that resulted in West Indians in England and the United States traveling different routes to reach a convergence in racial consciousness. And finally, we considered the changes in Barbadian society during the 1960's that made segments of the population particularly receptive to the political formulations and assertions of racial pride that emerged in West Indian communities in the metropoles.

The paradox of the situation lies in the juxtaposition of increased political autonomy at home, signified by formal independence from Britain, and increased economic dependency as North American influences penetrate the island – at the same time that Barbadians themselves are moving into the very societies responsible for their subjugation, past and present. Here they achieve an economic well-being unattainable at home, while rediscovering the political and social subordination from which islanders are just emerging. They discover, as West Indian social scientists point out, that West Indians remain in perpetual bondage to the world outside (Singham and Singham 1973).

Perhaps it is a big leap from our data, but the process we are describing is suggestive of a continuing dynamic whereby the nature of this exposure to other groups contributes to shared understandings that may become the important elements in building a West Indian and even Caribbean-wide identity based on the recognition of common problems bequeathed by colonial history. The potential for such unity which experiences in the metropoles are providing is being paralleled by other forces operating toward similar ends. Though the various European colonialisms which dominated the West Indies in the past divided the islands from each other by setting up exclusive links between each island and the metropole, the new imperialism comes in different forms and with different effect. Just as the rivalries of Euro-American nationalisms have no place in the multi-national corporations which increasingly dominate world capitalism, so do the same corporations disregard the boundaries of the former colonies when expediency and economic interest impel them to. Imperialism itself, then, in its actions as well as the reactions to it, is pushing the islands toward one another. But of all these forces, those at work in the metropoles, where Barbadians, Jamaicans, Puerto Ricans, Haitians, Pakistanis, West Africans, etc., encounter one another in territory which is no one's home ground, where despite their differences they share a common position and common problems, may yet prove to be the most decisive for forging a basis for concerted political action.

REFERENCES

Antillean Caribbean Echo
   1971   December 11.
Barbados Development Plan
   1965–1968   Bridgetown: Government Printing Office.
BEST, LLOYD
   1970   The February revolution. Tapia 12. (Reprinted in *The aftermath of sovereignty*, 1973. Edited by D. Lowenthal and L. Comitas, 106–330. Garden City, New York: Doubleday/Anchor.)
BLAUNER, ROBERT
   1972   *Racial oppression in America.* New York: Harper and Row.
BROWN, JOHN
   1970   *The un-melting pot — an English town and its immigrants.* London: Macmillan.
BRYCE-LAPORTE, ROY S.
   1970   "Crisis, contraculture, and religion among West Indians in the Panama Canal Zone," in *Afro-American Anthropology.* Edited by N. E. Whitten and John F. Szwed. New York: Free Press.
   1972   Black immigrants: the experience of invisibility and inequality. *Journal of Black Studies* 3 (1):27–59.
   1973   "Family, household and intergenerational relations in a 'Jamaican' village in Limón, Costa Rica." in *Family in the Caribbean.* Edited by Stanford N. Gerber, 65–94. University of Puerto Rico: Institute of Caribbean Studies.
DEAKIN, NICHOLAS
   1970   Ethnic minorities in the social sciences. *New Atlantis* 2 (1):134–159.
   1971   A survey of race relations in Britain. *Ethnies* I:75–90.
DESPRES, LEO
   1973   "Ethnicity and ethnic group relations in Guyana." Paper presented at the annual meeting of the Southern Anthropological Association, March 1973, Wrightsville Beach, North Carolina.
DUNN, R. S.
   1969   The Barbados Census of 1680. Profile of the richest colony in English America. *William and Mary Quarterly*, third series, 26(1):31–30.
FANON, FRANTZ
   1967   *Black skin, white masks.* New York: Grove.
FORSYTHE, DENNIS, *editor*
   1971   *Let the Niggers burn! the Sir George Williams University affair and its Caribbean aftermath.* Montreal, Quebec: Black Rose Books.

GONZÁLEZ, NANCIE L. SOLIEN
1969   *Black Carib household structure: a study of migration and moderniza-
        tion.* American Ethnological Society Monograph 48. Seattle, Washing-
        ton: University of Washington Press.

HAMILTON, BRUCE
1956   *Barbados and the Confederation, 1871-1885.* London: Crown Agents
        for Overseas Governments and Administrators.

KATZNELSON, IRA
1973   *Black men, white cities: race, politics and migration in the United
        States 1900-1930 and Britain 1948-1968.* London: Oxford University
        Press.

LAMMING, GEORGE
1953   *In the castle of my skin.* London: Michael Joseph.

LEWIS, GORDON
1969   Protest among the immigrants: the dilemma of minority culture.
        Political Quarterly 40 (4): 426–435.
1971   An introductory note to the study of race relations in Great Britain.
        Caribbean Studies 11 (1): 5–29.

LOWENTHAL, DAVID
1957   The population of Barbados. *Social and Economic Studies* 6(4): 445–501.
1972   *West Indian societies.* London: Oxford University Press.

MANNERS, ROBERT
1960   "Methods of community analysis in the Caribbean," in *Caribbean
        Studies: A Symposium.* Edited by Vera Rubin. Seattle: University of
        Washington Press.
1965   Remittances and the unit of analysis in anthropological research.
        Southwestern Journal of Anthropology 23 (2): 179–195.

MARSHALL, PAULE
1959   *Brown girl, brownstones.* New York: Random House.

MAYNARD, EDWARD S.
1972   "Endogamy among Barbadian immigrants to New York City." Un-
        published dissertation, New York University.

MIDGETT, DOUGLAS
1971   "Twice removed: West Indian or Black British?" Paper given at
        annual meeting of American Society for Ethnohistory, Athens,
        Georgia.

OXAAL, IVAR
1971   *Race and revolutionary consciousness.* Cambridge, Massachusetts:
        Schenkman.

PEACH, CERI
1968   *West Indian migration to Britain: a social geography.* London: Oxford
        University Press.

PHILPOTT, STUART B.
1970   "The implications of migration for sending societies: some theoretical
        considerations," in *Migration and anthropology: Proceedings of the
        1970 American Ethnological Society annual meeting.* Seattle, Wash-
        ington: University of Washington Press.

REID, IRA DE A.
1939 *The Negro immigrant: his background, characteristics and social adjustment, 1899–1937.* New York: Columbia University Press.

ROBERTS, GEORGE W.
1955 Emigration from the island of Barbados. *Social and Economic Studies* 4 (2):245–288.

ROSE, E. J. B., *et al.*
1969 *Colour and citizenship: a report on British race relations.* London: Oxford University Press.

SCHERMERHORN, R. A.
1970 *Comparative ethnic relations.* New York: Random House.

SINGHAM, A. W., N. L. SINGHAM
1973 Cultural domination and political subordination: notes toward a theory of the Caribbean political system. *Comparative Studies in Society and History* 15 (3):258–288.

SUTTON, CONSTANCE R.
1969 *The scene of the action: a wildcat strike in Barbados.* Ann Arbor, Michigan: University Microfilms.

TAJFEL, H., J. L. DAWSON, *editors*
1965 *Disappointed guests: essays by African, Asian and West Indian students.* London: Oxford University Press.

ZUBAIDA, SAMI, *editor*
1970 *Race and racialism.* London: Tavistock.

Jungle Quechua Ethnicity: An Ecuadorian Case Study

NORMAN E. WHITTEN, JR.

The Jungle Quechua

The vast majority of aboriginal peoples living in eastern Ecuador (the Oriente) in 1972 belong to one of two cultural divisions: they are either Quechua, or they are Jívaro. The latter are well known to

This paper is based primarily on five months of preliminary ethnography undertaken during the summers of 1970 and 1971. The research is sponsored by the University of Illinois, Urbana, and the Instituto Nacional de Antropología e Historia, Quito, Ecuador, and is funded by the National Science Foundation (Grant No. GS-2999). I am grateful to the Director of the Instituto, Arq. Hernán Crespo Toral, for his constant interest and encouragement in this preliminary field investigation. Considerable thanks also are due five assistants who worked at various stages of the preliminary project: Cynthia Gillette, Nacanor Jácome, Marcelo Naranjo, Michael Waag, and Margarita Würfl. Michael Waag also commented critically on an earlier draft of this paper. Confidentiality promised to the subjects of research now prohibits me from thanking those who helped the most — the Quechua and Jívaroan close associates now caught up in the international scheme of "becoming" Indian while confronting cataclysmic changes in their environments.

The major result of this preliminary research was a proposal to undertake a year of intensive ethnography with the Lowland Quechua, beginning in late August, 1972. This research, a joint project with Dorothea S. Whitten, is also funded by the National Science Foundation (continuation Grant No. GS-2999) and supplemented by funds for research assistance by the University of Illinois Research Board and Center for Comparative International Studies. The study has three basic aspects. In the first, Dorothea S. Whitten, Marcelo Naranjo, and I continue our study of Jungle Quechua ethnicity and adaptive strategies in the face of rapid change in their natural and social environments. In the second, John P. Ekstrom is completing a year's study of colonist strategies of land acquisition between the Pastaza and Curaray River drainages. The third aspect, designed and now being carried out by Theodore Macdonald, involves continuities in Quechua world view and symbolic domains, particularly as they relate to their position in the indigenous shaman system of highland and lowland Ecuador.

anthropology and are regarded as bona fide indigenes. The former Indians are the largest aggregate, numbering approximately 35,000 or more (Burbano Martínez, et al. 1964). They speak Quechua [1] as a first language and live a tropical forest life. Yet they are frequently mentioned only in passing by authors describing the Oriente. Within Ecuador they are often lumped as "Quijos," (e.g. Porras 1961; Ferdon 1950; Peñaherrera de Costales and Costales Samaniego 1961), reflecting their presumed tribal-linguistic origin west of the Napo River along the eastern cordillera of the Andes; or, they are lumped as "Yumbos" (Peñeherrera de Costales and Costales Samaniego, et al. 1969; Burbano Martínez, et al. 1964), which suggests that they are acculturated highland Quechuas who moved into the tropical forest and there mixed with other groups (particularly the Záparos). When compared to the Cofán, Secoya, Siona (Piojé), Huarani (Auca), Awishiri (Auca), Záparo, and Jívaroans (Untsuri Shuara — see Harner 1972 — and Achuara), the Quechua of east Lowland Ecuador are usually regarded as sufficiently assimilated to lowland *blanco-mestizo* culture as to preclude careful attention. All indigenous people of Ecuador contrast ethnically with the category *blanco–mestizo* (defined below in the section on internal colonialism).

The Jungle Quechua of the central Oriente may be linguistically divided into three major dialect segments:[2] northwest, northeast, and southern (Orr and Wrisley 1965). The northwest dialect, called Tena, is found along the upper reaches of the Napo River and its headwater affluent the Jatun Yacu. The dialect continues through the adminis-

---

[1]   I am using a standard, familiar international spelling for the word "Quechua," Ecuadorian usage prefers *Quichua*, or *Kichua*. In Ecuador the term is pronounced "Keéchuwa."

[2]   Cultural differences between Jungle Quechua of the southern dialect group and the northern group are extensive, and beyond the scope of this paper to list. Suffice it to say here that the Quechua-speakers of the Bobonaza basin — the "Canelos Quechua" — are Upper Amazonian peoples who have been adapting for centuries to the zone best identified with the Bobonaza River north to the Curaray River and south to the Pastaza River. This is the area carved out as the archdiocese of Canelos. In spite of their proximity to the Andes and their language, they have a fundamentally tropical forest way of life, which they have applied in some areas to *montaña* existence. The Canelos Quechua are, in many ways, more similar to Jívaroan speakers in cultural content than to the Quijos Quechuas (Tena dialect). Ethnic derivation is, in historical times, a merger of Záparoan, Achuara Jivaroan, some Jívaroan proper and more recently, Quijjos Quechua cultures. Achuara and Záparoan are the most important contributors to culture content. Ancient Omagua and Cocama Tupian influence is probable. The exact origin of the Quechua language in this zone is unknown at this time, but ancient tropical forest derivation cannot be discounted. A general ethnography of ethnic derivation, world view, and contemporary adaptation is now in preparation.

trative towns of Tena and Archidona, and on up the Sierra to near the present town of Baeza. It runs down the Napo to the settlement of Ahuano and south to Arajuno, cutting across the Puyo-Napo Road at Santa Clara. The northeastern dialect, called Napo, goes on down the Napo River, and is spoken on such north-Napo tributaries as the Suno and Payamino Rivers. The southern division, called Bobonaza, begins south of Santa Clara and Arajuno and extends to the Pastaza River. Quechua on the Curaray, Bobonaza, Conambo, and Pindo are all of the southern division, though other further dialectical differences do exist. The territory between the Curaray and the Napo is not inhabited by Quechuas — it is exclusively Auca (Huarani, Awishiri) country.

Culturally, the northern and southern divisions of Quechua territories are distinct, and their relationships with highland and other lowland indigenous peoples are also different.[3] The people of the Tena-Napo dialects and Bobonaza dialect regard one another as different; their aboriginal histories and histories of contact are different, and their present socioeconomic status is quite different, though perhaps convergent. The Tena-Napo groups represent expansions around Catholic mission bases from the sixteenth century on to the present (Oberem 1971). Quechua language clearly came from the missions (cf. Steward 1948: 509–515). Their history is one of continuous serfdom to the missions and *haciendas,* and their present socioeconomic position is analogous to that of the infamous highland *Huasipungueros.* They are generally called Yumbos, Napos, and Quijos. For clarity and convenience I will refer to them as "Quijos Quechua." (For a recent monograph on this culture see Oberem 1971.)

Native people of the Bobonaza, Conambo, and Curaray drainages seem to have been buffers between warring groups of Jívaroans, Záparoans, Awishiris, and others from the time of first contact. Missions may have been built in existing refuge areas, and while such missions may have solidified such refuge zones, it may not be accurate to say that the missions created these zones. Throughout southern Quechua territory internal bilingual and bicultural activities between Quechua and Achuara Jívaroan are maintained by marriage. Intermarriage with the Jívaro proper, "Untsuri Shuara," also exists. This pattern of marriage with otherwise warring Jívaroan groups seems to have at least

[3] For example, shamans from the Canelos Quechua are regarded as the most powerful in the world by the Jívaro (see Harner 1972), and highland Indians from near Ríobamba regularly visit Canelos Quechua shamans. But, other highland Indians such as the Salasaca and the Otavaleños generally avoid Canelos Quechua shamans and go directly to shamans and curers in Tena and Ahuano.

a 200–years' time depth. Also, on the Curaray, Corrientes, and Pindo Rivers, Záparo–Quechua bilingualism and biculturalism exists — here people in the river bank settlements are "Quechua," but many "become Záparo" in the forest. In the latter capacity not only is Záparoan spoken, but aggressive raids against Huarani Auca households have reputedly been made in the recent past. Some Záparo–Quechua bilingualism still exists on the Río Bobonaza. Finally, more profound influences on Quechua life in the southern areas have come from the extension of trade network (for furs, gold, medicines, and cinnamon) and from the rubber boom of the late nineteenth century to early twentieth century than from the establishment of *haciendas* as in the northern case.

From this point on, my paper deals with the southern dialect, with the Quechua of the Bobonaza drainage — the "Canelos Quechua."

The people in this southern area REFER to themselves in Quechua as *runa* 'indigenous person'. They also use the term *Alama* 'friend' or 'mythic brother',[4] among themselves to ADDRESS those who come from the Bobonaza or Curaray drainages and are southern Lowland Quechua speakers. In Spanish they use the term *gente* 'People', as a reference for themselves. (When speaking Spanish all Jungle Que-

---

[4] The derivation of the term *Alama* comes from a myth segment, dealing, in various ways, with older brother/younger brother authority and tension. In brief, an older and younger brother were on a huge stone in the middle of a great river, having been placed there by a giant condor. The older brother called a great cayman which came to the rock to help the brothers across, but the younger brother jumped down first, crossed, and by the time the cayman made the return trip for the older brother the younger had disappeared. Walking through the forest, lost, and searching not only for the brother, but also for a lost homeland, the older brother reached out to break off a piece of tree mushroom (*ala*) and as he pinched it the mushroom cried out "ouch, my mythic brother, don't pinch me, real brother" (*aiai alajma ama tiushi huaichu huauqui: aiai* 'ouch', *ala* 'mushroom, mythic brother', *j* possessive, *ma* emphasis, *ama* 'no', *tiushi* 'pinch', *hua* 'to me, *i* command, *chu* negative complement to *ama, huauqui* 'real brother'). On saying this the tree mushroom transformed into the younger brother who rejoined his sibling and they went on to more adventures.

There is more to the *ala* complex than this, for ancient peoples had the ability to send their souls (*aya*) into special rocks and logs when their bodies died, from whence a mushroom would emerge to await a wandering *runa* who, in hunger, would pinch the mushroom and awaken the ancient *runa*. In this way, older and younger statuses can fluctuate, because, although the younger brother was lost, rediscovery of him through this process indicates abilities of soul transformation suggestive of ancient, older status. The term *ala* is used in direct address by all acknowledged male participants in Canelos Quechua culture and is, thereby, a crucial ethnic marker. On being called *ala* or *alaj* one must immediately reciprocate the same term, acknowledging mythic brotherhood, or he must reciprocate a pejorative, negative, ethnic term such as *auca* 'heathen', or *mashca pupu* 'barley gut', 'Ecuadorian intruder'.

chuas use *gente* in contrast with *blanco*.) There is no term other than *Alama* used to differentiate the people of the Bobonaza drainage from other Quechua speakers in highland and lowland Ecuador. In speaking Spanish, though, the Jungle Quechua of this zone use *gente* for themselves, and from that point distinguish themselves as people from both *runa llacta* (literally, 'indigenous land' — which is used as though it were Spanish, when speaking Spanish) and *blancos* (literally 'whites' — including Negroes). Jívaros and some colonists who have been in the area for a generation or more designate the Bobonaza Jungle Quechua as *Alama* (and in Jívaro sometimes as "Aram Shuara"), but this is regarded as mildly pejorative by the Indians when used contrastively by any but southern dialect Jungle Quechua speakers. Very few Indians north of Santa Clara on the Puyo-Napo Road even know the term *Alama*, and no one knows its meaning (see Note 4).

When speaking Quechua, the division of ethnic categories and territories is quite clear. The Indians themselves seldom refer to their own referent dialect group, except by implicit contrast, when making the following distinctions. In the west — the Andes — there are two 'lands': *runa llacta* and *ahua llacta*. The former is 'indigenous land' but is used in the area under study only to refer to highland Indian territory — regarded as all of the Andes. The latter term, *ahua llacta,* is literally 'highland' but refers politely to all non–Indian Ecuadorians. The *ahua llacta* term in Jungle Quechua is used as a synomym for the Spanish *blanco*. Neither the designation *gente* in Spanish, nor the designation *runa* in Quechua, is used for the Ecuadorian highland *blanco–mestizo*.

To the north there are two territories of Quechua which correspond to the two dialect areas, called respectively *Alchirona Llacta* and *Napo Llacta* (representing the northwest and northeastern dialect divisions). (Sometimes *Ansuj Llacta* is added to indicate Quechua settlements southwest of the Napo River, on a feeder river to the Jatun Yacu River.) To the north and south lie *Auca Llacta*, 'heathen lands'. In the north this includes the Cushmas (Cofán, Tetéte, Secoya, and Siona), who are but dimly known by reputation, and the hostile Huarani (called *Llushti Auca* 'naked heathens' and *Tahuashiri* 'ridge people' in Quechua). On the Curaray River, and recently along the Bobonaza as well, distinctions are made between the Huarani or "true" *Llushti Auca* to the west, now clustered on the Curaray above the mouth of the Villano and the Nushiño River, and the *Awishiri (Tahuashiri) Aucas* to the east, who now live between the Cononaco and Tivacuna Rivers. The legendary (in Quechua legend) *Puca Chaqui Auca,* 'red leg heathens' of the Tiputini drainage, are said to constitute a third division, and the Canelos Quechua insist that these unknown people speak another language and use bows and arrows. Oil company observations seem to confirm Canelos Quechua insistence on a *Puca Chaqui Auca* group. Also belonging to *Auca Llacta* in the north are Záparo speakers, most of whom are bilingual in jungle Quechua, and many of whom are trilingual in Spanish as well. Northern Achuara from the Corrientes and Conambo River systems are also part of *Auca Llacta*. (Tessmann [1930], Steward [1948], and Steward and Métraux [1948] give historical data supporting these divisions made by the southern dialect group of Quechua–speakers.)

Due east of Alama land, in Peru, live *Andoa Runa* in the most eastern territory of the culture area of the Canelos Quechua. Other *Auca Llacta* are said to exist there, especially the Candochi Jívaroans on the Pastaza, Záparoans from the Marañon River, and Cocama on the Tigre River. Within their own territory the Jungle Quechua identify one another by the administrative center closest to their settlement, unless they actually come from that area, in which case identity is by clan segment and actual residence. From west to east the major identifying settlements are the *Puyo Runa* (sometimes *Pinduj Runa*), which include all people from the Pinduj River south to the Pastaza River, north on either side of the Napo Road for a few kilometers, and northeast to Cabecera de Bobonaza. *Canelos Runa* includes people from east of Cabecera de Bobonaza to Canelos and from Canelos north to the headwaters of the Villano and Curaray River, east to Chambira, and south to the headwaters of the Copotaza River. *Paca Yacu Runa* includes those around the settlement of Paca Yacu north to Villano, and *Sara Yacu Runa* includes all people there south to the Capahuari River, north to the Conambo River, and east on the Bobonaza River to Teresa Mama. *Montalvo Runa* includes the territory north to the Conambo River, east to Peru, and south to the Capahuari. Each *runa* territory is divided into *llactas,* which have recognized living or dead founders and consist of intermarried segments of clans which trek *(purina)* periodically to identified zones, where they encounter other people from other *runa* territories similarly engaged. Sara Yacu–Canelos is seen as the cultural hearth of contemporary Canelos Quechua culture, but the greatest population concentration is between the Pinduj and Pastaza Rivers. The people themselves see their origin area as somewhere around contemporary Yurimaguas, in Peru.

Because of the designation of Canelos as the stereotypic center of southern Quechua culture, because the people of this zone have so frequently been designated as the "Canelos tribe" in the literature, and because the designation "Canelos Quechua" is becoming increasingly accepted in Ecuador, I shall hereafter refer to the people of the southern Lowland Quechua dialect as "Canelos Quechua." The reader is warned, however, that in the Dominican and administrative site of Canelos, proper, there exists MORE INTRUSION from Quijos Quechua and highland Quechua than with any other area of Canelos Quechua territory, including Puyo. Figure 1 indicates the major geographic and ethnic divisions made by the Canelos Quechua in contrastively defining their position vis–á–vis other non–white ethnic categories in the Ecuadorian Oriente.

Marriage between the Canelos Quechua and both cultural groups of Jívaroan has taken place for at least two hundred years. The Canelos Quechua have virtually absorbed the Záparo speakers in the last fifty years, and marriages with highland Indians, occasionally highland whites, and Indians from both northern dialects today take place. For the Canelos Quechua, *Indígena* 'Indian' or preferably *nativo* 'native' is synonymous with their way of life, and they aggressively insist that the appropriate synonym in Spanish for *Indígena* is *gente*. Incorporation of Jívaroans, usually classed as *Auca* will be discussed below, when presenting some aspects of the Canelos Quechua kinship system.

Although the Canelos Quechua are not homogeneous in their ethnic make–up, they are nonetheless a self–identifying, if highly individualistic, indigenous aggregate with clear cultural markers; and as an aggregate they are not merging into *blanco-mestizo* culture. We must understand the expansion of Lowland Quechua ethnicity as a rational response to expanding opportunities in the money economy under the continuance of internal colonialism in Ecuador.

Economically, the staple of Lowland life is *yuca* 'manioc'. *Chagras* 'cleared fields' cover from one to three hectares. Land is cleared with ax and machete by a man, his sons, and sons–in–law, more often than not without help of kinsmen or friends, although *mingas* 'reciprocal labor exchange' may take place. Men plant plantains, bananas, corn, and naranjilla. The same men carry the manioc stems to the clearing; then women do the actual planting, keep the *chagra* clean, harvest the *yuca*, carry it to the house, prepare it, and serve it. Sweet potatoes and some *yautía* are also grown on the *chagra*, and these are also the responsibility of women. Palm shoots, *chontaduros*, *yautía*, a variety of fruits, peppers, tomatoes, and herbs are grown in

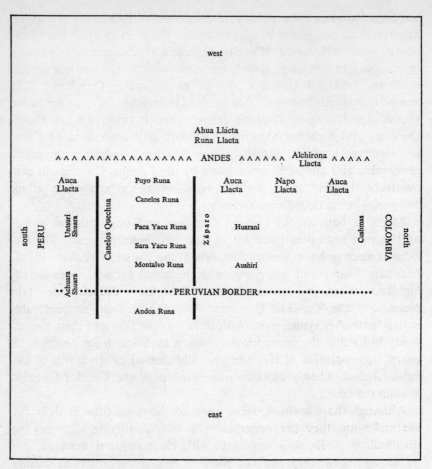

Figure 1.   Ethnicity and Territory as seen by the "Canelos Quechua"

kitchen gardens in back of the house as well as on the *chagra*. Near Puyo the *naranjilla* (*Solanum quitoense* and several other species) is grown as a cash crop; otherwise, the Canelos Quechua have few crops of cash value, though they are ringed on their western and northern flanks by sugar and tea plantations.

Manioc beer *(chicha* or *asua)* of very low alcoholic content (more of a gruel) is a staple of life, and the making and serving of *chicha* constitutes a focal point of symbolic interaction within the household. The masticated *yuca* is stored in large pottery jars, *(tinajas* or *asua churana manga)* and served in thin, finely decorated bowls *(mucahuas)*. All pottery is made by coiling. Women make their own *tinajas* and *mucahuas* and guard small secrets pertaining to color, design, and ways to get the thinnest possible sides and rims. Knowledge and techniques are passed from mother to daughter or from mother to son's wife. The pottery is fired without a kiln. This is the finest pottery made today in the Ecuadorian Oriente, and most, if not all, pottery sold in the highlands as "Jívaro pottery" comes from the Canelos Quechua. Indeed, some Jívaros marry Quechua women and bring them to their own houses in order to have a better pottery than the Jívaro women can provide.[5] Black pottery cooking pots *(yanuna manga)* and eating dishes *(callana)* are also made, sometimes with thumbnail decorations *(sarpa manga)*.

Fine decorated pottery for intra-household use is not disappearing with the introduction of metal pots and pans, but the black pottery is rapidly dwindling. People buy the new goods, or trade other things to obtain them, but they maintain at least one or two *tinajas* for *chicha* storage and at least one *mucahua* for serving.

Several fish poisons, such as *barbasco,* are grown in the *chagra* to be used during relatively dry times of the year, when the rivers run quite low and clear. Hallucinogens such as *Ayahuasca* (three *Banisteriopsis* species) and *Huanduj* (several *Datura* species) are grown, together with *Huayusa,* tobacco, and a large variety of medicinal and magical herbs. Men fish with spears, traps, weirs, lines, and nets, and hunt with traps and blowguns. Although many Quechua men make curare poison, using some forty or more plant and other substances, more powerful curare for the blowgun darts comes along trade networks originating in the east. Peruvian Achuara bring poison to Conambo, Montalvo, Copotaza, and Sara Yacu, and Copotaza Achuara or Conambo Achuara carry it on westward. Muzzle–loading shotguns are also used for small game, and cartridge guns are becoming available. Long treks *(purina)* to gather turtle eggs, to hunt for large quantities of meat, to catch and dry large fish, to keep a distant *chagra,* and to buy the appropriate black, red, and white clays for pottery decoration are made by a family once or twice a year, sometimes alone and sometimes with a larger kinship or settlement group.

Travel is frequent among the Canelos Quechua, and it is usually by

---

5 A crucial aspect of Canelos Quechua cultural perpetuity is bound up with the transmission of knowledge and secrets in pottery making. Three souls go to make up each storage jar and drinking bowl: the clay giver soul, the woman's own created body soul, and the household soul. These souls and the knowledge behind each are transmitted generation by generation through women, just as special knowledge of the clan souls acquired through psychedelic experiences are transmitted generation by generation through males. In my future ethnography I will devote considerable time to analysis of such cultural continuity.

foot. The rivers are too rapid and untrustworthy as far as depth goes (sometimes flooded, sometimes quite low) to provide stable avenues for transportation on the Pastaza east to Ayuy or on the Bobonaza east to Canelos. The Curaray, itself, meanders so much that it is about as efficient to travel on foot from one point to another as to make one oxbow turn after another by canoe. Nevertheless, canoes are used when cargo is to be moved, and the Canelos Quechuas are excellent canoe makers and superior boatsmen.

The nuclear family is a very tightly knit unit with man and woman sharing equally in decision making, in spatial mobility, and in upward socioeconomic mobility in some cases. Residence is ideally matripatrilocal but generally bilocal. There is no term for this unit except the Quechua term *huasi*, 'house', and the Spanish terms *familia* and *casa* are used synonymously for *huasi*.

The maximal kinship grouping, and segments of this grouping, are referred to as *ayllu*. The *ayllu*, as the maximal clan, is a stipulated descent system from a common animal ancestor, often a variety of puma or jaguar. Each *ayllu* is today identified with a set of surnames and extends through much of Canelos Quechua territory and on into other culture areas, as well. For people in any clan segment, extended clan (also called *ayllu*) reckoning is from father or father's father back to his father's wife. Within the extended clan there are tightly knit stem kindreds, reckoning from an old, founding shaman. These kindreds are also called *ayllu*, but because of the intertwining of *ayllu* membership through marriage with other *ayllu* segments within a territory, the resulting intermarried segments often refer to themselves by the territorial term, *llacta*.

Each *ayllu* (maximal and extended) maintains its special culture, transmitted to intimate residential in–laws. In this transmission special concentrations of knowledge, or culture, concatenate into the territorial *runa*, which expands and contracts with the *purina* system and fissions across *ayllu* lines in the *llacta* system. In this way shared knowledge embedded in the dispersed *ayllu* of antiquity is transferred repeatedly across *ayllu* boundaries and maintained through conflict and competition in the *llacta* system. *Ayllu* members maintain their *ayllu* ideology, however, through visionary experience, through mythology, and through actual travel. They can re–activate the maximal *ayllu* concept after many generations through the system of shared descent from a common animal ancestor and through shared possession of the souls of the deceased.

In ascending order of kin and neighbor units, a child is born into a *huasi* 'household' unit, in which the woman's cultural maintenance through pottery tradition and the man's maintenance through *aya* 'soul' acquisition assures each newborn of a place in a maximal clan extending back into mythic time. The *huasi* itself exists within a *llacta*, defensible territory, which was established by a founder in alliance with other founders of *ayllu* segments. These minimal *ayllu* segments within a *llacta* are stem kindreds. Beyond the stem kindred is the extended clan, which includes localized and dispersed kinsmen within and beyond a *runa* territory. And beyond the extended clan is the maximal clan, the everlasting system of stipulated descent into mythic time and structure. The ancient relationships among founders of maximal clans, during the time when all animals were human and humans crawled on the ground like babies, are repeated today as myths and are thought to provide the basis for integration of the Canelos Quechua, long before humans came to dominate their sector of the biosphere.

A developmental sequence exists which ties male *huasi, ayllu,* and *llacta* founders to the knowledge of mythical times. On marriage a male must, by taking *huanduj datura,* converse with the soul–master, *Amasanga,* and have the soul–master cure him of magical darts *(supai biruti)* sent by jealous suitors of his wife. Also, the bride must visit the wife of the *Amasanga,* the *chagra mama* or *Nunghuí mama,* to get her sacred stones and knowledge to make the manioc grow. If a man wishes to head a stem kindred then he must, through a long period of time, acquire the status of *yachaj* or 'shaman', becoming both curer and potential mystical killer; and when, if ever, he seeks to found a *llacta* he must have made pacts with the various spirits *(supai)* and souls *(aya)* of the territory, in which process he becomes a *potential bancu* 'seat' for the souls and spirits. He usually does not serve as *bancu,* however, because retaliation for the evil done by the spirits and souls through the *bancu* leads many people to attempt to eliminate the *bancu's* social capital — his family, neighbors, and friends — by witchcraft and assassination.

As the process of soul acquisition and making pacts with spirits goes on, something else also occurs due to the constant outward movement of affinally related clan segments: A MAXIMAL CLAN EVOLVES WITHIN A TERRITORY. This maximal clan is often named after a given area. Terms such as Puyo Runa, Canelos Runa, Sara Yacu Runa, etc. then take on another meaning, for not only do the territories exist as interrelated clan segments, but certain clans come to dominate, and knowledge of the *runa* territory suggests the dominating clan. The territorial clans represent a process of "social circumscription" (Carneiro 1970) overlaid with territorial circumscription. Segments of extended clans do cut through these territorial boundaries, however, as do alliances formed through intermarriage. Such cross–cutting of the circumscribed territorial clans suggests an evolution toward an incipient, as yet acephalous, ethnic state of southern Jungle Quechua.

All maximal clans of the Canelos Quechua include Achuara Jívaroans as members of Quechua extended clans. Also, in many of the maximal clans there is one Achuara or even Untsuri Shuara local group (caserío) which insures intra–indigenous ethnic contrast (Quechua versus Jívaroan) WITHIN the maximal clan itself. This ethnic contrast between two very different indigenous peoples, together with the countervailing complementarity through cross–cutting intermarriages, is an essential element in the definition of Canelos Quechua ethnicity and social structure and is a key to continuity of indigenous identity during times of rapid change.

The term ayllu may refer to the caserío when this local group consists of only one segment of the extended clan; otherwise it refers to the speaker's own descent group within the llacta, or caserío. If the speaker has no descent group members in the caserío he will use ayllu to mean members of the descent group of his wife, or deceased wife. Ayllu is regularly used to denote extended clan and, when involved in territorial disputes with Jívaroans or with colonists, ayllu as maximal clan is invoked. In this latter sense indigenous ethnicity is stressed over intra-indigenous divisions, and the concept of common, INDIGENOUS DESCENT, together with the acknowledgement of extensive networks resulting from stipulated clan intermarriage, is used vis–à–vis outsiders. Such a process of assertion of common descent of otherwise contrastive Indian ethnic identities is well under way in several parts of the Oriente, one of which is the Comuna de San Jacinto, near Puyo.

The Jungle Quechua call themselves Christians, and so distinguish themselves as opposed to all other Indians, except the highland Quechua. Practices such as genuflecting and kissing the hand of priests and nuns are ubiquitous. There are few churches in the caseríos, and where these exist a priest (or evangelist) may visit a few times a year, on the occasion of special fiestas. More generally, the central church for the Lowland Quechua is in a major town, or outlying post (Puyo, Canelos, Sara Yacu, Montalvo, Jesús Pitishca). Everywhere, though, other worlds associated with the sky and an inner earth, and other spirits, creatures and souls associated with the tropical forest and treacherous stretches of rivers, are talked about and visited with the aid of hallucinogens.

THE COMUNA DE SAN JACINTO DEL PINDO

The Comuna de San Jacinto del Pindo was established by executive decree in 1947 by the then national President, Dr. José María Velasco Ibarra. This decree was necessary due to the extreme conflict between colonists and Indians in and around the town of Puyo. Puyo is only nine kilometers east of Shell Mera, the town founded by Shell Oil Company in its explorations beginning in 1937. Indians were inhabiting the area around Puyo (along the Pinduj — now Pindo–Puyo — Rivers) and at the mouth of the Pindo where it joins the Pastaza long before 1899, when a priest (Alvaro Valladares) and some Indians (Jívaroan and Quechua) arrived from Canelos. Long a trading site for furs, gold, cinnamon, and wood, Puyo began to expand rapidly as a national frontier town when Shell Company completed the Baños–Shell Mera Road in the mid–1930's.

There followed about fifteen years of highland colonist settlement in Puyo, which meant squeezing out the Indians, who were apparently vociferous in making their land claims known as more and more settlers moved onto their *chagra* plots and began to raise sugar cane for the production of *aguardiente* 'rum'. The 1947 Presidential decree supposedly was made not only due to Indian-highlander conflict, but also due to growing national attention to the Indian plight in this area, stemming from explorers' accounts. One of the most important guides to the Oriente lived near Puyo, and Velasco Ibarra himself was supposedly respectful of this guide and the others of his extended clan (including one of the many powerful shamans of the area — see Eichler 1970: 109). This guide presumably had enough important contacts among prominent Ecuadorians to force some attention to Indian problems among colonists and traders. Also, it seems, many highlanders seeking to exploit the Oriente were sorely in need of Indian guides and labor, and they turned to the Puyo Runa for such help. It benefited all to have a permanent Indian aggregate with marginal dependence on Puyo's money economy but able to subsist on its own when labor was not needed.

Whatever the specific historical causes, the *comuna* was established just south of Puyo. Its 16,000 hectare territory is bordered on the east by the Puyo River, just after its junction with the Pindo-Puyo, and on the west and south by the Pastaza River. The northern pinnacle begins at the Caserío San Jacinto (the oldest official *caserío* on the *comuna*) and runs southwest to where a bridge now crosses the Chinimbimi, a branch of the Pastaza. Today, eleven official *caseríos* of from 25 to

120 people and at least two other dispersed *llactas* ring the *comuna,* and throughout the *comuna* people also live separately, on particular *chagras,* but with identity claimed to one or two *llactas.* The estimated population of the comuna de San Jacinto during 1973 is 1,600.

The *comuna* is ringed by sugar and tea plantations on all but the eastern flank, and one road cuts the *comuna* en route to the tea plantation south of the Pastaza. This road cuts through a rocky, fertile alluvial plain called *La Isla* 'the island' (because the Chinimbimi fork and Pastaza River enclose it). Here, along the road, there are more than 150 colonists illegally settled, almost all in conflict with the *comuna* members generally, while many form cooperative dyadic relationships with particular individuals from all of the *caseríos.* At the terminus of the road (Puerto Santa Ana) there is an all colonist *(colono)* settlement at the base of a hill, with an all Untsuri Shuara Jívaroan settlement on top of the hill.

In spite of cash cropping around the *comuna,* the *comuneros'* only recourse to cash is the *naranjilla* and sale of forest products (including medicines, wood, furs, and a variety of off–and–on products bringing little cash, such as pottery, tourist lances, beads, and live animals). Basically, the *comuneros* farm their manioc and plantain *chaqras* and supplement their diet with poultry, wild birds, fish, and small game. The major change in this has been the impact of cattle during the past eight years.

The *comuna* is loosely governed by a *cabildo,* with elected president, vice president, secretary, treasurer, *síndico* 'lawyer', and a *vocal* 'spokesman,' from each of the *caseríos.* The election is held annually, and thus far has resulted in officials who are bilingual and bicultural, but who are the children of prominent or high ranking, extended clans, or the male affines attached to prominent, high ranking clans. Deals made by the *cabildos* with prominent *colonos,* including the governor of the province, have improved their financial standing; a stratified system of high ranking *cabildos,* having differential access to money through public officials in need of *comuna* land and/or labor, has occurred. However, the intra–*comuna* prestige game involves conspicuous giving (Erasmus 1961), with rank accruing to the giver. Ranking on the *comuna* leads, usually, to uneven access by the *cabildos,* which in turn places them in a position of economic betterment vis–à–vis most other *comuneros;* but the need for conspicuous giving within the *comuna* tempers this class system, and suggests one of ranking evolving into stratification (see Fried 1967). Thus far there is no whole clan of Quechuas on the *comuna* with differential access, though in-

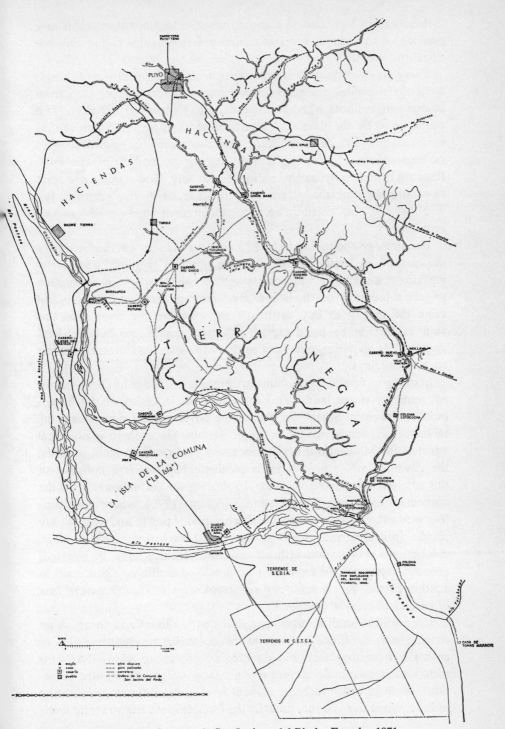

Figure 2.   Map of the Comuna de San Jacinto del Pindo, Ecuador 1971

dividuals from high ranked clans do manage to place themselves in a position of differential access to local power domains channeling national resources.

Every single *comunero* is concerned with male fertility and female fecundity. Families are generally very large — ranging upward from one or two children when the parents are eighteen or nineteen to a dozen or so by the time the parents reach their forties. Some fathers continue to sire children into their seventies or eighties. This rational serious concern with exploding the population of the Puyo Runa is tied directly to the political economy. The *comuneros* want to totally populate their territory and other territories, knowing full well that this plan depends on gaining increased access to the money economy.

The strategy adopted is to build new *caseríos* only on the border of the *comuna,* as territorial holding units, while at the same time entering into contractual arrangements with colonists who are attempting to gain a foothold on the island. By "renting" land to *colonos,* and using the money to buy cattle off the *comuna,* the people of this area are trying to build capital resources (cattle, marketable land areas) while acquiring new land and at the same time protecting their *comuna* holdings.

In order to do the latter, constant protests are lodged against colonists renting *comuna* lands. This must be done in Quito, at the Ministerio de Previsión Social, for this is the governmental department established to administer the *comuna* system. Since there is no local agent of the Ministerio it is also necessary to depend on local officials, the governor and political heads *(teniente político, jefe político)* of the adjacent administrative units. In dealing on the national level the *comuneros* enter one power domain (Adams 1970), where only conflict with *colonos* is stressed and where superior power and support are sought. In dealing with the local or regional level of the same domain, conflict AND cooperation with officials and colonists must be stressed; economic support and expansion of promised facilities (e.g. a road in another part of the *comuna)* are requested *often with the result of loss of ground on original grievances.*

More will be said about power domains (national and local) in an ensuing section. Suffice it to say at this point that pro tem transfers of authority from the Ministerio de Previsión Social to the IERAC (Instituto Ecuatoriano de Reforma Agraria y Colonización) are sometimes made in order to bring a local level competitive domain to the Indians. When this is done, though, *the Indians lose their strategic dual-*

ity of national–regional domain manipulation. They then must cope
through a unified national–regional domain — one that has as its
charge furtherance of COLONIST EXPANSION and, hence, INDIAN DISEN-
FRANCHISEMENT AND TERRITORIAL ENCAPSULATION.

The expansion of *caseríos* on the *comuna* is taking place rapidly,
and is accompanied by local–level clamor by the Indians for national
facilities on the larger *caseríos*. For example, there is a Catholic church
at San Jacinto and a Protestant one at Puyo Pungo. There are now
schools at Unión Base, Rosario Yacu, Río Chico, Chinimbimi, Puyo
Pungo, Amazonas, and Playas del Pastaza. Children are taught or
preached to in Spanish. In the schools, teachers are recruited from
various parts of the nation. They live in the schoolhouse, and teach
there for about eight months of the year. The sixth grade is the highest, from which some children go on to school in Puyo, this being paid
for by their families.

The experience of the Comuna de San Jacinto del Pindo is being
copied by a number of other people in definable *runa* territories that
are becoming bounded by colonizing non–*runa* from the highlands.
East of the Puyo–Napo Road there are two other *comunas* (San
Ramón and Arajuno), and still more are talked about. The *comuna*
at Canelos has now become quasi–official by executive decree, and
there is talk all down the Bobonaza of establishing *comunas* at the
sites of the various administrative towns. In fact, the term *comunero*
is being increasingly applied to all Indians, whether or not they live on
the *comuna,* and many, if not most, *blanco–mestizos* knowing anything at all about the residence of Indians think that *comuna* means
caserío and are surprised, or even bewildered, to find that *comuna*
refers to the grouping of maximal clan segments in a given area. The
Indians always explain their social–territorial structure to non–Indians in kinship terms, noting the intersection of extended clans in the
past. When pushed, for example, by curious *blancos* in Puyo as to
why there are many families from different backgrounds and with different origins, the reply is that such families were previously related
in grandparental generations through marriage, so that *all present comuneros are descended from a common, ethnically diverse, breeding
population.* By invoking this rule of stipulated ethnic descent the *comuneros* become, in their own eyes, a distinctive race — different
from all *blanco–mestizos* and generally related, but nonetheless distinct, from all other Indians.

I will say more about the Comuna de San Jacinto after setting forth
more of the relevant social environment of the Jungle Quechua by

reference to internal colonialism, expanding infrastructure, colonization, and the relationships between power domains in this frontier cultural ecological setting.

INTERNAL COLONIALISM

Internal colonialism refers to situations "... where an independent country has, within its own boundaries, given special legal status to groups that differ culturally from the dominant group, and created a distinct administrative machinery to handle such groups" (Colby and van den Berghe 1969: 3). The plural nature of Ecuadorian society has been documented repeatedly (see Jaramillo Alvarado 1936; Whitten 1965; Burgos 1970). What is usually assumed, though, is that expanded economic opportunities will result in the breakdown of plural segments and the establishment of a "mixed" or "mestizo" national ethnic category. Pareja Diezcanseco sums up a prevalent intellectual view on contemporary Ecuador:

Ecuador is not a country inhabited by white folk, for as an ethnic minority they only add up to scarcely one-tenth of the total population. Neither is it a country of Indians, for in that case its history would be one of regression, or else, of stratification ... the nation is *Mestizo* ... Once the Indians enter civilized life ... *the Mestizo part of the population will be more homogeneous* (1970: 88. Emphasis added.).

The swelling of the *"mestizo* part" of the country is seen by many, within and outside of Ecuador, as part of a growth of ethnic homogenization and a basis for the cultural and social revolution that will do away with a caste system where political and economic control rests with the very few *blancos*. But a large percent of the nation is Indian, and a small, but concentrated, percent is black (not mulatto). The national concept of *mestizo* contains a denial of *blanco* (white) supremacy and affirms roots to Indian and (sometimes) Negro, or at least Moorish–mulatto, ancestry. Such an IDEOLOGY OF MIXTURE allows for considerable EXCLUSION OF THE NONMIXED, including Highland and Lowland Indians, and ethnically distinct black communities in northwest, north, and southwestern districts. Furthermore, economic and political integration of Ecuador is taking place through internal colonization, particularly through an expansion of highland *mestizos* to lowland areas inhabited primarily by Indians in the east and blacks in the northwest (see Whitten 1965, 1968, 1969a, 1969b, 1974).

Casagrande, Thompson, and Young (1964: 281–325) and Gillette

(1970) give preliminary analyses of colonization in Ecuador. The former state:

The theoretical interest in studying colonization lies both in the processes whereby an already established sociocultural system is extended, replicated or reintegrated, and in colonization as a CREATIVE PROCESS, since colonists frequently must accommodate themselves to a new ecological situation, and to novel sociopolitical and economic arrangements (Casagrande, Thompson, and Young 1964: 282).

In an earlier work (Whitten 1965), I also took this approach to the predominantly black population of San Lorenzo, a northwest coastal rainforest town. I gave primary attention to the internal social and political structure of black *costeños* and thought of colonists as having to adapt to the new, local scene. But, in the view taken here, another important creative process must be stressed. This is the process of colonization from the high Andes to tropical lowlands. The process is characterized by a transposition of *blanco* ethnic values, reinforced through demographic shifts, causing local peoples classed as *negro* or *indio* to face a socioeconomic environment with an effective, continuing, ideational blockage to strategic resources exploited within their territories.

As highland *mestizos* descend the Andes they enter zones which lack members in the contrasting, upper-class, *blanco* category, and, it seems, in the absence of such *blancos* they assume membership in the *blanco* category themselves. As a consequence, those who would be *cholo* or *mestizo* in the *Sierra* become *blanco* on the coast and eastern slopes. "*Blanco*–ness" is reinforced by generalizing the non–*blanco* ethnic contrast — lumping black *costeños* into one pejorative category and lowland Indians into another. In eastern Ecuador, Indians have again and again had their residences forced completely out of the commercial and administrative towns, while economic dependence on these towns continued to increase.

It seems to me that the process of breaking up specific Indian linguistic-ethnic units ("tribes") is leading not to increased assimilation of Indians to "*mestizo* ways" but rather to an expanding generalized category "Indian" *(Indio)* to which *mestizos contrast themselves for virtually all purposes, when new opportunities in the money economy arise.* National and labor policies designed to speed up change in the *mestizo* sector, then, increasingly retard opportunities for those classed as *Indio*.

The crucial environmental factor for the contemporary Lowland Quechua is the expanding, contrastive ethnic category *blanco,* which includes the *mestizo* in the absence of upper-class *blanco* culture-bearers. *Blanco-mestizo* ethnicity forces Quechua ethnicity to intensify, and the strategies played in the arena of expanding and generalizing ethnicity have powerful economic consequences for both ethnic categories, *particularly when one ethnic category (the Jungle Quechua) is encapsulated by national policies of "Indian protection" while the other* (blanco–mestizo) *is given wide powers through the national policy of colonization.*

By "ethnicity" I mean *patterns of human interaction which form the basis for categorical social relations with observable, or projected economic consequences.* Categorical social relationships are characterized by stereotypic criteria, as distinct from structural relations which are characterized by group membership or network relationships which are characterized by extant exchange patterns between interacting individuals (see Southall 1961: 1–46; Mitchell 1966: 52–53; Banton 1967; Whitten and Szwed 1970: 43–48; Whitten and Wolfe 1972). Land access is intimately tied to the economic consequence of ethnic status.

In Ecuador today, Indian lands can only be legally protected from invasion by colonists with the formation of *comunas Indígenas* 'native comunes'. The formation of *comunas* is Indian–initiated but depends for administration on the Ministerio de Previsión Social; special laws pertain to the actions of Indians (and colonists) on the *comunas* (see Peñaherrera de Costales and Costales Samaniego 1962). The Instituto Ecuatoriano de Reforma Agraria y Colonización (IERAC), by contrast, is established not only to do away with *latifundia* holdings in the highlands, but also to encourage as rapid a penetration as possible of colonists into the Oriente, particularly in the zones where oil exploration is underway and where the pipeline and access roads are being built. Colonists are by definition *blanco* in the Oriente in contrast to all people classed as *Indio.*

All Oriente people classed as Indio *or* Indígena, *fall into a national power domain which is essentially static. It must await Indian protest before it will even investigate infiltration and invasion of legitimate Indian land. All people classed as* colono (blanco) *in the Oriente fall under a domain of national expansion and dynamic bureaucratic manipulation aimed at opening new land claims for non–Indians.* More will be said about the domains in the ensuing section.

In terms of oil exploration, Indians are generally regarded as "hunters" of the interfluvial zones and so are hired primarily to set up camps, to stay in the forests, and to work only "on the line" for the oil companies. *Blancos,* by contrast, are seen as new potential agriculturalists, are employed near camps and near towns, and are regarded as the proper spokesmen for all workers (including the Indians).

Quechua has long been the national trade and work language for communicating with all lowland Indians, while Spanish has been used primarily for the *blancos.* Today special bilingual line bosses (mostly recruited from the Summer Institute of Linguistics school teachers) are hired to deal with real and potential "Indian problems," while problems of labor organization, minimal wage, etc., are regarded nationally as a strictly *blanco–mestizo* concern.

EXPANDING INFRASTRUCTURE AND POLITICAL ECONOMY

An infrastructure is the network of transportation facilities enabling economic expansion, together with the administrative and educational apparatus, which establishes a bureaucratic–information system facilitating the expansion based on transportation networks. Hegen (1966) provides a good base for the study of infrastructure expansion in the Upper Amazon up to the mid–1960's. In his study Hegen makes a dramatic, if unrealistic, statement related to colonists (pioneers), which draws our attention to the nation as a whole:

Pioneering creates sociocultural demands and establishes a tax source which in turn will supply funds to satisfy these demands. It will stimulate the establishment and growth of trade, manufacturing and service industries, and the general exchange of goods, based upon a money economy. It will lead to regional specialization, fulfilling thereby the requirements of the demand-supply complex. Above all ... pioneering will revolutionize the static social and political life of the people by integrating them into the responsible, decision-making processes of a modern democracy (1966: 36).

Although apparently writing his conclusion prior to the events themselves and making enormously overgeneralized statements about a political economy which is now in the hands of foreign companies and a national military dictatorship, Hegen does direct attention to the expanding infrastructure itself and its importance in opening previous frontier zones to national bureaucratic controls. The official, national expanding infrastructure "follows" the *blanco* settlements, which mark the first results of the colonization programs. Pioneer settlements are not distributed willy–nilly around the jungle, nor are they necessarily first established in the best river–bank agricultural zones. They tend to cluster in areas where resources of value to international commerce exist, at a given time, as well as in the areas already targeted for national development. Not surprisingly, the two areas — those designated for development and those of special interest to foreign concerns for resource extraction — often coincide.

Regardless of the strategic importance of *colono* settlement to national planning, however, one inescapable need must be met — the colonists must find a stable food supply. And they are usually totally ignorant of tropical agriculture. Where Indian settlements exist, the *colono* food supply becomes the native *chagra*. To understand the informal aspect of an expanding infrastructure, we must put native peoples of the Oriente into the picture and carefully note the cycle whereby new lands are "opened" by *blanco* pioneers muscling into Indian *chagras*. By the time an official agent of a responsible bureaucracy arrives via plane or helicopter to an area to investigate alleged irregularities, the colonists are in control of major manioc plots, planted by Indians but claimed by colonists, and the stereotype of Indians as hunters is used to force the natives away from their own productive agricultural lands. This forces the Indians to open new territories to be exploited later in the same manner, unless effective counter–strategies are concurrently enacted. The Lowland Quechua seem remarkably effective in devising counter–strategies that are peace–producing and accommodating in terms of warding off destruction of their population.

Good land for growing crops within any given *runa* territory is limited, and the Jungle Quechua often opt to remain near enough to the national infrastructure tentacles to press early claims during times of invasion. This gives them more opportunity for social network maintenance within a known geographic zone than is characteristic of other Indian groups. The Lowland Quechua are particularly effective in losing one thing to gain something else vis–à–vis colonists and in maintaining strength vis–à–vis various quasi–sympathetic and relatively helpful brokerage agencies (Catholic and Protestant missions, military bases, powerful *hacendados*, land speculators, and even some Peace Corps volunteers). This allows them not only to survive in such a situation of replacive colonization, but also to actually expand under such an impress. But the price of their expansion is often peonage, in one form or another, to one of the patronage "helpers."

If we were dealing with nineteenth–century and early twentieth century exploitation of natural resources (as we are when dealing with the history of the Jungle Quechua), we might by now be able to construct an adequate model of Indian–*blanco* relationships. Steward (1948: 507–512) did just this, though since then data turned up will demand a reexamination of his model sequences. But the penetration in the last five years of foreign oil companies (Texaco–Gulf in the north, Anglo and Amoco in the central *Oriente,* together with subsidiary exploration companies and subcontracting companies) and their new technologies, make it clear that the frontier itself falls within an expanding technological sphere superior to, and guided by, agencies more powerful than Ecuador's political economy. *Blancos* and Quechua alike fall into power domains of national bureaucracies and, also, supranational domains reflecting new levels of politico-economic integration (Wolfe 1963). These latter domains are most productively considered as competitive to national interests.

Richard N. Adams (1970) presents us with an exhaustive and highly productive model and methodology for the study of dynamic structure of power in contemporary nations. He defines "power domain" as

... any arrangement of units wherein two or more units have unequal control over each other's environment. Wherever there is a distinctive difference in the relative power exercised by two units with respect to each other, there is a domain, and the two units pertain to different levels of articulation. Units in confrontation at one level will usually pertain to distinct domains. (Adams 1970, p. 56).

Regarding the expanding infrastructure itself, a bit more needs to be said. The Puyo–Napo–Tena Road has moved to Cotundo east of Tena, and the Papallacta–Baeza Road (from the Sierra toward the Oriente) opened in 1971. The Baeza–Cotundo section is underway. The oil pipeline constructed by Texaco–Gulf in late spring, 1972, runs from just south of Esmeraldas up the western Cordillera and moves from just south of Quito to Papallacta and follows the Papallacta–Baeza Road. It swings north from Baeza following the Quijos River and Coca River northeast to the Agua Rico River and then due east to Santa Cecilia and south to Coca. The Coca–Santa Cecilia section is completed, with access road, and oil is now being pumped for foreign consumption. The construction of this roadway virtually obliterated the Cofán, Secoya, and Siona Indians in this area (see Robinson 1971).

REFUGE, STRATEGY, AND ETHNIC DISENFRANCHISEMENT

In the area around Puyo the infrastructure expansion is taking place in large part by foot and by plane. From a small airport at Shell Mera, which used to see a maximum of two flights a week, there were over 100 per day until around February, 1973. Most of these fly cargo to the oil camps, but many flights fly colonists and food for colonists. Neither the Jívaro nor the Quechua of this zone intend to let *blancos* invade their territory or take over their land. But they are perfectly willing to exchange usufructory rights to land on a temporary basis for cash that will allow them to expand their own territories. Quechua and Jívaro, as well as *colonos,* want to be near the loci of national interaction — the airports, the proposed roadways, and the basic walking trails. Because the terrain along the Pastaza and Bobonaza is very rugged, it is not clear that there will be roadways in the foreseeable future, though many are on the planning boards. This means that the Indians have a temporary refuge area from Puyo due east, even though the Puyo area is itself the most developed in the current Oriente.

But this refuge area will not last for long. Recently an airport has been opened at Canelos, and Montalvo appears to be the central Oriente analog to Santa Cecilia in the north. The Canelos Quechua are increasingly hemmed in, and maximal clan segments and *purina* treks are cut in their fringe areas by *blanco* penetration settlements. Their rational, firm desire, to participate in the expanding Ecuadorian economy results in dynamic adaptive strategies which are contingent on national acceptance for success. Practically, I think, they must be "allowed" to continue their legal *comuna* formation, while at the same time fully participating in *colono* expansion.

This mixed strategy, which insists on both boundary establishment and land acquisition, also demands a duality of ethnicity — Indian and bicultural. The former stresses communal ownership of property and the latter individualism. Such a mixing of survival requirements and their strategic presentation to representatives of different national bureaucracies may seem paradoxical, but from the Quechua perspective it is the only way to avoid being further hemmed in and bounded by "protective" measures which establish rigid *comuna* boundaries. The national concept of *comuna Indígena* suggests a reservation complex governed from afar as a total institution. It is supposed to be locally maintained by internal primitive democracy through total agreement by all indigenous members, themselves ideally living in blissful, child–like ignorance of their treacherous external social environment. Since, of course, no such group of Indians exists on or off any *comuna,* it is easy for developers and those seeking patronage roles to decide that the Indians are too disorganized to maintain "their" *comuna* structure and to use such a rationale to take an even heavier hand in rigidifying Indian territorial boundaries.[6]

The national concept might even now be transformed to reflect the Lowland Quechua notion of *comuna* as a corporate *holding company*. By this perspective the corporation allows for the carrying out of maximal clan subsistence pursuits, while at the same time allowing people variously to employ their individually and familistically held land and social "stock" to give backbone to expansionist, colonizing functions of their own, eventually increasing the assets of the *comuna*–holding corporation. I frankly doubt that Ecuadorian non–Indians will allow this to happen. They will probably continually seek to contain indigenous expansion. Indians themselves will probably continue to attempt to use the *comuna* corporation established through *blanco* containment strategies to break out, economically, politically, socially, and symbolically, unless all their energies are taken up in simply protecting their *comunas* from very real *blanco* invasion.

The well–known international process of Indian disenfranchisement and exploitation, as a complement to ethnic annihilation, rushes on in the Ecuadorian Oriente. The fixing of blame on the disenfranchised by the invocation of an "Indian problem" exacerbates Lowland Quechua territorial consolidation and leads to heightened ethnic awareness, to *blanco* discrimination against Indians, and to *blanco* patronage of those people who are socially and politically disenfranchised.

A pamphlet on Ecuadorian ethnocide (Robinson 1971) is receiving some justifiable attention in Latin America. The very real annihilation of surviving native groups in countries such as Ecuador cannot pass without such attention, concern, and hopefully remedial action. The focus here of my own preliminary report on Jungle Quechua ethnicity seeks to anticipate the complementary problem of total disenfranchisement and structural confinement of the survivors of national ethnocide.

---

[6] One floundering United States Peace Corps project recently gave "motivational training" to a valiant group of *comuneros* fighting for their very lives to hold their territorial boundaries against a massive onslaught of territory-hungry land-grabbers. At the same time, the Peace Corps saviors helped land-grabbers from the highlands to formalize their land claims on institutionalized Indian territory and even offered courses in new agricultural skills to the exploiters. The rationale behind the motivational training was that the Indians had not yet learned to live "communally" on their *comuna*!

POSTSCRIPT, AUGUST, 1973

From our work over the past year, I see the following as unfolding. As the pressures from the militaristic Ecuadorian government, Gobierno Nacionalista Revolucionario del Ecuador, working with the ideology of a "political culture *(cultura politica)*," increase on the Canelos Quechua, these valiant people seek more and more ways to adapt their lifeways to new exigencies in their environment. At one level, they enter a domain of rapid change, but at another they intensify traditional beliefs and practices which give the only meaning possible in a biosphere experiencing chaotic stimuli. As national planners observe the rapid change they assume that the Canelos Quechua are plunging toward *mestizo*-ship in the political culture. But the Indians are increasingly expanding their self–identification system at one level, and becoming more and more "Indian conscious" at another level.

It is apparent to any Ecuadorian or foreign planner, evaluator, or administrator that the Canelos Quechua have a dynamic set of lifeways which is puzzlingly nonnational. But because these people have fewer and fewer overt signs of stereotypic Indianness (they wear clothes, eschew face painting and feather wearing in the presence of *mestizos,* and speak a language which many Ecuadorians understand), differences are attributed not to cultural continuity but to disorganization resulting from rapid change. Our posit that people who survive, expand their population, and consolidate their social system in the face of chaos have a clear, nonanarchistic, social structure is generally dismissed, perhaps because it is too destructive of national and international ideology aimed at simplistic models of how the poor should behave.

I think the following two complementary positions regarding jungle peoples are the only allowable ones in Ecuador today: (1) We must mourn their passing, make great noises about ethnocide, condemning those who destroy indigenous peoples, and do much self-searching to see if, somehow, we are all guilty of the destruction of native life, and (2) We must respect the *mestizo* all the more, for he is the last living embodiment of nativeness; the native has become a national with civilized *blanco* values, and in the new *blanco–mestizo* lifeway lies both the future and the past of national consolidation.

Again, the complementarity of ethnocide–mourning, plus heightened *blanco–mestizo*-ness, establishes a basis for considering the contemporary Jungle Quechua as a flagrant contradiction to national ideology. Perhaps this is why so much contempt is heaped upon these people, even by those nationals and nonnationals who cry loudly for Indian rights. I suspect that all over the world there is a complementarity in the expansion of ethnic culture and its denigration by those who seek to mourn the passing of other traditional cultures and to "help" the expanding ethnic cultures reach a new, "nondifferent," position within the nation. The problem with such help, given the rationale sketched above, is that it is probably a force equally as destructive as planned ethnocide, for it grows from the same source and serves the same national purpose.

REFERENCES

ADAMS, RICHARD N.
  1970   *Crucifixion by power: essays on Guatemalan national social structure, 1944–1966.* Austin: University of Texas Press.
BANTON, MICHAEL
  1967   *Race relations.* New York: Basic Books.
BROMLEY, RAYMOND J.
  i.p.   Agricultural colonization in the upper Amazon basin: the impact of oil discoveries. *Tijdschrift voor Economische en Sociale Geografia.*
BURBANO MARTÍNEZ, HÉCTOR, LUIS ANTONIO RIVADENEIRA, JULIO MONTALVO MONTENEGRO
  1964   "El problema de las poblaciones Indígenas selváticas del Ecuador." Paper presented at the Quinto Congreso Indigenista Interamericano, Quito, Ecuador, October, 1964.
BURGOS, HUGO
  1970   *Relaciones interétnicas en Ríobamba.* Instituto Indigenista Interamericano Ediciones Especiales 55. Mexico.
CARNEIRO, ROBERT L.
  1970   A theory of the origin of the state. *Science* (August 28): 733–738.
CASAGRANDE, JOSEPH B., STEPHEN I. THOMPSON, PHILIP D. YOUNG
  1964   "Colonization as a research frontier: the Ecuadorian case," in *Process and pattern in culture: essays in honor of Julian Steward.* Chicago: Aldine.
COLBY, BENJAMIN, PIERRE VAN DEN BERGHE
  1969   *Ixil country.* Berkeley: University of California Press.
EICHLER, ARTURO
  1970   *Snow peaks and jungles.* New York: Crowell. (Reprint of 1955 edition with new introduction by Alfredô Pareja Diezcanseco.)
ERASMUS, CHARLES J.
  1961   *Man takes control: cultural development and American aid.* Minneapolis: University of Minnesota Press.

FERDON, EDWIN N., JR.

1950 *Studies in Ecuadorian geography*. Monographs of the School of American Research 15. Santa Fe.

FRIED, MORTON

1967 *The evolution of political society: an essay in political anthropology*. New York: Random House.

GILLETTE, CYNTHIA

1970 "Problems of colonization in the Ecuadorian Oriente." Unpublished M.A. thesis, Washington University, St. Louis.

HARNER, MICHAEL J.

1972 *The Jívaro: people of the sacred waterfalls*. Garden City: Doubleday, Natural History Press.

HEGEN, EDMUND E.

1966 *Highways into the upper Amazon basin: pioneer lands in southern Colombia, Ecuador, and northern Peru*. Center for Latin American Studies Monograph 2. Gainesville: University of Florida Press.

JARAMILLO ALVARADO, PÍO

1936 *Tierras del Oriente*. Quito: Imprenta Nacionales.

MITCHELL, J. CLYDE

1966 "Theoretical orientations in African urban studies," in *The social anthropology of complex societies*. Edited by Michael Banton. New York: Praeger.

OBEREM, UDO

1971 *Los Quijos*. Memorias de Departamento de Antropología y Etnología de América. Madrid.

ORR, CAROLYN, BETSY WRISLEY

1965 *Vocabulario Quichua del Oriente del Ecuador*. Mexico: Instituto Lingüístico de Verano.

PAREJA DIEZCANSECO, ALFREDO

1970 "Introduction," in *Snow peaks and jungles*. By Arturo Eichler. New York: Crowell.

PEÑAHERRERA DE COSTALES, PIEDAD, ALFREDO COSTALES SAMANIEGO

1961 Llacta runa. *Llacta* 12. Quito.

1962 Comunas juridicamente organizadas. *Llacta* 15. Quito.

PEÑAHERRERA DE COSTALES, PIEDAD, ALFREDO COSTALES SAMANIEGO, *et al.*

1969 *Los Quichuas del Coca y el Napo*. Escuela de Sociología de la Universidad Central, Serie de Documentos y Estudios Sociales 1. Quito.

PORRAS G., P. PEDRO I.

1961 *Contribución al estudio de la arqueología e historia de los valles Quijos y Misaguallí (Alto Napo) en la región oriental del Ecuador, S. A.* Quito: Editora Fenix.

ROBINSON, SCOTT S.

1971 *El etnocidio Ecuatoriano*. Mexico: Universidad Iberoamericana.

ROBINSON, SCOTT S., MICHAEL SCOTT

1971 *Sky Chief*. Thirty-minute color documentary film.

SCHEFFLER, HAROLD W., FLOYD G. LOUNSBURY

1971 *A study in structural semantics: the Siriono kinship system*. Englewood Cliffs: Prentice-Hall.

SOUTHALL, AIDAN
1961   "Introductory summary," in *Social change in modern Africa.*
        Edited by Aidan Southall, 1–82. London: Oxford University Press
        (for the International African Institute).
STEWARD, JULIAN H.
1948   "Tribes of the Montaña: an introduction," in *Handbook of South
        American Indians,* volume three: *The tropical forest tribes.* Edited
        by Julian H. Steward, 507–534. Smithsonian Institution Bureau of
        American Ethnology Bulletin 143. Washington, D.C.
STEWARD, JULIAN H., ALFRED MÉTRAUX
1948   "Tribes of the Peruvian and Ecuadorian Montaña" (sections en-
        titled "The Jívaro," "Zaparoan Tribes," and "The Quijo"), in
        Handbook of South American Indians, volume three: *The tropical
        forest tribes.* Edited by Julian H. Steward, 617–656. Smithsonian
        Institution Bureau of American Ethnology Bulletin 143. Washing-
        ton, D.C.
TESSMANN, GÜNTER
1930   *Die Indianer Nordost-Perus: grundlegende Forschungen für eine
        systematische Kulturkunde.* Hamburg: Cram, De Gruyter.
WHITTEN, NORMAN E., JR.
1965   *Class, kinship, and power in an Ecuadorian town: the Negroes of
        San Lorenzo.* Stanford: Stanford University Press.
1968   Personal networks and musical contexts in the Pacific Lowlands
        of Ecuador and Colombia. *Man: Journal of the Royal Anthro-
        pological Institute* 3(1):50–63.
1969a   Strategies of adaptive mobility in the Colombian-Ecuadorian lit-
        toral. *American Anthropologist* 71(2):228–242.
1969b   The ecology of race relations in northwest Ecuador. *Journal de
        la Société des Americanístes* 54:223–235.
1974   *Black frontiersmen: a South American case.* Cambridge: Schenk-
        man.
WHITTEN, NORMAN E., JR., JOHN F. SZWED, editors
1970   *Afro-American anthropology: contemporary perspectives.* New
        York: Free Press, Macmillan.
WHITTEN, NORMAN E., JR., ALVIN W. WOLFE
1972   "Network analysis," in *Handbook of social and cultural anthro-
        pology.* Edited by John J. Honigmann. Chicago: Rand McNally.
WOLFE, ALVIN W.
1963   The African mineral industry: evolution of a supranational level
        of integration. *Social Problems* 11(2):153–163.

Comments

CONSTANCE R. SUTTON

The six articles in this section address themselves to the forms of ethnic or racial identity that arise as a consequence of migration. The migrations referred to have in most cases taken place since the end of World War II and are voluntary migrations of peoples from less-developed countries to urban industrial centers. Except for the discussion of Sephardic and Oriental Jews who sought political refuge in Israel, the articles deal with cross-national labor migrations motivated mainly by the migrants' search for better economic opportunities. Though strictly speaking the case of the Winnebago and Pueblo Indians does not conform to the definition of a cross-national migration, the special status of American Indians in the United States makes it possible to discuss them in this category.

It is important to indicate from the outset both the conditions of migration and the type of society the migrants enter, for they are crucial determinants of the status, career, and forms of identity immigrant groups develop (Richmond 1969; Schermerhorn 1970). The comparative field covered by the articles is further delimited by the focus on low-status ethnic or racial minorities; none of the articles discusses groups that have relatively privileged social positions or control over valued economic or social resources. Moreover, what is being examined here is the phenomenon of urban ethnicity, the identities which result from group interactions that occur in urban contexts (see Cohen 1974).

Anthropological interest in migration and ethnicity as two distinct fields of inquiry is relatively recent. These two phenomena, though often

My thanks to Susan R. Makiesky for all her very helpful comments.

interlinked, have been approached with conceptual frameworks that emphasize different issues. There are few theoretical formulations that attempt to unite the two phenomena within a single framework. At present the literature consists of studies of limited comparative scope and articles that list and rank variables deemed relevant.[1]

The conceptual frameworks for comparative analysis of ethnic and racial groupings are only slightly more advanced, though recent efforts in this direction are promising (see, for example, Barth 1969; Cohen 1974; Despres 1975; DeVos 1972; Spicer 1971). The concept of ethnicity itself remains fluid and multilayered in meaning and reference. Some anthropologists share with political scientists an emphasis on the instrumental aspects of ethnicity as a strategy of political mobilization or a means of solving problems of group organization and group interest. Others concern themselves with its implications as a social identity determining intra- and intergroup interactions – an identity that competes with other status claims in various interactional settings. Still others see ethnicity as a symbolic system supplying a world view and turn to studying the cultural constructs that form the content of an ethnic identity. While all of these approaches have contributed to our general understanding, their integration is something still to be achieved.

The articles in this section restrict their concern to the transfer and survival of ethnic and racial identities and the generation of new identities. Though most migrant groups discussed work as unskilled, semi-skilled, and sometimes skilled laborers in urban industrial centers, they perceive their experiences in ethnic and racial rather than class terms. While the reasons for this are not extensively discussed, there is indirect evidence suggesting why this is the case. For migrants, the experience of discrimination is not confined to exploitation at the workplace, but is a more total experience related to their second-class civil-political status and/or their limited access to the public resources of the wider society, including its public services and the protection it offers its citizens of similar socio-economic status. And while it is the host society's immigration and labor recruitment policies that produce these problems, it is often from members of the host country's working class that migrants experience the most direct expressions of hostility. Moreover, immigrants are frequently exposed to the host population's ridicule or contempt for their cultural ways, and this tends to threaten their sense of social

---

[1]   Sterling's fairly extensive outline includes such variables as the nature of the host society, geopolitical relations between the sending and receiving societies, the immigrants, their skills, perceptions, goals, patterns of settlement, and the social ties immigrants develop in the host society and maintain with the home society (Sterling 1970).

identity. Thus it is not surprising that immigrants and their descendants express their grievances in ethnic or racial terms. It is for them a more encompassing reality than class and refers to a more total group identity. This is an issue which deserves more attention than I can give it in this brief review. But like earlier discussions of objective conditions and class consciousness, ethnic and racial identities – the circumstances in which they operate and the forms they take – pose again the theoretical issue of the relationship between objective conditions, social experiences, and group consciousness.

I find that the best approach for discussing the articles in this section in more detail is to consider the analytic perspectives they adopt. I see them exhibiting two forms of analysis: a micro-sociological approach, focusing on migration processes and the formation of immigrant communities; and a macro-sociological approach, emphasizing the societal structure and the position of ethnic and racial groupings within it. The first three articles by the Buechlers, Hodge, and Midgett use the micro-sociological perspective; the works by Green and Heller represent the macrosociological perspective, and the final study by Sutton and Makiesky draws on both approaches.

The study by the Buechlers of Spanish Galician migrants to Switzerland begins by distinguishing the cultural from the social aspects of identity, and, like all contemporary work, focuses mainly on the latter – the continuity of social identity, not cultural tradition. The Buechlers discuss the conditions that make for a continuity in interpersonal ties among Galician immigrants in Switzerland and between the migrants and those who remain back home. They see this as the main determinant of a continuity in ethnic identity. Ties to those in the home community take the form of social and economic exchanges encouraged by complementary needs and by the reluctance of immigrants to burn their bridges when their status in the host country remains uncertain. The Buechlers describe the pattern of chain migration that leads to the creation of ethnic communities which cushion the migrants' adaptation to a new environment. Their account of these processes will be familiar to those acquainted with the literature on European immigrant groups in the United States, although unlike the Galicians, the European immigrants were unable to easily sustain close interpersonal links with those who remained behind.

Undoubtedly, maintaining interpersonal links with members of the sending society is an important, though not necessary, factor in the persistence of ethnicity. So too, as the Buechlers note, is isolation from the host population, whether inflicted or voluntary, and the related exclusion from access to the economic resources and centers of power in the society. These matters take on greater importance for second and third generation immigrants and in turn raise even more interesting questions concerning persistence as well as change in identity and in its meaningfulness. The Buechlers tell us that it is difficult to discern the limits to the meaningfulness of Galician ethnic identity, and that it functions more in expressive than instrumental domains. We are also told that Galician migrants express concern about losing their cultural identity and that the Swiss are hostile to the idea of absorbing immigrants into the mainstream of their life. Nevertheless, the frequency with which Galicians marry members of the host society in the second generation is one indication that barriers to assimilation may not be too high. It would, however, have been helpful if the Buechlers had been able to tell us more about the second and third generation of migrants (of which there may be few at this time). And to round out the picture more fully and make it possible to engage in comparative analysis, we would want to know more about the structure of the host society, its policies toward immigrants, the extent of cultural similarities between host and sending societies, and their geopolitical ties.

Hodge likewise focuses on migration and the migrant, but he narrows his concern to the ability of American Indian migrants to exercise control over the nature and content of their identity and relates this to the structure of the sending group. He posits that loosely structured, open communities allow migrants to engage in situational selection of cultural elements and that this is conducive to a heightened ethnic identity. In contrast, tightly structured, closed communities present the migrant with a conflict of loyalties that often results in personal breakdown. In support of his thesis, Hodge presents two case studies, one of a Winnebago man who achieved a heightened sense of Indianness while pursuing his livelihood in the wider white society and making periodic return visits to his native Winnebago community, which is open and loosely structured. The other case study deals with a family from the tightly structured Bear Pueblo, whose migration brought about a muting or dislocation of identity. While background factors surely play a role in creating either a comfortable biculturalism or a conflict of loyalties, we need much more data before we can decide the precise effect of the specific variables to which Hodge refers; we also need to know how they operate in conjunction with other factors known to influence identity.

Midgett's work deals with a group of West Indian migrants to London and, like the Buechlers, he describes the processes of migrant community formation that result from chain migrations and ethnic clustering. However, he goes beyond analyzing the transfer and persistence of ethnic identity and presents an extensive and sophisticated account of the increasingly inclusive categories of ethnic self-identity that immigrants use and the situationally defined contexts that evoke expression of these different levels of identity. Midgett also tells us what cultural traits, events, and organizational forms are associated with each level. Furthermore, he introduces the important distinction between an ethnic self-identity and an imposed identity such as "West Indian," which Midgett claims is a census category and is seen in racial not cultural terms.

Midgett's article takes up the question of identity changes over time. He points out that for second generation West Indians in London, the village and island identities become meaningless and are replaced by a black identity which is imbued with positive meaning and thus challenges the racist assumptions of British society. Midgett notes the analogs with the United States Black Power movement and mentions the potential for the development of a "third world" consciousness. He sees these identity changes as a response to the treatment that Commonwealth immigrants receive in England and to their placement in a category that carries the stigma of their colonized status (see Katznelson 1973). By introducing these factors, Midgett moves toward a more explicit consideration of the role of the host society in determining ethnic and racial identities. A key question is how the policies of the host society combine with the migrants' background to influence the direction and content of second generation identity changes. A comparison of identity changes among Galicians in Switzerland with those described for West Indians in England would illuminate this point. Both countries pursue restrictive immigration policies but Galicians, unlike West Indians, do not have a history of being colonized by the host society. This colonial factor may play a large role in determining the ultimate status the immigrants will occupy in the host society and whether they will be seen as an ethnic or racial group, a point to which I shall return later.

In the articles by Green and Heller there is a sharp change in the focus of analysis. They replace the previous emphasis on migration processes and the formation of immigrant communities and identities with a macro-sociological perspective in which the host society becomes the primary unit of analysis. In this approach, the nature of group identity is determined mainly by the host society, its structures of domination, its social categories and ideology, its immigration policies, and its general handling of ethnic and racial diversity. Though the articles touch on only a few of these aspects, it is worth noting that this perspective shifts attention away from the SELF-DEFINING nature of group identity emphasized in articles that pursued a migrant perspective. Instead there is a stress on the identities ASSIGNED to immigrants by others. Interestingly enough, the host society's power to impose ethnic identities can operate to either support or deny the relevance of ethnicity. As Heller indicates, official policy in Israel attempts to mute the significance of ethnic differentiation in contrast to the way the United States and the Netherlands Antilles, as described by Green, impose an ethnic or racial identity on black foreigners.

The question of whether an identity is imposed or self-defined is related to the distinction between a racial and an ethnic identity. The difference between racial and ethnic identities has not received much attention from scholars, who instead have been preoccupied with comparing the consequences of cleavages based on race and ethnicity to those based on class (see Kuper and Smith 1969; Rex 1973; Zubaida 1970). The political consequences of this difference have been explored in terms of the conditions that foster an ethnic or racial consciousness in contrast to a class consciousness. Kuper (1971) spells out how these two phenomena differ in their social roots, their responsiveness to political appeals, and their aims.

That ethnic and racial groupings arise from different historical processes is a fact that has been obscured by merging them and discussing them as a whole.[2] Even a brief review of the history of domination and exploitation that produced these two groupings suggests that they will differ in their political strategies and group consciousness. Racial ascription, unlike ethnic ascription, is originally imposed on a population by a dominant group, usually in a colonial context. Its primary symbolic markers are phenotypical and characterological traits, not cultural heritage, and the traits selected are ones which contrast with those the dominant group values and believes it possesses. Ethnic ascription, on the other hand, is based on real or putative ancestry that predates the group's existence in the society into which it is now incorporated and hence gives salience to a cultural past independent of the group's current position. Thus an ethnic identity draws on selected elements of a cultural heritage to symbolize group distinctiveness, and these elements are not necessarily viewed by the group or outsiders as being in opposition to the culture of the dominant group. An ethnic identity, then, is a more self-deffining identity, and

---

[2]   Blauner's analysis of the difference between colonized and immigrant ethnic minorities is the only extensive treatment known to me of the difference between ethnic identities (Blauner 1972). In an article discussing the identities of Haitians, Puerto Ricans, French-speaking and English-speaking West Indian immigrants, I refer to the ambiguous position of some Caribbean groups in the host society's system of ethnic and racial categorization (Sutton 1973).

this in itself reflects an aspect of the group's relationship to the wider polity. If these distinctions are valid, they suggest that racially-based political demands and a racial consciousness will constitute a more direct challenge or threat to the dominant group – to both its culture and its forms of political control – than similar assertions by ethnic groups.

It is also true that ethnic and racial identities often coexist within a single group. In the articles by Midgett and by Sutton and Makiesky, this is shown to be the case for West Indian migrants in England and the United States. It is the main topic of Green's study, which compares the relative salience of ethnic and racial identities in Houston, Texas, and in the Netherlands Antillean islands of Aruba and Curaçao. She found the status assigned to black foreigners in these three areas was different. In the United States they were ranked higher than black Americans by white Americans and were defined mainly by ethnic rather than racial criteria; whereas in Aruba and Curaçao they were ranked lower than islanders, and ethnic traits rather than racial traits were more frequently mentioned as a rationalization for excluding them from the more intimate social life of the islanders.

In the United States, the institutionalized racial division between black and white produces its own complex but predictable ironies, as Green notes. For example, although the imposed racial status of French Creole black Americans supersedes their ethnic status, their distinct ethnic traits influence their relations with other blacks and with whites. The same ethnic traits evoke favorable responses from white Americans and unfavorable ones from other black Americans. Green's article highlights the complex interweaving of racial, ethnic, and socio-economic factors in the social structures and social categories produced by colonialism, slavery, and the plantation system.

A focus on the host society also directs attention to issues of political and economic inequality which are prominent in Heller's analysis of ethnic differentiation and stratification in Israel. Unlike the New World societies Green discusses, Israel avoids assigning distinct ethnic identities to Jewish groups of diverse cultural backgrounds and instead treats their differences and their status as a function of their social class position. This policy stems from Israel's commitment to the ideal of assimilating its diverse immigrant groups into a society based on a single overriding Jewish identity. But for Sephardic and Oriental Jews who constitute over half the post-independence immigrant population and who find themselves in subordinate positions economically, politically, and culturally, ethnicity is experienced as an important factor in their lives. This ethnic inequality created what Heller refers to as an ethnic/class consciousness, expressed in charges of ethnic discrimination and, more dramatically, in the short-lived Pantherim Shehorim movement.

Lipset (1974) has pointed to parallels between Israel and the United States, each with an egalitarian ideology and an assimilationist approach to white immigrants. Whether Israel's ideology and policies will have the same results for Sephardic and Oriental Jews that United States policies had for white immigrants remains to be seen. But the context in which this Israeli immigrant absorption policy is occurring suggests another and less comfortable analog, which Lipset also notes. This concerns Israel's treatment of its Arab population, which is, in some ways, comparable to the treatment of black Americans. It is leading Israel to become, like the United States, a racist society.

One drawback of the host society perspective is that it can overemphasize the role of the wider society in evoking ethnicity. This political (strucral) approach to ethnicity deflects attention from its cultural dimensions and its role in providing meaningful interpretations of social reality. It also deflects attention from ethnic and racial movements that arise as group responses to their status in society. The role that a group itself plays in defining its own identity became evident during recent years with the rise of ethnic and racial movements in both industrial and developing countries. This phenomenon, which entails collective efforts to reevaluate and redefine group identities, is directed at changing not only the personal meanings associated with an identity but also the group's status, claims and options in relation to the wider society. Thus the emergence of ethnic and racial consciousness points up the importance of the *interplay* between self-definition and definition by others in establishing group identity. To analyze this interplay it is necessary to integrate the migrant perspective with the host society perspective.

An attempt to bridge this gap between a micro- and macro- structural perspective is made in the article by Sutton and Makiesky. Like Midgett, they deal with West Indians in urban industrial centers, and like the Buechlers, they are concerned with continuing links between migrants and their home communities. Their focus, however, is not on the transfer or persistence of an ethnic identity but on the factors that have produced a major shift in the content and scale of identity, creating a new racial consciousness and political awareness among both migrants and those who remain behind. Their approach is comparative: comparing migration experiences prior to World War II with those after, and comparing the experiences of West Indians in England and in the United States, where despite differences in their treatment they are assigned the status of a racial or colonized group. In analyzing the sources and consequences of a change in consciousness, Sutton and Makiesky take into account a number of variables. Among these are: (1) the identities immigrants bring to England and the United States; (2) their perceptions and expectations with respect to each country; (3) structural differences in the ways West Indians are incorporated into the two host societies; (4) how West Indians react to their experiences in these two countries and the forms of group identity that emerge; and (5) the way the feedback of ideas fosters a new field of awareness and collective consciousness that is transnational.

In this analysis, the host-society approach helped to reveal how the group-polity relations in the host countries replicated aspects of the colonial relationship. The migrant perspective was basic for understanding the attitudes and experiences that shaped migrant reactions and for recognizing the bidirectional flow of exchanges that the migration process produced. This perspective further showed that not only had a widening in the scale of identity occurred, but that this new identity was transnational in content as well. Perhaps it foreshadows the growth of a new collective consciousness among peoples whose cross-national migrations result partly from the spread of multinational corporations. It may even be that the "reverse colonial migrations" of peoples seeking jobs and opportunities in the urban centers of industrial countries will be the seedbed from which sprout the future political challenges to multinational corporations.

From these and other studies we have learned that, contrary to earlier thinking, urban situations do not result in the demise of ethnicity. Instead ethnicity appears to be more pronounced in urban centers than in rural settings and this is true throughout the world. We are now beginning to understand that this assertion of ethnicity is a modern response to needs generated in urban contexts rather than an expression of traditionality. Though these needs vary enormously with the nature of the urban social structure and country under consideration, where ethnic and racial movements have occurred they appear to share a common trait: they are not, in the main, revitalization movements but movements with demands for the present and future. Moreover, issues of life style and culture are treated as political matters. This in itself represents a new challenge to cultural domination, which in the past has been seen as a legitimate or inevitable outcome of political and economic hegemony. And it is worth noting that this new analysis of the role of culture and identity among immigrants and their descendents is a long step away from earlier views which considered immigrants' cultures and social organizations in terms of their negative or positive effects in adjusting immigrants to the host society.

It is not possible to draw any new, large conclusions from the studies discussed here, for there is not sufficient sampling of either different migration contexts or of different structural conditions that influence the formation of identities. While the discussion touched on a number of important issues, it also highlighted certain neglected areas of research. Let me conclude by listing a few.

First, perhaps because we have been too dazzled with the notion of ethnic persistence and group boundaries, we have not given enough attention to the changes in identity that take place over time. Second, we have not taken advantage of the opportunities to apply the method of controlled comparison in our studies, comparing the same group in different countries and different groups in the same country. Third, more studies of ethnic groups that are privileged or hold interstitial positions should be undertaken and their strategies and responses should be compared to those of oppressed ethnic and racial groups. Fourth, there is need to explore how a former colonized status influences the way an immigrant group handles the issue of cultural identity and how this contrasts with the experience of non-colonized groups. Fifth, we should compare migration experiences in terms of their differential impact on women and men, examining the changes they produce in the sexual division of labor and in the relative statuses of the sexes and their social identities. Finally, we should identify the worldwide conditions that have given salience to ethnic and racial identities and prompted a growth in identity-oriented social movements.

It is safe to forecast that migration and ethnicity will continue to have an impact on the world. Cross-national labor migrations are likely to remain important, creating significant redistributions of culturally distinct groups. Ethnicity is not likely to diminish in vitality, though its forms and functions change. As anthropologists we have just begun to understand the significance of the phenomena of migration and ethnicity, and the articles here represent a contribution to what is bound to be a continuing effort.

Unfortunately, through an oversight, Whitten's article is not included in these comments — Editor.

REFERENCES

BARTH, FREDRIK
  1969   *Ethnic groups and boundaries.* Boston: Little, Brown.
BLAUNER, ROBERT
  1972   *Racial oppression in America.* New York: Harper and Row.
COHEN, ABNER, *editor*
  1974   *Urban ethnicity.* ASA Monograph 12. London: Tavistock.
DEPRES, LEO A
  1975   "Toward a theory of ethnic phenomena", in *Ethnicity and resource competitition in plural societies.* Edited by Leo A. Despres. World Anthropology. The Hague: Mouton.
DEVOS, GEORGE
  1972   Social stratification and ethnic pluralism: An overview from the perspective of psychological anthropology. *Race* (13)4:435–460.
KATZNELSON, IRA
  1973   *Black men, white cities: race, politics and migration in the United States 1900–1930 and Britain 1948–68.* London: Oxford University Press.
KUPER, LEO
  1971   Political change in plural societies: problems in racial pluralism. *International Social Science Journal* (23)4:594–607.
KUPER, LEO, M. G. SMITH, *editors*
  1969   *Pluralism in Africa.* Berkeley: University of California Press.
LIPSET, SEYMOUR M.
  1974   Education and equality: Israel and the United States compared. *Society* (11)3:56–66.
REX, JOHN
  1973   *Race, colonialism and the city.* London: Routledge and Kegan Paul.
RICHMOND, ANTHONY
  1969   "Sociology of migration in industrial and post-industrial societies," in *Migration: Social studies 2.* Press. Edited by J. A. Jackson. London: Cambridge University Press.
SCHERMERHORN, R. A.
  1970   *Comparative ethnic relations.* New York: Random House.
SPICER, E. H.
  1971   Persistent cultural systems. *Science* 19:795–800.
STERLING, PAUL
  1970   Towards humane pluralism? some problems in research and variable shuffling. *New Atlantis* (2)1:192–211.
SUTTON, CONSTANCE
  1973   "Caribbean migrants and group identity: suggestions for comparative analysis", in *Migration.* Edited by Otto Klineberg and George DeVos. UNSDRI Publication 5. Rome.
ZUBAIDA, SAMI, *editor*
  1970   *Race and racialism.* London: Tavistock.

PART TWO

Inequality, Power, and Development

Perceptions of Class and Social Inequality among the Yoruba of Western Nigeria

PETER C. LLOYD

With monotonous regularity and uniformity, the predicament of Third World countries is reiterated: their economies are almost stagnant with very little development in the "traditional" rural sector and a more rapidly expanding, but yet small, industrial sector providing too few jobs for the vast numbers of urban migrants .The differences in wealth between rich and poor remain as great as ever. In spite of the recent oil boom, these structures are generally applicable to Nigeria – or in particular to the Yoruba peoples in the southwest.

Though varying widely from year to year with changes in the producer prices and in yields, the real income of the cocoa farmers has not altered substantially in the past two decades. Higher yields due to pest control have been balanced by the cost of pesticides. Furthermore, the profits from cocoa accumulated by the bigger farmers and especially by the produce buyers and lorry drivers seem not to be spent on flamboyant houses and conspicuous consumption in the rural area but are invested in education or in city property. Approximately one-third of the total receipts from cocoa have, in the same period, been withheld from the farmers by the Marketing Board and used to finance the development of manufacturing industry and its necessary infrastructure; very little has been spent in the rural area. The real wages of the workers, too, have not risen substantially. The Abedbo commission, set up to review the wage and salary structure of the country, finally in 1971 recommended

This article is based upon my experience in Nigeria since 1949 but it relies specifically on research carried out in 1968 financed by the Nuffield Trust and in 1969–72 financed by the Social Science Research Council.

not only an increase of £36 a year for all those earning less than £200 a year but also an increase of £300 for those earning between £2,500 and £3,000. The gap between rich and poor was largely preserved; furthermore the disproportionate increase of the wages of the lowest paid workers was obliterated by the rapidly rising prices of basic foodstuffs following the Civil War – by 40 percent in the year 1970–1971 alone.

Education is increasingly a prerequisite for jobs in the "modern" sector. The Western Region government established free primary education in 1956 and most boys (and perhaps 80 percent of girls) do start in the lowest classes. There is, however, a dropout rate of over 50 percent in the six years of primary schooling as parents are reluctant to pay the costs – in books, uniforms, etc. – and deprive themselves of the potential income of the dull scholar who would seem to have little chance of passing the school-leaving certificate or of getting a well-paid job Secondary education is not free – the fees for tuition and boarding equal the year's income of most unskilled laborers. Although the universities, too, are heavily subsidized by the government, the fees charged put them beyond the reach of many bright youths. For although the number of scholarships has risen, the proportion of places held by scholarship holders has fallen – at Ibadan University for instance from almost 100 percent in the early 1950's to 40 percent a decade or so later. Migration to the cities continues apace as the rural youth sees no future in farming, finds it difficult to establish himself as a trader or craftsman owing to lack of initial capital or intense competition, or is unable to find a post requiring the level of education which he has successfully attained. Yet the number of wage-paid jobs in the cities increases but slowly as the expansion of government services depends largely on the ability to raise taxes and as most industrial development is in capital-intensive enterprises (the lucky workers being relatively well paid).

While stagnation and inflation cause increasing hardship among the poor, the elite continue to live in conspicuous affluence. Those dependent – as most were in the 1950's – upon their salaries, were hit in the 1960's by the absence of any increase in salary scales, though individually most of them benefited from annual increments and promotion. However, those near the top have used the size and security of their income and the power and influence inherent in their offices to invest substantially in property and business. A distinct cleavage is emerging within the western educated elite between those civil servants and professionals who live off their salaries and those with secondary sources of income. Both groups strive to educate their children well so that they in turn will enjoy the privileged status; but it is clear that the children of the rich predominate in the older and more prestigious secondary schools, while those of the poor seek entry, if at all, to the schools of inferior scholastic reputation.

Faced with this picture, as he sees it, of growing poverty and unemployment at one end of the social scale and elite entrenchment at the other, the Western observer senses that the tensions engendered ought soon to reach breaking point. Yet events fail his predictions. "Liberal" scholars sitting in their university offices, focus their studies on the frustration of the urban unemployed. Yet social anthropologists who have lived in the slums of Ibadan and Lagos fail to find large bodies of unemployed; their impression is of the prevalent dynamism and hope in the communities studied. "Radical" scholars are apt to define the urban migrants as a working class or proletariat and to imply that class consciousness will develop and that the urban worker will assume his revolutionary role in society. Yet on-the-spot observers report the virtual absence of any manifest class ideology. This is not to deny the absence of all forms of social protest. During the past decade, Western Nigeria has experienced the highway robbery and lawlessness of late 1965 which in part precipitated the military coup, widespread industrial strikes in 1964 and 1970, and the Agbekoya farmers' uprising in 1968–1970. Yet all of these fall far short of revolutionary movements.

In most of these attempts to analyze Yoruba society, the Western external observer has used his own concepts of class, unemployment, poverty and the like. Admittedly he has often qualified their use. The factory worker, in Lagos for instance, is in the same economic position as his counterpart in industrial Western society; but he is a recent immigrant to the city and not fully committed to industrial employment; again the proportion of industrial workers in the city's population is very small and they cannot be expected to influence greatly the attitudes of the masses. Our task – and it is one that is particularly appropriate for a social anthropologist – is to ask how the Yoruba urban worker sees the structure of social inequality in his society; and in particular to seek "closure" attributed to poverty and the high costs of education.

YORUBA PERCEPTIONS: ORIGINS

The image which a Yoruba man holds of the structure of his society derives from three principal sources: the concepts, and propositions relating them, which were current in traditional rural society and which (as a recent migrant to the town) he learned in his youth; his own experiences and those of his peers, articulated in interaction with these peers; the ideology dominant in the society and propagated by those controlling the means of communication. Traditional Yoruba society – as it actually existed in the past, as it is believed by present-day Yoruba to have existed, and as it continues to exist in many sectors – was egalitarian in the sense that though very great differences in wealth and power existed, privileged positions were generally open to all, and it was far from unusual for a man to rise to prominence from a humble home.

Kingship, in the several Yoruba states, was indeed hereditary; an eligible candidate had to be born to a reigning *oba*, though a rotation of the title through the constituent segments of the royal lineage was usual.[1] But the Yoruba *oba* was a sacred ruler, heavily dependent in the secular aspects of government upon his councils of chiefs. These men were appointed in one of two ways: in some kingdoms the senior titles were held corporately by the descent groups, the chief being selected by, and from among, members of the group with the proviso that the title should rotate between the segments – a proviso which ensured that most men were eligible candidates at some point in their adult lives. Wealth and a strong personal following within the descent group were prerequisites for success; a son of a previous (but not the recently deceased) chief often had a better chance than others, but chiefs were strongly poly-gamous and many men thus shared this attribute. In other kingdoms men passed upwards through a series of title grades, vacancies in a grade being filled by election by the existing members; again, the successful entrant needed wealth and popularity. While chiefs were rich men, they were also seen as the apices of a system of redistribution whereby tribute was converted into assistance.

In a society in which land was held corporately by descent groups or a village community (giving each individual member a right to cultivate as much as he was able but retaining to the group all rights over the alloca-tion of unused land) and in which farming tools – hoe and cutlass – were of the simplest kind, wealth from farming depended upon the access to and control of labor. Basically a man depended upon his own efforts and skills. A surplus might be invested in wives who, if he were lucky, would bear him many sons whose labor he would exploit from their adolescence to marriage. Hiring of labor was almost unknown, for no man was landless, but a wealthy man could summon work parties at the optimal times while the chief could call for labor to cultivate the farms attached to his title.

[1]   Descriptions of Yoruba tradition society are given in Lloyd (1965, 1962).

The wealthiest men in traditional society (save the most powerful chiefs) were usually the traders. But trade in most commodities was highly competitive and the profit margins small; the rich trader owed his success (or was seen to owe it) to his skills in manipulating the markets, his acumen in giving or withholding credit and his ability to cope mentally with all the operations involved in the large turnover of goods – itself a direct correlate of his success. The successful trader usually had humble origins; at least these are now stressed. But his wealth did not outlive him; it reached its peak in his forties and thereafter declined with his increasing senility; business activity lapsed if he took a chieftaincy title; upon his death his estate, such as remained, was subdivided equally into as many parts as he had wives with issue and thence between the children, so that none received a sizable sum.

Strong Yoruba belief in "destiny" did not preclude hopes that a man might improve upon his predetermined fate by upholding the norms of his society and duly propitiating deities, nor imply that one could not conversely worsen one's fate. A man's inexplicable rise to prominence might be attributed to his manipulation of supernatural powers; the unsuccessful man might ascribe his poverty to the witchcraft of others, though his fellows might see a ready explanation in his laziness or ineptitude. In Western society in the past two centuries we have tended to see inequality as socially determined and thus have sought to regain or restore natural equality. The Yoruba, in contrast, though understandably in view of the structure of their society, saw human inequality as natural, often using the analogy of the fingers of the hand. Man is born unequal and it is up to everyone to exploit what talents and advantages he has. In fact, while the Yoruba have a concept of equal – in terms of measurement – which is synonymous with our own, the ideas implicit in our own concept of social inequality are very difficult to translate into Yoruba. If asked to describe his "equals," the Yoruba man most often cites his age mates; for age is a most fundamental mode of ranking onto which a ranking by wealth or titled office are superimposed.

The traditional view of the open society has been reinforced during the present century. As has often been described, those now at the top of Yoruba society have come from the widest range of social backgrounds. Chiefs and wealthy men had the resources to send their children to school, but they too had most to fear and lose if these children, at the instigation of highly evangelical teachers, flouted local norms. Conversely those of low status saw in schooling a chance for their children to achieve a level of success that traditional society might deny them. The pattern is now changing but the average man obviously relies most on his own experiences and least on the inferences to be drawn from contemporary statistical data; furthermore while he knows that some of his own village age mates have done conspicuously well, he does not have access to the houses of the modern affluent city elite, where he would see that all the children are being groomed for positions of power and wealth in society and that the traditional attitude – that rewards are attributed to genius which is randomly distributed – no longer prevails. Similarly, the average man sees today that there are far more secondary schools (and indeed services of all kinds) than in his own youth; the chances of his own children attaining these schools are thus higher. What he does not clearly recognize is the disparity in the chances of his own children of receiving secondary education, measured against those of the elite; though he is of course quite aware of his inability to find the necessary fees.

Finally, Nigeria's political leaders have never, for obvious reasons of ethnic diversity, promoted a distinct ideology in the manner of Nkrumah in neighboring Ghana. There has been little radical criticism of the existing structure of society. In the late 1950's, the Yoruba-dominated Action Group extolled "democratic socialism" but this seemed to imply little more than gradualism and increasing social benefits. In his recent writing, Chief Awolowo has moved to a more radical condemnation of exploitation but at a level verging on mysticism; he gives no suggestion as to which among the exploiting groups are to be expropriated. Whether or not he is currently advocating cooperative farming, and while he did ostensibly support the Agbekoya, his own activities as a successful lawyer and those of his wife – a very wealthy trader – seem to belie any argument for the radical transformation of society. The ideologies fostered by the elite, whether moderate or radical, are so often couched in terms which seem, to the masses, to have little direct relevance to their daily lives; this is notably so in the case of the few Marxist pronouncements which tend to be a crude precis of the well known classics with no attempt to reinterpret them in the light of modern Nigerian conditions.

The poor do not read Chief Awolowo's books; but they do see the newspapers. In recent years there has been an increasing number of articles, often by university lecturers and the like, highlighting the grievances of poverty and unemployment and attacking the persistent corruption in high places – themes frequently echoed by the military leaders themselves. But such journalism, generated usually by the salary-earning elite that has lost the opportunity to become a propertied bourgeoisie, in specifying the nature of the ills rather than its remedy, serves as much to diffuse the tension in society as to crystallize it. The press continues to give great prominence to activities in which national leaders are portrayed either as equals with foreign leaders or democratically mixing with their own people, and to the achievements of individuals who have gained academic or financial success and thus a place among the elite.

MODELS

Sociological literature on stratification frequently distinguishes between objective and subjective models, and at its most arrogant, is apt to stress the "scientific" nature of the former and the ignorance or "false consciousness" implied in the latter. In my view, a man's image of his own society, however humble a member he may be, is rationally based upon the concepts and propositions employed by him and information available to him. (It depends, too, upon his ability to make logical deductions, but so does the description given by the external observer.)

In trying to describe how the Yoruba man sees his society, I believe that it will be useful to imagine that he uses two models, different in both their use and construction. The distinction is, I must emphasize, a heuristic device.

The first is the ego-oriented model which for convenience I term the cognitive map. The individual is at the center of a map which denotes the goals open to him and the routes by which these may be achieved. The detail of the map is provided by the individual's network of personal relationships – a network which can be described in terms of intensity, density, span, and such measurable attributes. It is these relationships which the individual manipulates to attain his goals. Using this model the individual sees himself within the moral community – "us" – which shares a system of values, as opposed to "them," those outside the community either by reason of much higher social status, territorial distance, or failure to maintain the norms of the community even though physically part of it.

The second model is the externalized analytical structure; the individual surveys his society in its entirety from without, as if he were on a mountain peak looking down upon it. Important here are the social divisions seen in the society and the relationships seen between them, e.g. Ossowski's categorization of class relationships as opposed, ladder-like, or functionally interdependent. But such an external observer sees society not only as it is but also as it might be. In other words he assesses the legitimacy of the present structure according to his own values.

It is this second model which the Western external observer uses; for, save in certain circumstances, he is not a member, or at most only a peripheral one, of the society. The individual who uses both models in viewing his own society must achieve a certain degree of congruence between them. But while every individual is continually using his cognitive map, the externalized analytical structure is employed – at least in a sophisticated manner – both by few individuals and on few occasions. Thus the image of society tends to be dominated by the ego-oriented cognitive map. In the following paragraphs I present my data on Yoruba attitudes in accord with these two models.

ATTITUDES

The sources of the data to be presented below are a series of structured interviews conducted in 1968 in Ibadan and answers to open-ended questions in a survey carried out in 1971 in Ibadan and Agege, Lagos. While, as a social anthropologist, I am sceptical of the validity of this type of response, I have nevertheless been impressed by the uniformity of the values expressed by respondents both to different interviewers and in response to differently worded questions. The responses have confirmed my impressions gained over many years of residence and research in Yoruba country.

First, how do the urban Yoruba see the different occupations in society? Informants were given four sets of three occupations, said to have a similar income but differing in other ways; thus senior civil servant (politically powerful but employed), transport (self-employed), and factory manager (an employer of labor though himself an employee); clerk, factory worker, and mechanic. Informants were asked to rank each triad and to say why they preferred their first and second choices. From the wealth of the responses some dominant themes emerged. The preferences for the top occupations tended to be expressed in terms of the power wielded – the civil servant's abstract power, the employer's direct power over individuals, the secondary school headmaster's prestige and influence within the community. While the possession of power over others is valued, of even greater importance is the freedom from constraint implied by self-employment. Almost all respondents said that it is better to be self-employed than an employee, emphasizing in a manner that seems surprising to a Westerner, the importance of a daily income (even in respect of the most hazardous occupation such as tailoring) against the liability of dismissal (even for the senior civil servant). This desire to be one's own master seems to stem from memories of slavery – the wage earned is often so described – and from the continued respect for age; in the modern sector a man may rise in salaried rank above his father (with less education) so the father ought to retire to self-employment before his sons start working. At the pinnacle of society for most Yoruba stands the wealthy businessman, a generous patron. To the poor urban worker he constitutes a reference point – in his own quarter there will be living such self-made men; to the educated man, business offers the chance of higher financial rewards and greater personal power. Two broad routes to the top are open to the Yoruba; the one by scholastic success, the passing of each examination ensuring one's move to a higher income scale; the other by entrepreneurship, the craftsman or petty trader developing into a workshop owner or wealthy trader and thence to the magnate controlling a number of quasi-related enterprises. The greater value attached to entrepreneurship is balanced by the security of academic success; thus no Yoruba parent argues that he will train his son as a trader rather than send him to school. But the primary school dropouts and failures are trained in a craft, putting them on the bottom rung of the entrepreneurial ladder. Thus occupations in the middle and lower ranks are seen in terms of the opportunities provided for advancement. Clerical posts are part of a career ladder and give one a chance for private study for examinations; factory work is a dead-end job in itself, but provides a chance to acquire skills that one may use in self-employment. The tailor who sits in his roadside shop and the shop assistant in the big department store have the opportunity to meet important men and so develop their personal networks.

To the question, "Which is most important to a man in getting ahead – hard work or a helper?" it was clear that both were seen as important, though the latter was clearly dominant. By hard work alone one could not achieve sufficiently to make a substantial improvement in one's status; but without hard work the opportunities provided by the helper or patron could be wasted; by hard work, too, one learned to value one's own achievements and those of others. In explaining the termination of their own scholastic career men referred to the lack of finance – parents were sick or dead, lawsuits drained family reserves, brothers had to have their turn in school; very few said that they left school of their own choice. In essays, schoolboys emphasized the need to work hard, arguing often that the qualities came more easily to a boy from a poor home than to one from a rich home where attitudes of indolence were learned. The poor boy would still need a patron to pay his school or university fees, and a good character would be important here in attracting assistance.

An overwhelming desire to get ahead is balanced, however, by the recognition that it is now hard to obtain patronage. First, the wealthy buyer or transporter of produce has less political influence under the military regime than in the days when he moved closely with party politicians. Second, both the more traditionally-oriented wealthy men, and even more so the educated ones are confining their financial assistance to an ever-narrowing circle of close kin. The expansion of educational facilities now provides them with an opportunity to raise their immediate families to elite status. Nevertheless the Yoruba man, in outlining his career history gives as much prominence to help given to him by patrons as we would to our own achievements; yet the help cited – "my master taught me how to trade" – often seems to indicate crass exploitation. But by singing the praises of his benefactor, the Yoruba man seeks to retain the relationship not only in the hope of further benefits but to indicate to others (who might victimize him) where his support lies.

Everyone has a social network; but not all societies emphasize the need to keep the network in good repair and to extend it. The network of the urban Yoruba is highly complex, for it includes members of his descent group and community both at home and abroad, schoolmates and workmates. With the rapid social mobility experienced in recent decades the network of any individual includes rich and poor alike. Although the educated elite live rather exclusively in the affluent suburbs and in government residential areas, individually they visit their home towns and are involved in community affairs, thus reinforcing the links with less successful kin and age mates.

Abraham's Yoruba dictionary translates *mekunnu* as a [nincompoop], a person of no account. Yet this term is now widely used to describe the "common man." Asked to describe themselves as *olowo* [rich] *mekunnu* or *talaka* [poor] most urban Yoruba replied *mekunnu*. A few said they were rich, citing ownership of a house, a car, or ample farm land, though others might not have described them in this way. Those who described themselves as *talaka* were emphasizing their failure to achieve their ambitions, for some were clerks and teachers! The self-rated *mekunnu* tended to say that they were not *talaka* because they could manage to provide clothes and daily meals for their families without recourse to theft.

In summing up the cognitive map of the urban Yoruba one emphasizes the open nature of the perceived society with stress placed on achievement and patronage and a high value attached to entrepreneurial activity. The importance of one's social network is stressed – a network which for most Yoruba spans the society from rich to poor even though restricted largely to members of one's own community.

Let us now turn to our second model. When asked what differences they saw among Yoruba people, respondents answered overwhelmingly in ethnic terms; the primary divisions, Egba, Oyo, Ifesha, Ondo, Ekiti, Ijebu, etc. were cited with examples of peculiar cultural traits. In the same vein they divided the population of their own town into indigenes and strangers. The deviant responses tended to come from illiterate farmers who had least contact with people of other ethnic groups. This is because both immigration to the town and the importance credited to the helper or patron heighten ethnic consciousness. Patronage networks are the basis, too, on which factions are formed. Ultimately most Yoruba towns were, before the military coup, divided in their allegiances to two or three political parties – AG, NNDP and NCNC – each of these major factions being led by professional men and traders and for the most part appealing to people of all social ranks (Ibadan is somewhat exceptional in that the indigenes saw themselves as poor in contrast to the wealthy stranger elements). Virtually absent from these responses was any division of society into GROUPS based on wealth or social rank. The Yoruba terms for rich man, *olowo*, honored man, *olola*, are usually used to describe individuals, not categories. Western class terminology is used infrequently (a recent newspaper article refers to "working-class girls," i.e. salaried teachers, nurses, and secretaries); it has no vernacular equivalent (unlike Hausa, which does differentiate aristocracy [*sarakuna*] from commoners [*talakawa*].

This does not mean that Yoruba are blind to differences of power and wealth; their desire to achieve high status shows an acute awareness of the competitive nature of their society. Differences in wealth are, however, seen as legitimate. Asked whether it was fair that a laborer should earn £8 a month while a university graduate started at £70, men emphasized the hard work and suffering (using a word meaning physical pain as well as deprivation) endured by the scholar together with the fair expectation of dividends from the financial investment made. But £8 was also seen as quite insufficient for a man to maintain his family. However, those who said that the income gap cited was unfair, tended to suggest only that laborers should earn £15–£20 as against the graduate's £70. We did not ask whether traders should be so rich; the answer was obvious from so many other statements describing the legitimacy of entrepreneurial activity. The wealthy traders are not seen as an exploiting class, though on occasion they may combine monopolistically. Individually, they may be castigated for lack of generosity or for cheating the customer (i.e. the produce buyer who pays below the Marketing Board's fixed price); but they are also the patrons *par excellence*.

The ills of society are ascribed by the common man not to the rich businessman but to "the Government." Asked, "Does the government benefit all?" many replied that it did – in providing social services and in reducing the level of violence (from its 1965 peak). But others, especially wage earners, stated that the government only looked after its own people. Thus the high salaries of politicians, military leaders, and civil servants are legitimate; criticism is leveled at the way in which these people, in awarding contracts or scholarships, benefit each other, and educate only their own children or those of close kin. They are the antithesis of the traditional *gbajumo* who is accessible to all; they are becoming an exclusive group. But many who are critical of the government in this way, nevertheless still aspire to enter the higher ranks of society.

In choosing between a rise in wages and free secondary schooling many (and especially the wage earners!) opted for the former arguing that wages were too low for subsistence or that with higher wages they could afford the school fees, or at least the thrifty ones would. Conversely, free education provided opportunities for all, yet many feared that scholastic achievements would be devalued (as free primary education has devalued the Primary 6 certificate); some far-sighted men saw that a wage rise would never be enough to meet school fees, so they opted for free education. The antipathy to a socialist (in our sense) society was further demonstrated in other responses that the best form of help which the government could give was to provide vastly increased loan facilities to farmers, small traders, and craftsmen.

In the early years of independence these demands and aspirations were articulated through the network of patronage which culminated with the political party in power. Now this chain is broken, for while many erstwhile politicians are now back in office as commissioners, these are now responsible to the military leaders, not to an electorate. The illiterate say apathetically that they cannot reach the ears of government; the literates speak of writing to the newspapers; neither talk of collective action. Yet for both groups examples of the success of this mode of protest is available.

PROTESTS

In the wave of highway robbery in Western Nigeria in late 1965, party thugs, paid off following the elections, were probably responsible. There was no evidence of any widespread organization. Individuals justified their actions by reference to the corruption of politicians, "They have made their pile, now I am making mine." However, the *Agbekoya* rebellion and the strikes were organized.

Tax riots have not been infrequent in Ibadan and its rural hinterland; in 1958 there was widespread plunder following the death in a car accident of Adegoke Adelubu, the popular Ibadan leader. The *Agbekoya* (farmers reject suffering) movement was restricted, however, to farmers, though urban dwellers clearly gave moral support and political leaders tried to capitalize the discontent.[2] The movement was centered in those areas of Ibadan most hit by cocoa disease, though it spread widely; here too its adherents were the poorer farmers (men who held land, though as tenants, and did not hire labor). High taxes, often demanded at inopportune times, combined with low cocoa incomes produced intense deprivation. The government-sponsored farmers' union was dominated by the rich farmers and traders; attempts at orderly representation to the military government and to the traditional chiefs of Ibadan had failed. The initial wave of riots (described in the Ayoola Report) died as the government ceased tax collection but was revived in July 1969 when it was recommenced. September saw the farmers' raid on Ibadan jail to release tax defaulters. In October the government reduced the tax rate and abolished other rates which had no relevance to the rural areas. In its later period the *Agbekoya* was led by Tafa Adeoye, an illiterate farmer. Upon the government's capitulation he cooperated with it in forming the Agbe Parapo farmers' organization; suddenly he owned a three-story house and a big car. Schisms both within the farmers' movement and between the local and national politicians trying to control it led to renewed opposition by Adeoye and to his detention in September 1970.

The general strike of June 1964 and the widespread strikes of January 1971 both arose from the government's inept handling of the reports of commissions of enquiry into wage structure[3]. Nigerian trade unions are generally "house" unions – each firm has its own union; in the large Western expatriate firms these now tend to be well-organized and to function successfully within the rules of bargaining; oriental firms tend to disregard or ban union activity. The Nigerian trade union leadership is, however, generally fragmented into rival factions reflecting allegiances to the WFTU and IFCTU, and ethnic and personal rivalries; it tends to be held in low esteem by the workers who see the career unionists as seeking their own aggrandizement rather than the social advancement of the workers. However, the union leaders did unite to urge the government,

---

[2]   The *Agbekoya* movement is described in *Report of the Commission of Enquiry into the civil disturbances which occurred in certain parts of the Western State of Nigeria in the month of December 1968* (The Ayoola Report) 1969, in Beer (1971), and in Williams (1972).
[3]   The strikes are described in more detail in Melson (1970) and in Peace (1972).

with the threat of strikes, to set up the Morgan Commission in 1963. Again in 1970 it united; and on both occasions demanded a minimum wage which was, given the existing structure of the economy, unrealistically high (£180 – with an upper salary limit of £960 in 1964, £580 in 1970). In 1964 the Morgan report recommended a minimum wage of £120 a year (for Lagos) – 50 percent above the previous minimum, though this was a compromise between what it felt was deserved and what the government, the major employer, could afford. The government's delay first in publishing the report and then its own white paper (which accepted a minimum wage of only £109) led to a stoppage of work which not only had the support of workers but of most of the population; a compromise wage together with a promise of further negotiation terminated the two-week strike.

In 1970 the union leadership, in a move viewed cynically as an attempt to win popular approval, called for an interim report from the Adebo commission; Adebo awarded a £2 a month increase for all workers earning less than £100 a year, backdated for several months. This "Christmas bonus" was received with satisfaction; but the government then announced that the increase should be paid only by those employers who had granted no cost of living awards since 1964. The better employers had raised wages in this period, though employer and employee differed in their interpretation of the basis of the increases – higher productivity or cost of living. They declined to pay, in accord with the government's ruling (made at their behest) and their workers, spontaneously though with the support of the LOCAL union leadership, went on strike; ultimately the employers capitulated. When the final report of the Adebo commission was published, recommending only another £1 a month for the lowest paid workers but substantial increases for salary earners, there was no significant protest from the union leaders or their rank and file.

CLASS CONSCIOUSNESS?

We revert to our original question: How far is class consciousness developing? As we have seen, it is an ethnocentric question, but nevertheless one which can help to draw together the data presented. To put it tritely, it all depends on what we mean by class consciousness. At a minimum, consciousness of inequality is presumed; this the Yoruba certainly display, both in their desire to achieve power and rewards and in their criticism of the rich. In seeking to improve one's lot one may either act individually, in competition with others, or collectively with others similarly placed to attain given ends; only the latter is usually termed class action. But this action can range from attempts substantially to preserve the status quo (raising wages in line with cost of living indices) to radical attempts to change the structure of society. To Marxists the latter is implied in the recognition by the working class of its historic revolutionary role. We thus have three possible levels of class consciousness: (1) recognition of inequality and a desire to do something about it; (2) collective action with those of similar interests; and (3) an attempt to change the structure of society. But in attempting to measure class consciousness we must recognize that it is displayed in some situations, not in others, and at some periods more than others.

Thus the factory worker or laborer aspires to establish himself as a self-employed craftsman and thence to become a wealthy trader. These long-term hopes based upon an acceptance of the structure of society are not incompatible with strike action to gain immediate wage increases – especially when the cause of the tension lies in the government's apparent reluctance to accept the recommendations of important commissions. Again the action of the farmers was directed specifically against the payment of taxes and rates for which they saw no commensurate benefit. Yet neither movement would have achieved such widespread support had there not been a very high general level of discontent with the government. However, the unpopularity of the government rests largely on its restriction of the avenues of social mobility; the elite are consolidating into a self-perpetuating group; the demand is to restore the open society – more scholarships, more loans.

Collective action within the work situation, viz. trade union efforts to increase wages or redress grievances, must be set against other forms of collective action of a very different basis. The urban immigrant is encapsulated within his local ethnic community; he belongs to its association; its members find him work or maintain him in sickness. While his friends are found among people of similar income, prominent in his social network are wealthy and powerful potential patrons. If one assumes the ideal worker to be one whose whole life is devoted to the class struggle, then the Yoruba worker is far removed from this state.

How far, moreover, can one expect the poor farmer or worker to articulate on an alternative structure of society, rather than to exploit the opportunities offered by the present structure? His resources for so doing – the concepts available, his own limited experience and information – all impede such intellectual activity. Leadership must come from the better educated. But the Agbekoya movement and, to a large extent, the strikes were both spontaneous actions which the political trade union leaders then tried to mobilize to their own ends, often introducing issues which were irrelevant to the original demands.

The discontent of the masses can be interpreted as frustration, both with the failure of living standards to rise and with their individual failure to better themselves. The cause is seen in the selfishness of those in power, the cure in increasing the opportunities of the poor to achieve high positions within an open society. The leaders who exploit this discontent also accept the existing structure of indigenous society, and as yet provide no visions of an alternative, better or happier, society.

REFERENCES

BEER, C. E. F.
    1971   "The farmer and the state in Western Nigeria." Unpublished doctoral dissertation. Ibadan.
LLOYD, P. C.
    1962   *Yoruba land law*. London: Oxford University Press.
    1965   "The Yoruba", in *Peoples in Africa*. Edited by J. L. Gibbs. New York: Holt, Rinehart and Winston.
MELSON, R.
    1970   "Nigerian politics and the General Strike of 1964", in *Protest and power in Black Africa*. Edited by R. I. Rothburg and A. A. Mazrui. New York: Oxford University Press.
PEACE, A. J.
    1972   "Industrial protest in Nigeria", in *Sociology and development*. Edited by E. de Kadt and G. Williams. London: Tavistock.
WILLIAMS, G. P.
    1972   "Political consciousness among the Ibadan poor", in *Sociology and development*. Edited by E. de Kadt and G. Williams. London: Tavistock.

Plantation Infrastructure and Labor Mobility in Guyana and Trinidad

BONHAM C. RICHARDSON

Studies of Caribbean migration have concentrated upon inter-island movements and out-migration to other parts of the world. These are the most noticeable types of human mobility characteristic of the West Indies. However, in the southern Caribbean there is a more subtle though no less important kind of mobility related directly to plantation settlement patterns. In Guyana (British Guiana until 1966) and Trinidad most rural villagers live in communities originally inhabited by part-time sugar estate workers of the nineteenth century. The rural transportation networks of these two countries are actually remnants of colonial plantation systems. Villagers in Guyana and Trinidad today continue to exhibit a high degree of spatial mobility in commuting to part-time jobs from their residences and back again. Overall similarities in colonial livelihood patterns among the two main ethnic groups in both places suggest that historical-economic determinants are more important than ethnic identity in explaining rural economic behavior in Guyana and Trinidad.

Historical evidence from two periods throws light upon this labor migration. After emancipation, ex-slaves in British Guyana and Trinidad established settlements on the peripheries of plantations. These black freemen commuted short distances to estates for part-time labor. After their indenture periods, Indians also settled near plantations. Though estates had grown larger and technically more complex by this time, they

Fieldwork in Guyana during the summer of 1967 and a one-year period in 1968–1969 was supported by grants and a fellowship from the University of Wisconsin at Madison. Research in Trinidad during the summer of 1971 was made available by awards from the American Philosophical Society, the National Geographic Society and the Society of the Sigma Xi. These research funds are gratefully acknowledged.

still required periodic inputs of human labor which were provided by the Indian villagers. The roads along which blacks and Indians originally settled have now become parts of paved rural infrastructures. Settlement patterns today in Guyana and Trinidad look much as they did throughout the nineteenth century. In neither country have the peri-plantation villages ever been self-contained "peasant" communities. Ecological problems facing villagers in both places have reinforced the necessity of seeking extra-village sources of income.

Today the populations of both countries are unevenly divided between the same two ethnic groups: (1) blacks and "mixed" descendants of African slaves; and (2) descendants of indentured plantation laborers from India, locally called "East Indians." There are small numbers of whites and Chinese in the cities of both places, and some Amerindians are in southern Guyana though all of these groups taken together would account for only about 5 percent of the total population in either country. East Indians are now about 40 percent of Trinidad's populace of one million, and they are slightly over half of Guyana's 750,000 people. Speaking very generally, one can say that a demographic dichotomy exists between the two groups, blacks dominating the urban areas of Port of Spain and Georgetown, and Indians, especially in Guyana, numerically superior in rural zones. The first free villages in both places, however, were black. Some of their settlements began a pattern which has persisted until today.

THE EVOLUTION OF SETTLEMENT NETWORKS IN GUYANA AND TRINIDAD

Guyana's sea-level coastal plain (see Figure 1), the area in which over 90 percent of the country's populace lives in the 1970's, has been reclaimed from tidal mudflats bordering the Atlantic Ocean. This reclamation was first accomplished by African slaves supervised by planters from the Netherlands and England. Early Dutch trading posts were first established at upriver sites, but by the early eighteenth century Dutch plantations were located along the estuaries of the Essequibo, Demerara, and Berbice Rivers. The Dutch colonies of the same names became British early in the nineteenth century. By this time, estates for the production of the tropical staples of cotton, coffee, and sugar cane were being established along the Atlantic littoral. This area is composed of fertile alluvial soil deposited by the equatorial current running from the mouth of the Amazon along the northeastern coast of South America.

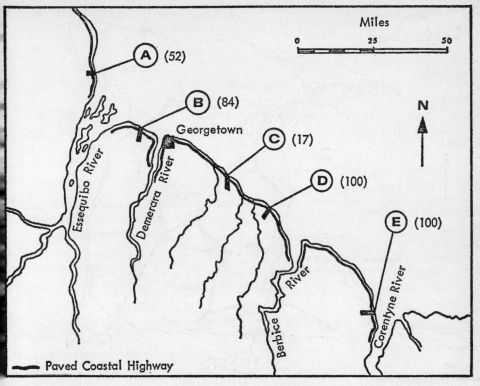

Figure 1. Coastal Guyana, showing study communities and number of villagers interviewed in each

Necessities for water control led to the distinctive rectangular shape of each of the coastal plantations. In each case a sea defense wall was erected at the foreshore. At the rear of each estate a backdam was built in order to protect the rear of the plantation from savanna swampwaters. These two water barriers were connected by long irrigation and drainage canals. Water was brought from the back of each estate, flowed through auxiliary canals and eventually spilled into the sea. The water movement through the plantation unit was powered by gravity. A large slave population kept water channels cleared of reeds, silt, and other debris which would inhibit the functioning of the plantation canals. The plantation settlement or nucleus, which included the housing units and agricultural processing buildings, was located near the water in every case. Thus, each coastal plantation had a rectangular shape with its settlement close to the ocean. In 1806 a coastal road was laid out linking the many estate nuclei (St. Clair 1947: 31–32). This highway had the effect of establishing a

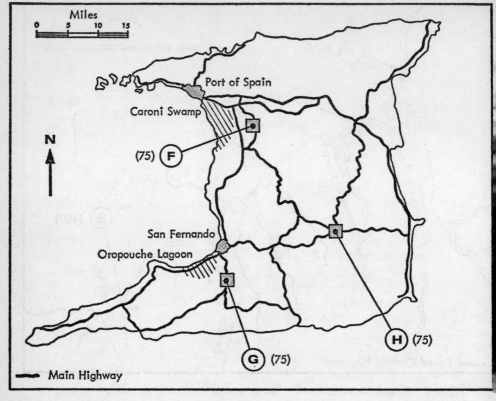

Figure 2.   Trinidad, showing study communities and number of villagers interviewed in each

settlement network from what had formerly been individual estates fronting the water's edge.

The earliest plantations of Trinidad (see Figure 2) were developed under Spanish rule until the island became British in 1797. The small estate zone was located in the extreme west central portion of the island near Trinidad's best natural port facilities and on the island's most fertile and level land areas. These early cane, cotton, and cacao estates were located on small yet navigable streams which emptied into the Gulf of Paria. Though swampy zones exist along certain coastal areas of the island, plantation owners avoided these areas and did not have to contend with the problems of water control facing the planters of the Guyana coastline. The few all-weather roads on the island in the late eighteenth century were in the vicinity of coastal estates near Port of Spain and San Fernando (Young Sing 1964: 100). The forty-odd years of British rule which preceded slave emancipation in the 1830's saw Trinidad change from a relatively unexploited island to one in which the production of tropical staples by slaves had become greatly intensified. Nevertheless, there were only about 20,000 slaves and their children in Trinidad at emancipation, a mere fraction of the number living in the older British islands of the West Indies.

There is an oversimplified generalization occasionally put forward uncritically by scholars concerning the aftermath of slavery in Guyana and Trinidad (Klass 1961:7; Ehrlich 1971:169). This is that upon serving their periods of "apprenticeship" from 1834 to 1838,[1] newly-freed blacks completely abandoned the estates for the freedom of the open countryside. Though complete data are unavailable, there is evidence that in both places groups of ex-slaves settled on the peripheries of plantations. By doing so, former slaves could continue to act as part-time laborers on plantations, thereby deriving cash income, and they could participate in this activity without having to remain within the physical and social confines of the plantations. As slaves in British Guiana and Trinidad, blacks had cultivated their own foodstuffs on plantation grounds and had therefore engaged in a semi-subsistence economy combined with the forced labor associated with the cultivation and processing of cash crops. After emancipation in both British colonies a distinctive settlement form developed as an expression of the continuing relationship between the ex-slaves and the plantations.

In Guyana freemen established communal settlements as groups, purchasing abandoned estates in the coastal zone (Farley 1954). These village settlements flanked the coastal highways; newly-freed slaves could thus walk back and forth to nearby plantations for part-time work. The ex-slaves had therefore replicated the settlement morphology of the coastal plantation: houses were near the road and farmland was inland. The villagers kept small livestock and grew provision crops on the parts of the village lands closest to the roadside settlements. They did not cultivate the entire rectangle of land owned by the community, often allowing the backlands to become swampy pastures (Farley 1954: 97). The overall impact of the livelihoods divided between plantation and village plots was to create a settlement pattern composed of strings of huts and houses extending from the plantation nuclei along the coastal road. The part-time livelihood pattern was also encouraged by the formidable water control requirements associated with maintaining a

[1] The date of emancipation for the British Caribbean is 1834. In both British Guiana and Trinidad, however, a transitional period of apprenticeship was decreed. Slaves still had to work, but they were clothed, fed, and paid beyond a certain amount of labor. Former slaves were legally freemen in both colonies on August 1, 1838.

typical rectangle of coastal land. The black villagers had neither the desire nor the technology to cope with the drainage and irrigation requirements of an entire village unit (Adamson 1972:61). It was simpler to cultivate patches of land close to the foreshore and main highway and to migrate to nearby plantations for day work.

Slave emancipation had roughly similar effects in Trinidad. In many cases black freemen merely settled "over the line" from sugar cane estates onto unoccupied land (*Report from the Select Committee on West India Colonies* 1842:47). As in Guyana, they could thus cultivate their own subsistence crops, yet they could also work for wages on the nearby estates. Hastily-passed legislation stipulated minimum acreages for ex-slaves and prohibited squatting on Crown Lands. These acts were ineffective, however, since plantation owners were reluctant to prosecute the squatters who comprised the only available labor force (Wood 1968: 51). Little is known of these peri-plantation villages themselves though one contemporary historian indicates a settlement morphology similar to that found in coastal Guyana at the same period in history:

Many villages had grown up in a haphazard and unplanned manner. The people had built huts wherever they pleased along the highway; these settlements were... like... long straggling villages without any centre... (Wood 1968:94).

Such a settlement pattern seems entirely reasonable considering the part-time nature of a villager's livelihood, which was divided between estate labor and individual provision farming plots.

CHANGES IN LABOR AND PLANTATION TECHNOLOGY DURING THE LATE NINETEENTH CENTURY

The synergism of slave emancipation, soil exhaustion, competition from both tropical canes and mid-latitude beets, and London's laissez faire trade practices had dealt the sugar colonies of Barbados, Jamaica, and the Leewards a mortal blow by the 1840's. In order for the West Indian sugar industry to survive, it had to shift to an area which had inherited neither overworked soils nor an infrastructure based upon antiquated means of producing raw sugar. Trinidad's relatively open spaces therefore beckoned planters from other areas of the Caribbean. British Guiana's fertile coastline was also relatively undeveloped and a source of attraction to those who sought to compete with sugar from other parts of the world.

If the southern Caribbean were to compete sucessfully for a share of the London sugar market, there would be the necessity not only for fertile lands but also for improved technology to produce raw sugar from each plantation unit far in excess of the earlier West Indian estate. The steam engine had been used to crush canes on the Guiana coastal plain as early as 1805 (Dalton 1855: 229). Later in the nineteenth century, vacuum pan boiling allowed for larger quantities of high quality sugar to be produced more efficiently in both Trinidad and British Guiana. Multi-stage rolling mills were installed in British Guiana in 1885 (Beachey 1957: 62–63). And all of these innovations, necessitating greater throughput of canes at each mill, meant that each should command a larger area and thus be spaced father apart from one another. The canals of the Guiana coast, macadam and gravel roads of Trinidad and, later, tramways in each colony provided more efficient transport for increasingly long distances from fields to mills. The culmination of the nineteenth century's technical and infrastructural improvements in the southern Caribbean's sugar industry was the establishment of the central factory St. Madeleine in southern Trinidad followed by similar centrals and a continuing consolidation of the sugar industry under more central control in both colonies (Beachey 1957: 84; Adamson 1972: 199-213).

After emancipation the existing estates in both Guyana and Trinidad continued to require large amounts of labor. The freed blacks of course provided part-time work from their locations on the fringes of estates. However, the planters disliked the relative independence of ex-slaves who divided their time between village and estate and were therefore regarded as "undependable." Gangs of blacks also bargained for higher wages. Such actions were especially effective at harvest time since ripe canes might rot in the fields if planters were unwilling to pay the workers more. Labor was actively recruited around the Caribbean by agents from Trinidad and British Guiana (Mathieson 1967: 44). Planters from each colony grudgingly acknowledged that a worker could earn as much in a few hours in Trinidad or British Guiana as he could in a day on other islands. An independent labor force was, however, less attractive to the planters than were the reliable, more docile indentured laborers from India who first came to British Guiana in 1838 and to Trinidad in 1845.

The indentured plantation workers from India were imported to the West Indies until 1917 (Nath 1950; Weller 1968). Almost 240,000 came to Guyana, 100,000 less to Trinidad, and a few to other West Indian areas. The principal recruiting terminal was Calcutta. Madras was established later as a secondary port of debarkation for migrant workers. Upon arrival in Trinidad or British Guiana, Indians were assigned to estates, usually for five-year periods. Indentured workers were housed in "ranges," long wooden barracks next to the mills and boiling houses.

By the late nineteenth century, the plantation's size had greatly enlarged from what is was in the days of slavery, though the relative location of workers to field and factory had remained the same. Indentured workers were awakened early, then walked long distances from barracks to fields in order to cut cane, plow furrows, or clean drainage ditches.

THE ESTABLISHMENT OF AUTONOMOUS INDIAN SETTLEMENTS

Upon completing his indenture period, an Indian could usually choose among re-indenture (two five-year indenture periods entitled a worker to repatriation to India at government expense), living as a free worker on the estate, or taking up land of his own provided by the colonial government. The latter option was important during the late nineteenth and early twentieth centuries as a number of Indian settlements were established along the Guiana coast and the sugar belt of western Trinidad.

Indians living in their own communities continued to derive much cash income from their labor on nearby plantations. Estate managers relied upon these laborers for part-time work, especially in field preparation and harvesting, though many stages of raw sugar production had become increasingly mechanized and less demanding of labor. In any case, it appears misleading to interpret the demographic changes of the late nineteenth century in Trinidad as a period in which "former indentured servants did cluster together to form villages" (Ehrlich 1971: 169). The villages in both colonies continued to radiate from the cane plantations in linear patterns just as those of black villagers had decades before.[2] The colonies of ex-indentured workers were economic adjuncts of the estates, not self-contained nodes of settlement. For instance, it was reported that Indian colonies in Trinidad did not "thrive" unless they were located near sugar estates (*Government of Trinidad and Tobago* 1888: 42); and in 1911, 74 per cent of the Indians in British Guiana engaged in agriculture were considered "agricultural laborers" rather than "independent farmers" though their dwelling places were evenly divided between "estates" and "villages and settlements" (*British Guiana Population Census* 1911: 70–71). By the late nineteenth century, Indian villagers in both colonies were becoming identified with their own village agricultural production, though this activity was usually a kind of semi-subsistence activity

[2]   Older residents of villages in both countries have all reported this type of settlement morphology for earliest Indian communities in Guyana and Trinidad.

nibbling at the edges of lands controlled by the large sugar cane plantations.

During the last two decades of the nineteenth century in British Guiana, rice emerged on the coastal plain as a subsistence crop cultivated mainly by Indian villagers (Mandle 1970). The grain was first exported in 1903, and it is now the main crop of Guyana's coastal belt.[3] The low-lying coastal soils are similar to those of Asian deltas in that they support padi crops of medium yield without a great deal of human attention to irrigation, drainage, or artificial fertilizers. On the other hand, sugar cane requires better water management, well-drained soils, and marketing expertise for sale of the final product; the cultivation of cane therefore remained under estate auspices where efficient, centralized water systems, maintained by organized gangs of laborers, ensured crops of highest yields. A symbiotic relationship thus developed between the large estates, whose canals and lands were managed under central control, and the nearby "free" villages with poorer water systems and cultivating subsistence rice. The estates required periodic labor, and the villagers, desiring wages over and above the small amounts of income derived from their grain production, supplied it. In some cases, marginal estate land was given over to rice production by estate laborers, and some of the first mechanical padi hullers in the colony were located on sugar estates.

It is noteworthy that the earliest areas of "free" Indian villages of Trinidad were in the areas of the low-lying swamplands of the Caroni Swamp and Oropouche Lagoon (see Figure 2). The best lands of western Trinidad had of course been preempted by plantations, leaving the ex-indentured Indians to cope with the same ecological problems facing their Guianese peers. Indian agriculture in Trinidad at first centered around rice, measureable quantities of padi coming from the "Caroni Savanna" as early as 1886 (*Government of Trinidad and Tobago* 1887: 11). Reports from the early twentieth century also indicate recurring flood hazards associated with Indian rice production in the Oropouche Lagoon (*Government of Trinidad and Tobago* 1903:16). Such hazards reinforced the necessity for part-time work on nearby estates. However, the demand for cane at Trinidadian sugar factories combined with planters' divided interests between cane and cacao, allowed the emergence of a class of small-scale cane farmers in the late nineteenth century who leased or bought well-drained lands above the coastal swamp zones.

[3]   There are now approximately 300,000 acres devoted to rice cultivation in Guyana. Sugar cane acreage accounts for about 100,000 acres located mainly near the mouths of the Demerara and Berbice Rivers. Guyana's caneland is almost totally controlled by large British-owned companies.

During this period in which Indian villagers in British Guiana and Trinidad were gaining a foothold on the peripheries of plantations, many blacks were drifting into urban areas. The definitive history of this demographic change has yet to be written, though several suggestions may be forwarded to help explain it. The oft-repeated idea that blacks abhorred agricultural work because of plantation memories has probably been overstated. In both places, the bulk of the work on estates was now done by indentured immigrants, forcing rural blacks to seek other means of acquiring incomes. Cheaper Indian labor had thus been substituted for more expensive black labor by the planter class in each colony, and the influx of thousands of indentured laborers had the overall effect of driving plantation wages down.

It has also been suggested that in British Guiana blacks had greater access to education and technical skills which led them away from plantation work (Despres 1969: 37–41). Blacks became identified with teaching and manning civil service posts in both colonies, occupational characteristics of this ethnic group which still hold true today in Guyana and Trinidad. In Guyana, the skilled mechanics and boilermen of the plantation factories continued to be mainly black even though fieldwork was done by Indians. The blacks in Trinidad also dominated these more prestigious and better-paying jobs in mills and boiling houses. Since the bulk of skilled mechanics on the island in the early twentieth century were blacks, they provided a convenient labor reservoir for the oil industry, labor for which continues to be dominated by workers of African descent.

Today, in the 1970's, East Indians remain predominant in the rural areas of both countries. The Indian villagers of Guyana are mainly rice producers while rural Indians of Trinidad are often cane farmers. In neither case, however, is the economic activity of the villagers confined to their own village lands.

CONTEMPORARY LIVELIHOOD CHARACTERISTICS AND LABOR MOBILITY IN RURAL AREAS OF GUYANA AND TRINIDAD

Contemporary livelihood data are presented here from eight villages in the two countries, five communities in Guyana and three in Trinidad (Figures 1 and 2).[4] Each of the eight communities is mainly Indian though

[4]   Approximately one month has been spent in each community. Village rice producers were interviewed in Guyana, and the different numbers of interviews in each community reflect relative village sizes. In Trinidad interviews were done on a house-to-house basis, regardless of residents' occupations, along lengths of rural roads.

there are black minorities in each one. Study villages were not selected using statistical sampling methods though each settlement may be considered representative of its district and of the rural areas of the two countries in general. The following discussion of contemporary village economics is based mainly upon personal interviews with 578 heads of households of the eight villages.

The average Guyanese padi producer controls about twelve acres of riceland, each acre producing about 1800 pounds of unhusked rice annually. He earns the equivalent of 1300 U.S. dollars annually from his padi production. Most rice growers cultivate one crop per year, planting in March and harvesting in September or October. Rice inputs are mostly mechanized. Plowing and harrowing is done by tractor while harvesting is usually accomplished with the use of combines. Agricultural machinery is either owned or rented from neighbors or relatives. Two crops of padi per year are produced in the communities west of the Demerara River, the area of the coast of highest labor inputs and least mechanization. Yields are always highest in these latter areas for the "big crop" which grows from March to September. In most of the coastal zone, which is east of Georgetown, rice producers grow only one crop annually using labor saving devices and techniques in rice cultivation thus freeing themselves to participate in other livelihood activities of the coastal region.

In Trinidad, sugar cane is the main village crop. The west central and south central parts of the island, the zones of densest rural settlement, are cane fields interspersed with forest, subsistence crops, and settlement areas. Over 40 percent of 225 randomly selected villagers in the three Trinidad communities controlled cane acreage either through leasing or direct ownership. A typical Trinidad cane producer farms about five acres of cane and earns the equivalent of 1350 U.S. dollars from this crop each year. Plowing land for cane is done by tractor. The crop is harvested by hand. A single planting of cane provides three to five successive "ratoon" crops so there is less planting overhead than that associated with rice, which involves planting for each crop. Fertilizer and weeding inputs are usual for each cane crop in rural Trinidad. In neither Trinidad nor Guyana is rural agriculture devoted to only one crop. Guyanese villages always have areas devoted to provisions such as citrus, beans, and rootcrops. Lower lying zones of Trinidad cane farming communities are almost always cultivated in patches of wet rice.

Environmental hazards continue to influence inhabitants of village areas in both countries. The typical rice community of Guyana is poorly suited to the production of a small-scale crop. The large coastal rectangles, originally designed for control by a single owner, are now inhabited by hundreds of padi producers. Many individual decisions, each partially dependent upon the levels of the main irrigation and drainage canals, are now made within each village. Poorly maintained master water canals hinder the flow of drainage and irrigation waters, thus accentuating the problems associated with both floods and droughts. In Trinidad the agricultural lands of the Caroni and Oropouche areas are now better drained than they were during their first habitation by ex-indentured Indians. Village farm lands continue to be located on lands peripheral to large estates, however. Small-scale Trinidadian cane farmers have to cope with steeper gradients in their canefields than do estate owners (Maharaj 1969: 130). Also, the rural roads of Trinidad not directly serving estates are invariably poor and are often impassable after heavy rains.

In both countries, there are thus ecological necessities for typical villagers to seek extra-community sources of livelihood. In rural Guyana, village water systems are usually poorly maintained; a rice producer there would be foolish to devote the majority of his time to rice husbandry only to see his crop seriously damaged by heavy rains at harvest time. In Trinidad, where the best lands are preempted by modern estates, marginal village lands have occasionally impassable roads. Without an active spatial link to a crushing mill, a cane crop is useless. In both places one therefore finds a high degree of livelihood diversification to offset the environmental hazards associated with village farm production.

Over half of the village rice growers from the five Guyanese villages had some sort of wage paying job (see Table 1). In communities close to existing sugar estates, near the mouths of the Demerara and Berbice Rivers, many villagers work as part-time estate laborers. Others act as

Table 1.   Non-rice sources of livelihood among the sampled village rice producers in Guyana

Village* (Total interviews)	Rice growers with full-time or part-time wage paying jobs	Rice growers who grow vegetables for market	Rice growers with cattle	Rice growers depending only on rice for a livelihood
A (52)	8	1	47	3
B (84)	43	31	61	4
C (17)	7	7	10	0
D (100)	72	8	20	4
E (100)	57	12	43	5
Column total (353)	187	59	181	16

* Differences in sample sizes reflect difference in absolute community populations.

carpenters, tailors, watchmen, fishermen, shopkeepers, drivers, and public works laborers on roads and canals. The last column of Table 1 puts the "other job" into perspective. Of the 353 padi producers interviewed, only sixteen had neither a wage job nor another source of income such as marketing vegetables or livestock. The "other job" is therefore not part-time work at all. To a typical Guyanese rice producer, the extra-village job represents an integral part of total livelihood. It represents the economic safety valve which compensates for a potentially poor padi crop; it also provides small amounts of cash throughout the year and not only at harvest time.

Similar findings emerged in Trinidad. Of the 225 interviewed households, many were devoid of major elements of agriculture. Sixty-seven households had neither sugar cane nor rice, fifty-seven had neither cane nor vegetables, and forty-one had neither rice nor vegetables. On the other hand, only ten had neither rice nor non-agricultural income, nine neither cane nor non-agricultural income, and eight neither vegetables for market nor non-agricultural income. Clearly, the crucial element of the diversified livelihood type of Trinidad is the extra-village job.

The livelihood diversification in Guyana and Trinidad always involves extra-community mobility. Farmers selling vegetables or livestock in neighboring villages may travel only one or two miles. Plantation work occasionally takes a village laborer up to ten miles from his community and back daily. Shorter distances are covered on foot, longer distances by bus, truck or a local route taxi which carries several passengers. Medium distances are usually traversed by bicycle. Typical commuting

Table 2. Commuting distances for all non-"village agriculture" workers from the three study communities of rural Trinidad

Distance in Miles	Village F (75 interviews*)	Village G (75 interviews*)	Village H (75 interviews*)	Row total
0–5	47	36	42	125
6–10	14	26	19	59
11–15	36	7	1	44
16–20	1	1	3	5
21–25	0	1	1	2
26–30	0	1	4	5
31–35	0	0	0	0
36–40	1	0	0	1
41–45	0	1	2	3
45–50	1	1	6	8
Column total	100	74	78	252

* Though each interview was conducted with the head of household, often more than one member of the household worked outside his or her village of residence.

distances in Trinidad are shown in Table 2. These data show no well-defined commuting distance threshhold for rural Trinidad. The high number of commuters in the eleven- to fifteen- mile category for village F, for instance, reflects the distance to Port of Spain. It is remarkable that several villagers travel almost fifty miles one way to work each day. In both Guyana and Trinidad, the contemporary extra-community livelihood mobility always takes place along the paved highways which continue to link villages to estates as their mud versions did one hundred years ago.

The contemporary East Indian padi cultivator of rural Guyana is therefore similar to his counterpart of the nineteenth century. He supplements village agricultural work with other jobs requiring extra-village mobility. The mobility depends upon the coastal highway which is a paved version of the early coastal road. The highway is therefore not only a relic landscape feature, but it also continues to act as a directional element for contemporary livelihood activities. Structurally, the settlement network is the same as it was at the time of slave emancipation. Not accidentally, livelihood activities are also much as they were at that time.

The situation in Trinidad is structurally analogous to that in Guyana though there is not a single public highway along the coast. The highly mobile rural populace of Trinidad commutes to work along such main thoroughfares as the Southern Main Road between Port of Spain and San Fernando which is "not really a road at all" but a patchwork of older north-south and east-west plantation roads which were linked up to connect the two largest towns of the island (Lamont 1933: 141-142). Trinidad's historically mobile labor force has readily adapted to serve as both part-time workers and daily commuters into Trinidad's urban centers of Port of Spain and San Fernando.

In neither Guyana nor Trinidad has a self-sufficient agrarian-based peasant society been established. Historically, the rural populace of each place has divided its time between village farm plots and plantation work. Though the areal extent of plantations in both places has decreased, the highly mobile rural workforce continues to divide its time between village agricultural niches and other jobs. The diagnostic settlement form, found in each place, is both a spatial manifestation and a determinant of the propensity for labor mobility on the part of rural Guyanese and Trinidadians. At the time of emancipation estates in both colonies were surrounded by linear settlements of freemen. As the large corporate plantations evolved in the late nineteenth century, similar linear settlements, this time inhabited by Indians, came into being. Ribbons of rural settlement continue to characterize each country. In Guyana this spatial form has been likened to a rural *strassendorf* (Lowenthal 1960:46). In Trinidad it is held partially responsible for a lack of village cohesion and difficulties in realizing rural amenities (Maharaj 1969: 118).

CONCLUSIONS

A hypothesized "plantation determinism" helps to explain both historical and contemporary economic behavior among small-scale rural inhabitants of Guyana and Trinidad. The evolving plantation system of the nineteenth and twentieth centuries has etched distinctive similarities into the cultural landscapes of both ex-colonies despite sharp contrasts in their overall environmental characteristics. Infrastructural linkages have provided settlement matrices into which inhabitants have drifted after their plantation experiences. The blacks at the time of emancipation and Indians after indenture have displayed remarkably similar livelihood patterns. These patterns have been directed by the peri-plantation settlement networks, networks which have themselves been formed by the relationships between estates and part-time workers. In explaining rural livelihood behavior, the plantation experience, not ethnic identity, seems to be the independent variable.

Nationwide livelihood differences between the two main ethnic groups in Guyana and Trinidad do of course exist. Blacks are clerks, teachers, and mechanics, and they dominate urban areas while Indians are rural dwellers associated with agrarian activity. This demographic dichotomy developed in the late nineteenth and early twentieth centuries when Indians replaced blacks as plantation workers. The evolving plantation, with its need for a continual supply of cheap labor, merely substituted one ethnic group for another. Members of both ethnic groups, seeking group identity, thus became roughly divided into urban and rural areas. Ethnic identity was important for participants in this period of demographic change, especially when one group was culturally different from the other. But there was little from Africa or India which helped to determine this population pattern. In other words, there is nothing inherently "urban" about descendants of West Africans, and many of the Indians recruited for Caribbean plantation work had artisan and urban background in India (Nath 1950: 36; Weller 1968: 13).

An extension of this argument is that the well-known animosity between Indians and blacks in the two countries may be partially grounded in the economic rivalry between the two groups in the nineteenth century, rivalry centered around plantation jobs. Black freemen in Trinidad seeking higher wages at mid-nineteenth century could not help feeling bitter to see another group taking their places for lower wages. It is reported that in British Guiana in the nineteenth century "the planters always relied on the potential of hostility that was latent between Negro and East Indian" (Adamson 1972: 266). And it is probably more than coincidental that the zone west of the Essequibo River was the calmest area of the coastal plain during Guyana's racial violence of the early 1960's. In the Essequibo area there are no estate or mining jobs at stake.

Such a view complements most research done among the Indians of the West Indies, much of which has been biased toward the study of non-economic elements of culture among Caribbean Indians (Schwartz 1964, 1965; Smith and Jayawardena 1958, 1959) and has therefore tended to reinforce the idea that this group is understandable principally on the basis of its ethnic identity (Despres 1969: 32–33; Klass 1961). Anthropological predilections have been in devoting efforts toward determining the persistence or dissolution of sociocultural variables from India or of studying Caribbean Indians as part of a "plural society." In contrast, this tracing of the evolution and persistence of plantation-based village settlements and economic activities provides a different filter through which to view the East Indians of the West Indies. Such a view is somewhat similar to those put forth by West Indian economists dealing with the Caribbean as an economic region (Beckford 1972; Best 1968).

The ethnicity variable could be appealed to, of course, in explaining the close areal correlation between rice acreage and concentrations of Indian villages in Guyana. Indeed, early padi production in British Guiana was accomplished by indentured estate laborers using methods they had recalled from India. In Trinidad, however, ex-indentured workers from the same areas of India opted for cane farming soon after indenture. All things being equal, cane farming has always been more remunerative than subsistence farming in the British Caribbean partially because plantation crop-biased market outlets have been directed toward serving metropolitan, not local, needs. A more reasonable explanation for the high incidence of rice farming in Guyana is that the ecological constraint associated with water control has never allowed the emergence of a cane farming peasantry of any size along the coastal plain. Even today small-scale Guyanese cane farming is limited to a few village zones which border contemporary plantations and benefit partially from estate water control systems. Also, it must be remembered that rice was a village staple in each of the three black villages of Guyana analyzed twenty years ago by Raymond Smith (Smith 1956: 26–32).

The part-time character of livelihood in both Guyana and Trinidad throws light upon the persistent dilemma associated with finding a convenient typology for rural West Indians (Frucht 1967; Mintz 1953; Norton and Cumper 1966). Spatially, the rural inhabitant of Guyana and Trinidad is indeed neither entirely "peasant" nor totally "proletarian" but some of each. He has always moved, often daily, along the continuum between his community of residence and the rural representatives of metropolitan markets, the plantations. It is this individual mobility, not the exploitation of a single, locationally static niche, which has been the essence of livelihood in much of the rural Caribbean since emancipation. Such mobility blurs contemporary cultural distinctions between urban and rural areas of the West Indies. There is no city-country dichotomy here based upon the stereotyped portrayal of an underdeveloped area characterized by an urban elite surrounded by a countryside of economically traditional peasants.

The mobility exhibited by rural Guyanese and Trinidadians is not "migration" in the sense that it involves a permanent move from point a to point b. The movement described here is reversible. It provides the human linkage between sources of work and areas of residence. It is therefore not adequate to analyze this movement using traditional migration models which emphasize origins influenced by "push factors" and destinations enhanced by "pull factors", the two polar opposites separated by intervening opportunities. The oscillation between village residence and outside work has an inertia of its own in Guyana and Trinidad. This inertia has been imbedded in the landscapes of the two areas by plantation systems of two hundred years' duration. Outside change, such as marked alterations of the infrastructural linkages, will be required to alter the system.

There are now first signs of infrastructural change in both countries related to the growing cities of Port of Spain and Georgetown. These changes have begun to alter commuting and occupational patterns of the populace living nearby. A stretch of limited access highway exists between Port of Spain and San Fernando which is unrelated to plantation needs but has been designed to facilitate transportation between Trinidad's two largest cities (Mulchansingh 1970: 44). Indian farmers west of Village F have recently substituted vegetables for cane in their fields because they now have a high speed route into Port of Spain. Good roads also connect Port of Spain and Arima which is on the eastern end of an urbanized corridor extending along the foot of the island's northern range of mountains. Similarly, the attractiveness of Georgetown and coastal road improvements in recent years have inspired commuting "into town" from villages of East Coast Demerara which border contemporary sugar cane plantations. A recently-planned highway is supposed to extend east from a point south of Georgetown and parallel Guyana's coastal highway (*Barclay's International Review* 1972: 56). This highway would perhaps develop its own settlement nodes. Changing infrastructures in both Guyana and Trinidad now and in the future may effectively refocus the attention of rural inhabitants toward the largest cities of the two countries and alter the work migration influenced by old plantation roads.

REFERENCES

ADAMSON, ALAN H.
1972   *Sugar without slaves: The political economy of British Guiana, 1838-1904*. New Haven: Yale University Press.
BARCLAY'S INTERNATIONAL REVIEW
1972   Guyana. *Barclay's International Review* (August): 55-56.
BEACHEY, R. W.
1957   *The British West Indies sugar industry in the late nineteenth century.* Oxford: Basil Blackwell.
BECKFORD, GEORGE L.
1972   *Persistent poverty*. New York: Oxford University Press.
BEST, LLOYD A.
1968   A model of pure plantation economy. *Social and Economic Studies* 17:283-326.
BRITISH GUIANA POPULATION CENSUS
1911, 1912   Georgetown.
DALTON, HENRY G.
1855   *The history of British Guiana*. London: Longman, Brown, Green and Longmans.
DESPRES, LEO A.
1969   Differential adaptations and micro-cultural evolution in Guyana. *Southwestern Journal of Anthropology* 25:14-44.
EHRLICH, ALLEN S.
1971   History, ecology and demography in the British Caribbean: an analysis of East Indian ethnicity. *Southwestern Journal of Anthropology* 27:166-80.
FARLEY, RAWLE
1954   The rise of peasantry in British Guiana. *Social and Economic Studies* 2:87-103.
FRUCHT, RICHARD
1967   A Caribbean social type: Neither "peasant" nor "proletarian." *Social and Economic Studies* 16:295-300.
GOVERNMENT OF TRINIDAD AND TOBAGO
1887   *Reports of the wardens and assistant wardens for 1886*. Council paper 27. Port of Spain.

1888   *Reports of the wardens and assistant wardens for 1888.* Council paper 15. Port of Spain.

1903   *Wardens' reports for 1902–1903.*Council paper 114. Port of Spain.

KLASS, MORTON

1961   *East Indians in Trinidad.* New York: Columbia University Press.

LAMONT, SIR NORMAN

1933   *Problems of Trinidad.* Port of Spain: Yuille's.

LOWENTHAL, DAVID

1960   Population contrasts in the Guianas. *The Geographical Review* 50:41-58.

MAHARAJ, DAYANAND

1969   "Cane farming in the Trinidad sugar industry." Unpublished doctoral dissertation, University of Edinburgh.

MANDLE, JAY R.

1970   Population and economic change: The emergence of the rice industry in Guyana, 1895-1915. *The Journal of Economic History* 30: 785-801.

MATHIESON, WILLIAM L.

1967   *British slave emancipation, 1838-1849.* New York: Octagon.

MINTZ, SIDNEY W.

1953   The folk-urban continuum and the rural proletarian community. *The American Journal of Sociology* 59:136-143.

MULCHANSINGH, VERNON C.

1970   A model approach to the understanding of the transportation network of Trinidad, W. I. *Caribbean Quarterly* 16:23-51.

NATH, DWARKA

1950   *A history of Indians in British Guiana.* London: Thomas Nelson and Sons.

NORTON, A. V., G. E. CUMPER

1966   "Peasant," "plantation," and "urban" communities in rural Jamaica: a test of the validity of the classification. *Social and Economic Studies* 15:338-352.

REPORT FROM THE SELECT COMMITTEE ON WEST INDIA COLONIES

1842   London: House of Commons.

ST. CLAIR, THOMAS S.

1947   *A soldier's sojourn in British Guiana, 1806-1808.* Edited by Vincent Roth. Georgetown: The Daily Chronicle.

SCHWARTZ, BARTON M.

1964   Caste and endogamy in Trinidad. *Southwestern Journal of Anthropology* 20:58-66.

1965   Patterns of East Indian family organization in Trinidad. *Caribbean Studies* 5:23-36.

SMITH, RAYMOND T.

1956   *The Negro family in British Guiana.* London: Routledge and Kegan Paul.

SMITH, RAYMOND T., CHANDRA JAYAWARDENA

1958   Hindu marriage customs in British Guiana. *Social and Economic Studies* 7: 178-94.

1959   Marriage and the family amongst East Indians in British Guiana. *Social and Economic Studies* 59:321-376.

WELLER, JUDITH ANN
  1968 *The East Indian indenture in Trinidad.* Rio Piedras, Puerto Rico: Institute of Caribbean Studies.
WOOD, DONALD
  1968 *Trinidad in transition: the years after slavery.* New York: Oxford University Press.
YOUNG SING. GLORIA E.
  1964 "The evolution of the present pattern of agricultural land use in the island of Trinidad in the West Indies." Unpublished doctoral dissertation, Queen's University, Belfast.

The "Native Reserves" (Bantustans) and the Role of the Migrant Labor System in the Political Economy of South Africa

BERNARD MAGUBANE

> The Colored people are generally looked upon by the Whites as an inferior race, whose interests ought to be systematically disregarded when they come into competition with their own, and should be governed mainly with a view to the advantage of the superior race. For this advantage two things are considered to be especially necessary: first that facilities should be afforded to the white colonists for obtaining the possession of land theretofore occupied by the Native tribes; secondly: that the Kaffir population should be made to furnish as large and as cheap a supply of labour as possible.
>
> EARL GREY (1880; quoted in Morel 1969:30)

In the study of reserves and migrant labor we have inherited a distorted understanding of their role in relation to the large capitalist economy. The reserves, we were told, were merely places in which Africans were to be protected for their own sake in the era of white conquest, and now the reserves are being seriously developed for eventual autonomy. Thus the reserves and the larger society are considered as separate entities, rather than as two sides of the same coin: development and underdevelopment, affluence and poverty. In this paper I will illustrate that the reserves are the method by which capital exploits labor to reap super profits.

The statement quoted above, made by an agent of British imperialism, in actual fact sums up the essence of what South Africa calls her "native policy." If the capitalist mode of production was to appear and develop it was necessary to do more than deprive the immediate producers of the means of production and make them "free" paupers; wealth had to be concentrated in the hands of the conquering settlers. The process of "imperialization" involved the restructuring of African subsistence society in such a way that peasants in the reserves could never become economically self sufficient again. The process which deprived Africans of their means of subsistence and reduced them to wage labor is not unique. Marx wrote that one of Wakefield's great merits is connected with his discoveries regarding the colonies:

First of all he discovered that in the colonies the ownership of money, the means of subsistence, machinery and other means of production, do not suffice to stamp the owner as a capitalist unless there exist, as a correlative wage workers, other persons who are compelled to sell themselves "voluntarily." He made the discovery that capital is not a thing, but a social relation between persons, and a relation determined by things. Mr. Peel, he says lamentingly, took with him from England to Swan River, Western Australia, means of subsistence and of production to the value of £50,000. He had the foresight to take with him, in addition, 3000 persons, men, women and children, members of the working class. But, on arrival at his destination, Mr. Peel was "left without a servant to make his bed or fetch him water from the river." Poor Mr. Peel, who had provided for everything, except for the export of the English relations of production. He had forgotten to bring these with him to Swan River! (1957:850).

When the English appeared in the Cape Colony in 1906, they brought settlers with capital who were expected to find their workers among the indigenous population. Their problem then was how to avoid the fate of Mr. Peel. Behind the wars of conquest and the "setting" aside of areas for African occupation is a more pervasive and sinister aspect of capitalist society – the need for a class of laborers to be exploited. For British imperialism, Africans were not just going to be conquered and decimated: they were to be relegated to a condition in which they would be dependent in every aspect on their conquerers for their livelihood. The imposition of capitalist productive relations engendered a profound crisis in African societies that were now being confined in the reservations.

One of the great achievements of Marx was to show that the specific exploitative relations of capitalism are recreated in the colonies in a different manner than in the metropolis:

It is otherwise in the colonies. There the capitalist regime encounters on all hands the resistance of producers who own the means of production with which they work, and who can gain wealth for themselves by their own labour instead of working to enrich a capitalist. The contradiction between these diametrically opposed economic systems works itself out in practice as a struggle between the two. When the capitalist is backed up by the power of the mother country, he tries, by forcible means, to clear out of his way the modes of production and appropriation that are based upon the independent labour of the producers. Whereas in the mother country, self-interest constrains the political economist, the sycophant of capital, to declare that the capitalist method of production is theoretically identical with its opposite; in the colonies, self-interest compels him to make a clean breast of it, and to acknowledge frankly that the two methods of production are antagonistic. To this end he shows that the development of the social productivity of labour, cooperation, the division of labour, the large-scale application of machinery, and the like, are impossible without the expropriation of the workers and a suitable transformation of their means of production into capital. In the interest of what is called "national wealth", he casts about for artificial means which will ensure the poverty of the common people. His apologetic armour, therefore, crumbles away bit by bit, like touchwood (1957:848–849).

The last sentence is extremely important. From the very beginning of white settler colonization, the colonists decided that the African population was suitable for the most brutal, insidious and cruel spoilations. In the process of harnessing their labor, a policy of conquest was begun that would not destroy the population but that would deprive it of its land and subsistence and thus reduce it, in effect, to a mere instrument in the process of capitalist prosperity. The Africans were subjected to both expropriation and appropriation. That was the secret alike of conquest and of the setting aside of the reservations in which they would find it hard to continue any form of independent subsistence. From their labor the settlers secured the surplus that provided them with the much needed capital. In his article, Mafeje (1973) describes the objectives of capitalism in the colonies:

In its imperialist form the objective of West European capitalism was NOT transformation of traditional societies, wherever it found them, but rather their incorporation so as to secure markets and supplies of raw materials... It did this by undermining or reconstructing traditional society in such a manner that it could satisfy its needs, without necessarily reproducing itself as a genuine mode of production. The primitive accumulation it engendered via the world market did not lead to a new and expanding SOCIAL division of labour as in Europe. Instead, it contrived to maintain some semblance of traditional society on non-traditional terms...

We, thus, see that in these countries the logic of predatory capitalism has not been a replacement of the old social formations by new ones but rather an establishment of a hybrid social formation.

By analyzing the history and evolution of the so-called native reserves, I hope to demonstrate in this chapter how these hybrid forms are created and maintained.

The great advantage of confining African labor in the reserves is this: there not only are Africans who are to become wage workers reproduced cheaply over and over again, but the reserves are also used as dumping grounds for the human waste that is discarded in the urban and mining industries. As a result a "perfect" number is maintained of the needed African labor in the so-called "white" areas. The so-called "African" areas suffer from the indispensable economic and social dependence on the "white" areas – a dependency which the capitalist sector wants to maintain by all the political means at its disposal and which the social scientist falsely represents as an aspect of a dual society or a plural society.

In a prototypical essay, W. A. Lewis characterized the economic relations of what he calls a dual society as follows:

The fact that the wage level in the capitalist sector depends upon earnings in the subsistence sector is sometimes of immense political importance, since its effect is that capitalists have a direct interest in holding down the productivity of the subsistence workers. Thus, the owners of plantations have no interest in seeing knowledge of new techniques or new seeds conveyed to the peasants, and if they are influential in the government, they will not be found using their influence to expand the facilities for agricultural extension. They will not support proposals for land settlement, and are often instead to be found engaged in turning the peasants off their lands. (cf. Marx on "Primary Accumulation"). This is one of the worst features of imperialism, for instance. The imperialists invest capital and hire workers; it is to their advantage to keep wages low, and even in those cases where they do not actually go out of their way to impoverish the subsistence economy, they will at least very seldom be found doing anything to make it more productive. In actual fact the record of every imperial power in Africa in modern times is one of impoverishing the subsistence economy, either by taking away the people's land, or by demanding forced labor in the capitalist sector, or by imposing taxes to drive people to work for capitalist employers. Compared with what they have spent on providing facilites for European agriculture or mining, their expenditure on the improvement of African agriculture has been negligible. The failure of imperialism to raise living standards is not wholly to be attributed to self-interest, but there are many places where it can be traced directly to the effects of having imperial capital invested in agriculture or in mining (1954:139).

The dependence of wages in the capitalist sector upon earnings in the subsistence sector is reminiscent of the development of German capitalism in the 19th century as described by Engels:

Here we see clearly: that which at an earlier historical stage was the basis of relative well-being for the workers, namely, the combination of agriculture and industry, the ownership of house, garden and field, and security of tenure in the dwelling-place, is becoming today, under the rule of large-scale industry, not only a worse hindrance to the worker, but the greatest misfortune for the whole working class, the basis for an exampled depression of wages below their normal level, and that not only for individual districts and branches of enterprise, but for the whole country. No wonder that the big bourgeoisie and petty bourgeoisie who live and grow rich from these abnormal deductions from wages are enthusiastic over rural industry and the workers owning their own houses, and that they regard the introduction of new domestic industries as the sole remedy for all rural distress (n.d.: 15).

The genesis of capitalism in South Africa in some respects was not unique. It had aspects similar to the German variant but sharply differed from it both in the cause of development and ultimate results. The capital that was invested in the development of South Africa's rich mineral resources was mature capital and it depended for its super profits on the impoverished masses of African workers confined in the reserves. The chief characteristic of the labor from the reserves has historically been its inability to meet even the minimum African subsistence needs.

The process that transforms, on the one hand, the social means of subsistence and production into capital and, on the other hand, the immediate producers into wage labor, differs under different circumstances. Engels, for instance, points out that:

When in the decline of the Roman Republic, the free Italian peasants were expropriated from their land, they formed a class of "poor whites" similar to that of the Southern Slaves before 1861; and between slaves and poor whites, two classes equally unfit for self-emancipation, the old world went to pieces. *In the middle ages, it was not the expropriation of the people from, but on the contrary, their appropriation to the land which became the source of feudal oppression.* The peasant retained his land, but was attached to it as a serf or villein, and made liable to tribute to the lord in labor and in produce. *It was only at the dawn of modern times, towards the end of the fifteenth century, that the expropriation of the peasantry on a large scale laid the foundation of the modern class of wage-workers who possess nothing but their labor-power and can live only by selling that labor power to others.* But if the expropriation from the land brought this class into existence, it was the development of capitalist production, of modern industry and agriculture on a large scale which perpetrated it, increased it, and shaped it into a distinct class with distinct interests and a distinct historical mission (Marx and Engs 1962: 10–11; emphasis added).

The development of capitalism in South Africa shared these general patterns. As long as Africans had free access to (relatively) plentiful land it was difficult for the mines and agriculture to satisfy their labor needs. The methods had to be devised to create free-wage labor for diamond and gold mines, and these methods illustrate how basic the land question was.

Marx laid down the axiom of the genesis of capitalist relations of production. That is for capitalist accumulation to work, two different kinds of commodity possessors must come face to face: on the one hand, owners of money, means of production and subsistence, who are eager to increase their capital by buying other people's labor; on the other hand "free" laborers, the sellers of their own labor power, in a double sense (that is, they themselves neither form part and parcel of the means of production, as in the case of slaves and bondsmen, nor own any means of production, as is the case with peasant proprietors; they are, therefore, "free" and unencumbered by any means of production of their own).

In the opening passage of the *Pre-capitalist economic formations*, Marx puts it this way:

One of the prerequisites of wage labor and one of the historic conditions for capital is free labor and the exchange of free labor against money.... Another prerequisite is the separation of free labor from the objective conditions of its realization – from the means and material of labor. This means above all that the worker must be separated from the land, which functions as his natural laboratory. This means the dissolution both of free petty landownership and of communal landed property, based on the oriental commune. In both these forms the relationship of the worker to the objective conditions of his labor, is one of ownership: this is the natural unity of labor with its material prerequi- sites. Hence the worker has an objective existence independent of his labor. The individual is related to himself as a proprietor, as master of the conditions of his reality. The same relation holds between one individual and the rest... (1965:67).

As the South African capitalist economy developed, peasants were progressively pushed to the reserves where they were then recruited to spend a large portion of their time working for wages. The peasants drawn into the capitalist market became willy nilly imprisoned by their dependency on wages which in turn perpetuated their exploitability.

As the cash nexus was firmly established, migrant labor relations were structured as a permanent way of life for people in the reserve. The circulation of labor between the mine-head and the reserves was main- tained and reproduced on a continuously expanding scale by various economic and "legal" means to meet mining and other industries' need for cheap labor.

Rosa Luxemburg demonstrated how mature capital, greedy for super- profits, depends in all respects on the exploitation of noncapitalist strata and social organizations existing side by side with, and integrated into, the capitalist structures.

Since the accumulation of capital becomes impossible in all points without non-capitalist surrounding, we cannot gain a true picture of it by assuming the exclusive and absolute domination of the capitalist mode of production.... Capital needs the means of production and the labour power of the whole globe for untrammelled accumulation; it cannot manage without the natural resources and the labour power which all territories provide. Seeing that the overwhelming majority of resources and labour power is in fact still in the orbit of pre-capitalist production – this being the historical milieu of accumulation –

capital must go all out to obtain ascendancy over these territories and social organizations. And in fact, primitive conditions allow of a greater drive and of far more ruthless measures than could be tolerated under purely capitalist social conditions (1965: 395–400).

The exploitation of gold mining accelerated the incursion and penetration of the "native" reserves by labor recruiters who siphoned off the so-called able-bodied males for labor in the mines.

The relations between the capitalist gold mining sector and the reserves is a classic demonstration of the workings of internal colonialism as well. André Gorz has advanced the important concept that colonialism is not simply the external practice of one country against the interests of another. On the contrary, he maintains, and rightly, that it is from the first an internal practice (Gorz 1971: 22–28). That is, the capitalist state invariably internalizes the colonial form of exploitation for certain areas and people.

When diamond and gold mining developed between 1864 and 1900, it constituted the first genuine branch of capitalist industry in South Africa. The internal colonialism that is articulated in the reserve system was simultaneously a way of prolonging the life of mining capitalism, and a way of very effectively limiting the development of these areas. Only the man power of these areas had to be "set free" in order to be enrolled in the active sphere of capitalist production. As Rosa Luxemburg explains:

The emancipation of labour power from primitive social conditions and its absorption by capitalist wage system is one of the indispensable historical bases of capitalism. For the first genuinely capitalist branch of production, the English cotton industry, not only the cotton of the Southern states of the American Union was essential, but also the millions of African Negroes who were shipped to America to provide the labour power of the plantations, and who later, as a free proletariat, were incorporated in the class of wage labourers in a capitalist system. Obtaining the necessary labour power from non-capitalist societies, the so called "labour-problem", is even more important for capital in the colonies. All possible methods of "gentle compulsion" are applied to solving this problem, to transfer labour from former social systems to the command of capital. This endeavor leads to the most peculiar combinations between the modern wage system and primitive authority in the colonial countries (1965:362–363).

Rosa Luxemburg illustrated the last point by quoting Bryce, an English Minister who had visited South Africa and who described a model pattern or a hybrid form of incorporation of the African in the diamond mines.

When Africans were first pressed to labour in the mines as wage earners, they were retained for six or nine months. In the rest of the year they were supposed to take part in their traditional subsistence, based on land. But the major

portion of African lands, as we have seen, had been seized in the wars of conquest. The remaining land soon became overworked and "over" populated.
Thus with the opening of diamond and gold mining wage labour became a
major source of subsistence and urban areas the main areas for earning a livelihood. The most striking sight at Kimberly, and one unique in the world,
is furnished by the two so called "compounds" in which the natives who work
in the mines are housed and confined. They are huge enclosures, unroofed,
but covered with a wire netting to prevent anything from being thrown out over
the walls, and with subterranean entrance to the adjoining mine. The mine is
worked on the system of three eight-hour shifts, so that the workman is never
more than eight hours together underground. Round the interior of the wall
are built sheds or huts in which the natives live and sleep when not working
(Bryce in Luxemburg 1965: 363).

To develop the mineral-rich Witwatersrand, the government and the
mine owners resorted to political and economic measures unheard of
in England: it transported on a temporary basis tens of thousands of
peasants who had been forcibly robbed of their land and freedom. The
migrant labor system created conditions in which African labor would
be reduced to a pure commodity, whilst maintaining an illusion of respect for traditional authorities. The communal ownership of the land
called the reserves is perfectly suited for this illusion. In these areas, the
conquerors have maintained, as far as possible, the outward structure
and genealogy of traditional African systems of authority, i.e. the kings
or chiefs and emasculated traditional institutions. But all these functions
are subject to the ultimate authority of the Minister of Bantu Affairs,
who can veto what he finds inimical to the interests of the larger capitalist reality for which the reserves were created in the first place. As a result of this and subsequent measures of the colonial state, African exploitation became more intensive.

When pre-capitalist societies are confined and objectified in the way
they are in the reserves, they experience regressive decay. Whatever
institutional growth they may require either is denied, because it departs
from ancient ways, or is distorted to serve the objective aims of the
colonizer. The formalized structures of the decaying traditional institutions are maintained as means of social isolation. People of the
reserves are sealed off from relationships with people in other communities, in particular, those in urban areas. They are even sealed off from a
relation with their physical environment. The reserves meant, among
other things, that Africans, after being forced off the land which they had
traditionally occupied, could not move to areas of economic growth
except as temporary migrants. The reserves are an "original" form of
creating cheap labor in South Africa.

Even as early as the middle of the 19th century, when Africans were being dispossessed of their best lands, one of the main determinants of the extent of land appropriation was the amount of African labor to be made available to the white settlers. This explains the scattered, spotty nature of the reserves today. The policies adopted in different places at different periods with regard to the maintenance, disposition, and size of the reserves were determined by the economies of the regions. When Natal began to develop sugar cane plantations, allowing for the presence of a sufficient number of Africans in close proximity to potential white exploiters was a basic strategy in carving-up the lands of the Zulu people. For instance, in rejecting Sir Harry Smith's policy of segregation, Earl Grey suggested that natural and permanent locations for Africans be established with sufficient intervals between them for the spread of European settlements, in order that "each European emigrant would thus have it in his power to draw supplies of labour from the location in his more immediate proximity" (Grey in Van der Horst 1971:16). Sheila Van der Horst explains that the same policy had been followed earlier in the Eastern Cape:

In embarking upon the policy of introducing European settlers into Victoria East and later into British Kaffaria, the administration was in fact creating what were to become in part pools of labour, even though at the time the predominant motive was to achieve security by breaking up the cohesion of the tribes and introducing European ideas and institutions (1971:17).

What is called in South Africa, NATIVE POLICY, was a strategy with three aims; breaking up the military might of the African kingdoms, laying the foundations of "law and order" required for a maturing of the new "economic" ways of exploitation, and creating conditions which facilitated both the incorporation of Africans as labor power and the creation of class support in the persons of "reformed" traditional rulers entirely dependent on the British.

The consequences of the policy of juxtaposing African reserves and areas settled by whites is described as follows by Van der Horst:

The effects of the intermingling of Europeans and Native settlement and the imposition of European government were many-sided. The mode of living of the natives, who had combined agricultural and pastoral subsistence farming, had to be modified. For one thing, it required more land than was now available. But, in the Cape Colony, the contact with Europeans tended for other reasons also to break their former self-sufficiency. New wants were awakened and new obligations, notably taxation, were imposed. All these developments necessitated change, the abandonment of that condition of self-sufficiency in which each household had produced the greater part of its own requirements (1971:25).

As a result of these internally contradictory developments, changes occurred in the structure of African societies: a large part of the male population was set free to be enrolled as a class of wage earners in mining and other industries. Alienated from subsistence this class cultivated desires and habits which made it look upon the substitution of its subsistence with consumption of capitalist goods as natural. Once the organization of the capitalist process of production is fully developed, its momentum breaks down all resistance by the precapitalist mode. The basic compulsion of economic needs ushered in the process of "voluntary" subjugation of the peasants to the capitalist milieu. But as Rosa Luxemburg points out:

Direct force, outside economic conditions, is...still used, but only exceptionally. In the ordinary run of things, the labourer can be left to the "natural law of production" i.e., to his dependence on capital, a dependence springing from and guaranteed in perpetuity by the conditions of production themselves (1965:364).

The reservations were thus designed to deal with economic as much as with political and strategic consequences of colonial economic integration. However, for reasons ideological or otherwise, there is a general reluctance among bourgeois theorists to analyze the South African reserves as an aspect of capitalist society, and hence there is a refusal to see the poverty of the reserves as having been generated by forces inherent in the characteristic features of the accumulation process of capitalism.

Before they were physically subdued, African traditional societies with plenty of land confronted the requirements of capitalism with difficult problems. The wants of an African living within his subsistence agriculture, cultivating his *mealies* (corn), were confined to a *kaross* (skin cloak) and some pieces of home-made cotton cloth. The prospects of leaving his family to work in a mine, in order to earn wages with which he could buy things he had no use for, did not at once appeal to him. James Bryce observed that,

The white men, anxious to get to work on the goldreefs, are annoyed at what they call stupidity and laziness of the native, and usually clamour for legislation to compel the native to come to work, adding of course that regular labor would be the best thing in the world for natives. Some go as far as to wish to compel them to work at fixed rate of wages, sufficient to leave good profit for the employer (1969:23)

In the struggle between the traditional and capitalist modes, the white settler government created the laws to make it easy for the capitalist mode to win. The effective reduction of land for African occupation necessarily limited development of the subsistence sector. In the process, earning money became an unavoidable necessity. In the impatience of the employers, the unavoidable cruelties of capitalism revealed themselves in full glare of day in the methods used to recruit labor for the goldmines. By force and coercion Africans were divorced from their former means of subsistence in a most frightful manner. The record, so far as the activities of the Chamber of Mines is concerned, is stained with pages almost as dark as those which disfigure the earlier records of imperialism in India and America. Rosa Luxemburg quoting Bryce's observations in South Africa tells us that:

Here we see that the Negroes are compelled to work in the mines and plantations of Kimberley, Witwatersrand, Natal, Matubelaland, by stripping them of all land and cattle, i.e., depriving them of their means of existence, by making them into proletarians and also demoralising them with alcohol. (Later, when they are already within the "enclosure" of capitalism, spirits, to which they have just been accustomed, are strictly prohibited – the object of exploitation must be kept fit for use.) Finally, they are simply pressed into the wage system of capital by force, by imprisonment and flogging (Bryce in Luxemburg 1965:364).

With the discovery of diamonds in 1866 and gold in 1884, the evolution of the "native policy," i.e. the creation of the native reserves, began to take shape. The entire country having been conquered and brought under a unified system of government, an effort was made to avoid competition among the various employers and to streamline the method of distributing African labor among hitherto competing employers. Before 1910, Van der Horst wrote:

The mines, and the expanding industries which served them, competed for the factors of production, for land, for capital and for labour. Complaints about the scarcity of labour became widespread, particularly in the coastal colonies where the construction of railways and harbours and the needs of the growing towns competed with the farmers in the market for native labour. In Natal the government renewed the efforts which it had already made to increase the labour supply by limiting the right of natives to occupy land outside the reserves, by taxation, and by the importation of Indian indentured labourers. In the Cape Colony, which was granted responsible government in 1872, attempts were made to promote the supply of Native labour by legislative and other administrative action of one kind or another. The South African Republic tried to meet its own labour needs by intercepting natives who were making their way to work on the diamond-fields (1971:64).

One of the reasons for the creation of the union was the need for a unified native policy to avoid such competition. Only a centralized administration, it was argued, could apportion African labor to satisfy the conflicting claims made upon it. Cecil Rhodes had already amalgamated the rival diamond mining companies to form the DeBeers monopoly in 1889. After the formation of the Union in 1910, Africans were soon to learn that their new masters had harsher ways of dealing with problems of "laziness' and labor scarcity. The cornerstone of Union native policy was to have total control over African labor and to distribute it in an authoritarian way among the different industries.

Historically, several mechanisms of forced labor have successfully supported primary production like mining and cash crop farming. The native reserves and migrant labor became but one version of the classic instances for creating a sufficiently large labor force that is not "completely" dependent on wages and for which the employer can deduct the whole surplus value by paying only supplementary wages for what the worker produces in the land. In the reserves it is always easy to impose noneconomic "inducements" and to institutionalize working class powerlessness. That is the secret of the extraordinary persistence of the reserves.

Though Cecil Rhodes has been called the father of the native reserves and the migrant labor system, English settlers in Natal, faced with the refusal of the Africans to work in the sugar cane plantations the colonists were establishing and lacking the means to compel the Zulu people to work for them, had forced the British government to import 6,500 indentured Indians between 1860 and 1866. Sir George Grey had seen the results of the use of indentured labor in the cane fields of Mauritius, and when he visited Natal in 1855, he approved the importation of Indian laborers. He reported to the Secretary of State that;

One measure which would greatly tend to promote wealth and security of that Colony [Natal], and render it of value and importance to Great Britain, would be to encourage the introduction of coolie labourers from India (Grey in Van der Horst 1971:61).

This scheme, however, could only be a stopgap measure. In the diamond mines an average of 30,000 Africans were employed annually in the first seven years of production. And the discovery and exploitation of gold only aggravated the shortage. Thus it became increasingly necessary to begin a crash program to manufacture a labor force out of African peasants. In 1876, Mr. M. X. Merriman was under extreme pressure to bring in Chinese coolie labor, and he wrote:

In the Cape the government is called upon to survey mankind from China to Peru in the hope of creating and maintaining a class of cheap labourers who will thankfully accept the position of helots and not be troubled with the inconvenient ambition of bettering this condition (Merriman in Van der Horst 1971:118).

Instead of looking to India and China for labor, a commission was appointed in 1893 – the Commission on Labour in the Cape Colony – which made suggestions that every male African should be taxed, with full remission if he could show he had been away from home in employment during the year. So in 1894, as Prime Minister of the Cape Colony, Cecil Rhodes passed the Glen Grey Act. Its objects were: (a) to encourage individual land tenure and (b) to establish a simple system of local councils. This became the surest method of accelerating the dissolution of the traditional social structure based on the communal ownership of land. Rhodes wanted to put an end to peasant "laziness." These two provisions (though praised by liberals as progressive) were intended to negate "tribal" communism and to encourage naked self-interest and egotistical calculation based on the cash nexus.

With the creation of local councils, the chiefs became agents of the colonial power. As if this were not enough, the act also imposed a tax of ten shillings on every male African in the reserve who was not employed by a white person or engaged in cultivating an allotment, or who had not worked outside his district during the previous twelve months. Moving the second reading of the bill, Rhodes, speaking as Minister of Native Affairs, explained:

If you are one who really likes the natives you must make them worthy of the country they live in, or else they are certain, by an inexorable law, to lose their country; you will certainly not make them worthy if you allow them to sit in idleness and if you do not train them in the arts of civilization (Rhodes in Hepple 1968:197).

The agents of British imperialism were past masters in Orwellian talk. The ideology of CIVILIZATION through work was merely a smoke screen for the most sinister scheme of proletarianization of the African peasants ever developed. What Rhodes was telling the Africans was that the reason for not killing them was to make them work. In time the African would learn the bitter lesson that laboring in the mines at wages that made fortunes for the mining capitalist had become an unavoidable necessity. They would also learn that economic bondage and wage slavery were not spasmodic but permanent features of the new system.

After the Boer War, the mining industry found itself desperately short of laborers. Despite pressure, and mainly because of low wages, Africans were not coming forward in sufficient numbers. In December of 1903, a labor commission reported a shortage of 129,000 African laborers in the mines and estimated that by 1908 the shortage would swell to 365,000. The Chamber of Mines, with the support of the press, embarked upon an intensive campaign to win support for the importation of Chinese coolies. The Milner government, which not only saw the gold-mining industry as key to its imperialist ambitions but also believed that the maintenance of British power in South Africa depended on the exploitation of South African gold, agreed to the policy of introducing indentured Chinese labor. As Simons and Simons put it:

There was no time to spare, in the view of Milner and the owners; they wanted a ready-to-hand proletariat at the lowest possible cost who would restore the mines to full working capacity without delay, satisfy share holders, attract new capital, save Milner's reputation and the Transvaal from bankruptcy. They would not wait for taxation and land seizures to turn African peasants into work seekers (1969:81).

Meanwhile, a commission would look into the best way to structure a political system that would compel the Africans to work whether they liked it or not. The indentured Chinese labor, like the Indian laborers, could not be a permanent substitute for local labor.

Before the Anglo-Boer War, there had been 90,000 Chinese indentured laborers in the mines. During the war they had scattered and only 30,000 remained. After the war, the mines needed some 200,000 laborers at three shillings per day (60 cents), the highest wages the Chamber of Mines was prepared to pay. Quite obviously this demand could not be permanently met by an imported and indentured labor force. Without a scheme to produce abundant, cheap African labor, there could be no extraction of gold on a permanent basis, and therefore no prospect for attracting foreign capital to expand the only industry that could make South Africa a worthwhile part of the British Empire.

The importation of Chinese coolie labor was thus a bad stopgap measure. In fact, the treatment of Chinese laborers had become an important political issue in Britain itself. In the Transvaal, Botha and Smuts, who were elected to the government in 1906, had pledged not only to repeal the Chinese Labour Ordinance but also to admit no more Chinese. The repatriation of those Chinese whose contracts expired began soon thereafter. By 1910 all Chinese had left South Africa except for a handful who evaded the net and became petty traders and shopkeepers (cf. Hepple 1968:201).

Having been deprived of cheap Chinese labor, the Chamber of Mines was forced to turn its eagle eyes on the local resources. In March, 1903, the South African Customs conference was convened to discuss the whole question of the shortage of labor in South Africa. Among other things it concluded that the native population of southern Africa south of the Zambezi did not "comprise a sufficient number of adult males capable of work to satisfy the normal requirements of the several colonies, and at the same time furnish an adequate amount of labour for the large industrial mining centers" (Van der Horst 1971:168).

This was a somber conclusion. In July 1903, the Transvaal Labour Commission was appointed. Its terms of reference were "to inquire what amount of labour is necessary for the requirements of the Agricultural, Mining and other Industries of the Transvaal, and to ascertain how far it is possible to obtain an adequate supply of labour to meet such requirements from central and South Africa" (Van der Horst 1971:168). The recommendations of this commission were put into effect three years after the formation of the Union of South Africa, by the passage of the 1913 Land Act. This act became one of the most effective instruments in creating a landless class of Africans who could be easily compelled to take up work with the mines and white settlers who needed their labor.

The immediate object of the act was to abolish the system of "farming-on-the-half" and to eliminate squatter locations. Farming-on-the-half was a system whereby Africans, who owned their own plough and oxen, entered into a partnership with a white landowner and worked the land, sowed their own seed, reaped the crop, and then handed over half of it to the farmer in return for the right to cultivate, graze stock, and live on the land. The abolition of this system uprooted hundreds of Africans from land that had become white-owned farms. These displaced peasants were sent wandering the roads of the country with no place to establish new homes. According to Francis Wilson:

Few laws passed in South Africa can have been felt with such immediate harshness by so large a section of the population. The system of farming-on-the-half which had flourished ever since whites gained control of the interior, was dealt a blow from which it never recovered. The next three decades were to see the almost total elimination of that class of rural Africans who, in the words of Sol Plaatje's policeman, had once been "fairly comfortable, if not rich and (who) enjoyed the possession" of their stock, living in many instances just like Dutchmen (1971:128).

Wilson then deals with long-range effects of the act:

In the longer term, the Act served well to fuse those idealists, who felt that partition alone was a realistic means of protecting Africans from total domination by whites, with those more selfish and more numerous people who wanted economic integration, without the uncomfortable social and political consequences. For the new law set aside sufficient land to tantalize the idealist without providing enough to enable all Africans to make their living there and so to be able to exist without working for the white man on his terms. In later years much political dexterity was displayed in using the reserves to maintain a policy which simultaneously won the support of idealists... without alienating the confidence of those voters for whom Africans were primarily units of labour whose presence was essential but only tolerable so long as they ministered to the needs of the white man (1971:131).

The South African version of the enclosure movement was extremely cruel. The expropriation and expulsion of the African peasantry from white farms, intermittent but renewed again and again, supplied the mining industry with a mass of proletarians entirely unconnected with the land and unfettered by possession of a house, garden, or field.[1] The thinning out of independent, self-supporting peasants was duplicated in the urban areas in 1923 by the Urban Areas Act and in 1954 by the Western Areas Removal Act, which abolished freehold that Africans had to land in Johannesburg and other urban areas.

From 1913 on, the Chamber of Mines and the capitalist farmers would have a regular flow of "temporary" labor. Furthermore, economic pressures increased when, in 1922, African taxation was transferred from the provincial administration to the central government under the Native Taxation and Development Act (Number 41 of 1925). In terms of this act, all African males between the ages of eighteen and sixty-five were made to pay a poll-tax of £1 per annum. *In addition, a local tax of ten shillings was imposed on every male occupier of a hut in the reserves.* The Native Economic Commission of 1930–1932, surveying the situation after twenty years of active legislation to extract the Africans from their subsistence, commented gleefully:

In the past difficulty was experienced in obtaining a sufficient supply of labour for industries of this country. The native in the tribal Reserves, accustomed to subsistence economy... felt no urge to go out to labour... The European Government, wanting labour for their industries, decided to bring pressure to bear on the native to force him to come out to work and did this by imposing taxation (in Hepple 1968:198).

The 1913 Land Act and subsequent acts in that genre proved one thing,

---

[1]   The forcible removal of Africans from one part of South Africa to another that began by the 1913 Land Act is being continued today on an even larger scale. According to a study just published, *Uprooting a nation* by Alan Baldwin, more than 1 3/4 million Africans have already been uprooted in South Africa and at least another half million stand ready to be moved along. The logic behind the removals is to shift the burden of responsibility to the Bantustans, and because the bulk of industrial growth is based in the white areas, blacks may return to work in a "white area" as migrant labor. "Migratory labor is thus the reverse flow of mass removals: Workers who, with their families, are pushed out of the towns... are often allowed to come back to urban areas when work is available, but this time as migrants; they cannot bring their families with them. Thus family life is being deliberately destroyed..." (Baldwin 1974:9).

The twin policies of removal and migrancy are being used as instruments for "transferring onto the newly created Bantustan administrations the problems of unemployment, overcrowding, poverty, and resettlement," the report says (1974:10).

if any proof was necessary, namely that "when capital finds itself face to face with relations which stand in the way of its needs for expansion and which would be overcome by economic process only gradually and much too slowly, it appeals to the state power and puts the latter into the service of forcible expropriation which creates the necessary force of wage proletariat..." (in Sweezy 1962:304).

For plantation and mining economies a large supply of cheap labor is a must. These industries in fact come to set the pattern in the structure of labor relations, wages, and employment. Cash-crop plantations and mines are extremely wasteful of manpower and thus always experience a chronic relative shortage, which impels the government to adopt even more stringent forced labor laws. With the ever increasing importance of mining in South Africa, it is not surprising that the reserves have been reduced to an increasing poverty: here the threat of death by starvation produces more helpless workers for the mines.

The primary responsibility of the mining industry for entrenching the reserves and migratory labor is not doubted. Hepple writes that:

In view of the considerable use made of migrant labour in the mining industry, its role in entrenching the system is worthy of examination. From the very beginning the gold-mining industry clamoured for cheap labour. The Chamber of Mines urged President Kruger to impose strict control on African labourers. They complained that because of inadequate pass laws and regulations for the control of African labour "it is impossible to secure such combination on the part of employers as would enable native wages to be reduced to a reasonable level." The cash wages of African miners was at the time about two shillings a day. Kruger complied with their request and enacted two pass laws (1968:199)

The 1913 Land Act expressed more than anything the extent to which "King Gold" enjoyed privileges as far as African labor was concerned. According to Wilson, "At the same time as the land legislation was being discussed and passed, mine owners were working out, not for the first time, an agreement whereby the average wage of blacks of any mine would not exceed a certain maximum, and there is a sense in which the Land Act was, for farmers, what the maximum-permissible-average agreement was for the mining magnates" (1971:128).

To sum up, the creation of the reserves, where Africans eke out a less than subsistence existence, became an important factor in South Africa's gold-labor-market structure. In the reserves, commodity labor power does not merely exist, it is also AVAILABLE in adequate quantities for the evolving capitalist sector. Starvation is a relentless goad pushing men out to places where they think they can earn money to support their families. Internal colonialism is the general result in the integration of non-capitalist organizations with capitalism. Working in the mines means, to use Marx's expression, the "martyrdom of the producer." It is inevitably accompanied by insecure existence for the worker. African existence in the reserves became vegetative, with no other purpose than to provide labor for an "exogenous" economy whose products were irrelevant and un-attainable to the African labor force itself.

THE ORIGINS OF THE "NATIVE RESERVES" OR BANTUSTANS[2]

The physical basis of the native reserves is complex; in the era of white settler colonization, they were initially the areas of the country to which Africans were progressively pushed and confined. According to Van der Horst:

The "Kaffir Wars" on the eastern frontier during the late eighteenth century and the first half of the nineteenth were essentially a struggle for land; a struggle in which the Bantu were pushed back until it was finally realized that conquest and expulsion proved no ultimate solution, but were the cause of further unrest (1971:13).

Today these areas have been modified by legislation into labor reservoirs and they are the only areas where Africans, whose labor is unwanted in either the urban areas, mining, or farming, are permitted permanent but dubious legal residence.

In 1964, a "new" legal maneuvre presented these areas as being prepared for independence. It promised that under certain conditions, they may be allowed to call themselves "independent states." These maneuvres are simply not going to achieve this. The so-called Black assemblies are and will remain powerless in matters of substance, since all power still remains in Pretoria. In a resolution 2671 (XXV) adopted on 8 December 1971, the Survival Assembly of the UND condemned the establishment of Bantustans in the so-called reserves as fraudulent, a violation of the principle of self determination, and prejudicial to the territorial integrity of the state and to the unity of its people.

After each act of conquest, boundaries were fixed by the conqueror, who then occupied some of the best land previously owned by Africans. The changes of the frontiers meant that the amount of land available for African use shrank, while each and every African kingdom and chiefdom was incorporated so that its people could become labor power for the

---

[2] "Bantustans" is a word coined on the analogy of "Pakistan" to denote the hoped for "separate" African states within the Republic of South Africa.

settlers. At no time were the reserves intended to support the population that ostensibly was to live on them, for the allocated land was not only insufficient in extent but also inferior in quality. Moreover, as mere subsistence production was impossible, the creation of a surplus with which to pay white-imposed taxes was wholly out of the question.

From the moment the Africans were pushed into these areas, they became totally and fully integrated into the developing "white" economy. Land scarcity forced them to work in the money economy permanently even though at intermittent intervals. But legislation decreed the scope, conditions, and specific application of their labor power. The political and social forms of organization that were imposed in the reserves did not grow organically from the indigenous society, nor were European type institutions grafted onto existing institutions. Whatever institution of rule is used today in the reserves was ruthlessly imposed in the service of the settler economy. In the reserves we can postulate a pure system of subordination achieved after numerous wars. Van der Horst explains:

Stripped of everything, and weary of war, [Africans] desired nothing better than to repair their fortunes by the labour of their hands, and from the first showed themselves tractable, and even grateful to those who received them; while the latter welcomed with delight skillful shepherds and excellent workmen, who were satisfied with very humble renumeration (1971:15).

The economic integration of the African, far from eliminating traditional dispersion, consolidated it. The British conquerors broke up larger states and created units over whom puppets were installed as rulers. This happened, for instance, in the case of the Zulu Kingdom. Extractive capitalism preferred to adopt the old structures to its needs, and through taxation it facilitated "economic assimilation." The relations between the reserves and white areas symbolized the essence of colonial capitalist relations, that is, relations between the buyer and settler of labor power, the center and metropolis, the colonizers and colonized, the master and servant. Like the relation of capital and labor in capitalist countries, colonial capitalist relations are based on the cash nexus and exploitation. Because they are unequal in structure and reward, they have to be maintained by force.

The constitution of the Union of South Africa, in 1910, was the most striking and specific expression of the fact that Africans were not citizens but a conquered people. Soon after 1910, the acts of parliament would begin to tidy the process of dispossession. In 1903 a government commission (already referred to above) declared (in paragraph 207 of its report) that:

...the time has arrived when the lands dedicated and set apart, as locations, reserves or otherwise, should be defined, delimited, and reserved for Natives by legislative enactment.

Further, it recommended that this should be done "with a view to finality" and thereafter that no more land should be set aside for African occupation. As a slight concession, it suggested that there should not be a prohibition on "deserving and progressive individuals among the Natives requiring land." However, the purchase of land by Africans should be limited in the future to certain areas defined by legislation: tribal, collective, or communal possession should be prohibited.

In 1910, a Parliamentary Select Committee on Native Affairs published a preliminary bill which embodied the conclusions of the commission, specially referring to the above-mentioned paragraph 207. Although the bill itself did not become law, the fundamental principle of territorial segregation which it contained became the policy of the Government.

The Native Land Act of 1913 was designed as an interim measure to maintain *inter alia* the *status quo* as regards land ownership, until the passing of a comprehensive and final measure: a commission was appointed to recommend the permanent lines of territorial segregation.

The Act stipulated that, without the consent of the Governor General, no African could acquire from a person other than an African (or *vice versa*) any land or interest in any land outside of the scheduled African areas. Nor could any person other than an African acquire any land or interest in any land in a scheduled African area without the approval of the Governor General.

The scheduled African areas consisted of the existing African reserves and locations in the rural areas of the Union, as well as (rural) land privately owned by Africans – a total of 10.7 million *morgen*. Tenure and occupation of the land in the townships was not covered by the Act.

The scheduled areas where Africans would be free to settle amounted to 10.7 million *morgen*, or a mere 7.3 percent of the total land area of the country. A further 5.7 percent of the area was to constitute "released" areas in which Africans would be freed from the general prohibition on buying land.

White farmers raised an outcry against "released" areas, on the grounds that whites would be prevented from obtaining more farms and that Africans would settle in these areas and cease to provide labor for white farmers.

White politicians began to reassure them that the actual release of the "released" areas would be contingent on the abolition of the voting rights held by Africans in the Cape. But the Act of Union (1910) and the promises not to betray the Africans were still too recent to trample on, and voting rights were not immediately abolished. Neither were the released areas actually released.

As a result, Africans, who were already land-starved, were deprived of the right to freely purchase and acquire land as a prelude to an indefinite promise of land concessions.

The anomaly of the Cape Colony (confirmed by the Act of Union) which gave Africans in the Cape Province the franchise and, thus, a claim to citizenship, was eliminated in 1936 when parliament passed the Hertzog Bills – the Representation of Natives Act and the Native Trust and Land Act. The first act took away the token franchise; in its place the Governor General was made the supreme chief of all Africans, while in parliament Africans were given three white representatives and a representative council to which they could take their grievances. The second act provided machinery for the acquisition and development of the 13 percent of the land intended for the subsistence of Africans when they were not employed in the "white" economy.

The principles laid down in the Native Trust and Land Act went far beyond those of the 1913 Land Act, which forbade the sale or lease of land outside the scheduled areas (that is, reserves) to Africans. The purpose of the 1936 act was essentially political — to establish once and for all that the conquered estate could not be acquired by Africans either through commercial purchase or political means.

The 1936 Native Trust and Land Act also dealt with the important issue of the control and direction of African labor. The Native Service Contract of 1932 was extended from the Transvaal and Natal to the Cape and Orange Free State. According to the Native Service Contract, landowners were obliged to choose between turning their African squatters into labor tenants, subject to the penal sanctions of the master and servant laws, or sending them to a declared native area. If a landowner could not prove that all his labor-tenants had rendered a minimum of 180 days of labor a year, he could be deprived of those considered surplus to his needs. The Native Service Contract complemented the Urban Areas Act of 1923, which declared that all Africans not ministering to the needs of the whites were to depart from urban areas. Thus the Hertzog Bills completed the scenario of conquest.

The struggle for land, which had lasted for three centuries, had now ended. The white settlers had won. Through the 1913 Land Act, the Urban Areas Act of 1923, the Native Service Contract of 1932 and the 1936 acts, the victims of conquest were finally being dispossessed and permanently reduced to "hewers of wood and drawers of water." From now on, they would be available as labor power when it was required by the various sectors of the "white" economy. That, of course, was the original rationale for sparing the lives of Africans — to force them to work for their new masters.

Land alienation transformed once self-supporting peasants into squatters, tenant farmers, or migrant laborers on the ill-gotten settler's farms or drove them into the mines and cities in search of work (This section is based on Hepple 1968: Chapter 13, 93–94.) With the passage of the various acts to which we have briefly referred, the Africans, like the Gaels of the eighteenth century, were forbidden to emigrate from the country in order to drive them by force to the mining centers (cf. Marx 1969:23).

In the history of colonization in other parts of the world, the reserves system has been a common device in the control and relocation of native populations by colonial governments. It is a system that is military and political in design but economic in practice. By controlling the movements of indigenous peoples, colonial governments try as far as possible to prevent any kind of political organization among them. At the same time, by leaving so little land available for "native" occupation they force the indigenous peoples to sell their labor, often very cheaply, to build the settler colonial economy which oppresses them further.

The South African Native Reserves (now renamed Bantu Homelands) today are great concentrations of poverty, disease, and ignorance, deliberately enforced in order to create the necessary labor for the "white" economy. They are centers of helplessness, of discouragement of initiative, of forced labor, and of legal repression of all activities or thoughts that the white rulers fear or dislike. The system represents, in a very real sense, the ultimate in deliberate human retardation. The Africans in the reserves are compelled by their physical hunger to do the hardest and the lowest-paying jobs. The political division of the land mass of South Africa into "white" and "Bantu Homeland" exhibits, more than anything else, the structural entrenchment of an inhuman social geography. The Bantu Homelands in the words of Mbeki are:

...South Africa's backwaters, primitive rural slums, socially eroded, and under-developed, lacking power resources and without cities, no industries and few resources of employment. They are congested and permanently distressed areas where the inhabitants live on a narrow ledge of starvation, where a drought... leads inevitably to famine. They are areas drained of their men folk, for their chief export is labour and while the men work on white owned farms, in mines and industry, their women folk and old people pursue a primitive agriculture incapable of providing even subsistence. The "homelands" are mere reserves of labour, with a population not even self-sustaining, supplying no more than a supplement to the low wages paid on the mines and farms (1964:82).

To make this system work, the chain of command extends from the State President and Minister of Native Affairs (now called Minister of Bantu Development) through the district commissioners in the reserve areas to the chiefs. By making the chiefs dependent on the salary paid by the government, the settlers transformed them into agents for requisitioning labor. The Bantu Homelands reveal the deliberateness and "incompletion" of the project of settlement! The destruction of traditional means of subsistence in order to ensure a constant supply of labor, the restriction of free land ownership to whites only, and the increasing constraints imposed by the towns on African entry and urban occupation, except as hired servants, all served to render Africans submissive and tractable in the hands of their masters, who then employed them as they wished and at the most minimal wages.

Through this deliberate policy, conquerors cultivated the assumption that Africans would be ancillary to European enterprise and yet would continue to live within the social, economic, and political system of the "traditional" society. This persuasion eventually formed part of the rationale for the lie that says that reservations are no longer reserves, but Bantustans.

Bourgeois social scientists have obfuscated the real meaning of the creation of the reserves in South Africa. The importance of the reserves for the whole development of South Africa lies in their "mutual" integration to the economy of the "white" state. It is a relationship based on a classic division between superiors and subordinates, between those who own capital and means of production and those who own nothing but their labor power. What would it mean to the mining and agricultural industries to be without reserve labor? The black worker confined in the reserves is the cornerstone of the two industries: gold mining and agriculture. African labor means the difference between profitableness and bankruptcy. From the exploitation of reserve labor comes the surplus value that is converted into capital invested in the urban-based industries.

In the light of the current debate regarding the future of these areas, I cannot overemphasize the fact that these areas, with a few exceptions, are the shrunken remnant of territories once occupied by Africans and are unevenly scattered over South Africa. The "white" state is a continuous land area, containing most of the natural resources, and most of the results of advanced development secured by the labor and skill of black and white workers — the most exploited of whom are, of course, the Africans. The so-called white area includes all large cities, seaports, harbors, airfields, and areas served by key railways, main roads, power lines, and major irrigation schemes. The enormously rich gold, diamond, and coal mines are located there, as are all main industries and seaports, worked by cheap black labor. The white area includes, as well, the best and most fertile lands for agricultural use (Mbeki 1964:82).

This asymmetrical economic geography is explained in official South African propaganda as the accomplishment of white capital, enterprise, and skills in exploiting the mines, agriculture, and industries; yet no mines or industries would ever have existed without the unceasing exploitation of black labor. In bourgeois social sciences the asymmetrical geography is explained as an example of plural or dual society. The far-reaching discriminatory laws and permanent violence that sustain the brutal exploitation of the Africans, making their tenure in any sphere of South African life extremely precarious, are thus observed. In fact, the superfluity of the white area issues out of the hunger of blacks, its prosperity out of the exploitation, impoverishment, and subjugation of millions of Africans, its exaltation out of debasement. Once the determinant influence of capitalist relations of production on the allocation of land and social resources is recognized, the surface irrationality and the amoral impoverishment of the reserves find their rational explanation.

The Afrikaans expression "too little to live on, too much to die from" is an apt description of the conditions in the reserves, where individuals exist in forced assemblage as groups to which extra-economic coercions and controls can be swiftly applied. The reserves should be conceptualized therefore as dormitories for cheap labor — severe handicaps are imposed on the African people, which depress their earnings, deny them skills, and put a premium on instability. With only a paltry budget and a pseudo-political status, the reserves are rural slums whose rhythm of toil is at the mercy of what happens in the mines and urban areas of what is called "white" South Africa.

In the reserves, we are dealing with regions whose social structures have been influenced a great deal by the demands made on their labor by the mining and cash-crop industries. With this recognized, the real dynamics of capitalist development and the structural imperatives behind the creation of the reserves are opened for analysis; then (and only then) does it become possible to assess the real significance of these areas in a way that does not mistake appearance for reality or mere surface phenomena for structural depths.

With the development of secondary manufacturing, a new demand for African labor was created. The problem of labor in one sector of the economy cannot be separated from its distribution in another. Because secondary industry is in general an urban phenomenon, requiring an infrastructure of services and supplies, urban counterparts to the Bantustans have developed. These are the "locations" or townships which are physically demarcated from the "white" cities whose labor they largely provide and in which all Africans are required to live under stringently restricted conditions. Needless to say, amenities are minimal and slum situations prevail. The structural relationship between the rural Bantustans and the urban locations is crucial here. While the migrants supply labor for the mines, those who are allowed to settle in towns supply labor to the secondary industry which is gaining in importance in the South African economy. The presence of Africans in urban locations demands day to day regulation; the pass system, the service contract, and other documents of eligibility demand an enormous police force and such a force is manned at strategic points by poor whites.

MIGRANT LABOR

Now that we have considered the forcible creation of the reserves as pools of labor and places where conquered African societies were confined, let us discuss the methods by which Africans were incorporated into the economy. Export of cheap migrant labor is not a purely South African phenomenon. Such highly developed countries as Germany, France, Belgium, the United States, etc., take thousands of migrant workers from the less developed countries on their periphery every year. As Castles and Kosack point out:

The employment of immigrant workers in the capitalist production process is not a new phenomenon. The Irish played a vital part in British industrialization. Not only did they provide a special form of labour for heavy work of a temporary nature on railways, canals and roads; their competition also forced down wages and conditions for other workers. Engels described Irish immigration as a "cause of abasement to which the English worker is exposed, a cause permanently active in forcing the whole class downwards" (1972:6).

Migrant workers in Europe have long filled the lowest paid jobs in city services: sweeping streets and mending roads. In the United States, migrant workers are employed to harvest vegetables, fruits, and tobacco in such states as California and Connecticut.

Labor migration in South Africa, although superficially similar to all capitalist societies in search of cheap labor that can be disposed of easily in times of economic crisis, has certain distinctive features of its own. Woddis has described the unique features of South Africa's migrant labor system:

First, it is a migration *almost overwhelmingly of adult males*, single men, or husbands unaccompanied by their wives and children, who have been left behind in the ruined countryside. Secondly, the migrants usually *take up employment for a strictly limited duration* – six months, a year, two years, but seldom longer. Thirdly, *the migration is repeated again and again in the life of the individual peasant-worker*, his career consisting of numerous short terms of employment alternating with periods at home in his village or the Reserve. Fourthly, whether he migrates from the countryside to a town or mining area within the same territory, or whether it is a question of "alien migration" across frontiers, it is *on foot*. Fifthly, it is frequently *connected with various forms of labor recruitment* which sometimes tend to be disguised forms of forced labor. *And sixthly, it is on such a scale and of such a character that it produces a completely disproportioned population both in the towns and in the rural areas, aggravates terribly the already acute agrarian crisis, and leads to a total disharmony of the economy of the African territories most affected by it.* From the standpoint of labor it has three further results; the constant change of personnel in employment which arises from this system *makes difficult the acquisition of labor skill, creates enormous difficulties for trade-union organization, and tends to depress wages* (1960:82; original emphasis).

Never in modern times has a country based its policy of employing more than 70 percent of its labor on such an extensive use of migrant labor as has South Africa. Why? What does it mean? We think of "modernizing societies" as societies in which there is a permanent shift of population from agriculture to industry. What about South Africa? South Africa of course is one country in the world that has a monopoly of gold, a mineral in universal demand, and it is this mineral that most heavily relies on migrant labor.

To begin, let us view the use of migrant labor in mining in historical perspective as provided by Maurice Dobb. In England, he writes:

When, the supply of labour for any new enterprise was insufficiently plentiful, for example in mining, it was not uncommon for the Crown to grant the right of impressment to the entrepreneur or to require that convicts be assigned to the work under penalty of hanging if they were refractory or if they absconded. This was done in the case of South Wales lead mines leased to royal patentees in Stuart times; from which apparently numerous convicts ran away, despite the threatened penalty, declaring that "they had better have been hanged than to be tied to that employment." Throughout this period compulsion to labour stood in the background of the labour market. Tudor legislation provided compulsory work for the unemployed as well as making unemployment an offence punishable with characteristic brutality (Dobb 1963:233).

In this passage Dobb draws attention to two facts — scarcity of labor in mining and the right of impressment granted by the Crown to the entrepreneur. We have already examined the considerable use of migrant labor in the mining industry, and its role in entrenching the system, despite many tongue-in the-cheek denials, is crucial. On June 20, 1955, in a paper entitled "Development and Progress in Bantu Communities" the late Prime Minister, Dr. Verwoerd, stated the reasons for the preference for migrant labor:

The migratory labour system under which the Bantu sell their working power and labour far from their homes, has been in force for generations. *We all know that for mining labour it is the best and presumably only practicable system.* It is my contention that strengthening of this system and its extention to most other fields of labour would benefit the Bantu, because the established business interests in the European towns will never permit the urban locations to grow into fully independent Bantu towns and because such development would, in any case, be contrary to government policy (1968 [1955]; emphasis added).

The hypocritical character of the assertion that migrant labor benefits the African is too obvious. But the statement also touches on the fundamental principles on which the migrant labor system is based: the need of gold mining for cheap labor. Furthermore, there is, on the one hand, the fear of a permanently settled African proletariat in the towns. That is, that migrant labor creates conditions in which the African working class is kept in a state of permanent disorientation, unable to organize and confront white supremacy where it is weakest. Hepple describes the advantages of migrant labor this way:

There is no doubt that the advantages of this kind kind of labour to employers are considerable. African mine workers are prevented from forming trade unions. Being compounded immigrants, they are insulated from the influences of trade unionism among free workers. Attempts to establish unions are quickly scotched, and the organizers severely dealt with. The exclusion of trade unionism has created the extraordinary situation that the industry is organized only to the extent of its white employees, who comprise a mere ten per cent of the workers employed (1968:204–205).

Other advantages of the migrant labor system are that African labor can be rationed and moved from one employer to another and from one branch of industry to another as required by the developing and expanding economy. In times of work shortages, Africans can be thrown out of work and dispatched to the reserves without causing social tensions. The system of labor bureaus facilitates the mobility of African labor. Describing the system of labor bureaus, the *South African yearbook* stated in its 1956–1957 issue:

The main object of the labour bureaux scheme is to canalize Native labour in accordance with the demand therefor. In order to facilitate matters for both employer and workseeker, each labour bureau is intended to form an avenue of contact between employer and workseeker. For this reason, employers are required to perform all their transactions in connection with the employment of native labour through the medium of the appropriate labour bureau. Such a bureau, being linked with the general network of labour bureaux, not only provides a system of contact between employers and workseekers – the only effective means of communication regarding Native workseekers – but also knows from day to day what the demand for Native labour is in various fields of employment. Hence a workseeker, either in the rural areas, or in an urban centre, is advised of the work available and the conditions of service attached to each category of employment. Once he decides to accept the employment offered to him, he is able to proceed directly to his employer, thus avoiding the frustration previously experienced by WORKSEEKERS who failed to find employment on their own. Although it cannot be claimed that the labour bureaux provide for all the needs of every employer or satisfy the wishes of every workseeker, it can nevertheless be stated that their scope is tremendous. During the period July 1955–June 1956, altogether 1,016,378 Native male workseekers were placed in employment through the labour bureaux (1956–1957:361).

Here then we have a full picture of how the African population is organized with maximum efficiency and bottled up in labor reservoirs. From the reserves, channels are created leading up to white farms and mines and wheresoever African labor is needed. As the secondary economy grew and the mining kingdom expanded, an unemployed (that is, "idle") African was an anomaly, a threat, and a menace. He must not be. He must be enrolled in the form of prison labor or free labor; if not, he must be weeded out and sent to the reserves to starve. Again I quote the *Yearbook*, which states:

The large number of unemployed Natives, especially juveniles, found in practically every urban area in the Union, is steadily being diminished through the efforts of both local and district labour bureaux. Large numbers of Native youths previously regarded as unplaceable and labelled as *tsotsis* (gangsters) are now being engaged for work and most employers have intimated that they are satisfied with the services of these juveniles (*South African yearbook* 1956–1957:360).

Since the famous declaration of the Stellard Commission in 1922, the migrant labor system and the rightless status of Africans working in white areas have been secured and entrenched by a complex system of laws and regulations that severely restricts the rights of African workers anywhere. Some of the laws recently passed are the Bantu Laws Amendment Act of 1964 and the Bantu Labour Regulations. A watershed in racial labor policies was passed on April 1, 1968, when the government finally established migrant labor as the only form of employment for Africans in urban areas. According to the terms of these regulations, all blacks entering the white areas to work may do so only on one-year contracts. While they may, and often do, return year after year, they can never qualify for permanent residence under Section 10 of the Urban Areas Act. A government minister declared that through these regulations "we now give judicial recognisance of our expressed policy of building our economy on contract labour" (quoted in *Financial Mail* 1968:198).

The true intent of the regulations introduced in 1968 was the abolition of Section 10 of the Urban Areas Act, which until then had made it possible for an African born in town or employed continuously by one firm or employer for ten years, to qualify for permanent residence in the town. Through the pretext that all Africans are migrant laborers, the government is in fact reducing them to what the late Prime Minister Verwoerd called "interchangeable" units of labor.

Given the political aims of the white state, an African with permanent rights in the city was a contradiction. As a vagabond he could threaten individuals in society; but as an educated property holder, a successful engineer, or a businessman, he undermined and threatened the whole superstructure of settler society. Therefore, patiently and systematically, all the anomalies and loopholes of 1910 are being removed.

The reserves cannot be treated solely as reservoirs for cheap labor. Nor can migrant labor be considered as an economic anomaly, South African's capitalism cannot be understood as an "economic" system in the narrow sense, divorced from the total social framework within which it grew and which sustains it. In a settler society likely to be threatened by African revolt, economic calculations mix with political and strategic considerations. The white settlers suffer from what may be called a minority status syndrome. They have always feared that someday they will be overwhelmed by African political power, if the various social and "racial" groups shared South Africa as a unified political state. To cope with this problem the various South African governments followed a strategy of "divide and rule." The various ethnic groups that made up the country were to be isolated from one another for the purpose of control and containment.

Thus the economic, political and strategic motives are inextricably intertwined in the establishment of Bantustans. The often quoted Landsdown Commission of 1944 particularly stressed the economic motives, especially the crucial importance of the gold mining industry:

The goldmining industry of the Witwatersrand has indeed been fortunate in having secured, for its unskilled labour, native peasants who have been prepared to come to the Witwatersrand for periods of labour at comparatively low rates of pay. But for this fortunate circumstance, the industry could never have reached the present stage of development – some mines would never have opened up, many low grade mines would have been unable to work with any prospect of profit; in the case of the richer mines, large bodies of ore, the milling of which has been brought within the limits of payability, could never have been worked, with the result that the lives of the mines would have been considerably reduced.

That the results accruing from this cheap native labour supply have had a profoundly beneficial influence on the general economic development of the Union is a matter that needs no demonstration. Not only has the earth yielded up a great body of wealth which would have remained unexploited, but vast amounts of money have been paid away in wages and put into circulation for the acquiring of equipment and stores necessary for the working of the mines and this, in turn, has had the beneficial effect upon the development of secondary industries (Union Government 1944: parts. 70–71).

The significance of the availability of "unlimited" supplies of cheap labor lies in the fact that only one portion of the capital invested in any productive undertaking directly contributes to the production of surplus values, and that is the capital laid out in the purchase of labor. Marx' categories of CONSTANT capital (i.e. capital invested in machinery, raw materials, and other accessories of labor) and VARIABLE capital (capital that is not only reproduced but is at the same time the direct source of surplus value) apply with particular cogency to the role played by reserved migrant labor in subsidizing the growth of industry in South Africa. According to Maurice Dobb:

It has always, of course, to be borne in mind that, when they spoke of plenty in connection with supply, both economists and factory-kings had in mind not only quantity but also price; and that they required the supply to be, not merely sufficient to fill a given number of available jobs, but in sufficient superabundance to cause labourers to compete pitilessly against one another for employment so as to restrain the price of this commodity from rising with its increased demand (1963:275).

That is, labor is cheap from the employer's point of view, when he contributes the least possible amount to the subsistence and upkeep of the laborer and when he can use the services of the laborer for the longest possible period, and in excess of the necessary labor time, to earn his upkeep. Slavery provides the most extreme and the most straightforward example of the process of exploitation. Slave labor was undisguised forced labor. Not only the means of production but also the workers were the property of the exploiting class. Everything created by the labor of slaves belonged to the slave owner. He supplied the slaves with the instruments and materials of production, and distributed work and the means of subsistence among them as he wished.

Migrant labor, confined in the reserves, is a variant of forced labor — hence its cheapness. Its resemblance to slavery is obvious at a glance. The fact that African migrant laborers are paid subsistence wages, as distinct from slaves or those working under forced-labor conditions, does not minimize the similarity. African migrant laborers are paid at the minimal subsistence level for single men, even when their families live with them in town. The rationale behind the wage structure is that wages merely supplement African subsistence farming in the reserve. The Native Recruiting Corporation told the Economic and Wage Commission of 1925:

The social and economic position of the Native is such that he is able to satisfy his needs by intermittent periods of service. Generally speaking, the Native postpones going out to work until the last possible moment, and the possession of additional funds merely enables him to remain in idleness a further period... The Corporation is convinced that any increase in the level of Native wages would be followed, to only a small extent, by an increase in the Native standard of living; that the main result would be that the Native would work for a shorter period than at present; and that consequently the Native labour available to industry in the Union would be reduced (Union Government 1944:66).

The close connection between land scarcity and availability of cheap labor was the corner stone in the creation of the reserves and use of migrant labor — hence the restriction on entry and permanent residence of Africans in towns.

By confining Africans to the reserves, where they were free to starve and die, the transition from exploitation of a slave labor to that of forced labor was disguised. Under slavery each worker represented a substantial initial investment for the owner/employer; thus it was in the interest of the owner of slaves to provide them with a satisfactory subsistence for themselves and their families in order to maintain their productivity and to assure their reproduction and replacement. This entailed additional investment beyond the purchase price. The reserve and migrant labor system in South Africa freed the employer of any expenses for the up-keep of his laborers. In the migrant laborer he bought only labor power and paid only for the laborer's subsistence, without heed to his family needs or further reproduction of new proletarians.

In general, the capitalist class under any circumstance goes to extremes to prevent the worker from selling his labor power above value. It often re-enacts the violence of "primitive accumulation" to swell the ranks of the proletariat and to ensure that there are always workers more than jobs, or what is called the "reserve army of labor." The existence of a mass of dispossessed workers, "free" to work or starve, is a necessary condition of capitalist production and accumulation. Under the political economy of South Africa, this general law is facilitated by the native reserves, legal-political enforcement, and the migrant labor system. The migrant laborer, to paraphrase Marx, stands in absolutely no relation to the objective condition of his labor; it is rather his labor power itself, which is placed in an organic relation to production alongside the other natural implements, e.g. cattle which are regarded as an appendage of the machinery if used as draft animals.

Besides economic benefits, there are psychological reasons why migrant workers are preferred for South Africa's political economy. In order to undercut the migrant laborer's claim to urban residence, he is forever forced to repeat the short history of his origin. Whereas, in the manufacturing sector a class of hereditary proletarians has crystallized out, having made a complete break with the country, in the mining industry the typical laborer is forced to be half-proletarian and half-peasant. A yearly outflow of the labor force from the reserves to the mining industry, depleting these communities of their manpower resources, results in a radical change of traditional attitudes and way of life without at the same time compensating the disintegration of the old order. Periodically returned to what are called homelands, the migrant, to a greater or lesser degree, acquiesces in his subjugation. According to Harris (1966–: 98), the sociological and psychological effects of migrant labor are that the peasant, who has been forcibly uprooted from subsistence and made a wage earner, is widely separated in space from his family; but this separation, while lasting for an uninterrupted period, is yet not so long as to break ties binding him to his family and the reserves.

The use of migrant labor shows that the domination of the working masses by capital is never based on violence alone. Capitalist rule is based on a whole range of mechanisms, some objective products of the economic process and others subjective phenomena arising through the manipulation of attitudes. Migrant labor is thus a deliberately contrived system whereby surplus value is extracted from the peasantry without incurring the political and economic consequences of a fully fledged and integrated proletariat.

Thus the employers of migrant labor enjoy many advantages: the initial investment required to obtain slave laborers is eliminated (police costs for maintaining and regulating this labor are high, but they are borne by the state as a whole and therefore do not enter into the profit calculations of individual firms), as is the necessity of maintaining their health and family through further investment. If a migrant laborer becomes unproductive or dies because his wage is not sufficient to meet his subsistence needs, he can be replaced with no additional capital simply by pressuring the government to make the necessary labor available. The cost of labor is thereby reduced to or below the cost of the individual laborer's subsistence. Burnett explains further:

Confined to a "reserve" of one form or another, the peasant is confronted with an insufficiency of land for the profitable pursuit of his traditional methods of shifting cultivation and pasturage, an insufficiency of capital and technical training to turn to a more advantageous form of agriculture or animal husbandry, and a resulting insufficiency of produce to feed his family and exchange for the cash required to pay his taxes and make the necessary purchases of imported goods. It is this condition which necessitates the outward flow of male, and to a lesser extent female, labor from the peasant communities into the European industrial centers. Low wages, short term contracts and other devices calculatedly prevent the vast majority of Africans from taking up permanent residence with their families in their place of employment, forcing them to leave wives and children at home and return to the reserves themselves after relatively short and intermittent periods of wage employment. This has resulted in what Wilson so vividly described as the "hungry, manless areas" of Africa in which peasants buy "clothes with hunger" (1973:22–24).

The "hungry manless" reserves are in a worse position than ever. In 1939 a government White paper on land policy said of the Reserves that "speaking generally," they were "congested, denuded, overstocked, eroded, and for the most part in a deplorable condition." Another typical and authoritative opinion was expressed in the ninth report of the Social and Economic Planning Council, an official body, which called attention to "the incapacity of the Native Reserves to provide even the minimum subsistence requirements under present conditions" (Davidson 1952:62). The African in the reserves is thus often pushed to work for menial wages by the real threat of death through starvation. The physical conditions in the reserves force streams of men into a search for casual employment in European domains or an outright exodus to the towns.

There is some similarity between the position of the Africans, as both tenants on the farm and migrant workers in the reserves, and that of former serfs in the agrarian centers of Europe at the beginning of the industrial revolution. Dobb gives two examples from the Russian and Prussian Empires; we quote him to stress the similarity. In the Baltic States, following the emancipation of serfs, the emancipated peasants were precluded from moving away from the locality, in order that they would remain as cheap laborers for the large estates. "In other parts of the Russian Empire after 1861 the institution of the village commune, with its collective obligations for taxes and other obstacles in the way of transfer of holdings of a peasant household — served to retard the flow of labor from the village to the towns [in order to be sent] from regions of surplus labor to the regions of growing demand in mill or mine" (Dobb 1963:275).

The extensiveness of the migratory labor system as used in the gold mining industry has been described by Houghton as probably the most fantastic labor set-up of any industry in the world:

Imagine an industry located in Paris drawing some 340,000 workers from as far afield as England, Scotland, Norway, Poland, Germany, Italy and Spain, and returning them to their homes once every year or eighteen months, and you have a European equivalent (1967:66).

Given this most peculiar situation, social scientists have been primarily interested in asking: What makes Africans travel thousands of miles to the South African gold mines? As with Houghton, they also often make comparison with some situations from the Western experience purely for purposes of dramatization and to denounce the evils of the migrant labor system without affecting the system in the slightest. However, the scope and extent of the migrant labor system in South Africa lead to the posing of far more fruitful questions. For example: What are the structures of command that compel men to leave wives and children and to travel great distances just to work under the most difficult conditions? Why should employers of African labor tolerate such a situation if in fact it has the disadvantages that bourgeois economists say that it has?

In the vast literature on this subject (some of which we have had the occasion to criticize [Magubane and O'Brien 1972:88–103]), the dynamics of the migrant system are often reduced to the motivations of Africans who "shuttle" between areas of work and the reserves because this helps (it is said) to stabilize their families. The causes of migration thus have been described as economic (e.g. the Africans' need for money to pay taxes and *lobola*); or political and social (e.g. the desire to escape from "tribal" obligations or from the dull routine of the "tribe"). Such subjective conceptions of migrant labor became most useful against those who criticized the migrant labor system, and these ideological assertions were repeated so often that they are now accepted as true. They have congealed to become the cruel folklore which must be debunked in order to illuminate the forcible expropriation of the migrants and their oppression.

Thus, for example, when discussing the effect of the reserves and recruiting system on the economic status of the urban African workers, Houghton reaches this comfortable conclusion:

The recruiting system has had important economic and social consequences. It does not create a permanent class of town dwellers, but is in effect the temporary transference of reserve Natives to the industrial centers to work for a period of nine months or more, after which they are returned to their homes in the Native territories. The recruited labourers *are not wholly dependent* upon their possessions in the reserves. They go to the mines to obtain cash to augment their farming income. *They can, therefore, accept wages that are less than sufficient to support a man and his family dependent entirely upon their urban earnings* (1967:36; emphasis added).

And later, he says that in addition to urban and recruited Africans:

There are a large number who, while they have come to town of their own accord, still have economic interests in the reserves and intend to return there eventually. These exert a depressing effect upon urban wages in much the same way as recruited labourers, for like them they are not wholly dependent on their urban earnings (1967:57).

These conclusions do not simply fail to weigh the effects of political manipulation — they never raise any serious questions about methods of compulsion on the determinant structures of the capitalist system. When Marx (1957) said that in the tender annals of bourgeois political economy, the idyllic reigns from time immemorial, he was referring to analyses like the above. We have seen that (in the actual evolution of South Africa's political economy) conquest, enslavement, robbery, and force played a great part in the production of cheap labor. To those facts the political economist applies the method of psychoanalysis to individuals who are victims of the system. The more loudly the facts cry out in the face of his ideology, the more the apologist of the system is forced to produce obfuscating psychological explanations.

Like "skill," the category "migrant labor" in South Africa has rarely been used to describe a real economic fact. As a descriptive term it is used for political and propaganda purposes, to justify low wages and labor regulation. Houghton writes:

Migratory labour cannot suddenly be abolished because the very survival of both black and white depends upon it, but it should be recognised for what it is – an evil canker at the heart of our whole society, wasteful of labour, destructive of ambition, a wrecker of homes and a symptom of our fundamental failure to create a coherent and progressive economic society... This institution is a symptom of a deep underlying weakness in the whole national structure. Perhaps the most insidious effect of the migrant system as a whole is that it perpetuates poverty, and prevents the raising of consumption standards of the mass of our population (1967:95).

Very little reflection is needed to understand that here we face not only a false conclusion, but also a deliberate apology. Any serious study of the migrant labor system must, of necessity, depart from an analysis of the superficial and must analyze migrant labor and "Native" reserves in the context of conquest and the labor requirements of extractive capitalist industries. That is, migrant labor is part and parcel of the political economy of capitalism and is a system devised and fostered by the state as an organ of capital. The decision to work as a migrant is not in the hands of African workers. Instead, this crucial set of decisions is mainly determined as a by-product of policies over which he had no say. In 1947, Schapera argued this point for the South African gold mines:

It is clearly to the advantage of the mines that native labourers should be encouraged to return to their homes after the completion of the ordinary period of service. The maintenance of the system under which the mines are able to obtain unskilled labour at a rate less than ordinarily paid in industry depends upon this, for otherwise the subsidiary means of subsistence would disappear and the labourer would tend to become a permanent resident upon the Witwatersrand, with increased requirements... (quoted in Wolpe 1972:434).

H. J. and Ray Simons agree with Schapera, but not for apologetic reasons:

The owners [of the mines] contended that the migratory system was "a fundamental factor" in the mining economy and essential to their prosperity. If the African "has not got the reserve subsistence to go back to" said Gemmil, the secretary of the Chamber, "we cannot afford a wage to make it possible for him to live in an urban area" (1969:86).

Gorz has examined the way in which the political and economic advantages of migrant labor work to subsidize capitalist accumulation in geographically selected areas. That is, migrant labor causes an artificial modification of the social and political structure of the indigenous and colonized population. And the migrants, fragmented and exploited, can be excluded from trade union action, which means a considerable decrease in the political and electoral weight of the working class and the weakening of its ideological force and cohesion. Economically, the importation of "ready made" workers amounts to a saving for the "country" for which the migrants work. The country of immigration does not have to pay for the childhood and adolescence of migrant workers, nor will it be responsible for supporting its migrant workers in their old age. The fact that most migrant workers are not accompanied by their families brings the "country" of immigration an additional and substantial saving in social capital (housing, schools, hospitals, transport and other infrastructural facilities).

On these counts alone – not to speak of the under payment of immigrant labor power, immigrant workers are super-exploited by the capitalist class i.e., they are a source of additional surplus value (Gorz 1970:70).

The contribution of the migrant laborers to the prosperity of the gold mining industry has been decisive. Brought up in the reserves in their youth and shipped back there in their old age, the urban-based capitalist industries save a whole range of social costs, and in fact shift the burden of these costs to the poverty stricken and underdeveloped "reserves". All that is produced over and above what is required to provide a bare living for migrant workers goes to the mine owners — this constitutes their profit, their "income." The reserves provide the towns their labor power and their men, without themselves having a right to the social benefits that are a spin-off from the capital accumulated through their activity. The reserves are made to fulfill the functions that capitalism prefers not to assume — the functions of social security for the migrant workers.

The development and prosperity of the settler sector depended directly and heavily upon the existence of labor from the reserves. Dr. Margaret Read points out that:

White employers on the whole are ready to put up with migrant labour provided the supply is constant, for the important reason that migrant labour is likely to be cheaper in the long run than permanent labour. Apart from a rising scale of wages, a permanent labour force would require social amenities, such as housing and recreation, of a more extensive and costly type than the migrant labourer will accept. Even more costly, whether at the employers' or the government's expense, would be the necessary provision for old age and unemployment. The white employers, provided they can get their labour at what they consider to be "reasonable wages", do not, naturally, concern themselves with the problem of whether the African working for them is undermining the economic life of his own village (quoted in Woddis 1960:94).

The studies of migrant labor by liberal sociologists, anthropologists, and economists discuss at length the effects of migration on the family life, the social structure, the economy, and the values of migrants, and they examine its consequences for the attainment or lack of skills among Africans, but they omit important questions regarding the profits that capitalists derive from this labor. At the same time, the conventional approach has tacitly accepted and thus reinforced ideas of the system of labor migration as a necessary evil, for it says that the reserves provide a place where Africans can have land free from fear of expropriation by whites.

By failing to come to grips with the political economy of the system of capitalism, social scientists have missed the underlying logic that has allowed such an obvious evil to continue for such a long time. The labels "homeland" and the "dual" or "plural" society are metaphorical terms for describing concrete policies for robbery and death. In the reserves, the specific meaning of a "dual" society can be observed at close quarters.

Davidson explains why migrant labor has continued:

Earnest commissions of medical men, missionaries, social workers, and officials have debated and debated on the disease, the abandonment of family life, the decay of agriculture, the breakdown of all serious tribal tradition, that are present in central and southern Africa today, and are intimately associated with the provision of cheap labour for the gold fields of the Rand. *The method of this provision – migratory labour – has been several times condemned by official investigations. But the Chamber of Mines has laid great stress on the fact that its policy was to employ cheap native labour; and the Chamber has had its way* (1952:94; emphasis added).

Houghton's description of migrant labor as a necessary evil reveals the dilemma facing bourgeois thought: that it must stop in theory where it must stop in social practice, i.e. it cannot supersede the reality from which its status and livelihood are derived (cf. Korsch 1970:47).

South Africa does not have two economies or two social systems, nor does it have "black" and "white" areas. Economically, socially, and politically the "Bantu homelands" and "white" areas are dovetailed parts of the larger imperial system, and any attempt to obscure this is an exercise in intellectual mystification. It is particularly important to emphasize this in the light of a school of thought that sees South Africa in terms of a "plural or dual society" distinguished by cultural cleavages. The Bantu Homelands and the migrant labor system are as much a problem of political economy as they are a problem of technology, town planning, or a strategic problem to contain revolutionary possibilities.

Marx rightly points out that the bulk of the labor force in capitalist society comprises unskilled workers expending time on routine operations. "Skilled labour counts only as simple labour intensified, or rather, as multiplied simple labour, a given quantity of skilled labour being considered equal to a greater quantity of simple labour... The different proportions in which different sorts of labour are reduced to unskilled labour as their standard are established by a social process that goes on behind the backs of producers, and consequently appears to be fixed by custom" (Marx in Eaton 1963:34).

The Carnegie Commission, appointed to investigate the "poor white" problem in the early 1930's, pointed to the characteristic rigidity and inflexibility of the labor market in the mining industry:

It is... quite certain that the task at present performed by Natives could not simply be transferred to White men, even if we were optimistically to assume that White men (under the conditions in the Witwatersrand mines) would achieve in larger output in purely normal labor. In 1930 in all the Transvaal gold mines non-Europeans received in wages over £7,000,000. A doubling – let us say – of these labor costs, the mining industry could not bear. But even twice the average native wage could not support a White family, for the average earnings of the non-Europeans were £33-8s per annum (Carnegie Commission n.d.).

Houghton and Horwitz directed their analysis to symptoms rather than primary structural causes of the migrant labor system. The socioeconomic conditions that prevail in the reserves or Bantu Homelands are conditioned by the need of cheap labor in the so called white economy to which the reserves are subjected. The need for migrant labor lies deep in the nature of the South African capitalist system. Specifically it lies in the difference the use of migrants make for the profitableness of the mines.

Through centralized recruitment and wage fixation by the Witwatersrand Native Recruiting Association and the Native Recruiting Corporation, both under the auspices of the Chamber of Mines, mine owners were able to extablish a monopolistic position in relation to unskilled African labor. Moreover recruitment was not confined to South African territories alone (as we have seen), which would have limited the available supply and favored the possible bargaining power of the workers, but was extended throughout East and Central Africa, including the Portuguese territories and what were then the British protectorates. Thus by eliminating competition among the mining companies, the government and the Chamber of Mines instituted a method of collective exploitation which is greatly facilitated by the reserves and migrant labor.

Yet, when South Africa's political economy is discussed, the role of the state in providing the political framework for the social relations of collective exploitation obtaining in the mines is usually de-emphasized or even omitted. Alternatively, those analyses which recognize government influence almost invariably assume a conflict of interests between economic growth and political legislation. Such perspectives lead to severe limitations on a thorough understanding of apartheid labor policies, for it has been particularly in this significant area of labor recruiting that government labor policies have NOT been in conflict in any major way with those of the employers. Labor legislation is enacted as much in the immediate interest of the capitalist class as in the interest of the white settlers' state in general. Even Houghton recognized that the labor going to the mines was not subject to influx control laws:

Finally, perhaps one of the most powerful forces of all is the fact that legislation restricting the movement of Africans into urban areas does not apply to mine workers. Thus general influx control, by diverting men into mining, who might otherwise have sought employment in some other field, tends to increase the supply of mine workers and thus to depress wages in mining (1967:162).

The gold mining industry, the original focus and foundation of South African economic development, has waged fierce war against the peasant societies of southern Africa. It has fought to buy African labor as cheaply as it is possible; and it has enjoyed a favored position, always receiving priority in fulfilling its labor requirements. The mining industry will defend its sources of cheap labor with all its might. On a few occasions, when laborers in the mines demanded better conditions, the armed might of the state was used with untold ruthlessness to suppress these workers. Migrant labor and slave wages will be eliminated only when the gold industry belongs to the people, and when the African people assume their rightful place. The impending death of an illusion.

The migrant labor system draws Africans from all over South and Central Africa into the capitalist economy. Thus the migratory labor has created conditions which have spread the effect of capitalist exploitation over a far wider territory than anywhere else in the world. Since 1963, Mozambique (from where more than 100,000 migrant workers are recruited annually) has been in the grips of a successful war of liberation. Recently this movement caused the fall of the Portuguese Government. In Southern Africa, the revolutionary working class has been spread over every part of the country instead of being confined exclusively to the urban centers. This explains the steady, certain, and irresistible progress of the revolutionary struggles in the late 1950's and early 1960's to the most remote corners of the country. In southern Africa it is perfectly clear that a victorious movement in Mozambique will be felt even more in South Africa. The interests of South Africa in the Portuguese territories of Angola and Mozambique were not only confined to the labor these territories supplied, but the areas also provided a *cordon sanitaire* against the spread of guerrillas truggles to South Africa itself. If FRELIMO can gain control in Mozambique, it will not only stop the flow of labor to South Africa, but it will provide fraternal support to South African insurgents, who will establish bases and lines of infiltration to South Africa. Nusey (1974) writes, "In five swift weeks [the April Coup in Portugal] has stripped away the comforting security of Mozambique and Angola, shaken the delicate coexistence between Black States and White States throughout Southern Africa, drastically bruised the White and boosted the Black morale and thrown the future into doubt."

The success of the guerrilla struggle in Mozambique and Angola, and recently in Zimbabwe, will have a definite impact on the South African labor market. Of the 370,000 Africans who work in the mines, only about 100,000 come from within South Africa, mostly from the Bantustan of the Transkei and Ciskei. The majority of the miners are what South African law classifies as "foreign natives," recruited from Malawi, Mozambique, Lesoto, and Bottswane. James Gemmill, general manager of the mine labor organization, expressed the fear of the miners in these words, "If we were thrown on our own devices for labor, we'd be busts" (Gimmel 1973).

When the struggle does get underway the revolutionary struggle of the urban areas will never be in a position to suffer defeats by the reactionary rural areas thanks to the mining industry and the migratory labor system.

In conclusion, the labor used in the gold mines reveals the most carefully planned structures of exploitation. The big mining companies are impersonal, professional corporations. They are rationalized in terms of personnel, production, marketing, advertising, etc. At all times the need to reduce costs gave mining capitalism its drive towards expansion and domination of the whole African labor force in South Africa. In the growth and entrenchment of migrant labor, we see how the superstructure was created by individuals capable of consciously planning the exploitation of resources to eternity, based always on social domination of the Africans.

Finally, in view of the greater expansion of the mining industry due to the external demand for gold, the domestic labor force will be subjected to even greater regulation and exploitation, especially when the guerrilla movement in Mozambique makes it impossible for South African recruiting agencies to get the necessary labor. This will create even more tensions in the domestic labor scene and negate even more the whole bogus idea of Bantustans.

REFERENCES

BALDWIN, ALAN
   1974   *Uprooting a nation.* African Publications Trust.
BRYCE, JAMES
   1969   *Impression of South Africa.* New York: New American Library.
BURNETT, DON
   1973   *Peasant types and revolutionary potential in colonial Africa.* Richmond, British Columbia, Canada: L.M.S. Press.
CARNEGIE COMMISSION
   n.d.   *The poor white problem in South Africa,* volume one. Carnegie Commission Report.
CASTLES, STEPHEN, GODULA KOSACK
   1972   Common Market migrants. *New Left Review* 73:3–22.
DAVIDSON, BASIL
   1952   *A report on southern Africa.* London: Jonathan Cape.
DOBB, MAURICE
   1963   *Studies in the development of capitalism.* New York: International Publishers.

EATON, JOHN
1963   *Political economy*. New York: International Publishers.
ENGELS, FRIEDRICH
n.d.   *The housing question*. New York: International Publishers.
Financial Mail
1968   Article appearing July 19, page 198.
GEMMILL, JAMES
1973   Article in the *New York Times*, October 23.
GORZ, ANDRÉ
1970   Immigrant labor. *New Left Review* 61:70
1971   Colonialism at home and abroad. *Liberation* 15(6):22–28.
HARRIS, MARVIN
1966   "'Labor emigration among the Mozambique Thonga: cultural and political factors," in *Social change: the colonial situation*. Edited by E. Wallenstein. New York: John Wiley and Sons.
HEPPLE, ALEX
1968   *South Africa: a political and economic history*. New York: Praeger.
HOUGHTON, D. HORBAT
1967   "Some economic problems of the Bantu in South Africa," in *The political economy of South Africa*. South African Institute of Race Relations, Monograph Series 1.
KORSCH, KARL
1970   *Marxism and philosophy*. New York: Monthly Review.
LEWIS, W. A.
1954   Economic development with unlimited supplies of labor. *The Manchester School of Economic and Social Studies* 22(2):139.
LUXEMBURG, ROSA
1965   *The accumulation of capital*. New York: Monthly Review.
MAFEJE, ARCHIE
1973   "The Fallacy of 'dual economies' revisited: a case for east, central Africa and southern Africa." Unpublished manuscript.
MAGUBANE, B., J. O'BRIEN
1972   Migrant labor in Africa: a critique of conventional wisdom. *Critical Anthropology* 2 (2):88–103.
MARX, KARL
1957   *Capital*, volume one. London: Everyman's Edition.
1965   *Pre-capitalist economic formations*. Translated by Jack Cohen, edited and with an introduction by E. J. Hahsbown. New York: International Publishers.
1969   *Genesis of capital*. Moscow: Progress Publishers.
MARX, KARL, FRIEDRICH ENGELS
1962   *On Britain*. Moscow: Foreign Language Publishing House.
MBEKI, GOVAN
1964   *South Africa: the peasants revolt*. Baltimore: Penguin African Library.
MOREL, E.D.
1969   *The black man's burden*. New York: Monthly Review Press.
NUSEY, WILF
1974   Article in the *Star*. June 8. Johannesburg.

SCHAPERA, I.
1947 *Migrant labour and tribal life*. London: Oxford University Press
SIMONS, H. J., RAY SIMONS
1969 *Race and class in South Africa, 1850–1950*. Baltimore: Penguin African Library.
South African yearbook
1956–1975 *The official year book of the Union of South Africa and Basutoland, Bechuana Protectorate and Swaizland* 29. Pretoria.
SWEEZY, PAUL M.
1962 *The theory of capitalist development*. New York: Monthly Review Press.
UNION GOVERNMENT
1944 *Landsdown Commission*. Union Government Report 21.
VAN DER HORST, SHEILA T.
1971 *Native labour in South Africa*. London: Frank Cass.
VERWOERD, H. F.
1968 [1955] "Development and progress in Bantu communities," quoted in *Daily Dispatch*. April 12, 1968, East London.
WILSON, FRANCIS
1971 "Farming 1870–1966," in *The Oxford history of South Africa*, volume two: *South Africa 1870–1966*. Edited by Monica Wilson and Leonard Thompson. New York: Oxford University Press.
WODDIS, JACK
1960 *Africa: the roots of revolt*. London: Laurence and Wilhart.
WOLPE, HAROLD
1972 Capitalism and cheap labour power in South Africa: from segregation to apartheid. *Economy and Society* 1(4).

Labor Migration in Papua New Guinea: Primary School Leavers in the Towns – Present and Future Significance

RICHARD CURTAIN

HISTORICAL BACKGROUND OF LABOR MIGRATION

Papua New Guinea is known primarily as the anthropologist's untouched enclave in which Stone Age Man can be studied either as a people completely isolated from outside influence or in the preliminary stages of European contact. Thus, one thinks of Malinowski and the primitive trade cycle of the Kula ring, or the many works on the cargo cults. However, Papua New Guinean society has been considerably more penetrated by the "colonial situation" than anthropology has inferred.[1]

Balandier has stressed the importance of recognizing the pervasive nature of the "colonial situation" as a specific historical factor influen-

This paper owes much to John D. Conroy of the Department of Economics, University of Papua New Guinea, under whose direction the writer did the research. We have collaborated on an earlier paper, which sets out the findings in a more directly empirical fashion (Conroy and Curtain f.c.). Needless to say, the views expressed in the present article are my own responsibility. I am grateful to the following persons for having helped me to locate the interviewees from the original 1968 survey: Karukuru Sere, Mariosu Avosa, Sepoe Karava, Meokoro Opa, Stanislaus Paisai, and Joseph Keviame. A special thanks to Doctor Helen Safa, Nelson Keith, and Eileen Tannachion for reading and commenting on the article.

[1] A recent article on social scientists in Papua New Guinea notes how the country has long been viewed as virgin territory: "In Papua New Guinea, as recently as 1968, almost two thirds of the 47 intensive studies (4 months or over in duration) by social anthropologists and sociologists were directed toward traditional institutions, while only 15% focused on such new institutions as trade unions and schools. The remainder were concerned with a mixture of traditional and new institutions, such as 'cargo cults' and changing patterns of land use... In short, a sizable proportion of post-war anthropologists in New Guinea seem to have deliberately sought out the kind of community long regarded as anthropology's happiest hunting ground" (Clark and Ogan 1973: 43–44).

cing all parts of the total society. Therefore the first fact to take into account in studying Papua New Guinea is that:

There is domination by a racially and culturally different foreign minority imposed in the name of a dogmatically asserted racial, ethnic or cultural superiority, on a materially inferior indigenous majority (Balandier 1961: 54).

After the 1850's, South Pacific slave-trading had been replaced by "blackbonding," a system of "indentured" labor under which the relationship of the worker to his master was brought within the law – a legal fiction, when one party to the contract could not know what he was being bound to. Bougainville and Buka under the Germans provided many recruits, as did southeastern Papua under British administration (Rowley 1966: 58; Brookfield 1972: 31).

In 1906 Australia took over control of Papua from the British. Although before World War II it was commonly thought that Papua was a model colony, its governor, Sir Hubert Murray, strongly insisted that the only way "the barbarous peoples" could be advanced to civilization was through participation in European enterprises (West 1968: 137). The Australian military administration in the League of Nations mandated territory of New Guinea was an even stronger supporter of European plantations, with less concern for the protection of the "native."

One of the key mechanisms utilized to "mobilize" the New Guinean labor force was the head tax. This tax was specifically used to force the young adolescent and adult males into indentured labor contracts. According to Viall (1938: 391), who was an officer of the prewar New Guinea administration, a tax of ten shillings was imposed on all able-bodied males starting from fifteen years of age (exemptions were for "natives" under indenture, village and mission officials, students, the sick, or men with four living children by one wife). He states that for most villages the only way to pay the tax was through returning indentured laborers. "In a few fortunate subdivisions no native need leave his home to earn money unless he wishes to do so" – that is, if there were opportunities for casual labor such as unloading shippings or being near a rich reef from which cowrie shells could be collected to sell to the government for buying food at inland stations. Viall's conclusion: "But generally the only way a youth of 15 to 20 can earn money is to go away under contract."

While legal provisions stipulated set terms of service, accommodations, wages, etc., the concern was actually to safeguard future supplies of labor by not destroying village life and thus decreasing the population. Penalties such as flogging, imprisonment with or without chains, and fining were commonly imposed in New Guinea until the 1930's. Penal sanctions (fines and imprisonment) in both territories were not abolished until 1950! In practice, for some years at least, most workers were not informed of the new situation and continued to be threatened by the planters (Rowley 1966: 105–106; Worsley 1968: 46–50).[2]

The Central Highlands labor scheme is still in existence today. It was introduced in 1950 because of the strong pressure brought to bear on the administration by the European planter interests seeking to tap the half million population in this area. Despite the fact that the highlands had been completely sealed off from the outside world until after World War II, and that there was substantial evidence that diseases such as malaria, dysentery, and tuberculosis would play havoc among those taken to the coastal areas, the scheme nevertheless was instituted with perfunctory stipulations about inoculations, etc. (West 1958: 99–101).

Local adminstration officers soon saw that the highland people were reacting violently to the cultural change. Despite restrictions on recruitment for the whole area to a third of the adult male labor force (a figure in itself high in relation to what other colonial territories, such as the Belgian Congo, regarded as a safe maximum), there was serious over-recruitment in specific areas. In 1953–1954, out of fifty-four clans in the Upper Chimbu census subdivision, twenty-one were over-recruited. By September 1952 (just six months after the first contracts expired), reports were coming in of a marked decrease in enthusiasm to engage in coastal labor (West 1958: 101, 105).

In areas where the conditions of work are known and alternative cash income opportunities are available, the "agreement labor scheme" continues to be markedly unpopular. Labor recruiters have some success (10,000 workers are recruited yearly), but this is in parts of the highlands where there is minimal cash cropping and little contact with the outside world (Ward 1971: 85).

So much for the assumptions of labor operating under conditions of a free market situation. Head tax was used as a means of forcing the Papua New Guinean to search for work in the plantation economy or to trade by selling coconuts or copra. The legal assumption has always been that the recruit was a free contracting agent. And often social scien-

[2] West's 1958 account of "Indigenous Labour in Papua New Guinea" is far from making the critical inferences I have made. His tone is that of a wholesale acceptance of the colonial administration's rhetoric. In contrast to the "colonial intellectual" is Stephen Reed, an American sociologist. Reed's work (1942) on prewar New Guinea starts from the totality of the colonial situation and analyzes in detail the caste-like superordinate-subordinate power relations between the colonizers and the colonized.

tists have carried this assumption over into explaining why Papua New Guineans became contract laborers:

This step, as with any shift of residence whether short or long distance, requires that the potential migrant weigh up the information available to him about his likely destination and assess whether it offers better prospects than this home situation.... The agreement system contract labour has made possible long-distance movements from areas whose people would otherwise have no chance of breaking out of the traditional realm (Ward 1971: 85).

This explanation fails to account for the fact that the contract is and has been the legalizing of a coerced push into the "modern" cash sector, a direction not by any means synonymous with internal and self-reliant development.[3]

INDEPENDENT MIGRATION

After World War II, when the "winds of change" began to blow in Africa, Papua New Guinea remained under heavily paternalistic control. Hasluck, the Australian Minister for External Territories, stated in 1958 that Papua New Guinea would still need a strong colonial administration for another thirty years. However, 1962 was the most decisive year since European colonization. In that year a United Nations Mission, led by a former British colonial governor, Sir Hugh Foot, strongly castigated the Australian government for its gradualism, and demanded immediate preparation for independence.

As a result, a World Bank report in 1964 laid the basis for the country's first five-year plan. Widespread introduction of cash cropping was encouraged, as was secondary and higher education. Localization of the public service in the middle levels was begun, and a representative House of Assembly was instituted. The towns, which had been from the beginning colonial creations, began to expand under the influx of expatriate bureaucrats. Local urban industries soon followed, to cater to the wealthy Australian short-term employee. Jobs became available in the building and construction sectors, public authorities, and domestic service. Especially in Port Moresby, the rate of increase in employment has accelerated rapidly over the last few years (Langmore 1970: 7).

[3]   The report of the most recent United Nations Development Programs Mission takes as one of its assumptions that impelling people to enter the cash economy merely in order to build up the size of the cash economy has no merit. The approach should rather be to seek to create conditions which will facilitate the earning of incomes by employment or self-employment for the satisfaction of those wants for which money is required (Overseas Development Group 1973).

Because of their new dependency on the cash sector, Papua New Guineans have begun to migrate to the towns to find work in the new expansion. The latest available figures (1971) estimate Papua New Guinea's urban population to be 212,643, an 8.5. percent of the total estimated population. The annual rate of increase (1966–1971) has been estimated at 10.8 percent (Ward 1972: 3). While the overall proportion of the population in urban areas is low compared to other underdeveloped countries (reflecting the very recent changes in the economy), the rate of increase is very high. If such rates were to continue, then nearly a half of the country's population will be living in urban areas in less than twenty-five years. Estimates for Port Moresby's population (now at 50,000) have been put at 250,000 by 1990 (Langmore 1970: 29). The rate of in-migration may fall, but not before many more people have come to town and natural increases have become an important component of urban growth.

Of an estimated population of 2.2 million (1966 census), 44 percent has been categorized as still wholly engaged in subsistence farming. A further 37 percent of the population is claimed to be in a so-called "transitional" sector, where subsistence farming is still the main activity, but where the people also have some part in the monetary sector. Thus, in 1966, it could be said that 81 percent of the population was still wholly or mostly dependent on subsistence agriculture. Since then, while the proportion in the "transitional" sector has undoubtedly risen greatly, the combined total in both the transitional and wholly subsistence groups has probably not fallen much, despite the growth of employment in other sectors. In 1966, 19 percent of the population was wholly dependent upon cash income from the monetary sector for its living (Shand 1971: 4).

The model Papua New Guinean cash cropper (transitional sector), according to Waddell and Krinks (1971), is a subsistence producer who spends less than 10 percent of his time on cash-producing activities. He disposes of cash crops either in minute quantities or else rather infrequently, but at the same time he is actively engaged in transactions of goods, labor, and valuables, including money, within the "traditional" system, to which he remains primarily committed. Away from the model picture, there is vigorous growth of "local indigenous entrepreneurs" ("big fellow man bilong bisnis") in parts of the Central and Eastern Highlands and in the Gazelle Peninsula, in such activities as transport, coffee- and copra-growing, and trade stores (Finney 1969).

Nevertheless, this should not hide the fact of the minor share of the economy held by Papua New Guineans themselves. The indigenous share of the monetary sector product was roughly 38 percent in 1960–1961, while that for later years shows a significant and continuing decline to 32 percent in 1969–1970. At the same time, the expatriate share of the monetary sector income rose from 62 percent in 1960–1961 to 68 percent in 1969–1970. Of the total increase in monetary sector income over the nine years (227.8 million Australian dollars), only 29 percent accrued to Papua New Guineans, and the rest to a group which represents less than 2 percent of the total population (Shand 1971: 18–19). Expatriates heavily predominate in the ownership of the larger businesses. They lease the great bulk of the plantation land. Apart from coffee, none of the major export crops were expected to come predominantly from indigenous holdings by 1974–1975 (Clunies-Ross 1971: 475).

In line with the new "developmentalist" approach, the country's economic base is changing from its colonial plantation economy to small-scale cash-crop farming and expatriate-owned urban industries. The 1970 Minimum Rural Wage judgment was a key signpost showing the change of focus in the economy. As Langmore (1971: 59) commented:

Both reports [pertaining to the judgment] apply national economic analysis to the New Guinea situation. This refreshingly cuts through the defensive planter oriented ideology which has dominated thinking about wages for 20 years. The aim of rational economic development is given precedence over short term sectional interests.

However, as I shall discuss later, the "developmentalist'" simple equating of "rational economic development" with urban-centered economic growth is open to substantial doubt.

PRIMARY SCHOOL LEAVERS IN PORT MORESBY

A key area in the growing rural-urban migration is the "primary school leaver."[4] Papua New Guinea has 42 percent of its population under fifteen, and the current objective of the administration is to have 50 percent of all school-age children enrolled in schools. By 1974 fully three quarters of the students completing the primary course will finish their schooling at that point. Although some thousands will attend vocational training centers, this will only delay their attempts to enter the modern sector work force by a year. The increase in actual numbers

4   "Primary school leaver" in the Papua New Guinean context refers to a person who has completed the first six years of school and for various reasons has not gone on to high school or the equivalent.

of primary school leavers is substantial, and there is every indication that they will become a significant social group among the unemployed within the urban areas.

Over four months in early 1972, the author interviewed some fifty-three former Standard VI[5] pupils. The interviews were part of a longitudinal study of a sample of 819 Standard VI students attending thirty-five primary schools in seven rural districts in 1968. The students were ques-primary schools in seven rural districts in 1968. The students were questioned at that time about their occupational and locational aspirations and expectations, a procedure which permitted certain conclusions to be drawn about their likely propensity to migrate after leaving school (Conroy and Stent 1970). In 1969 and again in 1970, mail surveys were conducted to trace the whereabouts of the members of the sample. The second of these placed about 95 percent of the group, and it was concluded that the high expectations of migration by schoolboys in 1968 were being fulfilled (Conroy 1972).

Of the fifty-three found in Port Moresby in 1972, fifty could be classified as independent migrants.[6] These fifty formed a substantial majority of all independent migrants from the 1968 sample who had found their way to Port Moresby at the time of the survey[7] (See Table 1).

The migrants interviewed came from the schools in the Gulf District (a coastal area some 200 miles west of Port Moresby) and the Southern Highlands District (midway between Papua and New Guinea). The greatest number (forty-six) were from the Gulf District, but the four Southern Highlanders were of particular interest because they represent the advance guard from an area which has yielded, as yet, few educated migrants to the towns.[8]

---

[5] The final year of primary school is also referred to as Standard VI.

[6] The following definition of an independent migrant was adopted: Those persons coming (or remaining) of their own volition to reside in Port Moresby and excluding the following cases:
a) Persons transferred by their employers to Port Moresby (as in the case of a man who enlisted in the army at home and was transferred to Port Moresby for training).
b) Persons coming to the city specifically to pursue further education of a type not available at home.

[7] The thirty-five primary schools attended by the members of the sample group were in New Guinea, as well as in Papua. Through University students, formerly of the same schools, the writer was able to trace the whereabouts of most in the 1968 survey. Some had migrated to Rabaul, Lae, or Mt. Hagen. Many were still in secondary school Form IV.

[8] In actual fact, not all could be called strictly speaking "primary school leavers"; 55 percent had completed standard VI only, and an additional 22 percent one year of vocational school but about 22 percent had attained a Form I to Form III level of education.

Table 1.   Independent migrants contacted in Port Moresby

	Male	Female	Total
In work force	37	3	40
Unemployed	6	4	10
Total	43	7	50

Expectations and Reality

The discussion which follows draws upon the raw data of the 1968 survey to describe the age, family background, and migration expectations of the fifty individuals. At the time of their interviews in Port Moresby in 1972, the mean stated ages of the migrants were 18.8 years for women and 18.2 years for men. This figure for males was significantly higher than the mean of 17.5 years (in early 1972) for all males (including both migrants and non-migrants) contacted in the 1968 survey. This may indicate that age has an influence on migration, and suggests that more movement will occur as the mean age of the group rises.

In 1968, 60 percent of the group had described their fathers as farmers, but it is likely that the fathers of the others were also engaged to some extent in agriculture. For example, the fathers of some of the migrants contacted in Port Moresby in 1972 were village pastors, but they and their families were doubtless largely self-supporting in garden produce. Probably at least 70 percent of the group came from families whose income was derived largely from subsistence activities.

In the initial survey made in 1968 by Conroy and Stent it was concluded that:

the overwhelming majority of final year primary [students] ... interviewed ... aspired to enter modern monetary sector employment. For many students this involved a desire to work in urban centres where such employment is available. Sutdents living in areas where wage employment is limited or largely performed by illiterates were most likely to express a desire to migrate (Conroy and Stent 1970: 309).

The information in Table 2, extracted from the 1968 data, shows quite clearly that most of the group contacted in Port Moresby had made plans to migrate while still at primary school. Only 14 percent expected to live and work at home, while 86 percent anticipated traveling away from the home district. Of these, fully 60 percent named major urban areas (Port Moresby, Lae, Rabaul, Goroka, Wewak, and Madang), while the remainder named various minor urban areas. Nor was there anything very

Table 2. Expectations in 1968 of future location

	Number	Percent
Own subdistrict	7	14
Elsewhere within own district	7	14
Port Moresby subdistrict	18	36
Other major urban subdistricts	12	24
Other	5	10
No answer	1	2
Total	50	100

fanciful about these plans: by 1971 various of their classmates were to be found in practically all of these places (Conroy 1972:367). That these school leavers came to Port Moresby is less important than the fact of their clear intention to migrate in the first place. Once a young person in the Gulf District decides to leave home, practical considerations draw him almost invariably to Port Moresby.

Similar considerations would appear to make Mount Hagen or Gorka (major towns in the Highlands) the most obvious destinations for the Southern Highlanders, especially given the expense of the air fare (the only transport available) to Port Moresby. None of the four migrants from that district had expected to move to Port Moresby, but all anticipated leaving their home district. Their final destination points to the greater information about more job opportunities in the capital city.

The group's strongly expressed expectations of urban living is reflected also in the form of an equally strong expectation of wage employment in urban occupations. Table 3 offers a comparison of the occupations anticipated in 1968 with those actually held in 1972 by the forty migrants working at the time of the interviews. Only two students had expected to become farmers; the bulk of the group expected to find modern sector jobs of a largely urban nature, or jobs which (as in the case of teaching) would probably necessitate migration from home.

Conroy and Stent concluded from the 1968 survey that in the aggregate the expectations were unrealistic in the face of the rising qualifications demanded by employers and the sheer growth of the numbers of school leavers. As Table 3 shows, the occupations aspired to and those actually achieved by the forty with jobs in 1972 were somewhat divergent. Nevertheless, most found work at some time and many were in jobs that paid above the urban minimum wage.

Langmore projected that from 1967 to 1973 urban employment opportunities for Papua New Guinea would expand from 40,600 to

Table 3. Expected and achieved work-force status*

Expected in 1968					Achieved in 1972				
Manpower class	Number	Percent	Occupation	Number	Manpower class	Number	Percent	Occupation	Number
A Professional, managerial, etc.	–	–			A	–	–		
B Semiprofessional, higher technical, submanagerial	6	15.0	Teacher Pilot Forestry officer	4 1 1	B	–	–		
C Skilled	17	42.5	Skilled trades Teacher Clerical Customs officer Ship's Officer	9 4 1 2 1	C	1	2.5	Potter	1
D Semiskilled	14	35.0	Army/police Tradesman Typist/clerical Nurse	3 8 2 1	D	15	37.5	Tradesman Clerical Shop assistant Typist Army	4 4 5 1 1
E Unskilled	2	5.0	Farmer	2	E	22	55.0	Clerical Manual Storeman Shop assistant Child care	10 6 3 2 1
No answer Never employed	1 –	2.5 –				– 2	– 5.0		
Total	40	100.0				40	100.0		

* Applies to work-force members only. The classification is based on the practice of the Papua New Guinea Manpower Planning Unit and the wage rates paid to respondents in 1972.

67,530 (a suggested annual rate of growth of 9 percent). These are mini-mum rates only (Langmore 1970:7). It has been difficult, however, to assess the degree of actual employment during this period.[9]

Recent studies by Conroy (1972) and by Conroy and Vines (1973) of the records of the Administration- and Mission-run labor offices (which record only the better-skilled applicants), have shown a 40 percent increase in unemployment from early 1968 to early 1971. There was also a statistically significant rise in the overall educational level of applicants. Only 23 percent of the applicants were placed in employment, but education very significantly increased a job seeker's chances of successful placement. So it would seem that the probability of primary school leavers finding jobs is greater in the present market situation, and this information carried back to the rural areas will substantially affect the rate of rural-urban migration from this group in the future, as long as the development strategy is based on the present assumption of free operation of market forces.

One feature of Table 3 is the unimportance of clerical work in the expectations of the group, contrasted with its importance in reality. The oft-repeated conception of how African school leavers in a similar situation have rejected manual work, hoping for positions as white-collar workers, does not seem to be borne out here. The expectations of the school leavers were not to eschew manual work. The reality for this group of migrants, however, proved to be that while many hoped for employment in trades and few for jobs in offices, labor market oppor-tunities dictated that many should work in offices and few should gain admission to skilled manual work.[10]

The forty work-force members had held a total of sixty-one jobs since leaving school, an average of about 1.5 jobs per worker. However, while one man had worked at seven jobs, twenty-three of the group had

[9] The 1966 census recorded only 478 as unemployed in Papua, a symptom of the colonial context under which the census was taken. The unemployed in an urban area are periodically subjected to arrest on vagrancy charges and repatriated, hence the suspicion of any administration inquiries.

[10] The Professor of Economics at the University of Papua New Guinea, Professor Clunies-Ross, has taken the view that education is the primary determinant: "It is generally accepted that education favors urban drift.... If there is any escape it would seem to lie in radically altering the character of primary schooling" (1971: 486). A recent econometric study of Ghanian migration statistics concluded: "Education is negatively related to migration. There is no evidence that education except insofar as it increases income potential and lessens an individual's abhorrence of cultural and social adjustments has any real effect.... Thus in our empirical analysis the simple dissatisfaction hypothesis concerning the effects of education is refuted" (Beals, Levy, and Moses 1967).

remained in a single job, so that in general the turnover of labor has been slight. At the time of the survey, six young men, or 16.2 percent of the male workers, were unemployed. They had been out of work for periods ranging from one week to thirty-three months. The first of these men had just arrived in Port Moresby. For the group of forty workers as a whole, approximately 17 percent of the time since entering the urban work-force (in Port Moresby and elsewhere) had been spent in involuntary unemployment.[11]

The mean wage received by thirty-one males working at the time of the interview was $20.30 per fortnight, which compared favorably with the Port Moresby minimum wage of $16.00 for adult unskilled males, especially considering the group's mean age of 18.2 years. If salary increases over a period of time are taken to indicate the acquisition of skill and experience on the job, there were seven males who had progressed with their current employer from a salary below the mean to one above it. One of the girls had a similar record. Clerical positions generally paid below the mean, and semiskilled manual jobs above it. Assuming economic rationality and some knowledge of the labor market among Standard VI leavers, awareness of this wage differential may help to explain their pattern of employment preferences in 1968.

Those who accord schools the central role in producing rural alienation and a wholesale drift to the urban areas, have to a great extent missed the point.[12] Education is not the complete molding of a malleable entity, it is a somewhat light veneer superimposed on a person who has a far more complex interaction with his immediate past and future. In short, the Standard VI school leavers, when they leave home for urban jobs, are doing so not because they are primarily acting according to a newly-imposed set of values, but because objective economic conditions show that there is a reasonably strong probability that they could earn a steady and (relatively) high income in the towns. This means that as a means to avoid the resulting lopsided resource allocation to the urban areas, a piecemeal effort such as a rural-oriented educational system will

[11]   Non-work-force participation was defined as follows: "The voluntary unemployed in urban areas include short-term visitors, those genuinely resting between jobs, and those whose supply price exceeds the wage for the occupation for which they are qualified, and who are not actively seeking other employment" (Conroy and Vines 1973: 7).

[12]   Both Foster (1965) and Callaway (1963: 358) reject this colonial conventional wisdom for Africa. Foster comments on an occupational choice survey of 210 students in Accra: "These results by no means substantiate the view that middle-school liberates desire or expectations of white collar employment. Rather do they indicate the remarkably moderate level of aspirations and expectations and the eminently realistic view of the occupational structure that these children have" (Foster 1965: 208).

have little effect on stemming the outflow. Complementary changes in the whole structure of the country's economy are called for. Callaway, writing about the African school leavers, makes the same point.

Curriculum reform alone will not solve the employment problem. The fact is that school leavers' views are determined outside the school, in the society and economy. As long as they see in farming a poor and stunted life, they will seek what seems to them better opportunities of the cities. What is wanted, first of all, is a really effective general policy towards agriculture which would demonstrate that improved farming can bring as much money and as rewarding a life as other occupations (Callaway 1963: 360).

Motivations for Migration

Within Papua New Guinea there is some debate as to the importance of various motives in the migration process. One group sees "the pull of the attractions of the towns, the 'bright lights' which for many villagers exerts an emotional pull that must be extraordinarily strong" (Ward 1970: 58) as the prime motivation. Other commentators such as Belshaw (1963: 20), Ward (1971: 97), and Brookfield and Hart (1971: 396) have stressed the same point. A second school of thought stresses the primacy of the economic motive:

There is very little in the bright lights hypothesis that cannot be explained in terms of a wholly rational and understandable desire for a higher level of real income.... Economic cash and returns appear, generally, to dominate the behaviour of migrants (Conroy 1972: 16).

Conroy's conclusion is supported by Oram's study of the Hula (1968: 271), and by Salisbury and Salisbury (1970), as well as by his own work (Conroy and Stent 1970).

The debate is not trite, because the way one sees migration seems to reflect one's views as to whether or not rapid urbanization is inevitable. The Wards both place a strong emphasis on the imperative of the "rapid expansion of the towns as essential to economic and social progress." They view rural-urban migration as an inevitable process, to be not only tolerated but actively encouraged.

Conroy has taken the position that urbanization is a constraint on development, and while he does not advocate the reversal or halting of urbanization, he has called for a control of the rate of its growth.

In attempting to investigate the causal factors that produce rural-urban migration, one cannot simply rely on the migrant's own "definition of the situation."[13] Therefore the next section attempts to outline the socio-economic conditions in the different rural areas from which the migrants have come, and hence the context in which their decisions are made.

When asked in 1972 "Why did you come to Port Moresby?" 75 percent of the worker group gave reasons directly connected with finding employment or earning money. The remaining reasons ranged from the basically economic ("no good clothes in the village," "friends said everything was free and there were plenty of jobs") to the functional ("brought my brother's wife to town"), the passive ("my brother told me to come"), or the merely curious ("to find out what Moresby was like," "Just go have a look").

The strong tendency toward an economic motivation for migration has been amply demonstrated in similar studies in Africa. In a wide-ranging review of the literature on African labor migration, Hutton states that, "virtually all studies are agreed" as to the "overwhelming importance" of economic factors (1970: 14).[14]

The artificially high wage rates in the modern sector (due to direct foreign investment, the capital intensive technology, high skill demands, welfare legislation, and trade union pressures) mean that it becomes quite rational, particularly for the young school leavers, to migrate to the towns even on the remote chance of a wage job in the modern sector. In the case of Papua New Guinea in 1968, the average urban wage was more than twice the average rural wage, and the latter itself much higher than the average income earned by export cash croppers. In addition there has been a recent decision to increase urban minimum wages by almost 75 percent by the end of 1973. Thus, it becomes rational to migrate even on a 50 percent or 33 percent chance of a job in the town.[15]

The consequence of viewing rural-urban migration as essentially economically motivated brings the question down from the skies, wherein urbanization is seen as inevitable. To identify specific causal factors means, in vacuo, that the development strategists have a choice as to whether to control the urban influx or not. Economic motivation seen as the primary causal factor means that income differentials between town and rural areas can be manipulated to stem migration flows. However, the question of equalizing the income differentials or creating employ-

[13]   This would to be deny the importance of objective structural factors which may be unknown to the participant.
[14]   Two other summaries of the literature with regard to Africa draw the same conclusion (Hanna and Hanna 1971; 1968).
[15]   See Todaro (1971) for the outline of a model based on the factors of the rural-urban income differential and the probability of finding employment.

ment opportunities in the hinterland cannot be carried out in vacuo. A country like Papua New Guinea already exists in a specific politico-economic situation, that of neo-colonialism. This means that economic growth is seen as achievable basically through direct foreign investment, a process which necessitates the development of a sharp division between an educated elite and a small highly skilled labor aristocracy, and the urban unemployed and peasantry.

Under these social relations of production, to apply the classical Keynesian answer to the unemployment problem (creating additional jobs by more investment) will only lead to the paradox of actually increasing the rate of unemployment. This is because the new jobs created would only attract more rural migrants in addition to the unemployed already in the towns.

Adaptation to Urban Life

To understand more completely the significance of an urban existence to these primary school leavers, we need to examine further the context from which they have come, and their urban existence.

There were two geographically distinct groups of interviewees, the small Southern Highland group of four and the remaining forty-six who were from the Gulf District.

The Gulf area, situated on the Papuan coast some 200 miles west of Port Moresby, has experienced the colonization process profoundly. Work on the plantations, mission education, and absorption into the cash economy has long ago disrupted the traditional subsistence farming existence. At the same time, there is very little land suitable for cash cropping, and no guaranteed market for anything that might be grown. Before World War II, there was plantation work for indentured laborers, and during the war many from the Gulf District were used as carriers, etc. for an Australian army base in the area and in Port Moresby. After the war, many stayed in Port Moresby and started permanent squatters' settlements. Several Gulf people had acquired trade skills and were able to set themselves up as independent contractors, taking subcontracts from the Administration for jobs that ranged from digging ditches to building houses. Thus, jobs were created for kinsmen. Later most of the contractors joined the Administration as tradesmen.

Therefore, for the Gulf primary school leaver there has been a long-time tradition of migration to Port Moresby, and a substantial network of relatives was already existing there (Ryan 1968: 61–63). Hence, it is not surprising that the Gulf interviewees spent little time in the village after leaving school. Within a month 67.5 percent had left home, and within two months, 75 percent. Most made the journey with relatives or friends, and when they arrived in Moresby, were accommodated by close relatives. However, insofar as the independence of the decision to migrate is concerned, it is of interest to note that not one of the respondents, worker or nonworker, was living with his or her parents.

The young migrants had been absent from home for periods ranging from three and a half years to one week. In the meantime, fifteen, or 37.5 percent, had returned to the village for visits. These visits were during holiday periods or spells of unemployment, and mostly for periods of less than one month. Only three persons had made more than one trip home, and in only one or two cases does there appear to have been any attempt by an individual to reintegrate himself into the rural agricultural work force. While the objective evidence may make it seem that these migrants are on the way to becoming permanent urban dwellers, subjectively only about 20 percent declared themselves to be permanent or long-term residents of the town, while 30 percent projected short- to medium-term stays (from one to ten years). About 50 percent were unsure of their plans, or made conditional statements, such as, "I will stay while I have a good job." Those intending to stay permanently were, for the most part, in relatively well-paid jobs.

On several occasions spontaneous group discussions arose which involved the interviewer, some of the respondents, and interested bystanders of the same age group. On two occasions someone volunteered the opinion that the lack of companionship of his peers at home exerted strong pressure on a young man to migrate. If jobs were readily available at home, many agreed, people would prefer to stay there. One person suggested that if something like the Bougainville copper project were to come into being in the Gulf, people now in Moresby would go back home.

Three people expressed fear of fighting and "payback" killing between ethnic groups in town. Several others feared trouble with the police, who are increasingly active in the enforcement of vagrancy laws. This fear is a real barrier to the collection of social data, and is responsible for undernumeration and inaccuracies in urban census statistics. A degree of suspicion of the motives of the interviewer was evident on a number of occasions, but it was normally possible to dispel this by referring to the 1968 survey, which almost all respondents remembered clearly. It was also helpful to have the interviewer introduced to respondents by someone known to them, normally a university student.

Many said that Moresby was not an easy place in which to live. A person could not save much, and life there was more difficult than life at home because one needed money for everything. A Form III leaver, who came from a village with a sawmill, would have preferred to stay home and work if there had been a vacancy at the mill, because of greater opportunities to save. However nineteen, or 56 percent of those employed at the time of the survey, admitted that they were saving part of their earnings, while only seven, or 21 percent, claimed they were unable to do so. It was felt inappropriate to ask the remainder questions about savings, because of the circumstances in which the interviews occurred. Similarly, the presence of relatives and friends during the interviews inhibited the collection of any worthwhile information on the amounts being saved.

Leisure-time activities took place largely within social networks which were transferred from the village to the town. Even churchgoing (and more than 80 percent of the respondents attended church services at least occasionally) tended to occur within this context. This is not to say that people did not enjoy the attractions of urban life, but these may be less central to their experience than is often supposed.

In contrast to the Gulf migrants, with their poor rural agricultural possibilities in the village and their extensive network of kin in Port Moresby, the four from the Southern Highlands came from and into a very different situation. The Highlands area was not explored until the 1930's, and was off limits to European missions and commerce until 1945. It is from the Highlands, from certain areas with few opportunities for cash cropping, that the contract labor scheme can still recruit substantial numbers of workers (10,000 a year). But after the first few groups return, and along with the development of alternative means of earning money, "agreement" labor drops to a low level.

In the Southern Highlands, involvement in cash cropping opportunities has come only recently; therefore emigration has by and large been through the "Agreement labor scheme." The case of the four 1968 Standard VI school leavers who had migrated to Moresby independently is rare, but their behavior is very similar to the pattern becoming established among the Western Highlanders, as described by Strathern (1972) and the Salisburys (1970).

The attitudes of these four Southern Highlanders parallel Salisbury's description of the Siane in Port Moresby (Salisbury and Salisbury 1970). The Siane are described as viewing employment in town as a learning experience, and as an opportunity for the accumulation of capital for rural investment in trucks and trade stores. They regard themselves as merely temporary residents in Port Moresby.

Strathern has described the way Western Highlanders (more particularly those in close contact with Mt. Hagen and its economic opportunities as a regional center) distinguish carefully between "bisnis" (i.e., coffee, transport services, and trade stores) and wage labor. Business is strongly stressed as superior to labor, which is looked upon only as a means to establishing oneself in "bisnis." What makes working away from home appear worthwhile is the possibility of accumulating enough to start one's own business back at home.

The four young men who had migrated to Moresby showed this same ideology concerning "bisnis." They planned to stay quite limited periods in town, specifically to save money. They professed a desire to return to invest their money in rural projects such as cattle, or fencing a brother's coffee acreage. The four claimed to be saving money, and one at least had accumulated $50. This is all in contrast to the Gulf migrants, whose ambitions appeared to be directed more to achievement within the urban economic framework. Of forty-six respondents from the Gulf, only two mentioned ambitions for rural investment. One person planned to accumulate $600 over ten years and take an outboard motor home with him, while a married woman said that her husband was financing the erection of a permanent material house in their village.

Thus, in viewing the present significance of rural-urban migration in Papua, we have seen how the movement to the towns seems best explained not as the product of inevitable evolutionary or developmental forces, but as a result of the substantial income differential between the rural area and the towns. Where rural cash income opportunities exist or are likely to exist, the migrants seem only too willing to return home to earn a living there, after they have tried their luck at rapidly accumulating capital in the city.

FUTURE SIGNIFICANCE

Recent work on urbanization in the Third World has persistently criticized earlier heavily Western-oriented emphasis on the "generative" role of the city as the agent of economic development (McGee 1971: Chapter 1; Hunter 1972; Todaro 1971: 413; Sutcliffe 1971; Pi-Chao Chen 1972). As McGee has effectively shown, the historical process of urbanization in what are today the advanced industrial societies was a substantially different process from what it is in the Third World today. Economic development for most of the Third World is not an autonomous process;

it is heavily dependent on a subservient relationship to the metropolitan countries. The postcolonial city is not an inducer of social change and economic development; it is merely a part of the total pattern of dependency of neocolonial societies.

Hunter has condemned the orthodox approach of "developmentalism" as being disastrously inappropriate in the case of African societies. He cites grave miscalculations in both the economic and the social spheres. The strong emphasis was on industrialization as the first priority, along with the creation of a highly educated elite. In the decade 1960–1970, these policies culminated in Africans coming from the schools in numbers too large to be absorbed by the small modern sector. As a result, the cities grew at alarming rates, while the demand for jobs was growing even faster.

The creation of a modern sector through import-substituting industrialization (see below) could not provide employment because, firstly, there was hardly an external market for African industrial goods that was not already saturated by cheaper competitors from the advanced industrial areas. Secondly, the African rural economy, incorporating as much as 80 to 90 percent of the population, is a very poor internal domestic market, due to its virtual lack of cash purchasing power. Thirdly, the technology used through the agency of direct foreign investment absorbed relatively little labor for the capital invested. On top of all these difficulties is a population growth rate of 2.5 or 3 percent per annum – three times the growth rate of nineteenth-century England.

The demand in the post-independence period for rapid Africanization in the bureaucracy meant a corresponding extension and upgrading of education standards. This, in turn, made both the government and the physical structure in the capital cities deliberately more sophisticated and complex, increasing further the demand for high-level skills, with corresponding high wages.

But all the while the gap was growing between the government services and the capital city on the one hand, and the 80 percent rural population on the other. No amount of moral injunctions or

rurally biased curricula could persuade young people to remain in an unimproved agricultural sector or a rural economy deprived of even minor investment–feeder roads, telephones, electricity, storage space for agricultural produce, water supply, health services and transport and petrol for extension and other staff to improve the situation (Hunter 1972: 40).

Weeks, in an important series of articles (1971a, 1971b, 1971c, 1972b; see also Atkinson 1972) has attacked the current outcry among economists and others over the failure of employment to grow. He points out how the

solution to the "unemployment" problem, as defined, would only increase the economic and political dependence which is itself the source
of the problem. The failure of employment opportunities to grow is the
result of six factors that he outlines, which together form the "pack-
age" that constitutes the conditions of industrial development under foreign investment. The strategy is commonly called "industrialization
through import substitution."

1.   The PRIVATE demand of the local elite is centered on a high consumption pattern involving capital intensive goods. Similarly, the RURAL-URBAN
DISTRIBUTION of income is heavily biased towards the urban areas because of the elite's economic power to redirect state expenditures into
the services it desires. Thus, employment opportunities will be fewer
where there is a more unequal distribution of income because of the
resultant structure of demand.

2.   Artificially low interest rates and overvalued exchange rates cheapen
captial and encourage the use of labor-saving technology.

3.   Tax concessions on investment expenditure encourage excessive
capital intensity.

4.   The shortages of supervisory and skilled labor significantly constrain
employment expansion. Since training is expensive, automated machinery
is often more profitable.

5.   Foreign aid policies encourage the use of capital intensive techniques by the practice of providing for only the capital component of
the projects.

6.   Transfer of technology through the transnational corporations is
invariably that of technology developed for the industrial countries.

Weeks concludes:

It is clear that the so called "employment problem" is not a problem at all,
but a problem of fundamental structural imbalance in the economics of the
Third World. The imbalance is the consequence of the growth of a parasitic
industrial sector catering to a narrow market, using techniques which require
a small portion of the labour force and generate few linkage effects. The rest
of the economy where the vast majority of the population toils, enters the picture only to generate foreign exchange to import the necessary capital and taxes
to finance the "development" expenditure for the parasitic infrastructure. This
is the basic contradiction of economic "development" through capitalistic
institutions in the Third World (1972a: 31)

In Papua New Guinea, the neocolonial pattern is being clearly articulated.[16] In a recent white paper, the Administration, now ostensibly under

[16]   Even to speak of Papua New Guinea as being shaped by the neocolonialist pattern
is technically still somewhat premature, because the country is still administered as a

the political control of a de facto independent Papua New Guinea government, reaffirmed the central importance it saw in direct foreign investment as the agent of economic growth. The ridiculously generous concessions granted by the Colonial Authority to Bougainville Copper, Ltd. in 1968 will probably not be paralleled in the present negotiations with Kennecott Copper in its bid to set up another massive copper mine in the country. But the Australian government is very keen on encouraging such huge investments, as the resulting taxes will relieve the Australian treasury of its present $120-million annual grant to Papua New Guinea. Also, with Australia's very high labor cost factor, Papua New Guinea, as it develops a skilled work force, will increasingly be used by Australian capital as a source of cheap labor for the assembling of various goods for re-export to Australia.[17]

The question of labor migration must be seen within the politico-economic context of a growing inequality occasioned by a pragmatic policy of mixed capitalism. The country, following the pattern of so many others under neocolonialism in the Third World today, is subject to the same powerful forces, beginning with the common need to preserve a hospitable climate for private foreign capital. This means a fairly influential expatriate business community, protectively associated with the government, and an ancillary local business class. Integral to this pattern also is the formation of a salariat with incomes related to those in developed countries and to the levels of profit which the foreign firms export and receive. The consequences of all this influence profoundly every aspect of government development policy (see Leys 1971: 338).

This is not to imply that in such circumstances a revolutionary situation is being created, notwithstanding the economic surplus that is extracted from the peasantry. The satellites may remain quite stable, at least in times of international economic expansion. But this pattern of growth will not stop the increasing gap between the primate towns and the hinterland.

Two countries which have successfully instituted a wide-ranging set of policies to redress the rural-urban allocation of resources and skilled

---

colony by Australia. This means to a very real extent that its economic structure is still heavily affected by European ownership, and its towns are being developed to cater to the affluent expatriate public servants on temporary contracts.

[17] W. J. Henderson, Secretary-General of the Australian-Indonesian Business Co-operation Committee, has said: "The question of rapidly rising labour costs [in Australia] is causing grave concern in industry. People in charge of labour intensive companies are being attracted by the low labour costs in Indonesia" (*Melbourne Sun* 1972). This unusually frank statement applies equally to Papua New Guinea.

manpower are China and Cuba.[18] However, the Maoist and Cuban strategies of decentralization can be seen only in their totality; any attempt to abstract and apply their policies in a piecemeal fashion elsewhere will be unsuccessful.

REFERENCES

ACOSTA, MARUJA, JORGE E. HARDOY
   1973   *Urban reform in revolutionary Cuba*. New Haven, Connecticut: Antilles Research Program, Yale University. (Translated by Mal Bochner.)
ATKINSON, D.
   1972   The Third World: does employment matter? *Arena* 29.
BALANDIER, GEORGES
   1961   "The Colonial situation, a theoretical approach," in *Social change: the colonial situation*. Edited by Immanuel Wallerstein. New York: Wiley.
BEALS, R. E., M. B. LEVY, L. N. MOSES
   1967   Rationality and migration in Ghana. *Review of Economics and Statistics* 48 (4): 480–486.
BELSHAW, CYRIL
   1963   "Pacific Island Towns and the Theory of Growth," in *Pacific Port Towns and Cities*. Edited by A. Sphoer, Honolulu: Bishop Museum Press.
BROOKFIELD, H. C.
   1972   *Colonialism, development and independence: the case of the Melanesian Islands in the South Pacific*. Cambridge: Cambridge University Press.
BROOKFIELD, H. C., DOREEN HART
   1971   *Melanesia: a geographic interpretation of an island world*. London: Methuen.
CALLAWAY, ARCHIBALD
   1963   "Unemployment among African school leavers," in *Education and Nation-Building in Africa*. Edited by L. Gray Cowan, James O'Connell, and David G. Scanlon, 235–256. New York: Praeger.
CLARK, W. C., EUGENE OGAN
   1973   Social scientists. *New Guinea Quarterly* 7(4): 41–62.
CLUNIES-ROSS, A.
   1971   Dilemmas and expedients in Papua New Guinea's development. *Economic Record* 47:470–493.
CONROY, J. D.
   1972   Urbanization: A development constraint. *Economic Record* 46:497–516.
CONROY, J. D., RICHARD CURTAIN
   f.c.   Migrants in the urban economy: case studies of rural school leavers in Port Moresby. *Oceania*.

[18]   See Pi-Chao Chen (1972) and Acosta and Hardoy (1973).

CONROY, J. D., W. R. STENT
1970 Education, employment, and migration: an analysis of the aspirations and expectations of school leavers in Niugini." Paper presented at the 42nd Congress of Australian and New Zealand Association for the Advancement of Science, Port Moresby. Mimeograph.

CONROY, J. D., D. VINES
1973 "Definitions and dimension of urban unemployment in Papua New Guinea." Discussion Paper 43, University of Papua New Guinea Economics Department.

FINNEY, B. R.
1969 New Guinea entrepeneurs. *New Guinea Research Bulletin* 27. Canberra: Australian National University.

FOSTER, PHILIP
1965 *Education and social change in Ghana:* Chicago: Univ. of Chicago Press.

GARNAUT, ROSS
1972 Problems of inequality. *New Guinea Quarterly* 7(3): 52–62.

GUGLER, JOSEF
1968 "A theory of labour migration." Paper presented to the Makerere Institute of Social Research Conference.

HANNA, WILLIAM J., JUDITH HANNA
1971 *Urban dynamics in Black Africa.* Chicago: Aldine Atherton.

HARRIS, G. T.
1972 Labour supply and economic development in the Southern Highlands of Papua New Guinea. *Oceania* 43:123–139.

HUNTER, GUY
1972 Employment policy in tropical Africa: the need for radical revision. *International Labour Review* 105 (1):39–58.

HUTTON, CAROLINE
1970 "Rates of labour migration," in *Urban growth in sub-Saharan, Africa.* Edited by Josef Gugler. Kampala, Uganda, Makerere Institute of Social Research.

LANGMORE, JOHN
1970 "Economic and demographic forecasts," in *Port Moresby Urban Development.* New Guinea Research Bulletin 37:1–41. Canberra: The Australian National University.
1971 Agricultural Wages. *New Guinea Quarterly* 6(1):56–62.

LEYS, COLIN
1971 Politics of a peasant society. *British Journal of Political Science* 1(1):35–71.
1972 Politics in Kenya. *British Journal of Political Science* 1.

MCGEE, T. G.
1971 *The process of urbanization in the Third World.* London: G. Bell.

MELBOURNE SUN
1972 A quotation from W. J. Henderson. February 15.

ORAM, N. D.
1968 Culture change, economic development and migration among the Hula. *Oceania* 38(4):243–275.

OVERSEAS DEVELOPMENT GROUP
  1973   A report on development strategies for Papua New Guinea. University of East Anglia.
PI-CHAO CHEN
  1972   Overurbanizing, rustication and the politics of rural transformation – the case of China. *Comparative Politics* 4(3):361–386.
REED, STEPHEN
  1942   *The making of modern New Guinea*. American Philosophical Society Memoirs, volume eighteen.
ROWLEY, C. D.
  1966   *The New Guinea villager*. New York: Praeger.
RYAN, DAWN
  1968   The migrants. *The New Guinea Quarterly* 2: 60–70.
SALISBURY, M. E., R. F. SALISBURY
  1970   The Siane in Port Moresby. *Industrial Review* (Papua New Guinea) 2.
SHAND, R.
  1971   "Emerging policy issues in the development of Papua New Guinea." The Australian National University Research School of Pacific Studies. Mimeograph.
STRATHERN, MARILYN
  1972   Absentee businessmen: the reaction at home to Hageners migrating to Port Moresby. *Oceania* 43:19–39.
SUTCLIFFE, R.
  1971   *Industry and development*. London: Addison Wesley.
TODARO, MICHAEL P.
  1971   Income expectations, rural-urban migration and employment in Africa. *International Labour Review* 104 (5): 390–407.
VIALL, L. G.
  1938   Some statistical aspects of population in the Morobe district. *Oceania* 8: 383–397.
WADDELL, E. W., P. A. KRINKS
  1971   The organization of production and distribution among the Orokaiva. *New Guinea Research Bulletin* 24. Canberra: Australian National University.
WARD, MARION
  1970   Urbanization – threat or promise? *New Guinea Quarterly* 5(1).
WARD, R. G.
  1971   "Internal migration and urbanization in Papua New Guinea," in *Population growth and socio-economic change*. New Guinea Research Bulletin 42:81–106. Canberra: Australian National University.
  1972   "Urbanization in the Pacific – facts and policies." Paper presented at the 6th Waigami Seminar, Port Moresby. Mimeograph.
WEEKS, JOHN
  1971a   The political economy of labour transfer. *Science and Society* 35: 463–480.
  1971b   Does employment matter? *Manpower and Unemployment Research in Africa* 4.
  1971c   "An exploration into the nature of the problem of urban imbalance in Africa." Paper presented to the Conference on Urban Unemploy-

—   ment in Africa at the Institute of Development Studies, Brighton, England.

1972a Employment, growth and foreign domination in underdeveloped countries. *Review of Radical Economics* (Spring).

1972b Growth and foreign domination in underdeveloped countries. *Review of Radical Political Economics* 4(1):59–69.

WEST, FRANCIS

1958   Indigenous labour in Papua New Guinea. *International Labour Review* 77(2):89–112.

1968   *Hubert Murray: the Australian Pro-Consul*. Melbourne: Oxford University Press.

WORSLEY, PETER

1968   *The trumpet shall sound: a study of the cargo cults in Melanesia*. London: Paladin.

Migration and Ethnicity in Sub-Saharan Africa: Affinity, Rural Interests, and Urban Alignments

JOSEF GUGLER

The majority of the adult population in the cities of sub-Saharan Africa is rural born and bred. Once in town, many maintain close ties with their areas of origin, their "homes." Rural origin and urban-rural ties are major determinants of ethnicity as expressed in the cities of sub-Saharan Africa today. They establish affinities in the urban setting and carry the competition for resources among different regions into the urban arena. Economic and political interests are perceived in these ethnic terms and in turn mold new ethnic categories.

HOME PEOPLE

I am illiterate. If I should need to go to an office to ask for a favor, on entering the office, I don't care who is there, I'll first greet the people in Yoruba. If there's a Yoruba man among them, I'm sure he'll reply in Yoruba. Then I'll know I have a brother there (A trader in Jos, Nigeria [Plotnicov 1967:107f.]).

The majority of adult urban dwellers in sub-Saharan Africa are first-generation townsmen. They spend their early childhood in an ethnically homogeneous milieu, they share a common ethnic background with their schoolmates. The first years of schooling are in a local language in most countries; many secondary schools are dominated by one ethnic group. Childhood friends are thus usually drawn from a single small ethnic category.[1]

I wish to thank, without implicating, William G. Flanagan for helpful comments.
[1] A great deal of education in sub-Saharan Africa has been provided by missions, which tended to operate within linguistically homogeneous areas. Religious differences thus became part of ethnic differences. Sometimes this pattern is perpetuated in the

Much of the urban population of sub-Saharan Africa maintains close ties with rural areas of origin. The income of many urban male workers is insufficient to support a wife and children in town, and earning opportunities for women are usually severely limited. Thus there is often little choice but to maintain the family in the rural home area; the separation of home and workplace engendered by the Industrial Revolution is drastically magnified. Urban workers who are able to support a family in town will still frequently find that the way to maximize their income is to retain their rural interests in land and have their family exploit it. In much of sub-Saharan Africa land cannot be bought and sold; abandoning it means foregoing part of the family income without compensation (Elkan and Fallers 1960).

Even families that manage to establish themselves in town typically value the ultimate security the rural home area promises. In the face of a growing tide of urban unemployment and underemployment and of social security systems only recently initiated, rights to land back home continue to guarantee final shelter for many. When Tonga migrants eventually retire to their village in Malawi, for instance, they do not fall back upon a traditional social system that happens to have continued during their absence, they return to a community to which they have been actively and consciously contributing because they knew that they might ultimately have to rely on it (Van Velsen 1960).

People may have strong emotional attachments to the village of their childhood, to the kin and friends they knew. For most urban dwellers sheer necessity, income advantage, and/or provision for an uncertain future give a pressing economic rationale to such attachment. There is often, accordingly, a strong commitment to the rural "home" that is articulated in an ideology of loyalty. Considerable pressure is brought to bear on potential deviants.[2]

Rural-urban migrants usually make their first move to a town where

---

urban setting. Plotnicov (1967:78f., 293f.) reported from Jos, Nigeria, that the urban elite sent its children to the schools of the missions with which its ethnic groups were historically associated.

[2]   For further discussion see Gugler (1969a:146ff.); for an account of urban-rural ties among Eastern Nigerians, Gugler (1971).

Pons (1969:75ff., 99) impressively shows how rural involvement differed within one town, Kisangani, Zaïre, among ethnic groups. The high urban and high rural involvements of the Lokele tended to reinforce each other. For the Babua, high urban involvement went hand in hand with low rural involvement. Conversely, the Topoke had limited urban involvement but a high degree of continuing rural involvement. Underlying factors included the accessibility of home areas, the degree of success in the urban economy, and, for the Lokele, the opportunity to supply Kisangani with products from their home area and eventually to control the markets in fish, vegetables, and fruits.

they can expect to be received by a relative or at least a co-villager. Only between 8 percent and 13 percent of factory workers interviewed in Accra, Kumasi, and Takoradi, Ghana, reported knowing no one in town before they came; about two-thirds stayed with a kinsman upon arrival (Peil 1972:145, 164).

From the first contacts the immigrant makes with his fellow hometowners, there follows a tendency for persons of the same or similar origin to cluster. Leslie (1963:33) reports that when Dar es Salaam was very small and most of the immigrants came on foot, they tended to settle on the side of town reached first. As others following joined them and then "hived off" and built houses nearby, ethnic groups dominated the quarter nearest their place of origin. Such trends are checked somewhat where the choice of residence is restricted by housing shortages. More severe constraints arise where public authorities and/or employers closely control a major part or even virtually all housing. They typically discourage ethnically homogeneous neighborhoods.[3] However, in pre-industrial towns the division between the old town and new residential areas for strangers, the *sabon gari* of Nigeria, usually received administrative sanction.

Where ethnic clusters exist, ethnicity will be reinforced by organizations established on a neighborhood basis. Thus Zolberg ([1964]1969: 116, 357) reports that neighborhoods in the smaller towns in the Ivory Coast were ethnically homogeneous, and ward committees of the Parti Démocratique de Côte d'Ivoire were in effect ethnic communities as well. Party life thus contributed to the maintenance and even the reinforcement of affiliations based on ethnic ties.

Whether residentially dispersed or not, the recent immigrant will tend to make friends within his or her ethnic group.[4] There is the reassurance of

---

[3] In East London, South Africa, "Red migrants" would generally live with or near "home-people" and spend most of their leisure time with them. Rehousing in a "homeland" town, Mdantsane, has meant dispersal of most of these groups of "home-people" (Mayer [1961]1971:99ff., 299ff.).

[4] Where kin are few or not accessible at all, kinship is frequently used loosely. Clément (1956:374) has referred to this pattern as "neo-fraternity." In Kisangani, Zaïre, he found that the categories to which it was extended varied greatly according to the numerical representation of ethnic groups or villages in town.

For a model of particularism that distinguishes bases and levels of identification, friendship, unions, and organizations, see Gugler (1975). The ethnic basis is described as a set of concentric circles designating more narrowly or more largely defined ethnic groups which Ego identifies with, recruits his friends from, joins in unions, and supports in formal organizations. Socioeconomic position and religion are seen as alternative bases, each again offering different levels at which to define "we" and "they." The model thus focuses attention on both: alternative contents of particularistic attachment and action, and different levels of ethnic, socioeconomic or religious inclusiveness at which such attachment and action crystallize.

association with people known from back home, the pleasure of sharing familiar customs, the ease of conversing in one's own tongue. As the lament in a Kalela song on the Zambian Copperbelt went (Mitchell 1956:7):

You mothers who speak Tonga,
You who speak Soli, mothers,
Teach me Lenje.
How shall I go and sing?
This song I am going to dance in the Lenje country,
I do not know how I am going to speak Lenje.
Soli I do not know,
Tonga I do not know,
Lozi I do not know.
Mbwela is difficult,
Kaonde is difficult.

We should not be surprised when 50 percent of the workers in a survey in Ibadan and Lagos, Nigeria, report that their best friend is from the same village or town, or when 86 percent say their best friend belongs to the same "tribe" (Seibel 1968:201).

An extreme case of encapsulation was reported by Wilson and Mafeje (1963:47ff.) from Langa, a township on the periphery of Cape Town, South Africa. Bachelors originating from the same village or village section were found to have formed corporate groups, each of which would share a room, and cook and eat together, using a common supply of staples. When one fell ill, they would look after him; if he died they would repatriate his body. They would help one of their number who was unemployed or in trouble with the police. They tended to work in the same place and to join the same churches and clubs. They accepted control by the senior member and arbitrated disputes effectively within the group.

Usually the urban immigrant does come to establish social relationships with strangers. Neighbors come to know each other over time, or they unite abruptly in the defense of common interests, e.g. the residents of a housing project in their grievances against the authorities (Parkin 1969: 78ff.). More frequently such links will be forged in work groups or in cliques within the work group. In Cameroun, new immigrants seeking employment in the plantations tended to look for work where there were already others of their ethnic group. However, the overwhelming majority of workers expressed a preference for the existing pattern of camps containing men of many different ethnic groups, and rejected the possibility of living in ethnically homogeneous camps. Again, the great majority were against any ethnic grouping of work-gangs (Ardener et al. 1960:101ff.). In the same survey of workers in Ibadan and Lagos in which 86 percent reported that their best friend belonged to the same "tribe", 80 percent said they preferred working with people from different "tribes"; this position correlated positively with level of education (Seibel 1968:195ff.).[5]

ETHNIC UNIONS

Can one grow greater than his clan? (Western Ibo saying [Okonjo 1967:108]).

People recognizing a common origin may be residentially dispersed, they may be surrounded by strangers at work, but they can and typically do get together during their leisure time. In addition to their informal reunions "home people" frequently institute regular meetings, attempt to have all from "home" join in, and establish a measure of formal organization. The meetings are multi-purpose and elicit intensive participation. I shall refer to them as ethnic unions.[6]

Members of an ethnic union have a broad basis of shared values and norms derived from common origin. They are in communion, they can partake fully, they relax from the constraints of a foreign urban environment. But the role of unions is not limited to the provision of recreation in the company of those of like mind. Ethnic unions deal effectively with the problems confronting the immigrant. He is helped to find shelter and employment, he is attended if ill, he is given economic and moral support in bereavement, he is assisted if he is in trouble with the law. Reciprocity is thus strengthened by the establishment of institutional controls.

Ethnic unions are in a strong position to exert a socializing function. Their leadership articulates responses to the juxtaposition of old and new that characterizes the urban scene in sub-Saharan Africa. Ethnic unions introduce the new arrival *expressis verbis* to the rules of life in the urban setting. In Mitchell's (1962:128) terms, ethnic unions are active agents in historical change, and at the same time they intermediate situational change. Much of the socialization is latent. The member who is made to pay a standard fine for arriving late at a meeting, or for failing to attend without valid excuse, or for disorderly behavior during the meeting, may see this as an expression of the authority of the union, and its leaders in particular,

[5] There was considerable variation, though, according to firm; in the one firm that was ethnically homogeneous, 57 percent of the workers interviewed indicated a preference for working with people of their own "tribe" (Seibel 1968:389f.)
[6] The following account is based primarily on my research among Eastern Nigerians in 1961–1962; see Gugler (1971), which includes a brief discussion of variables that may explain differences in this respect in sub-Saharan Africa.

but he is also introduced to the rhythm and formalization of present-day urban life.[7]

The ethnic unions' control reaches beyond their own activities. Members are taken to task for actions that run counter to the norms of the union and/or damage the reputation of its membership with the public. Unions typically attempt to settle disputes among members by arbitration within the union, outside the courts.

Ethnic unions are at times referred to as voluntary associations. However, they are frequently quite indispensable to the immigrant's survival in town in economic as well as psychological terms. Furthermore, strong norms, underpinned by sanctions, may make membership quasi-compulsory. Morrill ([1963]1967:175) reported from Calabar, Nigeria, that the absorption of new Ibo immigrants into their respective ethnic unions was such a natural and inevitable thing that informants were simply unable to conceive of anything else.[8]

At the same time the member is typically given unquestioning support. In Achebe's novel *No longer at ease*, the Umuofia Progressive Union pays for the services of a lawyer for Obi, even though Obi has repeatedly acted against the wishes of the union and only recently shown great disrespect. After Obi has been condemned to a prison sentence the union continues to support him:

They had no illusions about Obi. He was, without doubt, a very foolish and self-willed young man. But this was not the time to go into that. The fox must be chased away first; after that the hen might be warned against wandering into the bush (Achebe 1960:5).

The support given individual members by the ethnic union may be analytically distinguished from the common interests it pursues, although frequently they coincide. In Achebe's novel the unconditional support the hero receives from the union is seen by the members to be in their own best interest as well as that of the Eastern Nigerian village they represent in Lagos.

A main interest of ethnic unions is usually with rural development. If many a union calls itself "Improvement Union" this refers to the improvement not of urban living conditions but of the home area. The unions

---

[7]   For an account of procedures, here of the unions of Western Ibo in Ibadan, Nigeria, see Okonjo (1967).
[8]   In a survey in Enugu, Nigeria, in 1961, 82 percent of the unskilled workers and petty traders interviewed and 57 percent of a sample of senior civil servants, professionals, and contractors reported that they were regularly attending and contributing to an ethnic union (Gugler 1971:410).

transmit new ideas and aspirations; they constitute an urban lobby for village interests; they provide counsel and finance for village developments, scholarships for its youth; they direct the role the local area plays in the wider polity.[9]

Members usually interact not only within the ethnic union, but are likely to associate in extra-union activities as well. One important consequence of this is the increased probability of in-marriage — which in turn further strengthens the ties among union members. Multiplex relationships between union members thus inhibit the development of cross-cutting loyalties in the urban setting.

Ethnic unions are the most prevalent type of groups characterized by intensive participation on the urban scene in sub-Saharan Africa today.[10] They condition the identification of their members, shape their interaction, articulate their interests — both in the urban environment and for their rural homes. However, intensive participation necessitates a small membership, fewer than a hundred it seems. Unless members are particularly well placed in the urban power structure, such numbers do not provide much political leverage.

POLITICS OF ETHNICITY

The argument that economic inequality is the trigger mechanism for political conflict between groups of differing cultural identities carries the implicit suggestion that resolution of the conflict lies in reducing the extent of the inequality (Lofchie 1971:274).

Neither networks of friends nor ethnic unions provide a sufficient base for political action in the urban and national arenas. But, supported by these primary links, wider groupings frequently are similarly demarcated in terms of origin. To the extent that the urban population is rurally reared and continues to be involved in rural affairs, administrative divisions of these rural areas are doubly significant: they provided the context in which

[9] For accounts of ethnic unions that were particularly successful in this respect see Smock (1971:27ff.) and Gugler (1969b:98ff.).

The conspicuous character of contributions made by or extorted from members is striking to a Western observer. The economically successful in particular are under constant pressure to increase their prestige via conspicuous investment in village developments rather than through conspicuous consumption. Their continuing commitment to the village, to their standing in the eyes of people from the village, both in the village and in town, is a necessary precondition.

[10] An important other type is the independent church which frequently has a similarly small, intensively involved, membership. For an excellent account of Pentecostal churches in Monrovia, Liberia, see Fraenkel (1964:162ff.).

they grew up, and they constitute the framework in which they press for improvements to be brought to their home areas. "Tribalism" defined in terms of these broader administrative units may then bear little relationship to any traditional structure and culture.

The "Bangala tribe" in Zaïre provides an extreme example of such "super-tribalism." Young's (1965:242ff.) account shows the irony of the "creative" role of expatriate explorers, administrators, and anthropologists. Stanley, the first foreign visitor to the region, first used the name "Bangala" and located them in a string of villages extending ten miles along the Congo River. Coquilhat estimated that there were 110,000 Bangala. He persuaded a great many from the area surrounding his Equateur station to enter the army and to become members of the crews for the river steamers. Recruitment extended rapidly, and with it the boundaries of the "Bangala tribe." The myth of the Bangala was given anthropological sanction when a volume dedicated to the Bangala was included in the important ethnological survey of the Congo directed by E. de Jonghe. An ethnic map was published that indicated that the "tribe" covered an enormous area extending from Coquilhatville 400 miles upstream, and running inland some hundred miles on each side of the river. Half a century later an ethnological study of the region concluded that there existed no Bangala group.

In the meantime the legend had been consolidated by the adoption of "Lingala" as a language for the army and administration, in mission schools, and at work. This river-trading language was especially influenced by Lobobangi, but included infusions from Swahili, Kikongo, and other more local river dialects; the simplified version used by Europeans refined out most of the inflectional elements difficult for non-Africans to learn. It was widely believed that this synthetic *lingua franca* was the Bangala language. In later years, in Kinshasa, all up-river immigrants were referred to as Bangala. An ethnic federation, Liboke-lya-Bangala, was organized which, according to one source, in 1957 had forty-eight affiliated ethnic associations and 50,000 members. Both Europeans and Africans tended to analyze Kinshasa society in terms of a Bakongo-Bangala duality, and the 1957 urban elections in what was then Leopoldville were generally described in these terms. One major Congolese political leader, Jean Bolikango, linked his political fortunes with the reconstitution of a "grande ethnie bangala."

The relatively small size of an ethnic union severely limits its capability to act as a pressure group. In order to become an effective lobby for rural interests, or more precisely for the interest urban dwellers hold in the development of their home areas, a wider base is required. Unions are thus induced to combine and to establish formal organizations at higher levels of integration. Eastern Nigerians usually defined such organizations in terms of rural administrative units. A subtle interplay may then be observed: administrative boundaries had usually been designed to follow traditional divisions, but where they did not coincide, a new identity in terms of shared interests in the administrative unit competed with traditional identity; more important, larger administrative units frequently transcended traditional identities and nurtured a wider consciousness as the population made demands on the administration.[11]

Effective political action in the urban and national arenas requires the support of a major segment of the population, hence the incentive to establish formal organizations at even higher levels — still on ethnic lines, but usually encompassing peoples who did not recognize a shared identity in the traditional context. Such an extension of ethnic identity, the emergence of the "super-tribe," usually finds its main strength in the urban setting. Here the ethnic organizations represent not only the interests of rural areas, but also those of a category of people of the same origin in town.

Intricate organizational structures are thus established. For one thing, an ethnic union maintains contact with unions representing its own home area in other towns; these may establish a headquarters in the home area. At the same time, within the town, the union is integrated into a pyramid of organizations representing increasingly larger areas of origin.[12] Eastern Nigerians typically had a three-tier structure: ethnic unions, their delegates meeting in the second-level organizations that represented major administrative units, these in turn sending delegates to a third-level organization such as the Ibo State Union or the Ibibio State Union.

While these third-level organizations were thus defined in ethnic terms by Eastern Nigerians, they did not represent traditional political units. The new structural alignments, however, followed lines of cultural affinity. When a group of Yoruba students and professional men founded Egbe Omo Oduduwa, a pan-Yoruba cultural society, in London in 1944, they were similarly motivated by interests that were political as well as cultural.

[11] In a town in Northern Nigeria I attended the practice dance of an organization representing the immigrants from an administrative district in Eastern Nigeria. People from neighboring villages that had been feuding over land for many years were dancing together. A few months later, in their home area, men were killed in renewed violence between the two villages.

[12] Ethnic unions and ethnic organizations alike are frequently referred to as "tribal unions." As can be seen from the discussion, the term is inaccurate, because most of these associations represent groups of origin much smaller than could be called "tribes" in any accepted sense of the term. The term current in francophone countries, *associations d'originaires*, is more felicitous.

Leaders of Egbe Omo Oduduwa were to be among the principal organizers of the Action Group when it was launched in 1950 to become one of the three major Nigerian parties for more than a decade (Sklar 1960).

Language is a key element in cultural affinity.[13] Common language or related languages make it easier to recognize shared identity and facilitate communication. Whether Bangala, Ibo, Ibibio, or Yoruba, in every case the new ethnic entity is circumscribed in terms of language. The story of the Bangala is the more striking because they have no cultural element in common but a synthetic *lingua franca*.

A common language or related languages unite the members of traditionally distinct polities and cement the "super-tribe." They define them in opposition to speakers of another language or language group. Language has accordingly come to be seen as a major aspect of "nation building." In six sub-Saharan states, Botswana, Burundi, Lesotho, Rwanda, Somalia and Swaziland, most of the population shares a mother tongue. Elsewhere a European language has been adopted as national language. However, these languages have generally remained foreign to the masses.[14] In contrast, the policy of Swahilization in Tanzania promises to equip all strata with the national language.

The various dialects of the Ibo were clearly different from the languages of their neighbors. However, there was considerable variation within Ibo, such that some dialects were barely mutually intelligible. Significantly, then, major efforts were made to evolve one standard Ibo speech and script. In addition certain elements of traditional culture, such as music and dance, were reaffirmed and a new pride in Ibo identity fostered.[15]

[13]   Most social scientists appear strangely insensitive to the importance of language in the everyday life of the masses, for the education and occupational career of the elite, and as the medium of ideology. Thus Mitchell (1956:22ff.) in a study of social distance among ethnic groups on the Zambian Copperbelt, takes rules of descent, not linguistic affinity, as his measure of cultural similarity. We are not even told how language differences relate to the two measures found to be significant: geographic distance in the traditional context and cultural similarity. Expections are discussed only in terms of the widely established reputations of some ethnic groups.

Note, however, that intelligibility between languages is itself a function of interethnic trends and relationships, a point strikingly demonstrated by Wolff (1959) with examples from Nigeria.

[14]   Van den Berghe (1968) has emphasized how the use of a European language as an official language, usually understood only by a minority, contributes to the increasing estrangement between elite and masses. Except for the first years of primary school, this language is the medium of instruction, and elite parents frequently use it with their children so as to further their educational opportunities.

[15]   At times customs are revived in order to cater to modern needs. Thus, in a village where age-grade celebrations had been abolished, age groups were brought to the fore of community life anew, and competition among age groups, a traditional feature, was directed toward village development (Gugler 1969b:103).

New structural alignments thus in turn develop new cultural contents.

Even where the boundaries of the ethnic entity have not changed, the perceived coincidence of ethnic difference and economic opposition may lead to a reaffirmation of cultural distinctiveness, to an ethnic renaissance Cohen describes this process among the Hausa in Ibadan, Nigeria, and concludes:

The situation will be entirely different if the new class cleavages will overlap with tribal groupings, so that within the new system the privileged will tend to be identified with one ethnic group and the under-privileged with another ethnic group. In this situation cultural differences between the two groups will become entrenched, consolidated, and strengthened in order to express the struggle between the two interest groups across the new class lines. Old customs will tend to persist, but within the newly emerging social system they will assume new values and new social significance. A great deal of social change will take place, but it will tend to be effected through the rearrangement of traditional cultural items, rather than through the development of new cultural items, or, more significantly, rather than the borrowing of cultural items from the other tribal groups. Thus to the casual observer it will look as if there is here stagnation, conservatism, or a return to the past, when in fact we are confronted with a new social system in which men articulate their NEW ROLES in terms of traditional ethnic idioms (1969:194).

Not surprisingly, third-level organizations of Eastern Nigerians were little heard of in towns where the majority of residents would have come under the jurisdiction of one such organization, but they played an important role where they represented a vocal minority. Thus, in Northern Nigeria Ibo always felt threatened and they formed the Ibo Northern Regional Union to speak and act for all of them. Severely handicapped in access to educational facilities, Ibo, through the Ibo Northern Regional Union, ran two primary and two secondary schools in Northern Nigeria. In Calabar, Eastern Nigeria, the Ibo Federal Union provided social welfare services unavailable through any other mechanisms in the city, and employed funds to insure that Ibo were not discriminated against politically in this area where they were strangers (Morrill [1963] 1967:176).

In parts of West Africa such organizational structures on ethnic lines were sufficiently effective in controlling most urban immigrants to have functions of public administration delegated to them by colonial authorities. In a number of countries they were entrusted with the collection of personal taxes. Official devolution of administrative and judicial powers to the leaders of immigrant groups went particularly far in Freetown (Banton 1957:11ff., 25ff., 142ff.; Kilson 1966:259ff.).[16]

[16] Such an arrangement obviously suited the colonial administration: a mosaic of "tribes" in the city was easier to control than an African working class; there was further

When party politics started, ethnic organizational structures became obvious channels of communication to urban voters and, through them, to the rural masses. Recruitment of members for the parties frequently followed these same lines. In fact, when the National Council of Nigeria and the Cameroons (NCNC) was founded in 1944, membership was organizational: the overwhelming majority of such organizations was made up of ethnic associations (Coleman 1958:264ff.).[17] Post (1963:382) notes how the *West African Pilot*, the organ of the NCNC, continually published affirmations of loyalty by Ibo clan, town, and village unions for several months preceding the federal election of 1959. The Ibo State Union also backed the NCNC, as it had done since its foundation in 1948.

That ethnic associations provided a training ground for leadership has been emphasized variously. The experience of running an organization and negotiating with other parties, as well as the ready clientele of the rank and file, furnished the basis for the career of many an African successful in politics or business enterprise.[18] It also reenforced lines of identifying and interaction among the rank and file, and dependencies on the part of the leadership.[19]

In such a climate, opposition over the allocation of the extremely scarce resources is easily perceived to follow ethnic cleavages. In fact, two processes have made a measure of identification of ethnic categories with specific economic interest a recurrent feature in the states of sub-Saharan Africa. During colonial rule some ethnic groups built up a considerable lead, be it because of better access to education, or because they were

---

the possibility of having some control exerted from the "tribal," i.e. the rural and usually conservative, end.

[17]   Similarly, the initial ties of the Sierra Leone People's Party (SLPP) with voluntary associations were with the Mende Tribal Committee and the Temne Tribal Union in Freetown. However, the ties were not based on organizational membership but provided by interlocking leadership. These links were more important than party branches in communicating the party's aims and policies to the literate and semi-literate urban population. Conversely, the associations gave the articulate supporters of the SLPP much more opportunity to initiate lines of action and policy for the party than did the party branches. At election time, and on other occasions as well, the ties between the SLPP and voluntary associations were a crucial factor in the popular backing the party received (Kilson 1966:241ff., 259).

[18]   In Aba, Nigeria, all the thirty councillors and all the regional and national politicians who returned to the city after the January 1966 coup held responsible positions in ethnic associations (Callaway 1970:139). In Kampala, Uganda, in the early 1960's, a large proportion of the leaders in the Luo Union and some Luo location unions were businessmen of various descriptions (Parkin 1969:158ff.).

[19]   For an extensive discussion of the politics of ethnicity, with special reference to Nigeria, see Melson and Wolpe (1971). They present fourteen propositions on economic competition among ethnic groups, relations between political and ethnic institutions, changes in ethnic groups, and situational selection.

recruited into certain occupations (most importantly the army), or because their land offered exceptional opportunities (e.g. the growing of cocoa), or because they dominated distribution of important commodities (e.g. Hausa control of the cattle trade in West Africa). Second, once an ethnic group was established in a privileged position, it wielded considerable influence over the opportunities open to others, and patronage tended to go to kinsmen, co-villagers, or any "brother." The position of such privileged groups became vulnerable, though, once the protective umbrella of colonial rule was removed. When Independence approached and universal suffrage was introduced they risked being outvoted, inasmuch as they constituted numerical minorities. At present voters in most countries are no longer in a position to change the status quo. However, elites face the constant threat that underprivileged groups may close ranks to redress the balance. In many countries the process appears to be self-perpetuating: where new elites have come to power, their bases of support are often similarly circumscribed in ethnic terms and they seem to find it necessary to give preferential treatment to their own ethnic group in order to main-this support.

REFERENCES

ACHEBE, CHINUA
   1960   *No longer at ease.* London/Ibadan: Heinemann.
ARDENER, EDWIN, SHIRLEY ARDENER, W. A. WARMINGTON
   1960   *Plantation and village in the Cameroons: some economic and social studies.* London: Oxford University Press.
BANTON, MICHAEL
   1957   *West African city: a study of tribal life in Freetown.* London: Oxford University Press.
CALLAWAY, BARBARA
   1970   Local politics in Ho and Aba. *Canadian Journal of African Studies* 4: 121–144.
CLÉMENT, PIERRE
   1956   "Social patterns of urban life," in *Social implications of industrialization and urbanization in Africa South of the Sahara.* Edited by International African Institute, 368–492. UNESCO.
COHEN, ABNER
   1969   *Custom and politics in urban Africa: a study of Hausa migrants in Yoruba towns.* Berkeley: University of California Press.
COLEMAN, JAMES S.
   1958   *Nigeria: background to nationalism.* Berkeley: University of California Press.

ELKAN, WALTER, LLOYD A. FALLERS
1960   "The mobility of labor," in *Labor commitment and social change in developing areas*. Edited by Wilbert E. Moore and Arnold S. Feldman, 238–257. New York: Social Science Research Council.

FRAENKEL, MERRAN
1964   *Tribe and class in Monrovia*. London: Oxford University Press.

GUGLER, JOSEF
1969a "On the theory of rural-urban migration: the case of Subsaharan Africa," in *Migration*. Sociological Studies 2. Edited by J. G. Jackson, 134–155. London: Cambridge University Press.

1969b "Identity — association — unions," in *University of East Africa Social Sciences Council Conference 1968/1969 Sociology Papers I*. Kampala: Makerere Institute of Social Research.

1971   Life in a dual system: Eastern Nigerians in town, 1961. *Cahiers d'Etudes Africaines* 11:400–421.

1975   "Particularism in sub-Saharan Africa: 'tribalism' in town.' *Canadian Review of Sociology and Anthropology*.

KILSON, MARTIN
1966   *Political change in a West African state: a study of the modernization process in Sierra Leone*. Cambridge: Harvard University Press.

LESLIE, J. A. K.
1963   *A survey of Dar es Salaam*. London: Oxford University Press.

LOFCHIE, MICHAEL F.
1971   "Observations on social and institutional change in independent Africa," in *The state of the nations: constraints on development in independent Africa*. Edited by Michael F. Lofchie, 261–283. Berkeley: University of California Press.

MAYER, PHILIP
1961   *Townsmen or tribesmen: conservatism and the process of urbanization in a South African city*. Cape Town: Oxford University Press.

MELSON, ROBERT, HOWARD WOLPE
1971   "Modernization and the politics of commununalism: a theoretical perspective," in *Nigeria: modernization and the politics of communalism*. Edited by Robert Melson and Howard Wolpe, 1–42. East Lansing: Michigan State University Press.

MITCHELL, J. CLYDE
1956   *The Kalela dance: aspects of social relationships among the urban Africans in Northern Rhodesia*. Rhodes-Livingstone Papers 27. Manchester: Manchester University Press.

1962   "Social change and the new towns of Bantu Africa," in *Social implications of technological change*. Edited by Georges Balandier, 117–129. Paris: International Social Science Council.

MORRILL, W. T.
1963   Immigrants and associations: the Ibo in twentieth-century Calabar. *Comparative Studies in Society and History* 5:424–448; reprinted in *Immigrants and associations* (1967). Edited by Lloyd A. Fallers, 154–187. The Hague: Mouton.

OKONJO, C.
1967 "The Western Ibo," in *The city of Ibadan.* Edited by P. C. Lloyd, A. L. Mabogunje, and B. Awe, 97–116. London: Cambridge University Press.

PARKIN, DAVID J.
1969 *Neighbours and nationals in an African city ward.* London: Routledge and Kegan Paul.

PEIL, MARGARET
1972 *The Ghanaian factory worker: industrial man in Africa.* London: Cambridge University Press.

PLOTNICOV, LEONARD
1967 *Strangers to the city: urban man in Jos, Nigeria.* Pittsburgh: University of Pittsburgh Press.

PONS, VALDO
1969 *Stanleyville: an African urban community under Belgian administration.* London: Oxford University Press.

POST, K. W. J.
1963 *The Nigerian federal election of 1959: politics and administration in a developing political system.* London: Oxford University Press.

SEIBEL, HANS DIETER
1968 *Industriearbeit und Kulturwandel in Nigeria: Kulturelle Implikationen des Wandels von einer traditionellen Stammesgesellschaft zu einer modernen Industriegesellschaft.* Köln: Westdeutscher Verlag.

SKLAR, RICHARD L.
1960 The contribution of tribalism to nationalism in Western Nigeria. *Journal of Human Relations* 8:407–418.

SMOCK, AUDREY C.
1971 *Ibo politics: the role of ethnic unions in Eastern Nigeria.* Cambridge: Harvard University Press.

VAN DEN BERGHE, PIERRE L.
1968 European languages and black mandarins. *Transition* 34:19–23.

VAN VELSEN, JAAP
1960 Labor migration as a positive factor in the continuity of Tonga tribal society. *Economic Development and Cultural Change* 8:265–278.

WILSON, MONICA, ARCHIE MAFEJE
1963 *Langa: a study of social groups in an African township.* Cape Town: Oxford University Press.

WOLFF, HANS
1959 Intelligibility and inter-ethnic attitudes. *Anthropological Linguistics* 1: 34–41.

YOUNG, CRAWFORD
1965 *Politics in the Congo: decolonization and independence.* Princeton: Princeton University Press.

ZOLBERG, ARISTIDE R.
1964 *One-party government in the Ivory Coast.* Princeton: Princeton University Press. (Revised edition 1969.)

Comments

ROY SIMÓN BRYCE-LAPORTE

The bringing together of the concept of migration with ethnicity, as the larger collection of essays does, is neither new nor surprising at this point. In fact, many of the people viewed as ethnics are so defined precisely because they tend to have migrated from or be associated with others who were known (or believed) to have migrated from societies or states other than those in which they reside at present. In some cases such migration may have been forced; other cases may have been induced by adverse conditions at home, attraction or curiosity toward an external situation, or some accidents of events which evoked the direct or indirect exercise of choice. Other ethnics may not have migrated recently (if they ever did so in socio-historical terms), but their homeland may have been invaded, annexed, or conquered by foreign settlers, in still another form of migration. As in the case of South Africa described by Magubane, the superordinate aliens may come to view themselves as natives as well. Whether they do so or not, they tend to reserve for themselves the role of standard bearers and value-enforcers who determine what is to be defined as civilized features of the national culture and identity, as well as who will be natives or nationals of this new country they have acquired. In the process of settlement and adoption of the conquered nation they may breed offspring among themselves (forming creole generations), interbreed with the natives, and bring or attract other immigrant groups, all of whom add to the multi-ethnic nature of the society, its culture, and its general stratified structure. All of this is not to suggest necessarily that all migrants are to be viewed as ethnics or vice-versa, since the two conditions or statuses can be mutually exclusive. It is being suggested here that precisely because of their mutual exclusiveness any juxtaposition, combination, or interrelation that may be conceived between them introduces complexities beyond those already associated with either concept in isolation. Thus, studies of migration and ethnicity necessarily involve great variety.

To begin, the sociological question may be asked, who is a migrant or when has migration taken place? This is a problem of both operational and theoretical proportions. For example, it is not immediately apparent whether Lloyd's observations hold only for urban migrants as distinct from other Yoruban residents of Lagos. In the other articles the definition of migration ranges from Richardson's reference to the daily commuting of peasant laborers of Guyana, themselves earlier victims of slavery and imported contract labor in their own history, to Magubane's, Curtain's, and Gugler's articles which focus on indigenous populations who were forced, induced, or attracted to move from their traditional place of residence to work and live in other distant and sometimes alien regions within their country, if only temporarily.

All the authors directed their attention to internal migration among subordinate peoples in the countries studied, though they could as well have treated either the dominant alien settlers or marginal intermediate middle groups as immigrants. Nor do the articles included in this section look at the phenomenon of international migration (although several articles do so in the first section). Such omissions point up the failure to demonstrate more fully the very complex relationships of power and migration, and to understand the sociological significance of these relationships to ethnicity and development. Are we to believe that the two levels of migration, superordinate and subordinate or international and intra-national, represent basically the same sociological conditions, operations, experiences and adaptations? Or, are they significantly different in terms beyond matters of their ideographic and ethnological details?

Presumably, the shift in locus of residence or crucial activities is already an insufficient factor in the definition of migration or migrants. Also to be considered are the factors of (1) purpose of travel, (2) frequency and duration of stay, and (3) distance and qualitative socio-cultural differences between original and present places of residence. Within the definition of migrant itself there are important distinctions or sub-categories as well, even extending beyond the previously stated ones of power and ethnicity. Pertinent to this differentiation among migrants or types of migration would be such considerations as sex and age distribution, generation, country of origin, language and culture, pheno-typical visibility, predisposition of host society to immigrants in general and particular, economic and political conditions of host society at time of arrival, wave of entry and size of wave, initial occupational roles, literacy and socio-economic attributes, and so on.

We must also distinguish migrations in which large numbers of people voluntarily and independently enter an already developed or established country (or region) in search of new opportunities and frontiers, and with the option of entertaining permanent residence and even acquiring citizenship from migrations that were forced or externally contrived and managed. Voluntary migrants may seek to retain distinctive identities, cultures, statuses, and communities apart from other groups in the society, as was historically true of some Caribbean migrants in Central America (cf. Bryce-Laporte 1970, 1973). Often, however, such voluntary migrants tend to be more readily disposed to pursue integration, assimilate into membership in the host society and, if not noticeably different, they will acquire such membership upon acculturation of the dominant culture. High visibility can become such an overriding factor that it may cancel the differences in orientation and status between these immigrants and their native or forceably transplanted ethnic peers, as experienced by the Caribbean migrants in the United States (Bryce-Laporte 1972).

The writers in this section are almost unanimous in their concentrations on the situation of nonwhite migrants whose sociological plight is connected directly to the fact that their new countries or areas of residence were sometime in the past conquered and colonized by alien whites – yet another variation of voluntary migration. People who invade alien populated countries with intentions of establishing settlements tend to want to dominate the recipient society and to coerce and exploit the local population as a source of cheap, low-status labor for development of the new frontier. The initial contact situation often is met by resistance, flight, or maladaptation and often results in the annihilation or withdrawal of the local people. The next step is to recruit, forceably or otherwise, a labor force from a third country. This, however, sometimes has to be the first step if the land was in the beginning insufficiently populated or if the impressing of a prospective working class from the metropolis itself has failed. The work to be done by such a labor force tends to be crucial, intensive but of low prestige and often is related to organized extraction, cultivation, construction, and perhaps maintenance or defense. The system tends to exhaust its human supply and must engage in control of labor, movement, and residence; it also must have a reliable method of heavy recruitment, and all this must be done without destroying the status and power systems or the racist ideology and legal systems by which these relations become institutionalized and legitimized. This was the case of most societies of the American hemisphere. It explains in part the role of plantation slavery as the predominant experience of generations of black immigrants in those areas of the world. And, as Richardson suggests, the slave plantation system has left its mark on the economic structure, land-man relations, movement patterns, and road systems in Guyana and Trinidad.

In South Africa, the situation was a bit different. As Magubane observes, early efforts by Europeans to enlist natives were not successful. While these indigenous people resisted, they suffered neither the annihilation of Caribbean Indians nor the weakening and withdrawal of North American Indians. Their fate was more like the skilled, sedentary, and sophisticatedly organized high cultures of mainland Latin America – colonial subjugation. The subsequent failure of South Africa to obtain European labor and to be able to exploit Oriental contract labor led to reinforced efforts to concentrate and exploit local labor, by various legal and coercive operations. Magubane points out that it was then that South African natives began to experience forced migration, forced labor, containment, and low status on a par with the earlier history of the transplanted West African slaves to America. Hence, it is not surprising that there is much parallel in form and function between plantation and mines, ghettoes and settlements, Jim Crow laws and Native Acts. The two timetables of experiential details were not simultaneous or congruent, but neither was this true of the development of these two areas. It may be concluded from these articles that a good part of the early migration and ethnic experience of blacks in various parts of the world is intricately tied up with the colonial stage of development which non-Western countries underwent as part of an emergent European capitalistic-imperialistic system.

Notwithstanding outright slavery, head tax, and other legal-economic devices of recruitment that were utilized in the Americas, Papua New Guinea, and South Africa, there have been other less contrived or coercive movements of black people, on both the international and internal levels. As Lloyd's article describes for Nigeria, many of these movements are induced by the "push" of economic and political adversities or natural disaster at home and the "pull" of employment possibilities and visions of difference in life-style and life-chances in other places, usually national cities, more urbanized societies, or established metropolitan centers. But as our writers correctly contend, such migratory dynamics are intricately tied to patterns of national and international inequality in development as well as to the neo-colonial relationship many black countries hold to metropolitan influence or local white expatriate control.

On one scale there is the internal migration in Papua New Guinea, Nigeria, and other parts of sub-Saharan Africa discussed in this section. However, there have been also the more massive historic movements of American blacks from the South to the northern and western states of their country; West Indians to Central and North America and Western Europe; Africans to Western Europe; and added to normal nomadism among some African peoples, there is the voluntary dispersal of others during the colonial period. And, there is today the massive migration across now established national boundaries by Africans due to drought, famine, unemployment, and also political-military adversities. It may be further pointed out that such massive migrations have never been limited to blacks or nonwhite populations. In this respect the inadvertently limited sample of populations represented by this section is as unfortunate and misleading as the limited variation in migration that they covered.

Gugler and Lloyd in particular point out that during colonial rule the colonized people – both native and strangers – were organized, differentiated, and stratified along ethnic lines. This involved variation not simply in cultural terms but also in power, privilege, status, role, and modernizing opportunities along ethnic lines. The legacy remains and it is observable in even "post" colonial societies that intergroup struggles and intragroup organizations continue generally to follow these ethnic lines. The topics of ethnic succession and struggles among non-Western peoples slightly alluded to in these articles, also gain in importance and complexity under such circumstances. On the one hand they may give rise to serious national and international crises. Quite awesome is the far reaching potential and transcendental nature of their explosiveness. The catastrophes suffered or perpetrated by ethnic representatives of belligerent states on each other can mount in cruelty and cost about as much as war itself. Such events abound in world history, as much as their more benign counterparts which take such forms as ethnic politics, pressure groups, fraternal and philanthropic organizations, and the like.

Various types of migrations (forced, induced and voluntary) have had much to do with the dispersed presence of blacks all over the world. Such migrations (also true of other peoples), have played an intricate part in the dividing of blacks, creating among them national, ethnic, and sub-ethnic groupings. Therefore, in varying historic moments, groups of blacks have occupied various roles in the native-alien conflict, at times even opposed to each other. But as was earlier stated, migration need not be seen solely as a divisive force; it also has a unifying function, and involves or contributes to the various levels of linkages. Many of these linkages are subtle and *sub rosa*, subversive in the general non-emotive sense of the word. Usually they have not been recognized for their worth by Western society and its established academic and political elements, and therefore are destroyed or disregarded. Similarly, much of what holds together these human groups across time and space, despite national and international adversities, of how such ethnic groups and human societies emerge and re-emerge, and of the function, process, and meaning of all this is missed in the morass of static social-scientific conceptualizations.

The world is witnessing the emergence of new levels of blackness, the universalization of black ethnicity, a new meaning to the Black Diaspora. There is observable an international tendency, especially among the "blacks" of the world, to establish linkages, symbolic and real, across the boundaries of societies vast distances apart and with significant differences in culture and scale of organization. Such linkages include the sharing of identities and ideologies, mutual definition of problems and solutions, coordinating of moods and movements, conscious interpenetration of cultures and aethetics, and so on. The more minute (not necessarily minor) differences among blacks are apparently being sublimated; terms such as "black", "Afro-American", and "African" have been acquiring symbolically generic properties – representing a rising consciousness of kind which transcends formerly accepted (or imposed) distinctions of tribes, statuses, shades, colonial states, religions, and language groups.

The articles in this section suggest that migration is both a reflection of and response to inequality. Inequality is of essence in those migrations which were forced or which were the consequences of coercive or contrived inductions. Voluntary migrations, on the other hand, represent reactions to inequality of opportunities due to various forms of inexactness and inequality among two or more loci of residence. These may be short-term (based on natural or historical occurrences), long-term (based on natural resources or conditions, technical and socio-economic development, political habitat, opportunity structures, and culturally defined offerings), or simply a result of the existence and importance of either or all of such considerations. Recent observations in the neo-colonial and developing world indicate that these countries (or regions within them) find it difficult not merely to fulfill the traditional or standard desires of their population, but also to match the rising expectations and increasing aspirations of their peoples. Voluntary migration then results from those persons dissatisfied with this inability and convinced that such satisfaction can be obtained in more developed areas. Not only are the notions of availability often obtained from developed nations but the new expectations and aspirations are also provoked by them, and they are reinforced by the myths and masquerade of migrants and expatriates.

The vexing problem is that such migration neither represents a final nor isolated answer. For the donor country, it may represent a safety valve but can also be part of a brain drain. For the host country it can be a cheap and crucial human resource but it can be the catalyzation of serious social, economic, and ethnic problems. Yet if left unbridled in either location such activated elements of the population may likely trigger national and international problems which may come to involve the very same metropolitan states and the very same native homelands in other forms of uneven relationships. But the departure of sensitive elements or their return after exposure does not resolve the explosiveness of their presence either. Emigration of any sort has not rendered any emergent country (or colonized state for that matter) free of the influence of its emigrants.

All this seems to relate to development – a term which implies controlled or directed change for the improvement of specific national or regional conditions. The role of migration and ethnicity within this context is no less complex and confounding than other areas considered in this brief commentary. Now, idealistic optimists tend to believe that, all things being equal, development will ultimately eliminate ethnic and socio-economic disparities among and within the developing societies. Related to a point made by Safa in her "Introduction", development can accentuate the process of inequality in most countries. In fact, it exacerbates the consciousness of inequality in intranational and international terms. It makes more pressing the need for positive multilateral and comprehensive schemes of development directed at true equality among and within nations.

All of this suggests not the obsoleteness of the traditional ethnographic concerns with culture shock, acculturation, ethnic organization, and assimilation, but their insufficiency as a range of topics in the light of the greater complexity of the contemporary situation. Also involved here is the adaptation to different scales, rhythms, qualities, and ideologies of life as a result of the rural-urban shifts, and to new role challenges within a context of a rapidly changing world, unstabilized political-economic situations, and constantly moving sectors of national populations. Ethnographers must turn their attention to providing the world with needed qualitative information (descriptive and codified) on varying activities and experiences of migrants. They must attend to the yet unheralded, in some cases unrecognized, linkages and organizations which migration represents and the trajectories of those various structural forms which emerge in the process of migration. They must begin to contribute their specific expertise and information into channels directed to the formation of comprehensive, multilateral views of development – views which (1) take into account problems of inequality and ethnic tensions, (2) do not simply accept migration as given but question its necessity, worthiness, and propensities, and (3) weigh the wisdom and feasibility of institutionalizing into policy and programs some of the unheralded structural forms and linkages that emerge out of the emigration syndrome. Finally, within this context, metropolitan ethnographers must demonstrate their sensitivity by offering appropriate opportunities for truly equal coparticipation with their "ethnic" colleagues in source countries and at various points along the migrant stream.

REFERENCES

BRYCE-LAPORTE, ROY S.
   1970   "Crisis, contraculture and religion among West Indians in the Panama Canal Zone," in *Afro-American anthropology: contemporary perspectives*. Edited by Norman Whitten and John Szwed, 103–118. New York: The Free Press.
   1972   The black immigrant: the experience of invisibility and inequality. *Journal of Black Studies* 3 (1): 29–56.
   1973   "Family, household and intergenerational relationships in 'Jamaican' village in Limón, Costa Rica," in *The family in the Caribbean*. Edited by Stanford Gerber. University of Puerto Rico: Institute of Caribbean Studies.

Biographical Notes

ROY S. BRYCE-LAPORTE (1933–   ) was born in the Republic of Panama. He received an A. A. from Canal Zone College, his B. A. and M. A. from the University of Nebraska, an Advanced Certificate in Caribbean Studies from the University of Puerto Rico, and his Ph. D. from UCLA. He has taught at the University of Southern California, Syracuse University, Hunter College, and is an Adjunct Professor of Sociology at the University of Pennsylvania. He was the first director of the Afro-American Studies Program at Yale University, and presently directs the Research Institute on Immigration and Ethnic Studies at the Smithsonian Institution. His primary interests are in comparative and historical sociology of New World black experience, development and new migration to the United States, and the critical sociology of knowledge and social theory of ethnicity and race relations.

HANS C. BUECHLER (1940–   ) was born in Switzerland and grew up in Bolivia. He studied at the University of Geneva (1962), at the Sorbonne, and at Columbia University (Ph.D. 1966) and has taught at the Université de Montréal (1966–1968) and at Syracuse University where he is presently an Associate Professor in the Department of Anthropology. His research interests include agrarian reform and rural-urban migration in the Andes and lately international migration in Europe. He is co-author of *Land reform and social revolution in Bolivia* (1969) and *The Bolivian Aymara* (1971) and author of "The masked media" (n.d.).

JUDITH-MARIA BUECHLER was born in Shanghai, China. She studied at Barnard College (B. A. 1959), Columbia University (M.A. 1966) and

McGill University (Ph. D. 1972). She has conducted field research in Bolivia on child development and peasant marketing and in Galicia and Switzerland on female migrants. She is co-author of *The Bolivian Aymara* and author of a number of articles on entrepreneurship in Bolivia and Assistant Professor at Hobart and William Smith Colleges, Geneva, New York.

RICHARD CURTAIN (1947–   ) has a B. A. in Sociology from Latrobe University, Melbourne and a M. A. in Sociology from Rutgers University, New Jersey. He spent four months in 1972 as a Research Assistant in the Department of Economics, University of Papua New Guinea. Currently he is a Research Scholar at the Australian National University and a participant in the A.N.U./U.P.N.G. Rural-Urban Migration Project in Papua New Guinea. Forthcoming are town chapters and, with Dr. Ross Garnaut, "Employment, incomes and rural-urban imbalance" in a *New Guinea research bulletin* on the 1973–1974 Urban end of the Survey. His Ph. D. thesis topic is "The policy implications of rural urban migration in Papua New Guinea."

BRIAN M. DU TOIT (1935–   ) was born in Bloemfontein, South Africa. He studied at the University of Pretoria where he received his B.A. (1957) and M. A. (1961) degrees, and at the University of Oregon where he received his Ph.D. (1963). He was a lecturer at the University of Stellenbosch and the University of Cape Town, and presently is Professor of Anthropology at the University of Florida. Recent publications include *People of the valley: life in an isolated Afrikaner community in South Africa* (1974), *Akuna: a New Guinea village community* (1975), "Dagga: the history and ehtnographic setting of *cannabis sativa* in southern Africa," in *Cannabis and culture*, edited by Vera Rubin (1975).

VERA GREEN is Associate Professor of Anthropology and Department Chairperson at Livingston College, Rutgers University. After receiving a B.A. from Roosevelt College and M.A. from Columbia University, she was awarded the UNESCO title of Fundamental Educator on the basis of field work completed at C.R.E.F.A.L. in Michoacan, Mexico. Ms. Green has a Ph. D. (Arizona) in Anthropology and has done research in Puerto Rico, Aruba, Curaçao, South India, and among blacks and Puerto Ricans in New York City. She is the author of several articles and of *Migrants in Aruba*.

JOSEF GUGLER (1933–   ) is Associate Professor of Sociology at The

University of Connecticut. Earlier he was Director of Sociological Research at the Makerere Institute of Social Research, Uganda. His research in Nigeria (1961–1962) and East Africa (1964–1970) focused on labor migration, urban unemployment, patterns of association in the urban setting, and urban-rural relationships; he has published a number of papers on these topics. He is joint author of *Urbanization and social change in West Africa*, forthcoming in 1975–1976. Presently he is analyzing a major survey, "Urbanization and social change in East Africa," which he directed in Dar es Salaam, Kampala, and Nairobi.

CELIA S. HELLER (1927–   ) is Professor of Sociology at Hunter College and the Graduate Center of the City University of New York. She spent her Sabbatical year (1970–1971) in Israel as Visiting Professor at Tel Aviv University and Bar-Ilan University. She received both her M.A. and Ph.D from Columbia University. Her areas of specialization are social stratification and comparative ethnic relations. Her numerous publications include: *Mexican American youth – forgotten youth at the crossroads* (1966); *Structured social inequality* (1969); *New converts to the American dream?* (1971); "Poles of Jewish background — the case of assimilation without integration in interwar Poland," in *Studies on Polish Jewry* (1974).

WILLIAM H. HODGE (1932–   ) received his B.A. and M.A. degrees from Washington University, St. Louis, in 1953 and 1954. His Ph. D. degree in Anthropology was awarded by Brandeis University in 1966. At present he is an Associate Professor of Anthropology at the University of Wisconsin-Oshkosh. For the past sixteen years he has been interested in a wide spectrum of topics related to the contemporary American Indian experience. In addition, his interests include whites and gypsies in the United States.

PETER C. LLOYD (1927–   ) is Reader in Social Anthropology at the University of Sussex. He spent fifteen years, 1949–1964, in Nigeria first conducting research among the Yoruba and later teaching at the University of Ibadan. His publications include *Yoruba land law* (1962); *Africa in social change* (1967); co-editor of *The city of Ibadan* (1967); editor of *The new elites of tropical Africa* (1966), *The political development of Yoruba kingdoms in the eighteenth and nineteenth centuries* (1970); *Classes, crises and coups* (1971); and *Power and independence: urban Africans' perceptions of social inequality* (1974). His present research interest is in the shanty towns of the Third World.

BERNARD MAGUBANE (1930–   ) was educated at the University of Natal (B.A. in Sociology and Native Administration, 1958; M.A., 1960) and at U.C.L.A. (M.A. in Sociology, 1964; Ph.D., 1967). He has been a lecturer at the University of Zambia (1967–1969) and a visiting lecturer at U.C.L.A. (January-June 1970), a Research Fellow of the American Friends Service Committee in Pasadena, California, in a study of the problems of unemployed young Negro males, and a Research Assistant for a U.C.L.A. School of Public Health study of habits associated with heart ailments. His M.A. thesis "Sports and politics in an urban African town" became the basis of a chapter entitled "Politics of football: the urban and district African Football Association" in Leo Kuper's book, *An African bourgeoisie* (1965). Papers by him dealing with social change in Africa have appeared in *African Social Research*, *Race*, *East African Journal*, and *The African Political Review*. He is now teaching at the University of Connecticut in Storrs.

SUSAN R. MAKIESKY received her B.A. from New York University in 1967 and is completing her doctoral dissertation in Anthropology at Brandeis University. She has done research in the West Indies in Antigua and Barbados on social and political change. She was Visiting Lecturer in Sociology at the University of the West Indies (Cave Hill Campus) in 1971–1972 and was an Instructor in the Anthropology Department of New York University during 1972–1973. She is currently Senior Research Scientist in the Anthropology Section of the Biometrics Research Unit, New York State Department of Mental Hygiene. Her special research interests include migration and ethnicity, political anthropology, Caribbean studies, and the anthropology of women.

DOUGLAS MIDGETT (1939–   ) currently teaches in the Department of Anthropology at the University of Iowa. He formerly taught at the University of Illinois, where he studied for a Ph. D. in Anthropology. He has done fieldwork in the West Indies and among West Indian migrants in London. In addition to interests in migration and urbanization he has done research in sociolinguistics and political development and has publications in both areas.

BONHAM C. RICHARDSON (1939–   ) received his B.A. (1961) at the University of Arizona and his M.S. (1968) and Ph.D. (1970) in geography at the University of Wisconsin at Madison. Besides doing fieldwork in Guyana and Trinidad, he worked in Grenada and Carriacou in 1973 on the interrelationships between ecological deterioration and labor migration. He is currently Book Review Editor of *Human Ecology*: *An Interdisciplinary Journal*.

HELEN I. SAFA (1930–   ) is Graduate Director and New Brunswick Chairperson of Anthropology at Rutgers University, the State University of New Jersey. She received her Ph. D. in Anthropology from Columbia University in 1962, on a study of a Puerto Rican shanty-town, which has been updated and published in 1974 as a monograph, *The urban poor of Puerto Rico*: *a study in development and inequality*. She has published numerous articles in the field of urbanization and development in professional anthropological and sociological journals and is presently on the Executive Council of the Latin American Studies Association. She is currently working on a comparative study of determinants of women's role and status in Latin American and American society.

CONSTANCE R. SUTTON received her M.A. in Anthropology from the University of Chicago in 1954 and her Ph.D. in Anthropology from Columbia University in 1969. She is Associate Professor in the Anthropology Department of New York University, where she has taught since 1960. During 1971–1972 she was Chairwoman of the Anthropology Department at New York University's University College of Arts and Science. Her field research has been in the Afro-Caribbean region, where she studied plantation workers in the late 1950's. She returned to the West Indies in the late 1960's and early 1970's to carry out follow-up studies on political and ideological change. Her monograph, *Protest and change in Barbados*, focuses on changing forms of political protest. Her current research interests include migration and ethnicity and women's model of social reality. She has served on committees of the American Anthropological Association, is a Danforth Associate, and is a member of New York University's Affirmative Action Council.

NORMAN E. WHITTEN, JR. (1937–   ) is Professor of Anthropology and Director of Research of the Center for Latin American and Caribbean Studies at the University of Illinois, Urbana. He received his B.A. from Colgate University and his M.A. and Ph.D. from the University of North Carolina, Chapel Hill. Publications include the following books: *Class, kinship, and power in an Ecuadorian town* (1965), *Afro-American anthropology* (1970), "Black frontiersmen" (1974), and *Sacha Runa: ethnicity and adaptation of Ecuadorian jungle Quechua* (forthcoming). He is continuing field research on the adaptive strategies of Indians and blacks in South America.

Index of Names

Index of Subjects